BIRTH
OF AN
INDUSTRY

BIRTH
OF AN
INDUSTRY

Blackface Minstrelsy and the

Rise of American Animation

NICHOLAS SAMMOND

DUKE UNIVERSITY PRESS

Durham and London

2015

Library of Congress Cataloging-in-Publication Data
Sammond, Nicholas, [date]
Birth of an industry : blackface minstrelsy and the
rise of American animation / Nicholas Sammond.
pages
Includes bibliographical references and index.
ISBN 978-0-8223-5840-4 (hardcover : alk. paper)
ISBN 978-0-8223-5852-7 (pbk. : alk. paper)
ISBN 978-0-8223-7578-4 (e-book)
1. Animated films—United States—History and criticism.
2. Animation (Cinematography)—United States—
History—20th century. 3. Blackface entertainers.
4. Minstrel shows. I. Title.
NC1766.U5S36 2015
791.43'34—dc23
2015003368

Dedicated to the Memory of

JOHN MCCLOSKEY MOYNIHAN

1960–2004

Animator, Author, Rogue

and

SARA ELIZABETH GARMENT

1960–2011

Poet, Translator, Swami

CONTENTS

NOTE ON THE COMPANION WEBSITE

Birth of an Industry has a digital companion that
features all of the media discussed here. To view
that media, as well as additional materials and
commentary on blackface minstrelsy, vaudeville,
and animation, go to
http://scalar.usc.edu/works/birthofanindustry

ACKNOWLEDGMENTS

Film and media historians have long noted that American animation is indebted to blackface minstrelsy. Yet that observation too often has added up to little more than a mere nod or at best a shaking finger—yes, the American cartoon's debt to the minstrel is undeniable and wrong, now could we please move on? This leaves an unanswered question: why did early animators decide to use cartoon minstrels to build an industry in the first place? Or if not why, how did they do it, and to what ends? It is not enough simply to remark on a thing, especially something as simultaneously ephemeral and significant as that, and then to say little more. Animation studies, often protective of the playful spirit of the 'toon itself, have until recently tended to avoid this sort of knotty question—bracketing animation's less than honorable history of representational, performative, and industrial practices of racism, misogyny, and homophobia—perhaps fearing that animation's subordinate status when compared to live cinema, its perpetual dismissal as childish, will be once more confirmed. With a winsome shrug, defenders of a form seen as itself vulnerable and perpetually disrespected sometimes seem to say, "C'mon, can't you take a joke?"

Those reticent to delve deeply into the less noble aspects of American commercial animation's past (or present) include not only its chroniclers but also animators, collectors, and critics who bristle at critiques of cartoons' crimes and misdemeanors when leveled by those who lack knowledge of the form's history and craft. Given animation's traditionally subordinate aesthetic status as a "low art," this defensiveness is very understandable. Yet, as it becomes ever clearer how integral animation is to cinematic practice, that attitude also becomes less acceptable. Now that

American commercial animation is finally reaping the dubious rewards of amalgamation, it needs all the more to answer for its shortcomings as well as for its virtues. Indeed, what this book attempts to demonstrate is that the two are deeply imbricated: animation's fantastic plasticity, its magnificent metamorphic flights, its gleeful disrespect for the boundary between the real and the imagined are profoundly of a piece with its worst fantasies about black bodies.

What this significant intersection requires, then, is careful study that joins the deep personal and institutional knowledge bases that mark animation history with a critical analysis of the role of race in that history, one that extends past mere finger-wagging indictments of racism. The danger in such a project is, of course, that neither side of the aisle will feel adequately represented in the telling. So this book, as an interdisciplinary work, will do its best to speak to (and back to) the substantial and interesting institutional memory of animation. Yet it will do so in ways that make respectful and proper use of the tools of critical race theory, which, more than merely charting racializing operations within a grander historical narrative of American popular culture, also mark how constitutive of that culture the intersecting racial projects of the twentieth century have been.

All of which is to say that writing near the crossroads of animation history and critical race studies is humbling. Where this book succeeds it does so primarily because of the counsel, ideas, and foundational work of the people whose work I have read or with whom I have discussed it over the years. Where it falters it does so solely due to my own shortcomings.

This project had its beginnings following a panel at the 1993 Association for Theatre in Higher Education conference, in a discussion between myself, Jon Nichols, and Mark Sussman regarding Jon's excellent paper on the "Helping Hand" animated glove in Hamburger Helper advertising. I am very grateful to Jon for initiating this topic. He did the framing; I've tried to provide the finish work, in which I trace the connections between the animated blackface minstrel, the industrialization of the art of animation, and fantasies of resistant labor.

My earlier work on animation has focused more on the industry's public relations than on its art and craft, and I thank Stephen Worth, Ray Pointer, Jerry Beck, and John Canemaker for their patient, thorough, and good-natured schooling in a history that is dense, complicated, and (as it should be) endlessly amusing. Likewise, the outstanding scholars of film and animation Donald Crafton and Daniel Goldmark have also at different turns served as patient mentors and exemplars of historical practice, and

I remain very grateful to them for their observations and corrections, and their unstinting generosity.

Although its central topic is cartoons, this project draws from, and perhaps adds a small amount to, a rich literature on blackface minstrelsy and on African American performance in American social, popular, and political history and has benefited enormously and variously from the writings, knowledge, insights, and criticisms of Jayna Brown, Daphne Brooks, Eric Lott, Kara Keeling, David Roediger, Arthur Knight, Linda Williams, Huey Copeland, Alice Maurice, Anna Everett, and Stephen Johnson. Since this work also trespasses in the precincts of early film history, it has gained much as it has crossed the desks of Charlie Keil and the taciturn and assiduous Rob King. Both of these men, at one moment or another, have suffered me gladly and corrected me gently, and I hope this book repays them in some small measure. At key moments, Thomas LaMarre, Paul Wells, and Suzanne Buchan have also offered, in person or through their writing, invaluable insight into the nuances of animation theory and practice and have supported this project and its offspring, the Early Animation Wiki (www.rarebit.org). I am also deeply indebted to my students, undergraduate and graduate alike, who constantly challenge me with vital and interesting questions and with their own vast collective knowledge of the convoluted terrains of animation.

I have always depended on the kindness of mentors. From the beginning of my academic career, Chandra Mukerji has been my role model in the rigors of interdisciplinary inquiry; she is a woman I admire deeply and whose scholarship and integrity I have tried to emulate. Charlie McGovern not only continues to school me in the finer points of cultural history but also stands as a paradigm of intellectual, institutional, and personal generosity to which I can only hope to aspire. For many years, Eric Smoodin (who has also educated me in animation history) and Henry Jenkins not only have generously supported my work but also have served as models of how to bring scholarship into productive and meaningful dialogue with the politics of popular culture. Mark Lynn Anderson, Eric Cazdyn, Anna McCarthy, Sarah Banet-Weiser, and Fred Turner have all been invaluable interlocutors; each sets an example for intellectual rigor, and all continue to teach me about the nature of the engaged life of the public intellectual. Cynthia Chris adds to that rigor the lesson that writing about funny things with humor is a craft—one at which she excels.

Spanning several different official archives and a host of less formal sites, this book would be nearly devoid of evidence were it not for the hard work of my assistants and researchers. During its key research phases, Alicia Fletcher served as both project manager and researcher, and she was ably aided by Sarah Barmak, Andrea Whyte, and Nathaniel Laywine. The Early Animation Wiki was initially developed and managed by Agnieska Baranowska and eventually masterfully designed and programmed by Claire Sykes and Michael Toledano, respectively. It has since been maintained and refined first by David Dennison and then by the diligent and thoughtful Alice Xue.

This book has a substantial online companion (http://scalar.usc.edu /works/birthofanindustry) that features many of the cartoons it discusses, along with ephemera such as minstrel playbills and manuals, as well as more recent examples of blackface minstrelsy. That companion was designed on the Scalar platform. I am very grateful to Tara McPherson and John Carlos Rowe for inviting me to learn Scalar and for generously providing the resources for developing the site beyond the scope of my meager design skills. Although all of my fellow Scalar summer campers educated me in the finer points of making the perfect online lanyard, I owe special thanks to Oliver Wang, Carrie Rentschler, and Jonathan Sterne for sharing their design chops with me. Alexei Taylor has been absolutely invaluable as a designer and mentor in subsequent rebuilds, and Eric Loyer and Craig Dietrich were also extremely supportive and giving of their time and talents. Steve Anderson, the developer of Critical Commons (www .criticalcommons.org), has been unstintingly helpful and generous at every phase of this venture, and I am one of many scholars deeply indebted to him.

Support for early research for this project was provided by the Dean of Arts and Sciences and the Connaught Fund at the University of Toronto, the Jackman Humanities Institute, and the Social Sciences and Humanities Research Council of Canada. Development of its web-based components was supported by the Andrew Mellon Foundation, the National Endowment for the Humanities, and the Annenberg Center at the University of Southern California.

At Duke University Press, Elizabeth Ault has patiently guided this book through the production process. Ken Wissoker has for many years been unstinting in his support and advice, and I owe him a debt of gratitude the size of an ACME safe for his good humor, better taste, and firm counsel.

The earliest days of this project were visited on Amy Greenstadt, who has for many years served variously as interlocutor, muse, and model of probity, mindful scholarship, and unsurpassed wit. Were I to find the proper words to thank her for all she has taught me, I probably would find that I had only borrowed them from her.

Finally, were it not for Aubrey Anable, this book would have realized few of the moments of nuance and wit it occasionally imagines itself to reach. A marvelous soul brimming with an odd admixture of compassion, loyalty, and deviltry and a scholar of remarkable flexibility and insight, she rarely shies from speaking necessary truths, naming the genuine and the false notes, or pointing out potential dead ends. Aubrey is a truly future-forward individual and the crucial difference between the light and the train at the end of my tunnel.

BITING THE INVISIBLE HAND

A tattered, makeshift curtain rises on a ragtag troupe of blackface minstrels preparing to offer their interpretation of Harriet Beecher Stowe's *Uncle Tom's Cabin* to a rural audience in a converted barn. So begins *Mickey's Mellerdrammer* (Disney, 1933), a telling artifact from early twentieth-century American popular culture.[1] In this cartoon short, Walt Disney Productions' wildly popular new star joins his "girlfriend," Minnie Mouse, and friends Goofy, Clarabelle Cow, and Horace Horsecollar in an amateur production of the classic abolitionist tale. As with many other versions of Stowe's melodrama staged in the late nineteenth and early twentieth centuries, the cartoon's racial organization seems a bit confused.[2] The short begins with the cast backstage, preparing. Minnie as Little Eva takes great pleasure in powdering her face and donning a blonde wig. Clarabelle blacks up with the aid of chimney soot from an oil lamp. Mickey—who will play both Topsy and Uncle Tom—inserts a firecracker into his mouth and lights the fuse: he literally blasts himself into blackness.[3] Once in costume, Mickey and Minnie take the stage, while in the wings Goofy, in a nod to nineteenth-century stage mechanics, manipulates a primitive pasteboard chorus of plantation darkies whose jaws flap while a phonograph plays Dan Emmett's "Dixie" . . . to which Mickey and Minnie tap dance.[4]

This mixture of abolitionist melodrama and blackface minstrel show may seem odd and contradictory, but it accurately captures one of the uses to which Stowe's tale was put in its long heyday. Yet what makes this scene truly strange and contradictory is that Mickey and Clarabelle were *already* minstrels before they blacked up (as was Minnie). With their white gloves, wide mouths and eyes, and tricksterish behaviors, Mickey and his friends

FIGS. I.1–I.3 In *Mickey's Mellerdrammer* (1933), Mickey Mouse, who is already a minstrel, uses a firecracker to black up further.

were just a few more in a long line of animated minstrels that stretches back to the beginnings of American commercial animation in the first years of the twentieth century. That in 1933 they seemed white enough that they needed to black up in order to clearly read as minstrels speaks to the state of animation at the dawn of sound film: they had become *vestigial minstrels*, carrying the tokens of blackface minstrelsy in their bodies and behaviors yet no longer immediately signifying as such. Their status as minstrels was becoming occluded by the rapidly changing conventions of cartooning and by the fading popularity of live minstrelsy itself. The historical operations by which popular continuing characters such as Mickey came to embody the conventions of blackface minstrelsy in the first place is the central topic of this book, even as, in the space of a few decades, those same conventions became obscured, though never erased.

This reading of the industrialization of the animation industry in the United States and its place in a larger history of blackface minstrelsy considers two notable details from animation history. One is unremarkable, the second less so. First, from its beginnings, the animation industry in the United States has been labor intensive and rationalized, and the industry itself has celebrated that labor in its public relations and in cartoons themselves. Second, many of the continuing characters that came to define the industry—Mickey Mouse, Felix the Cat, Bugs Bunny—are actually minstrels. In brief, this book considers the relationship between American animation's ongoing fascination with its own production, especially with the labor involved in making cartoons, and its long-standing debt/contribution to blackface minstrelsy. Since animation shares with minstrelsy as one of its fundamental tropes the regulation of unruly labor—as many blackface minstrel characters were based on a fantasy of the rebellious or recalcitrant African American slave or free person— understanding this simultaneous fascination with labor and with its discipline through racially charged characters is this study's central project.

Although this book charts the place of animation in the history of blackface minstrelsy (and the history of blackface in animation), it is also about how those histories might inform approaches to the material practices of animation as they relate to cartoon aesthetics. More than that, though, it explores how fantastic performative relationships between animators and their minstrel creations modeled larger social and discursive formations in the United States, especially those perdurable racial fantasies that linked caricatures of African American bodies and behaviors to concepts of enthralled labor and its resistance to domination. For the cartoon minstrel not only wears the gloves and painted-on smile of the live blackface performer, he (and in the case of cartoons it is most often "he") also shares the blackface minstrel's resistance to regulation, which is itself inextricably yoked to labor through the minstrel's indelible association with chattel slavery. Yet the cartoon minstrel does his live cousin one better in this regard: he is actually created by the very forces of regulation and domination he resists. So, while the lesser goal of this work is to carefully delineate the how and perhaps the why of cartoon minstrelsy, its larger goal is to link that analysis to a larger and longer history of racial iconography and taxonomy in the United States.

Blackface has made a comeback in the twenty-first century, especially on television, and it is usually presented nostalgically, as an odd historical anomaly and a stand-in for more racist times and unenlightened performers and audiences.[5] Perhaps the most sustained, famous, and controversial use of minstrelsy in recent years is Spike Lee's satire *Bamboozled* (2000), an uneven commentary about the impossibility of authentic black performance in American mass culture, in which an African American television producer's sardonic revival of an old-time minstrel show on prime-time TV becomes an improbable hit. Yet even in that film minstrelsy is treated as if it were archaic, outdated, anachronistic—a throwback brought out of mothballs to reveal the underlying racism that structures and informs contemporary mainstream entertainment industries.[6] Not quite. The old-time minstrel show may be gone, but blackface is a surprisingly vital tradition and a global one at that. Whether via South African rap group die Antwoord's video *Fatty Boom Boom* (2012), Australian comedian Chris Lilley's rapper character S.mouse in his *Angry Boys* series (2011), the tragicomic scene in the prime-time cable show *Madmen* (2009) in which Roger Sterling blacks up to sing at his daughter's wedding, or Billy Crystal reviving his impersonation of Sammy Davis Jr. for the 2012 Academy Awards, blackface as a performance practice is still very much a part of mainstream popular culture. Even though there seems to be wide consensus that blackface is racist and unacceptable, each week finds instances of professional and amateur blackface performance in the United States and elsewhere, inevitably followed by expressions of outrage that in no way deter the following week's performances.

Which is to say that minstrelsy is a past practice that (to paraphrase William Faulkner and Barack Obama) isn't even past.[7] Although blackface—with its much-disputed origins sometime in the eighteenth or nineteenth century and reaching its popular height toward the end of the

1800s—is alive and well today, it has always been a creature of its time: it refracts contemporary anxieties about the power and meaning of whiteness through nostalgic fantasies about blackness. This particular study takes as its starting point the relationship between imagined blackness and imagined whiteness at the beginning of the twentieth century, and more specifically with how that relationship was made manifest in famous continuing cartoon characters such as Felix the Cat and Mickey Mouse. More simply it asks, why the gloves? It traces how these relatives of live minstrels informed and inflected the conventions and practices of an emerging cartoon industry, and how, as that industry matured, those characters gradually became gestures toward minstrelsy's past rather than direct references to its ongoing practice. Describing this earlier moment in the history of animated minstrelsy may cast some light on why, in the face of overwhelming evidence that blackface is alive and well today, it is almost always treated as if it were a relic of a historically remote past that Americans have moved beyond—even as we demonstrate with pathetic regularity that we actually haven't.

That blackface as a tradition predates cartoons might seem to suggest that animation merely borrowed from minstrelsy. That reading is unproductive on two fronts. First, it plays into a long-standing and misguided critical tradition that sees blackface in cartoons as an exception or aberration, rather than as integral to the form. At the same time it underplays the syncretic practices that run through many popular American performance traditions—what more bluntly might be called a shared tendency toward theft. A diachronic ordering of minstrelsy, burlesque, vaudeville, movies, radio, and television is more or less chronologically accurate (as long as one ignores significant moments of overlap) but runs the risk of effacing the significant transit of talent between forms, and the outright lifting of techniques and routines from one form to another. American animation, which had its origins and developed many of its enduring conventions on the vaudeville stage, is not merely one more in a succession of textual forms; it is also a performative tradition that is indebted to and imbricated in blackface minstrelsy and vaudeville. Commercial animation in the United States didn't borrow from blackface minstrelsy, nor was it simply influenced by it. Rather, American animation is actually in many of its most enduring incarnations an integral part of the ongoing iconographic and performative traditions of blackface. Mickey Mouse isn't *like* a minstrel; he *is* a minstrel. Betty Boop's sidekicks, Bimbo and Ko-Ko, aren't references to minstrelsy; they, too, *are* minstrels.[8] This is more than a mere conceit: although blackface is usually thought of as a live performance tradition, it evokes in its tension between surface and interior—between the makeup and the face beneath—a fantastic black persona that is analogous in many ways to cartoon characters who dwell in the flatland on the surface of the page or cel, and again at the liminal boundary of the screen onto which they are projected. Both gain force and substance through their play at the frontiers between ontological realms. (This liminality is the central gag in the nostalgic Disney short *Get a Horse* [2013], which depicts the boundary between the past and present as between 2-D and 3-D.)

Because the history of cartoons is more widely known today than that of minstrelsy, this narrative begins with a briefly sketched delineation of blackface as a traditional form. Just as minstrelsy has occupied many different media over the centuries, the blackface minstrel show as a live, staged spectacle has gone through many permutations, which the scholarship around its early history has chronicled in detail.[9] This study takes as its paradigmatic structure the minstrel show in its heyday in the years immediately between the end of the Civil War and the beginning of the twentieth century. While the three-act blackface show that epitomized the height of minstrelsy's popularity was formally contiguous with earlier and later types of minstrel performance, it is no more or less authentic than that which preceded or followed it. Studying blackface, or any type of performance, it is important to avoid an originary fantasy that sees one historical moment as more genuine than another, and to consider (albeit briefly) the historically specific iterations of minstrelsy during different moments of social and racial formation. Indeed, part of what makes blackface minstrelsy such a peculiar performative creature is that *minstrelsy itself* is based on just such fantasies about origins. One of its founding and recurring ideas is that blackface performers reenact dances, songs, and conversations learned from actual black folk, whether slaves on the plantation or free blacks in northern cities. At the same time, however, that nostalgic fantasy has served as a useful cover for mounting critiques of the political, social, and cultural issues of the times in which it is being performed.

American commercial animation did not appropriate a more authentic blackface minstrelsy from the stage, becoming a more distant or debased version of its live predecessor by virtue of chronology. Blackface minstrelsy is such a durable performance form, in part, because it has always adapted to the social and material relations of its day. At the beginning of the twentieth century, live blackface performance was still popular but was in decline; the emerging technology and vernacular artistic form of animation offered a new home for the minstrel, one more suited to its historical moment yet still dependent on the modes of minstrelsy that had preceded it. Each generation of blackface minstrelsy is a fantastic iteration of those pedestrian acts of casual racism that draw on and feed a racial imaginary, made strange only when they are pried away from the immediate circumstances that naturalize them. For that reason, rather than starting right into a comparative history of live blackface performance and animation—which is what much of this book does—I will pause here and offer up three other, distinct moments in the history of blackface, ones that may seem at first to have little to do with cartoons. As iterations in an ongoing history of blackface minstrelsy of which animation is one more element, each of these moments' oddity and historical specificity may better set the stage for understanding the cartoon's particular performative and iconographic place in that history. These three distinct instances in the history of American blackface—one from the early twentieth century, one from the 1960s, and one from a few years ago—may make it easier to get at how minstrelsy has persisted for so long, even after it ceased to be considered popular or even acceptable, and how minstrels, whether performed by living persons or drawings, serve as fantastic embodiments of the historical contradictions of the racial formation of the times in which they live. The first of these moments, though, actually does coincide roughly with the creation of American commercial animation in the first decade of the twentieth century.

MOMENT 1: THE BLACKFACE MINSTREL AND THE GREAT WHITE HOPE

On the Fourth of July 1910, heavyweight boxer Jim Jeffries, the "Great White Hope," stepped into the ring in Reno for the "Fight of the Century" against reigning champion Jack Johnson, who was African American. Jeffries lost. By most accounts, Jeffries, who had been enticed out of retirement by a large purse, had no personal or racial animus against Johnson. Many in the white press, on the other hand, did: they treated the fight as a matter of honor and Jeffries as having a duty to reclaim the championship for the white race.[10] Two weeks before the fight, the *New York Morning Telegraph* ran a photo of the Jeffries training camp, the caption of which identified Jeffries as "surrounded by his cronies and bosom pals," one of whom was the very popular blackface minstrel Eddie Leonard. In 1910, even though minstrelsy's popularity was in decline, Eddie Leonard was at the apex of his career. Having started with the Haverly Minstrels around the turn of the century, by 1903 Leonard was working for famed producer George Primrose, who owned one of the premier minstrel troupes of the day. Known first for his buck-and-wing dancing and his "wha-wha" style of ragtime coon shouting—a white fantasy of African American song—Leonard was a phenomenon on the B. F. Keith vaudeville circuit during the first two decades of the twentieth century.[11] By way of bona fides, Leonard also claimed that he and legendary African American tap dancer Bill "Bojangles" Robinson were close friends, having come up together riding the rails and performing in cabarets in the late nineteenth century. After Jeffries's loss, Leonard claimed in the same paper that two weeks of training in the heat and the thin mountain air of the Sierras before the fight had defeated the white boxer, not Johnson. "If the fight had been two weeks earlier," he suggested, "a white man would still be champion of the world." Leonard went on to recount telegrams that had exhorted Jeffries to "save the white race" and claimed that when the "negro left the ring [he] received not a hand; Jeffries, even though he had lost, was cheered heartily."[12] That a man touted as the "Great White Hope" apparently bore no ill will toward his opponent yet chose as a close friend a man famous for performing as a (caricature of a) black man, who also made free with expressions that smacked of white supremacy, may seem contradictory, or at least confusing. Surely, a man who claimed friendship with Bill Robinson wouldn't be invested in a white man's victory over an African American—yet he was. It would be easy to suggest that well, it was 1910, and well, times were different then. Yet times are always different—that's what makes them times.[13]

Moving beyond (or perhaps further into) the "it was the times" explanation, this welter of contradictions is susceptible to at least several interpretations. One explanation might be that Leonard's coon shouting, blacking up, and supremacist diatribes were consistent: nothing more than the racist diminution of African Americans. In this version, Leonard befriended Robinson in order to appropriate his techniques and knowledge and then deployed them in racist parodies, whose intent was eventually borne out by his statements regarding Jack Johnson. In a slight variation, known today as "some of my best friends . . . ," Leonard perhaps differentiated between the African Americans he knew as individuals, who were his friends, and the race as a whole, which he still held in contempt. Yet an-

JIM JEFFRIES' TRAINING CAMP, ROWARDENNAN, CAL., JUNE 20.

The Above Photo Shows James J. Jeffries at His Training Camp, Surrounded by His Cronies and Bosom Pals. You Will Note That Eddie Leonard, "The Minstrel," and One of Virginia's Native Sons, Is Seated Alongside of Jeff. Leonard Joined Jeff at Jeff's Invitation and Will Remain Until the Fight.

FIG. I.4 Blackface minstrel Eddie Leonard appearing with prizefighting "Great White Hope" Jim Jeffries shortly before Jeffries lost to the reigning champion, African American Jack Johnson. Courtesy of the Billy Rose Theatre Division, The New York Public Library for the Performing Arts, Astor, Lenox and Tilden Foundations.

other interpretation—by no means the last—might have Leonard understanding full well that his performances in blackface were not imitations of actual African American dance and song but delineations of fantastic creatures known as "darkies," who, though based on common stereotypes associated with African Americans, were understood to be unreal.

And so on. Each of these readings of the historical record taken singularly imagines Eddie Leonard, a poor boy who chose the stage over the floor of a Richmond steel mill, as somehow carefully and consciously articulating his relationship to race.[14] Taken as a complex, though, they outline a person whose intersubjective relations were various and whose emotional, ideological, and performative investments framed an inconsistent worldview unperturbed by its own contradictions. That is, there is no reason to believe that Eddie Leonard was not all of those things— hard-core racist, racialist opportunist, selective racist, and fabulist—all at once. This, in essence, is the exploded view of "it was the times," one that, rather than offering up the casual racism of the moment as an apology for behaviors and stances unacceptable by today's standards, or merely condemning that racism out of hand, asks instead how it achieved its effects regardless of intent—muddled or otherwise. Leonard made use of the racial formations and discourse of his day (a "day" that actually spanned the first four decades of the twentieth century) to his advantage and to that of his (primarily white) friends.[15] Whether he did so with malice or without integrity is rather beside the point. The work was done either way.

What this slight parable of the minstrel and the prizefighter points out is that racist stereotypes are effective, not just because they appeal to extant prejudice, but because they circulate across forms and discourses. In this instance the imbrication of the racist fantasy of the blackface minstrel with anxieties about the relative abilities of black and white prizefighters produced a matrix of racial discourse that simultaneously empowered and enriched the blackface minstrel even as it demonized and debased the black prizefighter. Though he was much maligned by the white press in his day, Jack Johnson is now remembered as a champion and a hero; Eddie Leonard was celebrated at the height of his career, yet died alone in hotel room in 1941, at a moment when blackface minstrelsy was increasingly disavowed as regressive, worthy at most of nostalgic fondness.[16] His obituary framed him as warmly remembered, but a has-been.[17] Racial formation, and minstrelsy as one of its performances, is not fixed; it is always historically contingent.

If blackface minstrelsy had begun a decline into seeming disrepute in the 1940s, by the 1960s and the height of the civil rights and Black Power movements, performing in blackface smacked of outright hostility. Nonetheless, in 1969, while working on the film *Putney Swope*, director Robert Downey Sr. had a problem he chose to solve through minstrelsy. At the time of its release, the film, a farce, was widely seen as a radical correction to mainstream racist representations of African American life, culture, and politics. In *Swope*, the title character, a black man working at a major advertising agency, finds that an unexpected turn of events leaves him in charge of the agency. Swope radicalizes the workplace, changing the agency's name to Truth and Soul, bringing in gun-toting Mau Maus as business associates, and producing ads designed to counter offensive stereotypes, to criticize the Vietnam War and senseless consumerism, and to assert black pride. So, what was Downey's problem? As he shot the film, he didn't like the vocal performance of Arnold Johnson, the actor playing Swope. Yet rather than cast a different actor, Downey dubbed Swope's voice in himself, apparently feeling no compunction about performing vocal minstrelsy. Truth and Soul, indeed.[18]

In addition to describing the relatively benign but nonetheless racist impulse behind Downey's choice, this anecdote also demonstrates that blackface as a traditional art form is not a relic of a past that died with Eddie Leonard in 1941 in a Philadelphia hotel; minstrelsy gets dredged up from time to time when it is useful. Blackface is a living performance tradition, the motivations behind it are often complex, and its modes and operations are always historically specific. In both of these cases, to describe a white performance of imagined blackness, either Leonard's or Downey's, as simply racist is reasonable, but at the cost of a nuanced understanding of what each of those white men might have imagined themselves accomplishing through their performances.

One such example of that white fantasy of the power of blackness is in the name Downey gave to the advertising agency that his imagined black executive created: Truth and Soul, Inc. In the film, truth is that which is spoken to power; the "soul" part refers to an essential, ephemeral, and often disputed quality associated with being black—one forged in pain, poverty, suffering, celebration, and hope and putatively offering access to a more genuine experience of the world—what in 1970 the band Funkadelic fondly and sarcastically boiled down to "a ham hock in your

FIG. I.5 A promotional poster for the Robert Downey Sr. film *Putney Swope* (1969).

cornflakes" and "rusty ankles and ashy kneecaps." Like the blues, an ineffable quality also intimately associated with African American life, "soul" refers to an essential being forged in adverse conditions, an emotionally nuanced yet vibrant lived experience, a virtually material perdurability in the face of oppression.[19] In the white liberal imagination (and guilt) of the late 1960s and early 1970s, the ideal blackness represented by Truth and Soul, Inc., was a token of realness, fueled by a nostalgic longing for an authentic experience of life lived without the social and material padding of a white, middle-class, suburban existence pejoratively called "plastic"— as in manufactured, inorganic, and unreal.[20] The imagined black radical of the late 1960s and early 1970s—whose material touchstones were the likes of Angela Davis, Malcolm X, Bobby Seale, and Huey Newton— was genuine precisely because of her righteous anger, her firsthand experience of suffering and social censure. Her ostensible access to the wellsprings of spiritual and cultural solace in the black community was imagined to exist in inverse proportion to white America's relative excess of wealth and privilege.[21] To have access to some part of the black community ("some of my best friends . . .") could create a delightful frisson of guilt and expiation in which white liberals such as Downey could imagine themselves as both condemned by and forgiven through those associations. Short of having black friends or of sympathizing with "the cause," indulging in black popular culture could provide a sort of expiation through consumption, albeit one that required regular reinvestment. In this light, Downey's vocal minstrelsy, his updating of Leonard's coon shouting, would not necessarily have read as minstrelsy at the time. When Arnold Johnson couldn't do justice to Swope's authenticity, Downey gave that "authentic" voice to Swope himself. Shortening the circuit, he channeled the anxious power of the 1960s white bourgeoisie into a ritual performance of self-abnegation, a self-flagellatory rite of confession through which one's own inauthenticity is ameliorated through contact with the very thing that seemingly produced it in the first place. Minstrelsy always invokes a tension between the authentic and the inauthentic.

Yet even the suggestion that an ongoing fascination with African American cultural and social life in the mid-twentieth century encompassed the anxious intersubjectivity of rising members of a primarily white middle class only goes so far in explaining the durability of the blackface minstrel, whether in voice or in body, whether in live performance or in cartoons.[22] For beneath the fantasy of poverty as virtue and suffering as truth lurks an originary fantasy of the minstrel: that of the rebellious slave. Reduced beyond poverty to property, beyond unemployment to chattel servitude, the eighteenth-century "plantation Ethiopian" was *King Lear*'s "thing itself," little more than an object first appropriated into bondage and then re-appropriated in blackface minstrelsy.[23] The central conceit of minstrelsy, that its performers had traveled to the plantation to witness (i.e., steal) the songs, dances, and wordplay of African American slaves (themselves stolen from themselves, made objects rather than persons) depended on an idea of the slave as a natural commodity, an owner of nothing, not even her own thoughts and gestures. Yet in the midst of this mise en abyme of theft, the minstrel figure appeared to repetitively reclaim itself through performances of misrecognition and wily resistance, through gestures of moral turpitude and the studied avoidance of physical labor. In the 1800s this figure was embodied first by Jim Crow, later by Tambo and Bones. In the twentieth century there are echoes of the minstrel in characters such as Lincoln Perry's Stepin Fetchit and Redd Foxx's Fred Sanford. In-voke blackface minstrelsy, though, and if we don't immediately think of Al Jolson we might well imagine the classic minstrel extravaganza of the mid-nineteenth century: the top hats, giant cuffs, and ridiculously wide lapels; the enormous painted lips, wide eyes, and wooly wig. These are its markers, and they also signify and condense the form's fraught origins in a rhetoric that supported chattel slavery—the fancier clothing invoking the northern urban dandy who misrecognizes the markers of civilization (the cuffs perhaps invoking manacles), the oversize eyes and mouths the childlike simplicity and brutish voraciousness used to justify the slave as subhuman—about which Hartman, Brooks, Moten, and others have written.[24] Yet blackface minstrelsy should also call to mind more recent attempts to call out and comment on the racial order of the day, from Ted Danson and Whoopie Goldberg's 1993 blackface performance at the Friar's Club to today's almost weekly YouTube videos of college students blacking up and pretending to be gangsta rappers. Which begs the ques-tion, when people black up today, what do they intend to signify and why? In an era in which Barack Obama's election as president of the United States is touted as proof of the end of racism, what is the "postracial" meaning of race?

Blackface has always favored the comic over the dramatic, and when people black up today it is usually in the service of a joke, the minstrel turn being well suited to comedies of embarrassment such as *30 Rock* (2006–2013). Like comedian Jimmie Walker's character J. J. Evans on the 1970s sitcom *Good Times* (1974–1979), Tracy Morgan's character Tracy Jordan on *30 Rock*—modeled on Morgan himself—is a buffoon whose representation of pathetic ghetto realness has been hotly contested on-screen and off, and whose scenes often involve contestations and jokes around difficult issues of race and gender. In the 1970s, Walker's portrayal of a ghetto youth squandering his talent as a painter for the sake of immediate gratification rather than mobilizing it for the greater good was criticized as reductive and stereotypical. This so much seemed to undermine *Good Times'* purported message of uplift that costars John Amos and Esther Rolle each left the show in protest at different moments during its run. How, then, to read, in the early twentieth century, Tracy Jordan's constant threats to leave *30 Rock's* show-within-a-show, TGS? Historically distant from the urban uprisings of the late 1960s that informed the reformist attitude of *Good Times*, Tina Fey's *30 Rock* operated in an ironic, "postracial" realm in which a stereotype, as long as it is accompanied by a wink, is justified.[25] So, for instance, its episode "Christmas Attack Zone" (2010) features Tracy showing his film *The Chunks Two: A Very Chunky Christmas* (a parodic nod to the Eddie Murphy *Nutty Professor* remakes) for families trying to celebrate the holiday in a battered women's shelter. It juxtaposes this awkward scene with a drag duet between Jenna Maroney (Jane Krakowski), in blackface as former NFL receiver Lynn Swann, and her boyfriend Paul (Will Forte) as Natalie Portman from *Black Swan* (Aronofsky, 2010). As Tracy (wearing a diamond-encrusted gold neck chain that reads "POVERTY") screens an offensive scene in which he plays all of the characters—all in fat suits and all projectile vomiting at a Christmas dinner—the show crosscuts to Jenna and Paul in drag, singing "Oh, Holy Night" to an unseen television audience. Tracy's oblivious offensiveness offsets and is offset by Jenna's clueless use of blackface for the sake of a visual one-liner.[26]

This was not the show's first use of blackface. In the episode "Believe in the Stars" (2008), Liz Lemon (Tina Fey), having overdosed on anxiety medication on a flight from Chicago to New York, hallucinates that the teenage girl sitting next to her is Oprah Winfrey. Meanwhile, in

FIG. I.6 In one of several blackface moments on *30 Rock*, Jenna (Jane Krakowski) and her boyfriend Paul (Will Forte) appear as Natalie Portman from *Black Swan* (2010) and the former NFL player and right-wing politician Lynn Swann.

the *TGS* studio Jenna and Tracy engage in a fierce argument about who has it harder, black men or white women. To settle the dispute, they trade places: Jenna blacks up and dresses as an African American man, circa 1974, while Tracy converts himself into a white woman in the style of *White Chicks* (Wayans, 2004). Lemon asks "Oprah" to intervene to settle the dispute. In the interim her medication has worn off, and the truth is revealed. In spite of this the teenage girl solves the problem as Oprah would have, and an argument that has troubled feminism since the nineteenth century is boiled down to teenage-version Oprah-isms: Tracy admits that he was hearing without listening, and Jenna confesses that she needs to go from being Tracy's frenemy to his BFF. The episode ends with the two singing Bill Withers's "Lean on Me" (1972) to each other.

This episode juxtaposes Lemon's absurd, drug-amplified racial insensitivity, which leads her to mistake an African American teenager for Oprah Winfrey, with two pampered narcissists using an argument about who is more victimized to indulge in attention-getting racial/gender cross-dressing. In the wink-and-nod moment following the election of an African American president, which somehow generated permission for media producers to more freely express racist stereotypes and sentiments under the dictum that a forthright acknowledgment of racism also provides for its ironic absolution, Lemon's anxious racism is meant to be endearing, as is Jenna's, as is Tracy's misogyny. This does not in and of itself make the writers of *30 Rock*, or Tina Fey, or Tracy Morgan, or Jane Krakowski any more or less racist than Eddie Leonard, or Walt Disney, or Robert Downey Sr. At best, it acknowledges more openly the difficulty of commenting on the operations of race outside the structural and institutional foundations through which racism is made substantial. This is perhaps why *30 Rock* located the excess of *The Chunks* and Tracy's oblivious bling in a women's shelter and paired Natalie Portman as ballerina with ballet-trained ex–football star and Republican politician Lynn Swann (nicknamed Swanny). This begs a couple of questions that will be taken up in chapter 4 and the conclusion: If you perform racist behaviors and stereotypes in order to demonstrate their absurdity, do you deflate them or invest them with new life by destigmatizing them? Is the comic depiction of racism itself racist?

Too often that is the last, rather than the first, question. That is certainly the case with Henry Sampson's otherwise admirable book *That's Enough, Folks* (1998), a survey of racist depictions of African Americans during the first fifty years of American commercial animation. A detailed and comprehensive catalogue, it seems content to call out the racism in American cartoons at the expense of a detailed analysis of its historically specific roots and uses.[27] Attributions of racism in and of themselves too often stumble into this sort of discursive quagmire of intent, where they may become framed as calls for atonement, which of necessity collapse the social into the individual. What the racist (or racializing) performers of 1840, 1910, 1969, and 2010 have in common—once we move beyond their individual and distinct modes of performance and their likely quite disparate intents—is a recourse to blackness as a fantastic primal realm and force (and it is treated as both). This contested and contradictory imagined state is simultaneously biological and social, unruly and contained, material and ephemeral, underpinning and threatening to disrupt or rewrite the social order. What is lost in the move to assign racist intent (or to absolve it) is a grounded understanding of what Richard Iton has referred to as the "black fantastic"—itself located in and around the profound importance of the black/white binary to the discursive production and regulation of relations of power in the United States.[28] This realm, this force, this matrix of meaning is present as much in the trivial productions of television programs (trivial but for their millions of viewers), indie movies, and prizefights as it is in larger moments such as in the highly charged debates over the election (and reelection) of Barack Obama or in the aftermath of George Zimmerman's acquittal in the killing of

Trayvon Martin.[29] For it is through the seemingly trivial that fantasies of blackness and whiteness circulate freely and with relatively little critical comment, stabilizing if not producing meaning. Where intent is invoked as an arbiter of meaning, the force and reach of circulation and reappropriation may become obscured.

For this reason cartoons, until relatively recently considered by most a juvenile and relatively ephemeral form of entertainment, are an important historical site for working through the fantastic relations between imagined blackness and whiteness. Early animation's play with metamorphosis, with the relationship between surface and interior, and with the boundaries between the page, the screen, and the worlds outside them, makes cartoons an important location for witnessing the creation and working through of the fantastic. On the surface, this rationalized, emergent industry would seem to have relatively little in common with the unruly live performance of blackface minstrelsy. For one thing, in the early twentieth century, when the animation industry was created, minstrelsy was already waning. Although I have suggested that minstrelsy is very much alive and well today, as a widely and regularly enjoyed popular stage entertainment, blackface had its greatest moment in the nineteenth century, while hand-drawn animation on film did not arrive until the twentieth. Yet in spite of that seeming historical distance, American commercial animation and blackface minstrelsy share far more than the surface similarities of the white gloves, wide eyes, and painted mouth, as a brief history of the form may begin to reveal. That is why it is important to see animators and the cartoons they made as inheritors of and practitioners in the complex of iconography, convention, and performance that is blackface minstrelsy. Cartoons didn't borrow from minstrelsy; they joined minstrels T. D. Rice, E. P. Christy, Lew Dockstader, Eddie Leonard, Bert Williams, and Sophie Tucker in minstrelsy's ongoing development as an art form, one with its roots in antebellum American popular culture and with branches in every mass entertainment of the early twentieth century.

AN ACCEPTABLE HISTORY: T. D. RICE LEARNS TO JUMP JIM CROW

To give a competent description of blackface minstrelsy in a few sentences is a daunting task. Though the form is only a few centuries old (and that dating is contested), a significant body of scholarship has grown up around it in the past twenty years or so. Initially, minstrelsy was a performance form often transmitted orally, or through the ephemeral traces of handwritten song lists, scripts, playbills, and journals. In spite of these limitations, scholars such as Dale Cockrell, W. T. Lhamon, William J. Mahar, Annemarie Bean, and others have done substantial and important work to chronicle minstrelsy's songs, jibes, jokes, and dances as well as to carefully describe the contested moments and meanings in its history.[30] And because minstrelsy has so often inflected the social and political issues of the day through the lenses of race and ethnicity—especially in the stump speech (a minstrel parody of electioneering) or in the banter between the interlocutor and his end men—David Roediger, Eric Lott, Michael Rogin, Louis Chude-Sokei, and others have done significant work on minstrelsy's place in the operations of emergent, shifting, and imbricated discourses of race, class, ethnicity, and power.[31] In that this book is concerned with the place of American commercial animation in the forms and conventions of minstrelsy, it does not attempt to substantially intervene in that literature. Rather, it is a very modest addition to those projects, an extension of the historical analysis of minstrelsy from the stage to the screen and from the live to the drawn.

What the best scholarship on early blackface agrees on is that minstrelsy, which came to the fore in the United States in the early nineteenth century, defies easy categorization as either simply racist or as resistant to the dominant racial power structure; as a tool of capitalist domination, white working-class ressentiment, or transracial affiliation. The answer to these sorts of either/or classifications is yes. Multifarious and inconsistent, blackface minstrelsy as it has been practiced in the United States since the 1820s is all of these things because its practitioners by no means form a unified body. An extremely popular antecedent to the mass entertainments of the late nineteenth and early twentieth centuries—such as variety, burlesque, vaudeville, radio, and movies—blackface minstrel shows shared certain conventions, such as applying burnt cork or black greasepaint to the face, accentuating the eyes and mouth to make them seem larger and wider, and wearing wooly wigs and outsized clothes and sometimes white gloves. But beyond those outward similarities, the meanings brought to and taken from minstrel shows were more nuanced and varied, depending on a variety of circumstances on both sides of the footlights.

Most accounts of the beginnings of blackface minstrel shows mark the conventional stabilization of the form around 1843 by Dan Emmett's Virginia Minstrels in Manhattan and soon afterward by E. P. Christy's Plantation Minstrels in Buffalo. Yet the person commonly and mythically

FIG. I.7 Minstrels Eddie Leonard and George Evans in blackface, c. 1904. Courtesy of the Billy Rose Theatre Division, The New York Public Library for the Performing Arts, Astor, Lenox, and Tilden Foundations.

FIG. I.8 Bosko the Talk-Ink Kid discovers he has an audience, c. 1930.

named the originator of the form, Thomas Dartmouth Rice, began black-ing up as Jim Crow long before either of these minstrel troupes estab-lished themselves or Stephen Foster began penning minstrel classics such as "Old Folks at Home" or "Old Zip Coon" (later somewhat euphemized as "Turkey in the Straw") in the 1840s and 1850s.[32] A legend that circu-lated as early as the middle of the nineteenth century had it that Rice was inspired to create the character Jim Crow when, sometime between 1828 and 1831, he witnessed an African American stagecoach driver in Cin-cinnati dancing and singing in a very eccentric way. Soon afterward, in Pittsburgh, Rice met an African American stevedore named Cuff whose ill-fitting clothes he felt would be perfect for his new character. According to the story, Rice rented the clothes right off of the man's back, leaving him nearly naked in the wings of the theater, and then combined the odd costume of one man with the song and dance of another to "jump Jim Crow."[33] Within five years, Rice was performing that act on stages in New York, London, and beyond, to much acclaim.

There are perhaps as many variations to this story as there are versions of the song and dance "Jump Jim Crow."[34] Yet what remains consistent across all of them is the theme of appropriation: Rice saw in the voice and movement of one man and the clothing of another useful elements for the synthesis of a fantastic and essential "darky." By these same sorts of tokens, the words "Virginia" and "Plantation" were important to Emmett, to Christy, and to many others who followed them, as was the oft-used epi-

FIG. I.9 A playbill for Christy's Minstrels describes the troupe as "the first to Harmonise Negro Melodies and Originators of the present popular Style of Ethiopian Entertainments." Courtesy of the Special Collections Research Center, University of Chicago Library.

FIG. I.10 Mickey Rooney and Judy Garland, in *Babes in Arms* (1939), perform nostalgia for the good old days of minstrelsy.

thet "Ethiopian." These terms were metonymic, signaling in shorthand a set of assumptions about the fantastic nature of imagined blackness. The conceit of the minstrel show was that the white (or black) performers who blacked up claimed to reenact genuine dances and songs they had observed poor free black laborers perform or had witnessed slaves do on southern plantations in the fields or in the hours after a day's hard labor.[35] Minstrelsy traded on an authenticity based on the privilege of observing African Americans, be they free manual laborers or captive slaves, seemingly converting the burden of their labor into merriment. And minstrelsy depended on a fantasy by which those workers and slaves provided access through their libidinous bodies to the primal forces of Africa and the wildness of nature.

The form of minstrelsy nostalgically invoked in films such as *Babes in Arms* (Berkeley, 1939) or *Holiday Inn* (Sandrich, 1942) stabilized following the Civil War. Prior to the war, small troupes such as Christy's or Emmett's combined blackface, odd costumes, tambourines, banjo, and "bones" to create a carnivalesque mockery of African American "folkways" through which the decorum of proper white civilization was also lampooned and perhaps momentarily called into question. By the 1850s the minstrel format had changed somewhat. What had started as a loose collection of songs, jokes, and dances became divided into two rough parts. Lott suggests that the basic initial division in the show was along a North–South axis, with the first half centered around a dandy such as Zip Coon or Dandy Jim and the second around southern slave characters.[36] In the 1850s, this division was expanded to include an *olio*, which came between the show's first and last parts and featured sentimental ballads, skits, stump speeches, and dances.

Regardless of the specific historical moment, though, class tension has always held an important place in minstrelsy. Though a full accounting of the nuanced and shifting relationships between race, ethnicity, class, gender, and religion that surrounded and infused blackface are beyond the scope of this study, it is important to point out that a common thread in the different historical moments of minstrelsy is a conventional association between the minstrel body and its labor (or lack thereof).[37] Performed in its early days primarily by members of the working class yet patronized by people from varied class backgrounds, minstrelsy, in its songs, its colloquy, and its stump speeches often spoke to the sentiments, aspirations, and frustrations of working people and to American ideals of individualism and self-making. Yet beyond that, the figure of the minstrel itself was located in a mythos of the black body as resistant to labor—whether forced or voluntary—that is, as inherently "lazy." Whether the frame for that performance leaned toward affiliation or toward racial animus, minstrelsy performed that fantastic, imagined black body as always existing in relation to its labor. Within that construct, discourses of authenticity and inauthenticity—the conceit that what was being performed had been learned/appropriated/stolen from *actual* African Americans—marked the minstrel stage as a liminal zone, a place *between* insincere, exclusive, and elitist civilizing forces and the primal and materially grounded existence of genuine (imaginary) African American life and culture. Blackface minstrelsy's anthropological conceit framed a fantasy of otherness and reinforced a racialized hierarchy of labor in which Roediger suggests that even an indentured Irish day laborer could feel a momentary sense of superiority—even if some of his friends and coworkers were free blacks.[38]

Following the Civil War, minstrelsy's basic format remained relatively fixed for the next seventy years. Its central characters were often the interlocutor—a well-spoken master of ceremonies—and Tambo and Bones, simple-minded rural black folk whose confused replies to the interlocutor displayed both their own rustic ignorance and his pomposity. During the final act, the performers would arrange themselves in a semicircle with the interlocutor in the center and one or more banjo players nearby. At the far ends of each arm of this semicircle were the tambourine and bones players, Tambo and Bones. Although in minstrelsy's earlier days the interlocutor also appeared in blackface (but often spoke with a cultured accent), by the end of the century he also appeared in whiteface.

Whether in blackface or white, the interlocutor increasingly represented the quasi-aristocratic elites in tension with the more plebeian Tambo and Bones.[39] This format continued as a stand-alone entertainment until the 1880s, when minstrelsy was gradually subsumed (via burlesque) into vaudeville—sharing the stage with Irish, German, and Hebrew acts, with jugglers, comedians, and performing animals—seeming to fade (as stage performance) only as vaudeville gave way to radio, movies, and television.

FROM STAGE TO SCREEN

This genealogy is important to the history of animation not simply because some of the first animators this study examines were vaudeville enthusiasts but because the earliest American cartoons were components in vaudeville performances themselves, deriving particularly from lightning-sketch acts and from minstrel performances. Cartoons (or vaudeville, or live film) were not a form of entertainment that supplanted a dying blackface minstrelsy; rather, they were a permutation of minstrelsy, a part of a complex of entertainments at the dawn of American mass culture of which live minstrelsy was a fading element and film, including animation, a rising one. The porousness between different modes of performance and media then (and now) argues against a notion of succession and for models of interconnection and appropriation; performers in one medium often worked in others and took with them from one medium to the next their signature material and schtick.[40] In vaudeville and in film this is generously called *homage* but more honestly called theft. Animation inherited this appropriative impulse from its forebears—with one animation house regularly lifting a character or gag from another with only minor emendations. And because the figure of the blackface minstrel itself was an appropriative fantasy of the black laboring body, a moment's consideration of the minstrel's physiognomy and its gestural economy will also delineate some of the most common visual conventions that animation's continuing characters shared with live minstrels and will set the stage for considering how those characteristics eventually became vestigial.

One of the most familiar tropes in classical American animation is characters wearing white gloves, which were also quite common in blackface minstrelsy. On Zip Coon, Long Tail Blue, or Jim Dandy, or on a blackface interlocutor, they could signify the false gentility of white manners on a black body, sitting obviously and uneasily on flesh itself painted on, or more generally a pretense to superiority. Recalling the hands of

"ZIP COON," POPULAR NEGRO SONG, AS SUNG BY MR. DIXON.

FIG. I.11 George Dixon as Zip Coon. Minstrel characters such as Jim Dandy or Zip Coon portrayed free African Americans as northern dandies whose ignorance and confusion belied their pretensions to sophistication. Houghton Library, Harvard University (012172093).

both the master and the house slave, the white hands of control, they controlled little; for all his pretensions to taste and sophistication, Zip Coon always remained a clown. According to Lewis, the gloves marked a satire of upward mobility and bourgeois racial tolerance, simultaneously a sign of class ressentiment and racial animus.[41] The addition of white (or no) makeup around the eyes and mouth and the reddening of lips played into common stereotypes of African Americans as slack-jawed and voracious yet simple, innocent, and easily frightened or excited—all infantile, consuming eyes and mouth.[42] Similarly, the minstrel body's relative plasticity, its freedom of movement—as when wheeling around to "Jump Jim Crow"—suggested a primitive freedom from the constraints of civilized behavior. The same sort of freedom marks the bodies and behaviors of continuing cartoon characters, from Felix to Oswald, and to (the early) Mickey Mouse.

Lott has described the minstrel's assumption of fantastic imagined black characteristics as an act of love and theft. Similar to what Stuart Hall calls the "ambivalence of stereotype," it expresses a desire for an imagined liberation from social norms (perversely based in subjugated bodies) combined with a simultaneous fear of that freedom, of the imagined raw sensual power of those bodies.[43] Minstrelsy replicated a white, primarily northern fantasy of African American life and culture, particularly of plantation life, as populated by lazy black folk wallowing in a sensual torpor, almost devoid of higher mental and moral functions. The minstrel's body—fluid, voracious, and libidinal—represented a freedom from the constraints of Protestant middle-class morality. At the same time, that body suggested the threat of a fall from grace, of labor's ongoing enthrallment to capital.

This potent fantasy made the interlocutor, a conduit between audiences and minstrels, a particularly important character. Well spoken, and in the latter half of the nineteenth century often white, he addressed the audience directly and interrogated "his" minstrels in a quasi-anthropological fashion, asking them about details from their lives or, when they said something particularly elliptical, insisting that they explain themselves. He was the butt of the other minstrels' jokes, and his inability to make them understand his simple questions demonstrated the limits of education and of class in the face of natural turpitude. Regulating the border between nature and culture, the interlocutor—a role early animators would adapt and adopt when they interjected themselves into the frame with their creations—performed an always failing regulation of the minstrels' fantastic minds and bodies. The dynamic between the interlocutor and his end men found its way onto the screen via several avenues. It reappeared condensed into the two-man vaudeville acts of teams such as Weber and Fields, Abbott and Costello, and Burns and Allen, and in the power struggles between animator-character duos such as Winsor McCay and Gertie, Max Fleischer and Ko-Ko, or Walter Lantz and Pete the Pup. Thus, the conventions of blackface performance reappeared directly in the iconography and performance styles that informed continuing cartoon characters, and indirectly through vaudevillian performance and staging that had itself drawn from minstrelsy. Both the trope of the controlling and manipulating animator as interlocutor and of the continuing cartoon character as obdurate and willfully practicing misdirection, like Tambo or Bones, became standard conventions in American commercial animation, continuing long after the performance of animation had left the vaudeville stage (see chapter 1). Yet within the first three decades of the twentieth century, as blackface minstrelsy diminished as a popular entertainment, the obvious associations between popular continuing cartoon characters and the minstrel stage became less evident. Except in the case of characters who were explicitly described as minstrels, such as Bosko the Talk-Ink Kid, by the late 1930s the associative links between cartoons and the minstrel stage were becoming increasingly vestigial.

Continuing characters—those characters who appeared in multiple installments and became trademarks of animation studios—often exhibited a number of physical features that marked them as minstrels. Not only Mickey wore gloves; so did Bimbo, Oswald, and many of the Warner Bros. characters. Most of these popular continuing characters also featured the wide, expressive mouths and eyes of the minstrel painted onto black bodies. Yet the markers of cartoon minstrelsy were not simply visual; they were also performative. Like the eccentric dancing and movement typified by "jumping Jim Crow," these characters had the ability to twist and deform their bodies, and they did so to express extreme emotions, to extricate themselves from intractable situations, or simply for the sheer pleasure of the act. In this, their personalities were those of a minstrel as well: they behaved as tricksters, indifferent or even hostile to the social norms of polite society, as well as to the laws of physics. It is for this reason that even the continuing Fleischer character Ko-Ko the Clown, who appeared in whiteface, yet who persistently punctured the cartoon's frame to rebel against his maker, was *performatively* a minstrel.

These cartoon minstrels, who have persisted to this day, are distinct from cartoon depictions of African Americans. In fact, they are of a different class altogether. There were some African American characters in early silent animation, and many more were created with the coming of sound film and the rise of swing music in the late 1920s. American animation, strangely, responded to jazz and African American popular culture with a plethora of intensely virulent and racist caricatures of famous musicians, and of African Americans in general, even as it celebrated the music and dance of the swing era. While related to the animated minstrel in important ways, these racist caricatures were also distinct, both in their explicitness and in their topicality and historical specificity. Even though they were distinct from their predecessors, these caricatures made literal many of the earlier, implicit associations that blackface minstrelsy had made to the plantation, to Africa, and to primal nature and that had become less explicit in continuing characters such as Bugs Bunny or Woody Woodpecker. Playing on a common association of jazz with "jungle

FIG. I.12 Warner Bros.' *Clean Pastures* (1937) performs the early sound era's more directly virulent racist caricature of African Americans, in this case of Fats Waller, Lincoln Perry, Cab Calloway, and Louis Armstrong.

music," these cartoons imagined a fantastic and often quite violent realm in which blackness linked Harlem, the Deep South, and Africa in a seemingly contiguous fantastic geography (see chapter 3). For that reason, it is important to understand the relationship not only between blackface minstrelsy and popular continuing cartoon characters but also between those characters and later caricatures of jazz greats of the 1930s and 1940s such as Cab Calloway, Louis Armstrong, and Fats Waller.

CONTINUITY AND DISCONTINUITY

Both this last example of swing-era racist caricature and the three moments of blackface that opened this chapter indicate a tension in the study of the history of minstrelsy generally, and of animation in particular. There is no doubt that animation went through rapid and significant technological and formal changes during the first fifty years of its development, yet assuming that this development has been unreservedly progressive—that the fading of explicit links to minstrelsy in American commercial cartoons necessarily indicates a gradual improvement in animation's articulation of racial formations—risks producing a narrative that glosses over profound and significant discontinuities in the form. Rather than becoming less racist as live minstrelsy faded, American commercial animation engaged in an intensification of racist imagery in its depiction of music generally and swing music in particular, as in racially problematic cartoons such as many of the Warner Bros. Merrie Melodies and Looney Tunes, in George Pal's stop-action Puppetoons (1932–1947), and in Disney's combination of live action and animation *Song of the South* (Jackson and Foster, 1946). Likewise, an implicitly progressive narrative occludes the ways popular commercial animation actively participated in (rather than simply reflected) the racial formations of the day through its circulation of fantastic embodiments of dominant notions about the relationship between blackness and whiteness in the United States. Cartoons created visual correlates that associated African Americans with slavery, the jungle, and animals, literalizing and animating long-standing stereotypes. Simply put, the demise of minstrelsy on the stage coincided with a period of far more intense racist caricature in American animation, one that ended only with the rise of the postwar civil rights movement . . . and then only slowly. Thus, what unfolds in the chapters to come is not a progressive history. It is an examination of different facets or nodes in a matrix of discourses that produced, policed, and regulated the meanings and uses of the black/white binary in animation (see chapter 4). This study ends in the 1950s—not because the relationship it describes between minstrelsy and broader swing-era racist caricatures became fixed, or because the coming of television somehow obviated the racial overtones of the cinematic cartoon minstrel, but because the rise of the civil rights movement and the momentary stabilization of regimes of labor in the 1950s and 1960s mark a significantly different moment in the ongoing formation of the racial binary, and of the associative links between the laboring and the racially marked body. At the beginning and end of this study I discuss the contemporary rise of a "new blackface today," a seeming revival of minstrelsy in popular mass entertainments coincident with regimes of precarious labor in the neoliberal and increasingly neofeudal moments of the early twenty-first century. Perhaps reviewing the regimes of an earlier, discontinuous historical moment will illuminate similar dynamics at work in our present circumstances.

To the degree that there is a narrative to this study, it does not unfold linearly. Instead it loops back on itself, recursively. Because one of the key tropes of animation is repetition, the examination of cartoons encourages a repetitive mode of reading in which the same objects and practices are viewed from different vantage points, as different facets of the same object. So the first facet of the industrialization of commercial animation this study takes up is that of *performance*, followed by the *labor* of making cartoons, then the role of animation in the alteration and regulation of *space,* both within and outside the screen, and then finally what the vestigial minstrel might indicate about *racial* formation in both the moment of its effacement in the 1930s and in the purportedly postracial moment we now occupy. Animation is one site in the vernacular struggle over emerging social formations of labor, race, gender, and class. An art form that celebrates creating audiovisual correlates for ideas, it is in many ways a nonpareil for witnessing struggles over the meanings and uses of those social formations.

Between roughly 1913 and 1916, animation shifted extremely rapidly from a cottage industry to a fully realized and rationalized industrial complex, and its vernacular response to its own rationalization also reveals how new regimes of efficiency and accumulation, and of the industrial absorption of creative workers, translated into those seemingly living commodities, the continuing, trademark characters those same workers produced. For although animation is a far less grueling job than rolling steel, building automobiles, or stoop harvesting, it shares with other rationalized industries an intensified division of labor that reduces tasks to manageable, repetitive components and which views the workers engaged in those tasks as necessarily interchangeable. So even though the stereotypical view of animators is of happy-go-lucky creative sorts whose work is more play than toil (like Disney's seven dwarfs), and even though the field is generally described by animators themselves as creative, it is also true that it is a demanding *industry*—hence the strikes in animation studios in the late 1930s and early 1940s.

Designing popular continuing characters as minstrels was not an accident of history; it represents a visual correlate for the satisfactions and frustrations of an industrial art. Animation, via its minstrels, was particularly suited to creating a visible and eventually audible vernacular expression of work experience in its products. Animation is an unusual industry in that the commodities it produces appear to be alive and independent yet so often struggle against the conditions of their existence. Like live minstrels, they embody a performance of comic protest. Animation's very innocuousness, its lack of seriousness, its propensity for caricature makes it ideal for the promulgation of displaced fantasies of racialized ressentiment. Animation's irreality becomes its plausible deniability, its traditional location in comedy its exculpation for its repetitive performances of violence against others. But more than that, the traditions of metamorphosis and boundary crossing make animation an immanent and evanescent medium for producing a hieroglyphics of racial discourse: as the white blackface minstrel played with the seeming immutability of race (and by extension with anxieties around passing and racial categories), so the cartoon minstrel calls into question the boundary between the animate and inanimate commodity, the person and the thing.

So this is a book that asks, quite seriously, where did Mickey and Bugs get their gloves, their huge eyes, and their capacious and voracious mouths, and why have they kept them for so very many years? It asks why these enduring and endearing continuing cartoon characters so often show so little respect for authority, so often rail against the conditions of their existence, and so rarely succeed in overcoming them. It attempts to answer these questions by considering American animation as a lineal descendant in the very American performance tradition of blackface minstrelsy, and in the process compares Mickey and Bugs to Tambo and Bones—and Walt Disney or Max Fleischer to (equally vestigial) interlocutors. The purpose of this comparison is not to tar American commercial animation as racist, nor to root out its contributing villains so that we can then enjoy its remaining nonracist fare. Nor is it an attempt, at the end of the day, to usher in through critique the sort of utopian postracialism that some have imagined as having been magically engendered by the fantastic figure of President Barack Obama. The purpose of this comparison is, rather, to puzzle out how an industry whose primary products act like living beings chose as a fundamental template for those creatures a being that is itself an imaginary commodity, a living, breathing embodiment of property rebelling against the conditions of its existence—and why that still makes people laugh.

PERFORMANCE

BUG VAUDEVILLE, OR, THE CURTAIN RISES
AND FALLS ON WINSOR MCCAY

Early animators were not artists as much as they were entertainers.
—Frank Thomas and Ollie Johnston, *The Illusion of Life* (1981)

In their epic review of animation technique à la Disney, *The Illusion of Life*, Frank Thomas and Ollie Johnston, two of Walt Disney Productions' "Nine Old Men," offer a historical snapshot that hints at common assumptions about the relationship between popular art and entertainment, and between high art and animation, in the early twentieth century. The notion that an animator was an artist (or draughtsman) first and an entertainer second (if at all) speaks of a division of labor that was increasingly common when the two men began working for Disney in the early 1930s. It had not been the order of things during animation's beginnings twenty years earlier. Thomas and Johnston were skilled craftsmen, animators who could draw Disney's trademark characters on spec and could faithfully contribute to the company's evolving and distinctive style of "full" animation. Yet they were not entertainers: as workers in a rapidly changing industry, they were aware of American commercial animation's origins on the vaudeville stage and its profound debt to that stage's traditions and conventions, which were based in, borrowed from, and shared the spotlight with vaudeville's antecedent forms: burlesque, variety, and blackface minstrelsy. In the 1930s, Disney was the premier animation house in the United States; in the two decades prior to its rise, though, American commercial animation went from an art form that sometimes incorporated film into live performances to an industrial content sup-

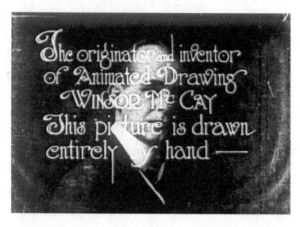

FIG. 1.1 In the opening title sequence for *Bug Vaudeville* (1921), Winsor McCay humbly claims to have invented animation.

plier for both major and minor Hollywood film studios. In the process of that transformation, the visual and performative tropes of vaudeville and blackface minstrelsy—well known to audiences of the day—gave rise to the basic template for trademark continuing characters such as Felix the Cat, Krazy Kat, Oswald the Lucky Rabbit, Mickey Mouse, and Bugs Bunny, with many other versions in between. That audiences today do not immediately recognize Mickey as a blackface minstrel is in part an effect of a widely shared belief that blackface minstrelsy no longer seems to be performed on a regular basis (though it is) and of the social and material changes that gradually remade the figure of the performing animator—the interlocutor to those cartoon minstrels—into that of an animation worker. Understanding the rapid transition from animation as performance to animation as industry requires setting aside a standard depiction of the history of early animation as a succession of favorite and famous texts (i.e., cartoons) and instead thinking of it as the development of a performative tradition into a commodity-based one. Thinking of animation first as performance, and later as industry, opens up a genealogy that traces the movement of animation's central conventions and tropes from the stage to the screen, a movement whose counterpoint is the organization of its creative workforce into increasingly rationalized and systematic divisions of labor—the products of which, strangely, regularly performed the labor that went into their creation.

The career of Winsor "Silas" McCay spanned the rise of the movies, the birth of American animation, and its rationalization as an industry.

McCay was the most famous of those early performing animators, and the story of his conception of animation (both the process and its products) as a vaudeville act, his departure from vaudeville, and the relationship between the two is illustrative of those changes. A talented artist, gifted performer, and tireless self-promoter, McCay began working in the 1880s, designing posters for the Barnumesque Sackett & Wiggins Wonderland and Eden Musée. After a few years designing posters and programs for dime museums, circuses, and traveling shows, McCay became a newspaper sketch artist—in part because of his skill at drawing the unusual and grotesque and in part because he could draw incredibly quickly and accurately. By the dawn of the twentieth century he had established himself as a newspaper cartoonist, first through editorial cartoons and then through Sunday cartoon series such as *Little Sammy Sneeze* (1904–1906), *Dreams of a Rarebit Fiend* (1904–1911, 1913), and *Little Nemo in Slumberland* (1905–1914).[1] Of these, *Dreams* and *Nemo* were particularly popular, and with them McCay gained acclaim as a master of perspective and of a sort of vernacular proto-surrealism, and this work led him to begin experimenting with the sequential art of animation. *Dreams* was so popular that it became a stage show and then was interpreted on film in 1906 by Edwin S. Porter. In that same year, McCay began an extremely successful vaudeville career, working as a lightning-sketch artist and developing stage acts that would eventually make use of his animated films *Little Nemo* (1911), *How a Mosquito Operates* (1912), and *Gertie* (1914).[2] In 1914, McCay's new contract with newspaper publisher William Randolph Hearst, for whom he worked as a cartoonist, forbade him from performing on vaudeville stages outside New York City. Although McCay's films continued to circulate, this effectively signaled the beginning of the end of a very lucrative and satisfying performing career.[3] McCay returned to the stage briefly in 1927, but by then vaudeville was in sharp decline—in part because of its replacement by movie/performance combination shows and by short-subject films, including cartoons (see chapter 3).

Winsor McCay died in 1934 at the relatively young age of sixty-seven, of heart disease probably hastened by alcohol. Yet he had already stopped producing cartoons in the early 1920s, a few years after he stopped performing animation for live vaudeville audiences. Of his final works, *Bug Vaudeville* (1921) clearly delineates McCay's sense of his importance to animation, while nodding to the rapid changes to moviegoing and cartooning that, during the late teens and early twenties, made him marginal in an industry he had helped to create. More than a visual epitaph for a fading showman, *Bug Vaudeville* offers a schematic of that marginalization, a means of reading changes to animation as an art, a craft, and an industry. In its self-reflexivity the cartoon performs a struggle to reconcile the contradictions between those three modes of production: art, craft, industry. Like many of the best cartoons of its age, the film tells a story that is as much about the social and material relations that obtained around its making as it is about the acrobatic Junebugs or butterflies on horseback it features. Like its maker, the cartoon is caught between celebrating an onrushing and tranformative technological modernity and recognizing in that transformation a pending obsolescence.

Even though McCay was only fifty-two when he made it, *Bug Vaudeville* seems a swan song. An opening title card announces that the short is part of a series made famous by McCay's comic strip *Dreams*; it is replaced by a picture of the animator himself, staring rather dolefully out at the audience. Superimposed over this is a characteristically brash claim: "The originator and inventor of animated drawing Winsor McCay. This picture is drawn entirely by hand." This announcement not only positions McCay as the creator of an entire type of cinema—a dubious claim, but one not entirely without merit—it also implies that what he does in this and other cartoons is different from what other animators do, the product of craft rather than industry.[4] Truth be told, pretty much all animated films at that time were drawn by hand, albeit not necessarily by a single person. But McCay's claim suggests that somehow the increasingly rationalized animation industry of the late teens had done away with the human touch of the artisan, of which he remained the epitome. This baleful still of McCay also speaks of his departure from the vaudeville stage, as do the title and topic of the film: in this still image, he sits motionless, staring out through, and somewhat obscured by, his bold claim.

The rest of the film is no less somber. A hobo enters the frame and settles down by a tree next to a rustic pond. A title card indicates that a handout of cheesecake he's gotten from an unseen woman has made him sleepy, and he's worried that it will give him queer dreams. Lying down to sleep it off, he immediately dreams that he is seated in the front row of an otherwise empty vaudeville house. (We see him there only from behind and in silhouette, as a head and shoulders and a set of applauding hands.) This now two-dimensional hobo watches a series of specialty acts—acrobats, pugilists, eccentric dancers, and the like—all of whom are bugs or spiders. Except for applauding listlessly at the end of each number, he sits completely still. Likewise, although every one of the numbers is ostensibly incredibly athletic and energetic, each unfolds at a lethargic and monotonous pace, and the expressions on the bug performers are anything but animated.

But the existential emptiness of the piece runs deeper. Each act is bracketed by the opening and closing of curtains, and each time the stage is revealed, its elaborate backgrounds display the easy mastery of perspective and rococo detail for which McCay was famous. Yet the bug performers repeatedly undermine the stability of those backgrounds, which in one moment are clearly drop curtains and in the next seem made up of discrete three-dimensional elements on the stage where the bugs move. That is, the bugs appear to move in and out of the backdrops, actually morphing the spatial relations of the stage as they perform. To put it another way, the spatial dynamics of the stage oscillate between two dimensions and three, as if what appears there could at one moment be merely a drawing and in the next become a thing of substance, inhabiting and helping to constitute the material world.

The last number in the show is titled "The Spider and the Fly." The curtain parts and a huge spider begins to perform a very lazy trapeze act, drifting slowly back and forth from upstage to down and from side to side. No fly appears. The spider continues to swing from side to side, then back and forth. As it swings forward, out over the audience, it descends on the hobo, lifting him up into the air, seemingly intent on eating him. With an intitled cry of "Oh Mama!" the hobo awakes . . . then slowly and silently stands and stares out at the pond. The end.

It would be easy enough to read this twelve-minute film biographically and be done with its contribution to animation hagiography. But juxtaposing the cartoon and its place in the history of American popular culture against the arc of McCay's career allows the film to speak to and for more. By 1921 the meticulous, time-consuming, largely solo-animator animation McCay practiced had been supplanted by a highly rationalized animation industry with a hierarchical division of labor, grueling production schedules, and a high weekly output (see chapter 2). For McCay, though, animation was first and foremost *performative*. This had certainly been true of his lightning-sketch act, traces of which remain in the live prologues of *Little Nemo* (1911) and *Gertie* (1914). Yet performance also lurks in the boastful intertitle at the beginning of *Bug Vaudeville* in which McCay throws down a gauntlet to other animators, dismissing what they do as somehow inhumanly mechanized.[5] Artisan-performers such as McCay were, like the hobo in *Bug Vaudeville*, a slowly and quietly dying breed. At the same time, vaudeville, while still quite popular, was beginning to give ground to an increasingly powerful movie industry, to which commercial animation was becoming a fully integrated adjunct. Occupying an indeterminate space between house and stage, the hobo is both a member of the audience and McCay's stand-in (he who dreams the characters to life). In this he invokes what Donald Crafton has recently described as "animation performativity," the cocreation of the animate world by the animator, his creations, and the audience watching the performance.[6] The spider, like the other denizens of the bug vaudeville troupe, moves in and out of the indeterminate space of the stage/background; unlike the others, he seems intent on consuming the hobo, absorbing him into an apparently dying form of performance, and of sociality. This short film is elegaic, paying homage to not one but two embattled performative forms: vaudeville generally and hand-drawn, performed animation in particular. For McCay, animation was more than simply a mode of visual narrative; it was an attraction centered around a performing animator who was part artist, part magician, and part raconteur. And vaudeville was more than simply another form of performance; it was a distinctly social entertainment in which performers and audience members sometimes engaged in a lively colloquy that punctured the boundaries between stage and house.[7]

In this light, the film becomes legible as a paean to a dying mode of artisanal production, and to the fading of vaudeville in general. But the strange spatial relations of the piece are as important as its dolorous, lethargic pacing and its sad sparsity. McCay was known as a master of depth of field and spatial relations in both his still and animated work.[8] In *Bug Vaudeville*, the confusion between the background and the plane of action is unsettling, and it seems unlikely that he would accidentally confuse the two. Whether the cartoon's indeterminate backgrounds are intended or merely strange happenstance, they present a troubled metaphysics, one in which the boundaries between audience and performer are occluded, as well as those between two-dimensional and three-dimensional space. The hobo, the lone human figure at this performance, is acknowledged at the outset as both its creator—it's his dream that produces the performers—and its consumer. Yet he himself is insubstantial: not only do the performers have more volume and substance than he does, they can move freely between the two-dimensional backgrounds and the ostensibly three-dimensional space of the stage, while the hobo is trapped in his seat and in silhouette. More than that, the movements of the performers actually morph the space itself, turning curtains into a stage and vice versa. In the end, the tramp's creation is so powerful that it attempts to absorb him into its lethargic, chthonic realm. He dreams of the vaudeville show that will consume him: in an empty house, it preys on the last live audience member, without whom there is no show. Animation, which McCay conceived of as a performative form, had transformed before his eyes into an industry, one in which the products consumed their producers—in which animators became anonymous workers and the characters, the product, were the stars. When the product consumed its producer, the boundaries between representational realms—the painted drop, the thin sliver of the stage apron, and the "real" world of the house—collapsed. In this short tale lies a history of spatial metaphysics and material relations, of an oscillation between the factory floor and the final product, of the performance of real social change at the level of both content and form.[9]

EFFICIENTLY PRODUCING FUN

This history is rather mundane, and very important because of its very plainness. Commercial animation in the United States was first created by a relative few practitioners, and at a very specific historical juncture—when motion pictures were emerging as a dominant form of entertainment. At the same time, in the first two decades of the twentieth century, modes of production (and their attendant social relations) were also undergoing a radical transformation: the industrialization that had begun in the previous century was approaching its apotheosis in regimes of efficiency, management, and regulation that are today often grouped under the sign of "Fordism." Within this rapidly changing social and material landscape, the roots of commercial animation's aesthetics, in tropes so common we scarcely notice them today (such as the convention of putting gloves on characters or of characters speaking directly to the audience), were bound to the interests, tastes, and cultural expectations of those early animators and producers as they navigated this changing social, material, and industrial landscape.

American animation came of age in a historical moment when the tensions between dying craft systems of industrial labor and an emerging rational industrial economy found their expression in regimes of efficiency (and in resistance to those regimes). The first two decades of the twentieth century witnessed a craze for popular systems of time and motion management, the two most notable of which were the "stopwatch studies" of F. W. Taylor and the self-aggrandizing time and motion cinematography of Lillian and Frank Gilbreth (later sentimentally memorialized in the book and film *Cheaper by the Dozen* [Gilbreth and Carey/Lang, 1948/1950]). Efficiency experts such as the Gilbreths and Taylor argued that the application of rationalized modes of management to production would increase productivity *and* the health and happiness of employees. Workers used to a degree of workplace autonomy, on the other hand, saw in the new regimes a loss of productive freedom and in automation the diminuation of their humanity.[10] While struggles over the rationalization of production in the late nineteenth and early twentieth centuries found visible and often violent expression in strikes and walkouts by laborers and in armed responses to those strikes by owners and by the state, a more fantastic expression of that struggle took place in animation—in the performed relationship between animators and their creations, enacted first on the vaudeville stage and later on-screen. In that performance, the animator created a cartoon character who by its very nature was rebellious, disobedient, and disruptive. Having intentionally created a difficult character, during the course of the cartoon short the animator performed the regulation, if not punishment, of the very bad behaviors that he himself had created.[11] In an emergent industry increasingly subject to rationalization, the animator performed a resistance to that rationalization through the product of that process, and, strangely, the punishment of that resistance as well.

Animation, then, offers more than simply an example of that historical change; it is a visible (and eventually audible) expression of the struggles inherent in that process. For in the repeating themes and characters of American animation one witnesses both the violence that lay behind regimented labor and its resistance by the products of that labor. This relationship was so deeply embedded in the cartoon that when vaudeville began to yield ground to the movies, the performing animator did not go softly into the night but lived on as a signature trope, a story repeated again and again, compulsively. As the performing animator was replaced in the 1920s by the producer performing *as* animator, who then performed the management of the labor of animation in the public relations of the 1930s, there remained nonetheless in each iteration a performance of labor, its resistance, and its eventual subjugation—all in the service of giving life to a cartoon.[12]

While it is possible to trace animation back centuries, to precinematic technologies such as the camera obscura, zoetrope, or phaenakistiscope, or to elaborations on the magic-lantern show such as Reynaud's Théâtre Optique—not to mention to the nonperformative realms of graphic arts in general and the comic strip in particular—in the United States hand-drawn animation had its public debut around the turn of the twentieth century, often in conjunction with staged performance.[13] There, cartoon-ing met the vaudeville stage in the form of the lightning-sketch. Popular even before the emergence of the cinema, on film the lightning-sketch act was of a piece with trick films, such as *Living Playing Cards* (Méliès, 1904) or *The Haunted Hotel* (Blackton, 1907). The lightning-sketch added the presence and mastery of the artist to early cinematic experiments in double-exposure, stop action, matte painting, and what Tom Gunning has called the "splice of substitution," all of which characterized the illusion-ism and misdirection of the trick film.[14]

In the lightning-sketch film, the indexicality of early animation, the act of pointing to the process of making, depended on the skill of the animator's hand and on the back-and-forth between the artist and his audience (or hers: early practitioner James Stuart Blackton performed in drag for a time). Topicality also lent a quality of immediacy to routines, as in the racist transformations performed in Blackton's *Lightning-Sketches* (1907)—in which he converts the word "Coon" into the image of a "coon shouter" or blackface minstrel and "Cohen" into a stereotypical image of a Jewish man—or in his and McCay's winking references to drink-ing, smoking, and other vices in acts that played on stages when temper-ance was a hotly contested issue for the middle-class audiences vaudeville chains were attempting to attract.[15] The lightning-sketch always involved the artist's intervention in and disruption of the seemingly stable world of his own drawing, revealing other meanings hidden within the apparent stability of an image or word. This type of early animation participated in an enduring legacy of the stage as a location for play and struggle—play with the vagaries of meaning in a quasi-pluralist society, play with the dissolving limitations of the physical world in an age of intense techno-logical invention and intervention, and play with the forces of manufac-ture in an emerging industrial society—articulated through the distor-tion, manipulation, and puncturing of spatial boundaries and through the previously impossible alteration of time into the unreasonably fast or

FIG. 1.2 James Stuart Blackton performs in *Lightning Sketches* (1907), glancing back at his audience to affirm their relationship to him as he transforms the words "Coon" and "Cohen" into racist caricatures.

the incredibly slow. Norman Klein has described the self-consciousness of early animation, the means by which animators reminded audiences of what Leo Charney and Vanessa Schwartz have called the "shock of the modern." Animators, by exposing the seams of the illusion through impossible transformations and with their own intruding hands, produced an *animorph*, the trace of a performance sympathetic to that dislocation: "All these fragments make a sum effect, a *condensed* narrative about decay or loss; in other words, the loss of control, the loss of the past, the loss of representation. I hesitate to call it a fable, because it is so architectonic. Perhaps I should simply call it a meta-fable, but the subject is how metamorphosis is built. The audience is supposed to sense the hand intruding."[16] While the increasing dominance of narrative cinematic realism in the live cinema of the decades to come would doom this sort of performative struggle to the ghetto of trick photography (and of what Gunning has described as a cinema of attractions), it would continue to persist and even flourish in drawing-based films.[17]

With the backward glance of the artist toward the audience, the lightning-sketch film divided its diegetic space into layers of proximity to the real world: it referred simultaneously to the object being created and to a bond between the performer and the audience witnessing that creation, with the additional audience pleasure in jokes about the contemporary cultural or political issues to which the routine referred.[18] The deepest space of creation (that is, the diegetic space most removed from the world of the audience) was the sketch pad or blackboard itself. There the creatures the animator drew lived for a moment before being erased and replaced, or metamorphosed into other things, other people, other animals. The next diegetic layer was the stage on which the artist performed, where a Blackton or McCay capered, demonstrating their mastery over the pad or blackboard. Next was the layer of the filmed audience, sometimes implicit, sometimes depicted. Finally, at the screen boundary the diegetic gave way to the theater where the lightning-sketch film was screened, a space the film often shared with other, live, performances. To generalize, early animated films—that is, films involving moving drawings—deployed a common trope of a mise en abyme that explicitly linked the real of the audience to the cinematic real, and to the drawn, treating all as contiguous realms.[19] Animation as performance, then, suggested an affinity between the performing animator, his creations, and his audience: all were animate beings, differing in kind and degree, but all engaged in the push-and-pull of maker and made, performer and audience. The implicit understanding in this metaphysics was that there was no clear boundary between the real and the ideal, and that the animator had the ability to make of the ideal something approximating the real—including the real of the social and material relations that obtained outside the theater door.

The work of the lightning-sketch animator offered access to other planes of existence, regions on, into, and from which something approximating living beings could be drawn.[20] As a performance tradition, this work suggested a spatial metaphysics in which those other planes of existence were made manifest through the animator's labor. Even camera-shy Emile Cohl—who produced elaborate and engaging drawn animation in France as early as 1908, and by 1913 was in the United States adapting George McManus's popular newspaper comic *The Newlyweds* for the American branch of Éclair—inserted his hand into the frame in *Fantasmagorie* (1908) and *The Hasher's Delerium* (1910).[21] Yet from the perspective of American animation's enduring tropes—self-reflexivity, the acknowledgment of its audience, and the tricksterish resistance of its main characters—certain animators stand out as having introduced performative signatures that quickly became conventions. There are practical reasons specific to the production of animation that make this conservation of convention common. But first and foremost, the *form* of animation itself, with its metaphysics of enlivening the inanimate, suggested a crossing over, a calling forth of life.[22] Even if not every animator expressed his craft on the stage, animation was understood from the outset as being at least as inherently performative as it was representational.[23] This was true of Blackton, of Felix the Cat producer Pat Sullivan, and particularly of Winsor McCay at the height of his career.

THE PLAY'S THE THING

Still, given how few cartoons were made before 1913 and how few films an artisan like Winsor McCay made during his lifetime, there is a danger of drawing overly broad conclusions from a relatively small sample, making someone like McCay stand in for an emergent set of practices of which he was only one lone and somewhat peculiar practitioner. Yet there are other antecedents. Blackton, who also has a strong claim to initiating American animation, as well as to early experiments in film technique and technology, not only preceded McCay with filmed sketch acts but also was a friend of McCay's, and his Vitagraph corporation shot the finished product of *Little Nemo* (1911).[24] (As Crafton points out, Blackton may have based *his* lightning-sketch films on works from England and France by the likes of Walter R. Booth and Georges Méliès.)[25] Similarly, only a year after he made *Dreams of Rarebit Fiend*, a live film based on the popular McCay comic strip, Edison director Edwin S. Porter made *The Teddy Bears* (1907), a comic retelling of how President Theodore Roosevelt got his nickname, which features a stop-action teddy bear dance that takes place in an indeterminate space located somewhere beyond a crack in a wall. Like a vaudeville act in the middle of a play, this dancing teddy bear scene is narratively and spatially dislocated from the film's plot, an animated interlude. And even John Randolph Bray, who with his wife, Margaret, played a key role in rationalizing animation, opened his first cartoon, *The Artist's Dream* (1912–1913), with the conceit of a sketch coming to life. Indeed, Bray credits the lightning-sketch with getting him into cartoons: "I was about fifteen, and we were living in a little town near Detroit, when I happened to attend a 'chalk talk' given by the cartoonist from the Detroit 'Journal.' His lecture was illustrated with drawings, which he made with quick, bold strokes before the eyes of the audience. My own almost popped out as I watched him; and I decided that night that I, too, would be a cartoonist."[26] And although the cartoonists Tom Powers and George McManus turned their comic strips over to other artists to be animated, even they made cameos in McCay's film version of his stage show.[27] In the American con-

FIG. 1.3 Felix the Cat imitates Charlie Chaplin in *Felix in Hollywood* (1923), a Pat Sullivan Cartoons creation that brought the two stars together.

text, at least, Blackton, and then later McCay and Bray, placed animation firmly in the tradition of the lightning-sketch, and it was widely accepted that the lines between media such as comic strips and film, and between independent texts and stage performances, were not fixed.

That syncretism would inspire the next generation of animators as well. Otto Messmer, the creator of Felix the Cat, claims that one of his earliest memories of animation was of McCay: "After he [McCay] did that mosquito thing [*How a Mosquito Operates* (1912)], that ran all over vaudeville theatres," Messmer recalled, "he used to appear personally in vaudeville. That was an act, you know. It was quite a thing to see drawings move."[28] Even before he caught McCay's act, Messmer had been moved by Blackton's early efforts, about which he reported, almost seventy years later: "Moving pictures began when I was a kid . . . about six or seven years old. My aunt took me to a theatre in Hoboken [New Jersey], all they had in those days was vaudeville; motion pictures weren't here yet. So they showed, as one of the acts, just a one-minute film showing motion; something moving. And the people thought it was terrific. You know. Actually a fella, I think it was J. Stuart Blackton, he just had a face changing expressions [*The Enchanted Drawing*, 1900]—and the people howled, you know—he did animate it." Messmer also claims that his boss, Pat Sullivan, got *his* start in a lightning-sketch act: "I know he [Sullivan] had a vaudeville act with a fellow named George Clardey. I never saw them. Guess I was a little too young then. . . . Sullivan would come out and he would draw like a whatdoyoucallit? Gra-feet-ti, draw a face, they had some kind of a trick where Calardey [*sic*] on the other side would, the face would animate. They would make a real red nose on this face and somehow or other Calardey would substitute a red balloon, blow it up."[29]

For Messmer, film and animation were part of continuum that included vaudeville. Although Messmer is generally acknowledged as creating and drawing Felix, Sullivan, his producer, took credit for the cat, a character that became incredibly popular during the 1920s—so much so that both Buster Keaton and Charlie Chaplin (of whom Sullivan's studio created an animated version) sent photos of themselves to Messmer so that he could incorporate their signature gestures into the cat's repertoire.[30] Crafton also reports that a young Keaton appeared on the same bill as McCay and Gertie and that parts of his *Three Ages* (1923) were inspired by McCay's act.[31]

This suggests, first, the importance of vaudeville's performative traditions, such as the lightning-sketch, to the development of American animation. Lightning-sketch artists, like other vaudeville performers, engaged in colloquy with their audiences and with fellow performers, and the interplay between the performing animator and his creation followed in that vein. Likewise, the classic vaudeville two-comic act was built around the running gag of the (seemingly) smarter partner failing to get his associate to see common sense, during which both partners enlisted the audience through double takes and asides. (Think of Laurel and Hardy, Abbott and Costello, or Burns and Allen, to name but a few; Abbott and Costello's "Who's On First" routine is perhaps the act's most famous example.) The same approach marked the conventional performance of their predecessors, blackface minstrelsy's end men Tambo and Bones. In minstrelsy, either Tambo would take the part of the more worldly minstrel, a spin-off of Zip Coon, or that role would fall to the (white) interlocutor, whom Bones would frustrate and amuse with his willful minsunderstandings. The trope of the comic duo, then, with its alloy of humor and annoyance, circulated and evolved between performative forms and media, including the sparring between the performing animator and his creation, and later in the direct address to audiences by continuing characters such as Bugs Bunny or Screwy Squirrel.

Beyond their conventional contribution to gag structure, these earlier stage forms played a significant role in the development of the aesthetics and styles of animators, or what Mark Langer has referred to as the "polyphony and heteregeneity" of forms that came together in American commercial animation.[32] For example, Dave Fleischer—before he and his brothers founded the studio that created Ko-Ko, Betty Boop, Superman, and Popeye—worked as an usher in the Palace Theater in New York, and he later recounted the influence of the vaudeville he watched there on his style and ideas: "What I enjoyed about that was watching the shows. I watched the laughs, and I watched the reactions. . . . There always was an act, something like acrobats in the beginning, then there was a singer, then a comedian, then they'd have a sketch, every week or whenever they changed programs. . . . Timburg [sic] and Rooney was a very famous act. An Irishman and a Jew . . . they were very funny. . . . If they played the Palace, I saw them. Weber and Fields were very funny."[33] Timberg and Rooney were a comic two-act that combined eccentric dancing with rapid-fire patter. Weber and Fields were another famous comic duo—Weber playing the clever half, Fields the simpleton—that began on the vaudeville stage and eventually appeared in films.[34] Like many vaudeville routines, these two-acts winkingly punctured the boundary between the performer and the audience, the smarter half looking to the audience for support, the simpler half gaining it through his or her innocent goodwill. Getting his gags from vaudeville, Fleischer based the look of Ko-Ko the Clown on a costume he'd made for a clowning job at Steeplechase Park in Brooklyn. This is the costume in which he was filmed when the Fleischers developed the animation technique of rotoscoping in the late teens. Norman Klein suggests that because the Fleischer animators would often adjourn to vaudeville theaters and jazz clubs after work, bringing what they had seen back to the studio, the Fleischer operation was first indebted to vaudeville aesthetics and later to the emerging swing music scene of the late 1920s.[35] Likewise, animator Dick Huemer, who grew up in the same neighborhood as the Fleischers and recalled seeing McCay's *Gertie* at the Cretona Theater in the Bronx, also traced his early influences in animation back to the vaudeville stage. Although popular histories of the rise of Hollywood often suggest that the movies killed vaudeville, in animation as well as in live cinema the two not only shared the stage, but traded performative conventions and practices as well.[36]

This genealogy of influences partially explains the convention of ongoing antagonism between so many performing animators and their creations, a tradition that continued whether the animator was onstage or not. In spite of animation's rapid industrialization, the performance of the *act* of animating continued throughout its rationalization, in the Fleischers' Out of the Inkwell series as well as in a number of the Felix shorts, Wallace Carlson's Dreamy Dud series, Walter Lantz's Pete the Pup, and elsewhere. (Producers Max Fleischer and Lantz favored appearing as the live animator dueling with his creation; in other studios' output, a metonymic photograph of an animator's hand indicated his performative presence.) Even after the introduction of sound, performative animation continued in a reduced form, from Hugh Harman and Rudy Ising's introduction of the minstrel character Bosko as a two-man act between Bosko and Ising (1930) to Disney's public-relations performances of the father–son relationship between Walt Disney and Mickey Mouse. Animation's ongoing celebration of the technology of industrial production (which Disney made central to its public relations beginning in the 1930s) shifted performances of skill from the vaudeville stage to the behind-the-scenes promotion of the animation studio as factory floor, and from the celebration of cartooning's raw labor to that of its management—but they were performances nonetheless.

When the animator or his metonymic hand appeared on-screen, though, the animated character inevitably resisted, as if embodying the frustrated labor of the animator himself. This struggle sedimented the convention established between McCay's fetishized piles of individual drawings and Emile Cohl's anonymous hand alternately aiding and tormenting Pierrot, through which the metaphysical power of animation was understood from its inception as ineluctably tied to the physical labor of its creation. The performance of animation was from the first also a performance of labor.

THE PERFORMANCE OF PREINDUSTRIAL ANIMATION

When he designed *Little Nemo* (1911) and *Gertie* (1914) McCay created the conceit that the lightning-sketch was the motivating force from which his animation sprang. There was a practical reason for this: both the fragmentary *Little Nemo* and *Gertie* were films *and* filmic elements in stage shows. (Compare them with his *How a Mosquito Operates* [1912], which, though included in his stage show, stands alone as a film.) In both films, McCay played himself as animator, a character somewhere between a circus ringmaster and the interlocutor of a blackface minstrel show, engaged in the push and pull of control and resistance.[37] Beyond this pragmatic explanation for their narrative structure—the filmed prologues of these animated shorts replaced a stage act that was itself modeled on a lightning-sketch act in order to retain the performative thrust of the animation—the use of the familiar lightning-sketch to introduce the unfamiliar form of animation points to the ongoing tension between conservation and marginal differentiation that marked vaudeville performance. Henry Jenkins has argued that vaudeville audiences were treated to the pleasure of repetition in the form of familiar jokes, songs, and routines and took yet more pleasure in witnessing the innovative skill with which individual performers remade familiar acts.[38] Likewise, McCay presented a new marvel (animation) via a comforting context (the lightning-sketch).

The setup for his early pieces was simple: socializing with friends and fellow artists such as George McManus and Tom Powers or comic film star John Bunny, McCay makes a bet about his ability to make still drawings come to life. A series of scenes then lays out the intense labor of animation, portraying McCay as a lone craftsman toiling over thousands of drawings, aided only by bumbling assistants. Finally, the finished product is revealed to his friends, and to an appreciative audience, as a lightning-sketch that comes to life. *Gertie* also ends with the stage trick of McCay seeming to ride off on the dinosaur's back, leaving the "real" world for that of the drawn. These performance films offered the spectacle of melding two distinct ways of presenting the act of animation. The prologues that precede the social event at which the bet is won (a generic social gathering for *Nemo*, a formal dinner for *Gertie*) depict animation as a craft and a solitary occupation. These apparent acts of revelation also *occlude* the details of animation's production, reducing it to the simple act of drawing.[39] Yet the scene of the bet's payoff, a framing device for the animation itself, contradicts the prologue's focus on labor by framing animation as the direct descendant of the lightning-sketch and presenting the cartoons as if they actually emerged ex nihilo there on the stage.

Ultimately, both of these frames—the prologue and the payoff—present animation as performative. Yet one offers that performance as the revelation of otherwise invisible labor, the other as the visible performance of drawing skill elevated to the level of magic. More specifically, the performance of the bet's payoff effaces that of the work that preceded it, replacing images of protracted labor with those of instantaneous legerdemain. McCay's performance for his friends suggests that animation is simply a lightning-sketch performed in long form, over months instead of minutes, and this gesture creates a historical continuity between the practices of the lightning-sketch and of film animation, effectively erasing the break between performative and productive practices that McCay had announced in earlier scenes. This origin story grounded in the labor of animation hints at the potential anonymity of the laboring animator, yet the device of the lightning-sketch attenuates that danger by relocating

FIG. 1.4 Winsor McCay performs the labor of animation for *Little Nemo* (1911) on a movie set that does not attempt to appear real.

the product of that labor as still under the control of McCay as a performing animator.

McCay also presented this spectacle as a complex interaction between competing planes of cinematic space. Unlike the relatively more realistic office set that the Fleischers would use for their Out of the Inkwell series (1919–1928), McCay's "studio" in his framing narrative was a patently obvious stage set, right down to its shaky trompe l'oeil flats depicting walls and its giant barrels indexically marked "INK" (like the huge bales labeled "PAPER" in *Little Nemo*). Likewise, the design of the sets for the bet payoffs in both films, and the framing and composition of the shots, reinforce the sense that those scenes are set within a proscenium, as does McCay's declamatory mode of address when he presents his creations to his friends. Occupying a space that is obviously a stage, McCay works his magic in a liminal zone between drawn space (itself further divided into fore-, middle-, and background), an on-screen audience that appears at the beginning of the film, and an implicit audience: us. Both he and Gertie acknowledge the presence of outside observers—McCay because he is performing for his friends, Gertie because she has been ordered to greet them . . . and so when she bows, it is both to them and to the film audience. The audiences who would have attended the live shows at which these cartoons premiered have become gestural referents, vestigially present in McCay's winking address to the camera.

Although at first glance the space of the studio and the space of the dinner might seem contradictory—one the space of a budding cinematic realism, the other closer to declamatory vaudeville—they are joined through McCay's performance: each is ultimately structured as a location for a vaudeville sketch, with what narrative there is in service of the gag. In the first, he demonstrates with significant self-reflexivity that his labor is invested in the thousands of drawings he has produced. In the second, that labor becomes manifest as the motive force behind a lightning-sketch that can live and change without the constant intervention of his hand. That hand had intervened already in the studio, and all that is required now is that he reinvoke its mastery through spoken commands. As John Canemaker has suggested, Winsor McCay was proud of his control over the products of his own labor, and Gertie in particular was its embodiment, obedient yet willful.[40] The conceit of the lightning-sketch cemented this relationship, as McCay performed the act of creation in long form, with his own body on the stage the embodiment of his drawing hand in motion.

That tension between obedience and willful resistance is important. Gertie's momentary petulance when she ignores a command, as she does several times during the short film, is a performance at a distance: having made a great show of creating Gertie, McCay now seemingly cannot fully control the product of his own labor—or he has created her resistance so that he may reassert that control after losing it.[41] That performance of control, of course, hinges on his ability to penetrate animate space, which itself depends on the permeability of the plane that separates the drawn world from the cinematic real. At the historical moment of its performance in the early teens, the control that McCay performed was passing from the individual artisan to the manager who oversaw increasingly divided labor: it is a performance of control being lost and a fantasy of it being regained.

EARLY CARTOON MODERNITY: GERTIE ON BROADWAY

From its opening sequence, *Gertie*, made seven years before *Bug Vaudeville* and arguably one of the founding texts of American animation, celebrates rather than mourns the performance of individual skill and of labor. The film opens with a lugubrious pan of the exterior of the American Museum of Natural History in New York and an equally slow establishing shot of McCay, fellow newspaper cartoonist George McManus, and other friends, riding in an open car. Fortuitously (an intertitle tells us), they get a flat

FIG. 1.5 Winsor McCay, in the style of a lightning-sketch artist, glances at the camera as he pretends that a still drawing of his dinosaur, Gertie, is animated in the live prologue to *Gertie* (1914).

tire outside the museum, and while their driver fixes it the friends tour the dinosaur exhibit. The group pauses to admire the skeleton of an apatosaurus (identified as a "dinosaurus"). Within moments, McCay has bet McManus that he can create an animated film of the dinosaurus in six months' time. So, the framing narrative for the film leaves the hurly-burly of Manhattan's streets to contemplate a relic that is located in an evolutionary time frame, then proceeds with a bet that has a time limit of six months. Time is of the essence. This is followed by a sequence of scenes portraying those six months in which we witness McCay single-handedly producing the ten thousand drawings required to bring Gertie to life, showing off the drawings to McManus, then revealing the completed film to his friends at a formal dinner party.

But McCay doesn't actually reveal a *film* to them. Instead he proceeds in the fashion of a vaudeville lightning-sketch act, first drawing his dinosaur on a blank pad of paper. Challenged that he had promised to make it move, McCay tears the drawing off the pad, revealing a rocky paleolithic landscape. He leans in and draws the snout of his dinosaur peeking shyly out from between some rocks, then invites her to come out. Having introduced this performance as operating somewhere between the pace of evolution (or extinction and fossilization) and that of the rapid new technology of film, McCay recapitulates the importance of time to his narrative by invoking another popular amusement. He offers up a lightning-sketch—the magical revelation of an artist's skill in transforming one object or person into another in real time—as an evolutionary precursor to animation . . . a craft that itself requires laborious operations that unfold over months (instead of seconds) and that he has just demonstrated in the framing narrative.

Cutting to a close-up that obscures the framing story, we watch Gertie emerge from her cave and perform tricks for us at McCay's bidding. At the end of the film, McCay seems to clamber into a corner of the sketch pad/ screen with a whip in his hand, climbing onto Gertie's back and riding off into the distance. In that final sequence the film changes from a study in time to one that troubles space. Far from being disjunctive, though, this shift encapsulates the historical moment when the film was made. It presents to its audience an understanding of the linearity of performative time and its immediacy relative to longer time frames. It contrasts this with the labor of animation, which is achingly slow in a performative time frame and blindingly fast in an evolutionary one (remember that we are witnessing the reanimation of the extinct *and* the performance of the evolution of new technologies of amusement). The performance is animation as magic: a long-extinct creature is brought to life through skill and imagination, and in the end the animator who created it slips into its prehistoric world.[42] The film is also a demonstration of the intense labor behind that magic: the act of animation requires months of planning, detailed drawing, and careful filming. Winsor McCay has chosen to perform the magic of animation by embodying the tension between the legerdemain of the lightning-sketch and animation's repetitive task of iterative drawing in the form of a reanimated dinosaur. He uses the omnipotent hand of the animator to overcome geologic time, and he uses film as the documentary medium that reveals the labor lurking behind the hand's magical powers, yet he then embodies and occludes that labor in a final product that is kittenish in its playful disobedience and massively lumbering toward extinction.

In the film, McCay seems to be in colloquy with the creation on his lightning-sketch easel, and he creates the illusion that the projection screen itself is a permeable giant sketch pad that permits him passage between the drawn and real worlds.[43] Even more, perhaps, than in the live version of his show, he presents himself as a master of time and space and of everything that dwells within the world he creates. In the filmic version, we are reminded of this at moments such as when he appears to feed Gertie—playing with scale by tossing a large pumpkin in to her from the stage, which then appears the size of a pea when she catches it in her mouth—with the bonus of having witnessed in the act's preamble the intense labor that went into creating that illusion. In this, *Gertie* offers up a crystallization of tropes that were already becoming conventional in the emerging form of film animation: the permeability of the screen surface, the performing animator as animating force, and the animated creature's awareness of its creator, its audience, and its own production. These performed gestures link a celebration of the intense creative labor of the craft to its fluid temporal and spatial metaphysics.

This was an evanescent moment, passing even as it emerged. While McCay celebrated his mastery over the cartoon world onstage, other animators and producers, such as Earl Hurd, Raoul Barré, Bill Nolan, Gregory La Cava, Paul Terry, and John and Margaret Bray, were laying the practical, technical, and hierarchical groundwork for an animation industry that would mass-produce this magic for a growing movie market. Indeed, in the same year that McCay produced *Gertie*, the Brays began hiring animators (as workers) to put out their Colonel Heeza Liar series (1913–1924). And while producers in the emerging live-feature market were articulating norms of narrative continuity that would consign gestures toward screen permeability and the fluid relationship between performed and textual space, such as those practiced by McCay and Gertie, to the ghetto of trick photography, McCay was still drawing attention to the metaphysics of animate space and its ineluctable link to the labor of creating it.[44]

At a historical moment when the social spaces of entertainment were being transformed (such as from vaudeville theaters and nickelodeons into movie palaces) and the social spaces of work were also undergoing radical change (through the rise of the Fordist factory), McCay's was a performance that ran against the grain of modernity even as it celebrated its advances. To reiterate, in the teens and early twenties, the United States witnessed a popular mania for tropes of efficiency and rationalization that linked time and space through the figure of the laboring body.[45] In industrial management, F. W. Taylor had popularized "stopwatch studies" of workers' movements, and Lillian and Frank Gilbreth then made films that charted the flow of work against the organization of work spaces, calling their research "time and motion study" (see chapter 2). Yet McCay's stubbornly preindustrial practices—he drew the action for virtually every frame himself, and (for his early films) on rice paper, not celluloid—actually flew in the face of efficiency. (In this vein, Scott

Bukatman has argued that in works such as *Little Sammy Sneeze*, McCay mocked the pretensions of time and motion study by appending chaos to the slow-motion study of Sammy's sneeze and its aftermath.)[46] In the live filmic preamble to Gertie's appearance, McCay's cinematographer piles individual drawings into an assistant's arms, higher and higher, until the pile falls to the ground, hopelessly shuffled. At least in its fantasy form, McCay's is an obstinately inefficient system, one that requires that the animator be ever-present in the frame, directing and controlling his workers and his creation, eventually escaping into the drawn world he has created. Like the lightning-sketch that McCay invokes in *Gertie*, the preindustrial animated films presented drawn space and the creatures that inhabited it as themselves performative: malleable, permeable, and under the ultimate control of their creators. These film shorts were proffered as artisanal products crafted to the particulars of the time and place in which they emerged. Yet even though this preindustrial film was made at the same time as films produced in the industrial mode, the fantastic relation between the animator and his creation that McCay performed became a durable convention in the products of the emerging animation industry, a standardized celebration of a relation largely fantastic from its very beginning.

From the perspective of distribution and exhibition, McCay's approach was a boutique version of animation not well adapted to producing a steady supply of product on a reliable schedule. The form's requirement of thousands of drawings for even a short film (ten thousand drawings yielding about seven minutes of film) effectively limited the field to those with both the talent and the willingness to engage in intense artistic labor; as a for-profit business with a very tight margin, it demanded labor and time-saving techniques as well. (It is worth noting that McCay made a great deal of his money performing, earning in some years over $1,500 a week for his performances.)[47] Within a few years in the midteens, animation was effectively reorganized from an artisanal model, with a sole animator directing a collection of amateur assistants (which had existed more as a performance than as a practical reality), to the systematic and highly organized production of animated shorts, with a producer managing a group of animators, themselves supported by journeymen and apprentices and, eventually, by departments of tracing, inking, and so on. From 1914 on, a flurry of patents for improved techniques of registration (the stable alignment of successive images on a drawing surface or photographic stage), reproduction (the lithographic and later xerographic mass production of

FIG. 1.6 Lillian and Frank Gilbreth's set for a cinematic time and motion study of a typist, c. 1914. Courtesy of Purdue University Libraries, Karnes Archives and Special Collections.

FIG. 1.7 Winsor McCay's cinematographer and his assistant pile drawings into McCay's assistant John Fitzsimmons's arms, performing the material enormity of the task of making *Gertie* (1914).

backgrounds), and materials (from inks and their carrier solutions to the use of celluloid ["cels"] instead of rice paper) contributed to rationalizing the production of animation and to intensified commercial competition. This intense legal and technical activity effectively transformed a craft that was performed into an industry that performed its performativity. These rapid technological developments, and their regulation through patents and licensing, beyond indicating the rapid rationalization of animation, signal the consolidation and control of the industry by producers and the accumulation of animators' labor power in the hands of their managers. Yet in spite of this, or perhaps because of it, the performative conventions McCay adapted from the vaudeville stage quickly became standard tropes in many mass-produced cartoons as well.

The point here is not to rehearse the tiredly glorious narrative of innovation and origin that crowds around every story of invention. Nor is it to romantically glorify McCay's idiosyncratic style as somehow producing a purer or more genuine form of animation. What is more important is that only a few scant years (at most) passed between what most historians of animation mark as its beginning in the United States and its industrialization. Yet in spite of the brevity of that interval, a number of the conventions McCay celebrated in his early films—self-reflexivity, the permeability of screen boundaries, the interplay between the animated character and its creator, and a metaphysics of time and of space linked to, but different from, that of the cinematic real—all have their antecedents in staged animation, and all became enduring tropes in film animation. McCay didn't invent these conventions; like any other show person, he adapted them from others on the vaudeville stage, who had in turn developed them from their antecedents in popular stage entertainments, such as burlesque and blackface minstrelsy.[48] Indeed, just as performed animation overlapped with its mass-produced cinematic "descendant," so vaudeville, burlesque, and minstrelsy coexisted at different historical moments. The reappropriation of conventions and tropes was hardly unidirectional: borrowing and reworking material was part of the creative process of popular performance at the turn of the last century, and in this way conventions circulated and metamorphosed between media over time.

Thus, revisiting the origins of American animation and considering whence some of its most enduring conventions derive—its self-reflexivity, the playful trickery of its trademark characters, its puncturing of screen boundaries (either the screen surface or the borders of the frame)—leads back toward a variety of staged entertainments, particularly vaudeville.

These tropes were established not only in the practical and theoretical working out of how to draw convincing narrative cinematic space, or how to model realistic motion and form, but also in the live performance of manufacturing, the demonstration of artisanal mastery in creating and controlling ostensibly living beings.[49] That this performance of animation featured the labor and materials of animation also hints at why the American cartoon, as living commodity, found its most durable form in a precursor to vaudeville, blackface minstrelsy.

HOW ARE YOU TODAY, MR. BONES?

Far from arbitrary in its signification, the minstrel, animate or otherwise, embodies both the American fantasy of self-invention and refashioning and its frustration and constraint. The minstrel is a meeting place for seeming immutability and absolute plasticity, a tense locus of contradiction wherein the possibility of transformation is simultaneously evoked and thwarted. Writing about morphing in cinema, Vivian Sobchack asserts that "the morph's effortless and elastic ease at 'realizing' itself is deeply uncanny: strangely familiar insofar as much of our physical existence is something transparently operational and continuous to us, unfamiliarly strange insofar as the realization of most of our conscious acts involves some degree of hesitation, difficulty, and effort." For Sobchack, the metamorphic act simultaneously encompasses the historically situated stories people who participate in cinematic, Western cultures tell about becoming and changing, about becoming an ostensibly autonomous self. It is a compressed and localized narrative in which all of the hesitations and obstacles, the impediments to our desires—and the fantasy of effortless change that they seem to thwart—all find their apotheosis in the morph: "Thus, in human terms, being is narrativized in time and space as the culmination of a laborious business—first in the effortful process of one's birth and then in the effortful progress of one's life. Hence the uncanniness of metamorphosis as it is figured generally throughout Western literature, marked as it is by the sudden appearance, quick physical change in space, and effortless transformation in time."[50] Like Klein's animorph, Sobchack's morph (the thing metamorphosing) speaks to us as much from the lacunae lurking within its transformation—those moments of either/or and neither/nor—as from a space of recognizability. Invoking the Bakhtinian chronotope, the intersection of time and space through language, to name the experience of metamorphosis in twentieth- and twenty-first-century arts, Sobchack describes the attraction of the morph as a condensation of the discontinuous and difficult process of personally becoming/being.[51] In an era bounded by Horatio Alger and Dale Carnegie, fantasies of self-making, self-improvement, and self-transformation were the ideological currency of the early twentieth century, and that fantasy found its popular expression throughout the vernacular arts. For example, as Rogin has suggested, for Jewish immigrants in the entertainment industry, such as Sophie Tucker, Eddie Cantor, and Al Jolson, blacking up or "coon shouting" was a way to reinvent themselves as (at least marginally) whiter than their immigrant roots seemed to allow.[52] Yet, as some of Rogin's critics have pointed out, performers such as Eddie Leonard also blacked up with greater regard for class advancement than for ethnic revision, and Jewish minstrels such as Cantor or Jolson, despite their successes in blackface (and out), never fully slipped the yoke of their own ethnicity and even winkingly celebrated it.[53] Yet despite those exceptions, what Rogin invokes is a shared fantastic sensibility in which, between the technologies and performative conventions of stage and screen in the early twentieth century, the purported mutability of human existence expressed in the American Creed of self-making and remaking was presented, critiqued, celebrated, and parodied.[54] The quick-change, the lightning-sketch, the transformation by hats, the blackface minstrel, and Felix the Cat's detachable tail were all of a piece.

Of course, as both Rogin and his critics have suggested, that mutability was not experienced equally by all. Even if the act of blacking up offered Jewish entertainers access to previously foreclosed precincts of whiteness, or provided ostensibly white entertainers performing in German, Irish, or Chinese acts further distance from the stigmata of ethnicity, to be African American was to stand as the baseline against which the relative mutability of others could be gauged, both onstage and off. Nowhere was this contradiction more evident than in the oxymoronic dictum "separate but equal" enshrined in *Plessy v. Ferguson* (1896): African Americans were by law understood to be simultaneously the same as, yet immutably different from (and implicitly less than) others.[55]

Within the melange of transformational performances that filled the vaudeville and theater stages at the turn of the twentieth century (including in movies), the seeming immutability of black skin added a transgressive frisson to blackface minstrelsy and its adjuncts. To black up was to invoke that immutability in the service of vernacular metamorphosis and in the process to reinforce its apparent impossiblity for African Americans.

FIG. 1.8 A photograph of a hand, presumably that of Otto Messmer, draws Felix the Cat, who impatiently awaits his completion as a highly mutable animated minstrel.

FIG. 1.9 Al Jolson makes a visual joke about the ethnicity under the burnt cork in *Wonder Bar* (1934).

According to Bukatman, this is where minstrelsy and animation—which share a playful relationship to regimes of similarity and difference—part ways: minstrelsy, he claims, is always grounded in racial and historical specificity, while morphing extends its possibilities beyond the specific to the infinite; the morph can become anything imaginable. For Bukatman, that makes morphing a "caricature of blackface."[56] Yet despite the seemingly limitless possibilities morphing afforded it, commercial animation in the turn-of-the-twentieth-century United States turned to the blackface minstrel to provide the *prima materia*—that which is always also itself no matter what it becomes—for its trademark continuing characters. While popular continuing characters could have become anything, in their resting state they were minstrels. Like the plasmatic material that Eisenstein imagined to be created in and through the act of animation, the minstrel, whether live or animated, always invoked the thingness lurking behind being human, that from which, as Sobchack reminds us, Americans were expected to transform themselves as they became American.[57]

All of which is to say, animation was not simply *influenced* by the performative conventions of vaudeville and minstrelsy. Rather, cartoons, vaudeville, and minstrelsy were all part of an early twentieth-century matrix of entertainments in which ideas and conventions were worked and reworked, adapted and revised. American animation shared the stage with blackface minstrelsy, where both were performed/practiced at the beginning of the twentieth century. Lightning-sketch animators such as J. S. Blackton, Pat Sullivan, and Winsor McCay developed a language of humor and wonder through the apparent free association between one image and the next, the transformation of one thing into another.[58] The repartee between minstrelsy's interlocutor and end men, Tambo and Bones, had also played on the free association of words and ideas, and the lightning-sketch was its visual equivalent. Just as Blackton could in a few strokes convert the words "Coon" and "Cohen" into their derogatory visual equivalents, the minstrel could demonstrate the plasticity of spoken language, its deformability to other purposes:

TAMBO, leaning on his head and meditating.
INTERLOCUTOR.—In what aesthetic garden of thought does your
    mind now wander?
TAMBO.—Eh?
INT.—You were meditating; and while gazing on your mobile face,
    I was forcibly reminded of a painting I once saw, representing—

BONES (interrupting).—The Russian bear driving the Hungry-uns from Turkey.

TAMBO.—There you go, *rushin'* your nose where your mouth shouldn't come.

BONES (to audience).—Were he a *Turk, he* would *gobble* it.

INT.—*Bear* with me gentlemen (reprovingly to Bones); and it would better become you, sir, not to *strut* your unsolicited wit before us at such an unseasonable juncture.

BONES.—All right; I'll *set* still and do *eggs*actly as you say.

INT.—Very well. Now, Tambo, I will repeat my question: What were you meditating upon . . . ?[59]

In this short exchange, dated roughly 1880, the interlocutor, Tambo, and Bones play with double entendre, converting recent news of alliances and struggles between Russia, the Austro-Hungarian Empire, and the failing Ottoman Empire into a reverie about eating, thence from a tale of world powers carving up the Baltic region into a gaggle of puns about turkeys gobbling, strutting, and laying eggs. As with the lightning-sketch, the gag required contemporary and historical knowledge, a pleasure in the mutability of terms, and a quick facility with language on the parts of both performers and audience members. Representing immutability itself, the minstrel performed as an engine of metamorphosis.

Viewed in this light, the minstrel show did not go into decline at the beginning of the twentieth century as much as it changed venue and medium. By the turn of the century, with the stand-alone minstrel show in decline and vaudeville absorbing minstrel acts, the blackface fantasy of a tension between the real and the ideal resident in black bodies was relocating to an emerging complex of mass entertainments, of which vaudeville was perhaps the first, but not the last. The rise of Bert Williams and George and Ada Overton Walker, who, after a start in vaudeville, combined minstrelsy with the Broadway musical to create elaborate stage shows, is a case in point. Without doubt the most famous African American performers of the early 1900s, and by 1910 some of the most famous and well-paid performers of any race, Williams and the Walkers mounted elaborate stage spectacles with names like *In Dahomey* (1902), *Abyssinia* (1906), and *Bandannaland* (1908). In these programs, Williams played a blackface minstrel character known for his self-abnegating routines, slow takes, and songs such as "Nobody" (from *Abyssinia*), which drew attention to and erased a black body wearing burnt cork. Ada Overton Walker was particularly famous for her version of Salome's dance of the seven veils and for popularizing the cakewalk, as was her husband, the comedian, dancer, and raconteur George Walker.[60] Williams and Walker shows, which often split their dramatic action between the United States or Europe and the African continent, played with the substantial and mythical relationships between African Americans and Africans, and with fantasies of African American authenticity.

It was through those terms that the company was praised when it seemed to properly perform "the Negro" and criticized when it seemed to veer from expectation, as in the comments of a Chicago critic on the opening of *Abyssinia* there: "The show is creditable, but it is not representative of them. . . . So it seems a waste of effort that they should try for such [Broadway] effects and meanwhile deprive us of so much that is both true and amusing and which only they can portray—we mean the real American negro, who sings from the heart out, dances with his whole soul and voices his droll and leisurely philosophy of life with such unction."[61] The "real American negro" of which the reviewer speaks was imagined as a fusion of body and soul, a fantasy used in this instance to complain about the troupe straying from the stereotypical conventions of minstrelsy, even as the form itself was fading. This widespread sentiment was echoed repeatedly, as in this review of the same tour:

> Nobody will deny that a negro can be one of the most amusing persons possible as long as he remains a negro. He is the most natural dancer in the world. He can sing simple melodies to perfection. He is a happy-go-lucky fellow who can rattle a pair of bones, pick a banjo, and laugh so heartily that every one within earshot must laugh too. . . . It is when he tries to speak, do, and look like a white man that he is at his worst. That is the reason Abyssinia failed last night. . . . Instead of bringing into the foreground the barbaric splendor of middle Africa, the simple melodies and characteristic dances of the colored race, the laughing, rollicking humor of the black man of all time . . . they constructed a loose-jointed copy of a Broadway musical comedy.

Even if the blackface minstrel show was in decline, the desire of white audiences to see African American performers enact its stereotypes remained strong enough to border on a command. Yet Williams and the Walkers were astute performers and business people and knew how to speak back to stereotype even as they confirmed its underlying logic. In an article in *Theatre Magazine* in 1906 titled "The Real Coon on the American

Stage," George Walker recounted that as he and Williams developed their act, "Bert and I watched the white 'coons' and were often much amused at seeing white men with black cork on their faces trying to imitate black folks. Nothing about these white men's actions was natural, and therefore nothing was as interesting as if black performers had been dancing and singing their own songs in their own way."[62] Even as he mocked white minstrels, Walker affirmed a notion of the superior naturalness of African Americans as "coons." Likewise, in the lead-up to a run of *Abyssinia* in Toledo, Ohio, Walker told the *Toledo Blade*:

> I attribute our success to our knowledge that to please an audience we must give them the real negro character. Few negroes will burlesque their own race; in fact, we don't have to be burlesqued if we stick to nature. That's where the average darkey loses out. We know that when we try to act like white folks, the public won't have us; there are enough bad white actors now. . . . There is no reason why we should be forced to do all these old-time nigger acts. It's all rot, this slap-stick-bandanna handkerchief-bladder in the face act, with which negro acting is associated. It ought to die out and we are trying hard to kill it.[63]

Walker's gentle yet provocative dig at the policing of boundaries between "white" and "black" acting, an insult couched in self-deprecation, should indicate the degree of the troupe's fame in 1907. His claim to want to end the worst of racist stereotypes demonstrates even more the reach of his celebrity. Yet at the same time, the "burlesque" Walker invokes seems in one light to be of actual African American life and culture, in another of those self-same racist fantasies, in which sticking to nature will of itself produce a burlesque. Yet even after several more years of fame, and of gently but firmly resisting reductive minstrel-based stereotypes, soon after George Walker's sudden and tragic death in 1911, the *New York Times* treated Ada Overton Walker to a review of her new show, *His Honor: The Barber*, that scolded her company for straying from the fantasy of the "real negro": "The same fault is to be found with this entertainment that has been found with numerous other negro shows. There is too much effort to imitate white performers and very little attempt at showing the racial cleverness of the performers. Had it not been for the characteristic staging of the choruses the performers for the most part might have been members of an indifferent burlesque company."[64]

Ada Overton's mistake, it seemed, and the mistake of other popular "negro shows" of the day, was in turning their backs on their native racial cleverness, which found its best expression through stump speeches, banjos, bones, and in the end, the cakewalk. Much less was said about what it meant to imitate white performers, the assumption being that theirs was the less native and more European stagecraft, admitting of finer sentiments but at the expense of exuberance and unbridled physicality. As Bert Williams put it in 1910: "The one new stage form which has been developed in this country is of plantation origin; I refer, of course, to minstrelsy. The only music that may be regarded as typically American is Negro music. Minstrelsy is now firmly imbedded [sic] in the American comic spirit; and syncopation or 'rag-time,' an African contribution, has tinged all the popular balladry of this generation." Deriving from the plantation, the minstrel show and its attenuated forms, Williams claimed, was the original American art. And, he continued, it was so not because of the original white minstrel performers but because of the African Americans they imitated: "My observation has led me to the theory that when a strange unassimilated element exists in a nation, it almost immediately finds its way to the stage in comic types, usually caricatured. So the first American comic role was the negro—'Jim Crow' and his fellows. Then with succeeding waves of immigration came the Irishman and the Italian. . . . But the negro, an unamalgamated element, has persisted through them all, without losing his ability to entertain."[65] Williams, himself a minstrel, collapsed Jim Crow and "his fellows" into the first American comic role, "the negro." The waves of immigration that followed, he hinted, "amalgamated" into whiteness eventually, and in the process of that amalgamation lost something essentially comic about themselves. The "negro," unamalgamated and existing somewhere between comic stereotype and actual African American life, could still (and always) entertain because he could not assimilate.[66] Given the support that Williams and the Walkers offered to budding nonminstrel talent in New York in the predawn of the Harlem Renaissance, which Chude-Sokei and others have discussed at length, it seems reasonable to assume that a reading of this sentiment as perhaps a little parodic, as playing on the very constructedness of "the negro," is well within reach.[67] Yet at the same time its deference to the powerful tropes of assimilation and the plantation fantasy of African American life could reaffirm for a white audience the very terms it seemed to call into question.

Why, in a discussion of the animated minstrel, this detour to examine a single troupe, only one of whom was a minstrel, that seemed to defy stereotype even as they played in and with it? First, to demonstrate that although the traditional minstrel troupe may have been in decline in the early 1900s, the blackface minstrel continued in related performance forms. But more than that, the discourse around the relative "realness" of Williams's and the Walkers' performances of fantastic African and African American characters offers an example of the persistence of the minstrel as a fantastic trickster figure, one still in active circulation at the dawn of American commercial animation. That persistence begins to suggest why, when animation producers developed characters that appeared to tread the boundary between the fantastic and the real, coherent expressions of a metamorphic, plasmatic, prime material, they might turn to the minstrel for a model.

On the vaudeville stage of the early twentieth century, as Jenkins has pointed out, not only was mutability important, but interchangeability between forms of performance was key.[68] Animation acts were but one of a variety of bits that made up any vaudeville program. Alongside the dog acts, the acrobats, dancers, and comics, there were also "Dutch" (German), Irish, "Hebrew," and blackface minstrel acts.[69] As Williams hinted in 1910, in a performance style that had its roots in working-class burlesques, a shared experience of oppression ideally allowed one to laugh at being stereotyped, because in theory everyone else in the theater had also gone through it at one point or another. The transformational ethos extended to what contemporary celebrants of the form described as vaudeville's "democratic impulse": the vaudeville house was imagined as a melting pot unto itself in both its transformational acts and (save for segregation) in the nearly free mixing of its patrons.[70]

Yet the mutability that vaudeville, animation, and minstrelsy shared was not shared equally, and the transformation of ideal forms took place against a seemingly fixed backdrop of imagined "real" blackness. The early minstrel show had been a peculiar animal, one in which the usually white performers who blacked up had traditionally claimed that they were re-enacting genuine dances and songs that they (or their forebears) had witnessed slaves perform on southern plantations.[71] Later minstrels, such as Eddie Leonard, who got his big break in George Primrose's troupe in 1903, or Al Jolson, who joined Lew Dockstader's spinoff from Primrose in 1905, maintained the conceit that the African Americans they caricatured were nostalgic, nineteenth-century throwbacks, denizens of the plantation or the Ethiopian show, or northern dandies such as Zip Coon or Jim Dandy. Even the African American minstrel troupe Brooker and Clayton's Georgia Minstrels touted a heritage that traced back to the planta-

THE BREAK DOWN

Portraying the Peculiar Characteristics of the Southern Plantation Negro

Plantation Banjo Song..E. Pierce
Duet—Walk in Joe ....T Vaughn and E Peirce
Ol' Zip Coon.............Raynor, Pierce, Vaughn, Abbott, and George Christy
Plantation Jig..Geo. Christy
Rail Road Overture...Full Hand
Picayune Butler...E. P. Christy
The Gal from the South...L. V. H. Crosby
Medley Chorus...E. P. Christy
Quartette---The Skeeters do Bite...Company
Farewell Ladies...E. P. Christy
Congo Green Dance with Specimens of Ethopian Statuary.....Peirce & G. Christy

FIG. 1.10 A detail from a playbill for Christy's Minstrels, which promises to portray the "Peculiar Characteristics of the Southern Plantation Negroe." Courtesy of the Special Collections Research Center, University of Chicago Library.

tion, with many of its members claiming (truthfully or not) to be former slaves.[72]

Because minstrelsy traded on access to an imagined blackness for its aura of authenticity (particularly in its early days), it was a performance form built on the free appropriation (i.e., theft) of others' material—first from (real or imagined) African Americans and then from other minstrel troupes—yet it conventionally stressed an intimate knowledge of the transitory routes between the real and the ideal.[73] At the same time, the figure of the minstrel pointed to the black body as an object available for (re)use, like the clothing that T. D. Rice borrowed from Cuff, and this idea circulated beyond the bounds of minstrelsy proper. And that black person, that black body, was always understood as socially less than but performatively more than his white counterpart. The interlocutor lorded it over Tambo and Bones, but they always had the last laugh. So it would be with the animated minstrel—the tug-of-war between interlocutor and end men became one between animator and animated.

The real and feigned appropriation of black performance that legitimized minstrelsy fed into and was supported by an assumption of freely circulating cultural goods in both burlesque and vaudeville. To be blunt, one of the central organizing principals in vaudeville was theft: performers regularly poached material from each other and just as regularly complained about that appropriation.[74] And with that borrowing came a practice of marginal differentiation, the changing of a bit or routine just enough to fend off accusations of outright lifting. In this practice, the audience's recognition of a bit's origins, conventions, and references was just as important as its uniqueness, and the sharing of common cultural information was central to the experience of vaudeville theatergoing. It provided both legibility and what Jenkins has called "affective immediacy," a hook, an instant identificatory link to the material.[75] Performers built on known tropes—popular songs, current events, hot dances, racial and ethnic stereotypes—and branded the familiar as their own through trademark voices, gestures, and tics. Audience pleasure lay in recognition, misdirection, and identification—knowing the material but not how it would be transformed in a given bit. Like the notion of "folk" art originating nowhere but in the ethos of a people, the stuff of variety performance depended on this fantasy of fungibility: the very authenticity of the material was its denial of absolute possession; likewise, the very realness of the originary performer behind the blackface minstrel depended on its/ his/her lack of control over his/her/its own person. The continuing animated character was built the same way: seemingly autonomous, its freedom was the fantastic construction of its maker, its rebellious nature a manufactured nod toward its ultimate constraint.

Gesturing toward empirical authenticity yet free to ignore nascent regimes of social-scientific falsification, minstrelsy and its descendants offered up a fantastic liminal realm between civilization and savagery, a realm where animation was happy to lease property. This faux anthropology operated on a continuum with the Zulu shows and traveling exhibits of native villages popular in the world's fairs at the turn of the century.[76] Even George Walker and Bert Williams performed the anthropologist. Pitching their new African-themed review *In Dahomey* (1902), Walker explained its origins:

> In 1893, natives from Dahomey, Africa, were imported to San Francisco to be exhibited at the Midwinter Fair. They were late in arriving . . . and Afro-Americans were employed and exhibited for native Dahomians. Williams and Walker were among the sham native[s]. . . . After the arrival of the native Africans, the Afro-Americans were dismissed . . . [but] we were permitted to visit the natives from Africa . . . and the study of those natives interested us very much. [We decided] that if we ever . . . [had] a show of our own, we would delineate and feature African characters.[77]

The distance between the African folk Williams and Walker studied and the characters they derived from them, and the indissoluble bond between the two, even as it reinforced their performance of mastery over racial charade, bound them to a fantasy of immutable originary blackness.

DRAWING THE COLOR LINE

As the reviews of this and other of their shows indicate, that delineation had in some degree to align with prevailing ideas of what blackness, savage or otherwise, looked and sounded like—and those notions followed from popular amusements such as minstrel and Zulu shows.[78] When it came to creating characters that were literally or figuratively black, the same expectations dogged the performing animator, and as Daniel Goldmark succinctly puts it, with the rise of cartoons "minstrelsy never died—it simply changed media."[79] So it wasn't just that early animators performed their craft on a stage also populated by minstrels, or that animators frequented vaudeville shows where they witnessed minstrelsy and its pale shadows

FIG. 1.11 In Disney's *Steamboat Willie* (1928), Mickey Mouse plays "Old Zip Coon" on a variety of farm animals.

(which some did).[80] It was also true of early animation, with its frequent colloquies between animators and characters, and between the animator and his audience, with its play with the tropes of creation and transformation—that when it chose the gloves, the wide mouth and eyes, and the somatic elasticity of the minstrel for its popular continuing characters, it also adopted the power dynamics of minstrelsy. Mutability—the ability to transform one's self or the world—far from being disinterested, was heavily invested in the racial formations of the day. This provides the backdrop (quite literally) against which to read early American animation's indebtedness to the minstrel show, and its use of racial alterity. Animation is related to blackface minstrelsy in its performative history, its visual iconography, and its description of power relations.

Drawn almost exclusively by whites, and in the early sound era voiced largely by white talent, animation had its own means of segregation, and its violation. Even in the silent era, the visual representation of blackness—whether in the literal form of the racist caricature of the human form or in the oblique form of the upright animal—followed the conventions of blackface minstrelsy in the large, pale lips, wide eyes, and elastic loping movements of the minstrel.[81] With the coming of sound, the voice followed the same rule: "black" characters spoke with the long, slow, southern, and stupid cadence of the minstrel. This minstrel trope was also repeated in cartoon music. For example, Disney's *Steamboat Willie*

(1928), famous (erroneously) for being the first sound cartoon, featured the rising star Mickey Mouse playing the tune "Turkey in the Straw," formerly known as "Old Zip Coon," very violently on various farm animals' bodies.[82] Even before that moment, with the rise in the teens and twenties of trademark animal and quasi-human characters (Felix, Krazy Kat, Ko-Ko, Oswald) the visual markers of minstrelsy—the mouth, eyes, gloves, and so on—were combined with the fantastic qualities whites also projected onto and through the minstrel: feral cleverness, musicality, joy, humor, agility, and resistance to oppression. As with Mickey's choice of music, these vestigial markings didn't necessarily *directly* signal blackness, yet it was always present, as Otto Messmer's explanation of Felix the Cat's origins makes clear: "[Producer] Pat Sullivan . . . had worked with Raoul Barré, see, so he started off on his own, doing his little Negro Pickaninny [Sammie Johnsin]. Which later on became almost Felix, at least in my mind anyway. Same kind of a, only he was a pickaninny. Now that was going along pretty good, but it didn't through the South, that little anti-Negro feeling. They wouldn't run the Pickaninnies."[83] For Messmer, the circuit was explicit: Sullivan had taken the standard racist trope of the "pickaninny," as common a stereotype on the page as it was on the stage, and translated it into cartoon form. Like Topsy in the many stage and screen versions of *Uncle Tom's Cabin* popular at the time, the pickaninny character was willful, energetic, mischievous, and potentially violent—everything that nonhuman characters such as Felix would be.[84]

Yet the minstrel was not chosen simply because it was playful and popular: deriving from a fantasy of forced plantation labor (or of northern black dandyism and lassitude), it signified a willful refusal to serve obediently. So, while Messmer may have taken up Sullivan's work already in progress, he also entered into a community of practice in which blackness and slavery signified very specifically, even when they did so indirectly. As a review of Sullivan's *Trials of a Movie Cartoonist* (1916) in *Moving Picture World* put it, "The figures that he draws become rebellious and refuse to act as he wants them to, so he has a terrible time to make them do his bidding. They answer back and say that he has no right to make slaves of them even if he is their creator."[85] (The short was made the same year as the first Sammy Johnsin cartoon, *Sammy Johnsin Hunter*.) The figure of the minstrel epitomized the rebellious commodity, and the performing animator (whether onstage or in in the press) produced that commodity, then punished it for the very refusal that defined it.

FIG. 1.12 A Blatz gum ad from a 1928 issue of *Photoplay* blithely asks, "Why Does a Pickaninny Love Watermelon?"—implying that his uncontrollable appetites will lead him to steal.

FIG. 1.13 Felix dreams of an ideal future in which he can eat endlessly in *Futuritzy* (1928).

PERFORMING LABOR (AND MANAGEMENT)
AND TRAINING AUDIENCES

REPORTER: How many drawings does it take to make an animated cartoon?

MAX FLEISCHER: Why, we make from twelve to fourteen thousand drawings for every picture.

REPORTER: That's a lot of work! That'll make an interesting story for my paper. Mr. Fleischer, can you let me see how Betty Boop does her stuff?

MF: Yes, I'll have her ready for you in just a moment . . . and I'll have her go through some of her stuff for you.

—*Betty Boop's Rise to Fame* (1934)

Even before studios such as Bray or Fleischer industrialized cartoon animation and perfected the public-relations gambit of the studio tour, early animators such as James Stuart Blackton and Winsor McCay built on the even earlier tradition of the lightning-sketch performance to demonstrate to their audiences the magical transformations, technical wizardry, and intense manual labor that went into producing a short animated cartoon. The theatrical convention of the technological reveal also attempted to train audiences in how they were meant to understand and relate to animated films. This training took two forms. First and foremost, it asked audiences to celebrate the magic of animation and the skill of the individual animator. Second, from McCay on, animators regularly touted the very difficult labor of animation as worthy of its own performance, and asked audiences to appreciate not just their art but also their *work*.

While it is important to remember that the live-action preludes to both *Little Nemo* and *Gertie* helped to take the place of McCay's curtailed live vaudeville performances, they nonetheless helped set the tone for future cinematic performances of the magic and labor of animation by other animation studios. But this sort of routine wasn't limited to the screen: it also found its way into both the trade press and popular journalism. Whether through a studio tour or an interview with an animator (usually actually a producer) or as the more fanciful interview with the character itself, the oddly contradictory tropes of celebrating labor *and* celebrating the magic of creation sometimes shared the same page.

Or was it a contradiction? Another way to understand the relationship between labor and magic was that the animated character embodied that contradiction, that it revealed labor as the force that animated the cartoon. While most commodities remain still and mute, unable to express the

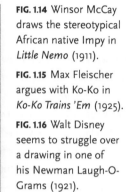

FIG. 1.14 Winsor McCay draws the stereotypical African native Impy in *Little Nemo* (1911).

FIG. 1.15 Max Fleischer argues with Ko-Ko in *Ko-Ko Trains 'Em* (1925).

FIG. 1.16 Walt Disney seems to struggle over a drawing in one of his Newman Laugh-O-Grams (1921).

social and material relations that have shaped their creation, the cartoon character can (like Marx's imaginary table gone mad) dance and jump about.[86] With the coming of sound, that commodity would gain a voice, too (although prior to that moment it had its share of dialogue bubbles and intertitles). The cartoon character, if not the entire cartoon realm (any part of which could come to life), embodied the labor of its making, was an expression of profoundly mundane magic.

The performance of animation as a feat of modern technology, then, hinged on that contradiction. Opposite the magic of bringing inert matter to life, early animators and their public relations touted the immense labor of producing volumes of images and the many hours required to make them into even a short film. For instance, the author of an anonymous article in the *Los Angeles Times* admonished her readers in 1916 that "few realize the enormous amount of work entailed in making one of the animated photo comics. Six cartoonists, twelve assistants and four cameramen are included in the average staff of a studio turning out animated cartoons. There are from 3000 to 4000 cartoons in each thousand feet of completed film and as each cartoon undergoes thirty-four processes, it will be seen that a thousand feet of animated pictures involves from 102,000 to 136,000 processes."[87] Less than a year later, John Randolph Bray, often credited with industrializing animation through force of will and cunning business acumen, would tell readers of the fan magazine *Photoplay*:

> In each foot of moving picture film there are about sixteen pictures, or sixteen thousand separate pictures to the thousand-foot reel. A one-reel cartoon contains, therefore, sixteen thousand sketches. A "struggling" newspaper artist . . . draws five pictures a day. Therefore it would take him, at that rate, three thousand two hundred days, or one hundred and six months, or nearly nine years to finish one reel of animated cartoons. In my studio we turn out not less than one a week. Allowing that there are twenty of us at work, it makes nearly six months work each to be done in one week. If this isn't "struggling," what do you call it?[88]

This was the flip side of McCay's performance of geologic time in *Gertie*. Here the magic of animation was quantified in man-hours, and the "struggle" was not for labor to be free of its exploitation but to realize itself in the products of others. Yet at the same time that animators (or their managers) detailed how arduous the job was, they also took great pains to suggest that their audiences' favorite creations were nonetheless living, autonomous beings. Writing in *Photoplay* in 1920, popular cartoonist Bud Fisher assured fans that "having created Mutt and Jeff doesn't mean that I control their destinies—not by a long shot. They control their own destinies pretty well. In fact, Mutt and Jeff now almost control Bud Fisher. They make him work hard for eight hours every day and prevent him from realizing his youthful ambition to settle down and live on his income at the ripe age of thirty-five or so." For Fisher, "struggle" had actually meant wresting copyright control of the characters from William Randolph Hearst, for whom he had worked until 1913. For a brief while, Fisher hadn't controlled the destinies of the characters he'd created. Yet in this instance, power relations are inverted: the creations own the creator, and they work him hard: "The thing that concerns me the most, of course, is the fact that to make one half-reel picture requires from 3,000 to 4,000 separate drawings. And 3,000 to 4,000 drawings to a picture, when pictures are coming out every few days, is a shirt-sleeve job that keeps a fellow hustling, let me tell you." Yet this seemed to suggest that his famous characters, even as they controlled his destiny, weren't actually alive or autonomous. So, after celebrating his own labor (almost all of which was not done by Fisher himself but jobbed out to Raoul Barré and Charles Bowers), Fisher does an about-face, telling his readers that "I say 'making motion picture cartoon stories,' but I don't make them. Mutt and Jeff make them. All I have to do is give them some scenery and they supply the action."[89] (The series carried this joke a little further in the 1920 short *On Strike*, in which Mutt and Jeff went on strike, demanded a pay increase and a fifteen-hour week, then attempted to open their own studio but failed, eventually returning to his employ.)

One of the performances of animation, then, was that of the public secret of the magic of labor and its alienation (aka mystification). On the one hand there was the long-standing convention of paternalism—as when Winsor McCay scolded his young assistant, John Fitzsimmons, or employed a tone with Gertie that fell somewhere between master and parent—of treating the animated character as if it were a pet, a line worker, or a child. Yet these creations were neither docile nor obedient: a running gag that reached its epitome in the struggles between Max Fleischer and Ko-Ko the Clown in the 1920s involved repeated attempts by characters to escape the film frame and the control of the animator's hand.[90] On the other hand the studios' repetitive performances of the mundane details of the labor of producing a cartoon, which seemed to run counter to its

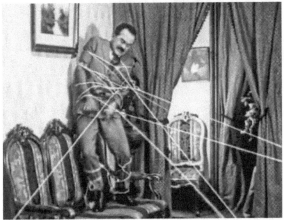

FIGS. 1.17–1.18 Made of magical and mutable ink, Ko-Ko the Clown multiplies and revolts against Max Fleischer in *Jumping Beans* (1922).

FIG. 1.19 A caricature of John Randolph Bray mocks the cartooning process in a feature in *Photoplay*, c. 1916.

magical aspects, presented animators as every bit as much workers as the creatures they spawned with their pens were actors. From McCay's performance of his voluminous output of drawings, and the herculean task of maintaining order in the face of always encroaching entropy, to the public-relations performances of Bray, Fisher, and others, the need to impress on potential audiences the sheer difficulty of animating a seven-minute short was framed within narratives of magic and mystery.

To reiterate: after McCay, the "animators" who publicly performed the backbreaking labor of making cartoons—Bray, Pat Sullivan, Max Fleischer, Disney, and others—even if they had once been animators, were producers. The "children" they managed were not the characters (those were product) but the animators who actually put in the long, repetitive hours in a process that animator Shamus Culhane, recalling working on Krazy Kat in the 1920s, referred to as a "sausage mill."[91] For animation producers—who faced increasingly demanding production schedules and tighter profit margins as animation found a larger place in short-subject catalogues—the rebellious charges they managed weren't their trademark characters but the animators responsible for actually churning product out on time.

This would eventually lead to a subsidiary performative trope of the animator as willful and childlike, captured in tales of Warner Bros.' Termite Terrace in the 1930s and 1940s, or in an account of the business of cartooning in a 1927 issue of *Moving Picture World* that asserted that a "movie cartoonist has to be more than *just a little bit crazy*, he must in most cases be a raving maniac. . . . It is not unusual in a cartoon studio to see several artists doing high dives off their desks, or playing leap frog, maybe doing a dry swim on the floor while several others stand by and watch to study the timing of the action."[92] This fantasy of the animator as childish and playful aligned him with the characters he was charged with producing and suggested that the effort of putting out a cartoon was really more play than work.

GET OFF THE STAGE!

Bug Vaudeville may stand as an elegy for the departing performing animator, but as such it says little about how that animator left the stage, or why. A thread that runs through *Before Mickey* (1982), Crafton's touchstone history of cartoons prior to the coming of sound, takes up the disappearance of the performing animator in the early twentieth century as animation changed inexorably from a craft to an industry. Presaging his recent work on performance and the relationship between animator, animated, and audience, Crafton noted that in the late teens and early twenties, the "films with human characters and then the films with animal stars represent the progressive retreat of the animator behind the screen." Arguing that at that point the 'toons seemed to become relatively autonmous beings, he asserted that the hand of the animator vanished, "its place now occupied by the characters who become agents of his will and ideas and through which his presence is known. . . . The animator opts for increasing invisibility while seeming to perform a service for the audience, entertaining them with these diverting adorable protagonists. But his invisibility does not mean he no longer exists. . . . His statements are no longer about his relation to his drawings, but about concerns shared with his audience."[93] This is an accurate and very astute survey of changes to the dominant visual and narrative conventions that had been instituted in the teens and twenties. Performing animators such as McCay, Blackton, or

Pat Sullivan were relatively rare and trod the vaudeville stage for only a few years before animation became rationalized. Yet in spite of their exceptional status, as a trope onstage animators remained a staple of the form long after individual animators stopped performing. Even as animation producers such as Bray, Sullivan, Paul Terry, the Fleischers, and Disney restructured animation on a production-line model, they retained and re-tooled the figure of the performing animator. Until the coming of sound, producers such as Max Fleischer and Walter Lantz appeared regularly alongside their characters. Even in the animation industry's early days, regimes of efficiency had negotiated this convention by replacing the moving body of the lightning-sketch artist with a close-up photo cutout of a hand holding a pen. While the registration pegs that held the drawings in place could guarantee continuity between one frame and the next, re-positioning the animator's hand from shot to shot proved more challenging. A live hand in the act of drawing, photographed in a sequence, could not maintain as stable a position relative to the image it was purportedly drawing: if, from frame to frame, it moved too far to the left or right, or closer or farther from the camera lens, it appeared strange and discontinuous with itself. A flat photograph of that same hand was more manageable and reliable: by virtue of its lack of movement, it seemed more like a real hand. So, while the convention of the performing animator continued, rationalization required that the animator himself be replaced by an indexical marker. Animators were reduced to line workers and replaced on-screen by performing producers and cutouts.[94]

Yet there is one noteworthy exception to take with this narrative: the animator did not necessarily *willingly* cede the screen to his creations, and the figure of the animated trickster that remained (and remains) owes more than a little of his resistant nature to the vestiges of the struggle that marked the departure of the animator in the face of industrialization. Winsor McCay was forced off the vaudeville stage by his boss, William Randolph Hearst; Emile Cohl's anonymous hand constructing and deconstructing his Pierrot in *Fantasmagorie* was replaced by producer Max Fleischer doing battle with a relatively autonomous Ko-Ko on a set meant to represent the animator's studio. Animation's celebratory performance of labor was rapidly contained within the emergent discourse of industrial management, and it was the product, the 'toon, that carried on the struggle in the absence of the animator.

The performing animator and his replacement by the cinematically performing animator-producer, or by the (photograph of a) hand suggesting his presence, were conventions worked out over time in the interplay between animation producers and their audiences, and each convention carried a complex of social meanings. That the live performance of animation was only briefly considered significant and enjoyable, and that in spite of this it persisted as a trope in film animation, points to a set of meanings generated in the interplay between the animator, his creation, and their audience that were significant to each party. It is not entirely the case that the animator left the screen because the performance of his relationship to the drawn world had been supplanted by more amorphous concerns that he "shared with his audience." The visible performance of craft *was* a shared concern, just as the disappearance of craft work in an industrializing society was a shared concern. So, that shift from the performing animator to his avatar was not simply a change in aesthetics distant from the social concerns of the day. The ways animation was made and received were of a piece with the modes in which those concerns circulated, and changes to the labor of animation and its performance echoed changes to the social and material relations of workers in other industries undergoing rationalization. The meaning of animation production as a performance underwent important changes in the teens and twenties that repositioned the animator as occupying a separate realm from that of his creation and as having a more limited commerce with that creation, just as the work of an individual assembly-line worker became one gesture in a series of gestures by other workers, more distant from the finished product itself.

Thus, at a moment when tensions between a craft system of industrial labor and an emerging rational industrial economy found their expression in fantasies of efficiency (and its resistance), the industrial organization of animation in the teens is more than simply an example of that historical change. It also offers a visible (and eventually audible) expression of the struggles inherent in that process, an expression that in its early stages centered around the playful yet contentious interactions between the animator and the creatures he made. Cohl made Pierrot in part to torment then reassemble him; McCay handled Gertie with stern commands and a whip, and she willfully disobeyed him; when the Fleischers introduced Ko-Ko in 1919, the clown regularly made it his business to escape the drawing board and wreak havoc in their (cinematic) real world, and so on. This is not to say that there weren't many cartoons in the first years of industrial animation in America that were less self-conscious, that featured relatively unremarkable characters, such as Carlson's Dreamy Dud and the denizens of Paul Terry's Aesop's Fables in self-contained stories in which the character offered little more than a wink and nod to the cinematic spectator. Even those less-revered cartoons, popular in their own day, acknowledged their audience, and in doing so hinted at their own autonomy from time to time.

Yet in those cartoons that repeated the trope of interaction between the performing animator and his creation, the nature of that interaction was one of struggle. The animator created characters who were by their nature willful and disobedient and which he was then obliged to discipline. This convention would all but define the figures who became the trademark continuing characters in American animation. Each would have a definite personality, yet that personality would always be one that resisted the conditions of its creation and questioned the limits of its existence. When it came to trademark continuing characters, the work of the commodity was to perform its subjugation, its resistance, and its final capitulation to the animator who created it.

So, one way to understand Winsor McCay's choice to foreground his own productive process, and the durability of that convention even after his methods had been superseded, is to read the continuing character as a commodity, the embodiment of the animator's labor. The continuing characters that became the popular center of American commercial animation by the early 1920s—Felix, Mutt and Jeff, Ko-Ko, Krazy, and others—were fetish figures who, in their struggles with their creators to escape or remake their world, encapsulated labor's struggle to claim some control over the means of production. Read in this light, the repetitive struggle of that commodity/character to become independent, and of the animator/producer to control it, becomes a ritual reenactment of industrial alienation. Self-reflexive, simultaneously involved in the mystification of apparent motion and the demystification of the creative process behind that motion, early American animation is a place and a process through which to understand the emergence of new regimes of labor and the production and regulation of bodies in those regimes. The drawn character was simultaneously the embodiment of the alienation of the producing artist *and* the product of his labor, and the space of animation (no less than the figure itself) was also implicated in that expression. A chronicle of early American animation as a history of labor necessarily involves recounting the *performance* of that labor, and the form in which that performance and that labor were embodied, the trickster or minstrel became the embodiment of that labor, the culturally and historically specific ideal for the resistance of the very industrial labor that created it, and the suppression of that resistance. Blackface minstrelsy, itself a performance of disciplining resistant labor, offered conventional form to that struggle, and likewise animation offered to blackface minstrelsy a new home for its performance of regulating fantastic black bodies.

CONCLUSION

By the end of the 1930s, the depiction of animators as childlike and of the work of animation as play would give way to strikes and the formation of animation-industry unions. The most important issues in those strikes were clear-cut rules for pay scales and job security, but another issue was that of acknowledgment: working animators wanted adequate screen credit for their work; many had grown tired of toiling relatively anonymously while directors, lead animators, and producers took the lion's share of credit.[95] Animation was a popular art form, yet it was also the product of intensive repetitive labor, and they wanted that labor acknowledged in more than just performative terms.

This was the dark side of that happy contradiction between magic and work: the product was magical; the work often wasn't. For betweeners, for tracers, for the ink and paint departments—for all of the divisions of labor that contributed to the industry's efficiency and economy of scale as it expanded—much of the labor that produced its magic was repetitive piecework. While certainly not as grueling as, say, coal mining, textile manufacture, or other line work, animation piecework could be exhaust-

FIG. 1.21 Hand-drawn labor hand draws cartoons to the jazzy beat of an in-house orchestra in Van Beuren's *Making 'Em Move* (1931).

ing, and doing it anonymously made workers feel less like Disney's seven whistling dwarfs and more like the mindlessly laboring brooms in the "Sorcerer's Apprentice" section of *Fantasia* (1940).[96]

Though rarely referred to directly, the less-than-playful quality of the grunt work of animation was lampooned in a few shorts, such as the Fleischers' *Cartoon Factory* (1924), or more explicitly in Van Beuren's *Making 'Em Move* (1931), but for the most part it remained invisible.[97] The latter depicted animation as a self-contained world in which cartoon characters slaved away to produce more cartoon characters—albeit happily and to catchy swing music. The earlier cartoon, continuing the Fleischer formula of an unending battle between Max and Ko-Ko, depicted a world in which Max as a mad animator created machines that automated the process, creating and destroying cartoon landscapes and characters—including a hybrid version of Max himself as a mindless automaton. In this instance, the cartoon seemed to nod toward the dehumanizing qualities of animation piecework, but offset that gesture by making Max, rather than his employees, both the instigator and victim of industrial automation. (As sympathetic to labor as that might seem, the Fleischers went so far as to move their studios from New York to Florida in the hope of avoiding unionization.)[98]

All told, as the 1920s progressed, the performing animator (or producer performing as animator) did, as Crafton points out, disappear from the screen. Yet the tension between magic and labor that the figure of the performing animator described didn't vanish. In fact, the performative convention hadn't been the only way tension had been described in cartoons. Another location for expressing the severe social dislocation that rationalization and industrialization had imposed on the craft—not just on animation but on social and material life more generally—was in the trademark characters themselves. For if Max Fleischer, Walter Lantz, or Rudy Ising performed the role of the animator as comic foil or straight man, Ko-Ko, Felix, Oswald, Mickey, and others performed the necessary other half of this dynamic, that of the disobedient, willful, and playful product rising up against its master. The animator may have gradually left the screen and the stage, but the other half of the duo remained, and it remained an expression of the tensions surrounding the laboring body. These continuing characters—who became ever more the center of the animation industry as competing studios struggled to gain brand recognition—derived from an extant story of a body resistant to impressment into regimes of labor: the blackface minstrel, a figure based on the fantasy of the happy and disobedient slave who, though compelled to labor, resisted in creative, amusing, and interesting ways. Although this, too, was a performative gesture, it was one with roots in fantastic responses to regimes of labor, and it is perhaps best understood in its historical relation to those regimes.

2

LABOR

The 1924 Out of the Inkwell short *The Cartoon Factory* offers a less than exacting depiction of the labor of cartooning in its early industrial period. In the cartoon's framing narrative, producer Max Fleischer attempts to automate the drawing process by adding electricity. First, a photograph of a hand (a match cut tells us it's Max's) draws the background, a cityscape. Max then attaches wires to his drawing pad, causing a pen to rise up and draw Ko-Ko the Clown. Max then attaches wires directly to Ko-Ko and torments him with electric shocks. Soon, as Ko-Ko strolls through town unawares, Max surreptitiously sketches a mobile cartoon-drawing machine into the scene—further eliminating the need for the increasingly elusive (and antagonistic) animator. In a visual pun that points out the relative flatness of animation at the time, the drawing machine sketches a turkey dinner, then a beautiful woman, each slightly higher in the picture plane than Ko-Ko, as if they were drawn on a wall behind him. It then erases both before Ko-Ko can take a bite or steal a kiss. After this, the clown hijacks the machine and rides it across the page, drawing the background as he goes. The machine, now under *his* control, draws a house and fills its interior with photographic images of furnishings, providing the schematically drawn house with a cinematically real interior. Ko-Ko then visits a machine shop where Max manically controls a Rube Goldberg machine that (after much effort) spits out a wooden soldier with Max's head on its martinet body. In the hijinks that ensue, that soldier comes to life as Max in the "real" house and begins madly scribbling more toy soldiers on its walls—who then come to life and join him in a war against the clown. Ko-Ko fights back, using the drawing machine to erase the oncoming horde and creating a cannon with which he barrages Max with cannonballs. Yet

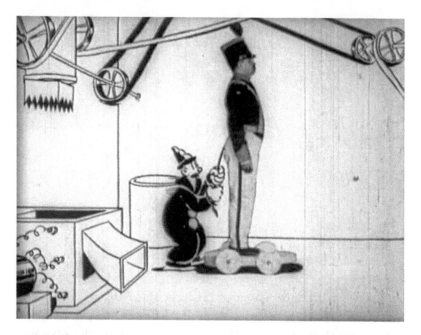

FIG. 2.1 In *The Cartoon Factory* (1924), a toy soldier version of Max Fleischer is machine-assembled and deployed in a war against his own creation, Ko-Ko the Clown.

Ko-Ko is eventually overwhelmed when the machine shop spews out more and more martinet Maxes. As the first Max soldier draws reinforcements on the "real" interior walls of a drawn house, Ko-Ko can only flee into the inkwell, as do the soldiers, while in the (cinematic) real world the actual Max twists dials and flips switches with glee.

The cartoon short performs the Fleischers' well-documented fascination with new technology, as well as a certain anxiety about the control of labor and its products.[1] In his discombobulated efforts to automate the process of animation, Max produces an unstable circuit between the real and the drawn cinematic worlds. Having demonstrated the potency of that circuit by torturing Ko-Ko, Max creates a mechanized, labor-saving (hence cost-cutting) automated amanuensis in the drawn world, a device that collapses product and production into the same realm. Inflecting the public-relations trope that treated animators as playful children, the cartoon reduces the production process into the work of one wacky machine—the control of which becomes vital in a playful struggle to lay claim to animate space. While Max uses the device to taunt Ko-Ko with objects of desire such as food and sex, Ko-Ko appropriates it to expand his territory and lay sovereign claim to it. In a conventional turnabout that has the animator resisting his creation, Max must defend himself against Ko-Ko's attempts to annex drawn space, including the "real" interior of the house. Depicted as a rigid, inflexible soldier (the exact opposite of the elastic, unpredictable minstrel figure), Max is driven to attempt to regain control by scribbling like a child on the walls of the house, generating ever more imperfect copies of himself. The production process in this instance seems not only to have spawned a rebellious product in Ko-Ko but also to have reduced its manager to a martinet who can only reproduce himself in his own degraded image, and can only maintain control in the cartoon world by insanely scribbling into a "real" space that he himself has created. His attempts to automate the process of animation seem to have yielded neither efficiency nor rationalization. The final shot of Max manically flipping a switch seems desperate and sad, as if the drive to increase productivity has eliminated in him a very basic humanity, or reduced him to a sadistic, infantile berserker, tormenting his creation out of frustration over his loss of control over the process and narrative space of animation.

This cartoon also suggests the tangle of relations of labor and management in an industry that regularly performed its own work process in its products. In reading shorts such as this, the challenge becomes one of separating out the representation of labor from the labor of representation, to consider carefully how the two were related to each other. Within an art form that rapidly transformed from a craft model into a Fordist industry, the standardization of artists as workers took place alongside the development of the continuing characters as blackface minstrels. Given that parallel development, a useful question to ask is, what might the minstrel have represented to the workers charged with its industrial reproduction? The nineteenth-century blackface minstrel represented the rebellious slave and her descendants: absolutely unfree labor resisting its subjugation through playful, subversive, and willfully incoherent behavior. Likewise, the animation producer, having given up the craft of animation for the business of cartoon production, performed opposite those continuing characters, updating the push and pull between minstrelsy's interlocutor and its end men. The animation producer's efforts to make his 'toons behave replicated the interlocutor's efforts to stop Tambo and Bones from making sense into nonsense. A vehicle for this repeated performance was the back-and-forth between the performing producer and his trademark character, the creation of a commodity that, often as not, would turn against its "maker" and ultimately be punished for that act. A dream of labor's revolt and its suppression, this scenario—while certainly not the only one in early American cartoons—was quite often repeated. And that it was so often repeated cannot be put down solely to animation's conservation of its tropes; were there not a public with which the images and story lines resonated, they would have vanished quickly. As Crafton has recently suggested, describing what he calls "coanimation," producers "must anticipate their fickle taste to survive, but, more pertinently, they must recognize that audiences do much of the work with their personal and collective energy . . . when they indulge their assumptions, exercise their imaginations, suspend disbelief up to a point, and fill in toons' personalities."[2]

That these struggles between products and producers resonated enough with early animation audiences to become an enduring trope suggests a common affective and cultural currency. Yet as fantastical and whimsical as many of these shorts were, they were grounded in the practical conditions of animation production. Repetitive performances of cartooning as a solitary activity that was grueling yet playful, whether by producers or their animated stand-ins, were not without a basis in reality. Unlike, say, workers in a Ford plant, laborers in animation studios—lead animators, animators, in-betweeners, backgrounds artists, and workers in tracing and (eventually) in ink and paint—did not stand in front of moving conveyor belts repeating the same basic motion over and over again for eight to ten hours a day. Yet they did engage in repetitive, task-oriented work, and each technological innovation the industry developed or adopted tended also to involve a greater division of labor and a more regimented approach to production. Behind popular fantasies of cartoon creation, an emerging American commercial animation industry undertook the same regimes of efficiency and regimentation in which other industries were engaging. The tensions and contradictions that flowed from that process, which by the late 1930s would lead to strikes by animation studio workers, provided the affective charge behind the minstrel–interlocutor relationship that played out repeatedly in animation's early days. So, a closer look at the labor of cartooning may help in describing how minstrelsy became central to the industry—and why it eventually became vestigial.

I never have had the least difficulty with any of my actors over salaries. . . . Perhaps you can't quite see the moving picture director in the role of the tender-hearted sympathizer with the hired help. But you must remember that my actors, as well as being my employes [sic], are my children.
—John Randolph Bray, "How the Comics Caper," *Photoplay* (1917)

Employees, children, chattel objects: in the liminal zone that American commercial animation created, cartoon characters, audiences were often reminded, existed at the whim of their creators. Just two years after Winsor McCay had been enjoined by his employer, William Randolph Hearst, from appearing on vaudeville stages outside New York, John Randolph Bray's coy performance of managerial skill transformed into genteel paternalism succinctly delineated the distance between actual labor and its performance in early American commercial animation. Though McCay had created only a handful of films since his first in 1911, his comical performance of the solitary and crushing labor of cartooning had become by the decade's end a widely shared performative trope. Yet as animation rapidly industrialized, that convention underwent subtle but important alterations, not the least of which was the transformation of the performing animator into the cartoon producer performing *as* animator.[3] Bray, and after him Pat Sullivan, Max Fleischer, Walter Lantz, and Walt Disney, could all draw with varying degrees of skill, yet all participated in serially creating a public-relations regime that converted an appreciation for the skill of cartooning into a celebration of managerial mastery. This discursive shift, which happened both on-screen and in public relations, changed the performance of bringing ink and paper (or celluloid) to life, then of controlling that unruly life, into one of the magic of industrial management. Using incredible powers of efficiency and organization to mobilize workers, animation producers animated their animators, who in turn performed the magic of bringing inert materials to rebellious life.

As that skill at animating creatures transformed into the metaskill of regulating animators, several important things happened. First, the performance of animation as onerous—represented so well by McCay's giant rolls of paper, barrels of ink, and mountains of drawings—was slowly erased and replaced with one in which that work was portrayed as playful and capricious. Articles in fan magazines, newspapers, and trade journals pointedly detailed the thousands of drawings that went into each cartoon short, and that enumeration demonstrated the efficiency of the industrial organization of a studio and its managers, its ability to corral the rambunctious energy of its animators into a highly rational and productive machine. At the same time, those PR performances elided the hierarchical relationship between the animation producer and the animator, which was reconfigured as a paternal relationship between the producer-cum-animator and his animated creations. In the same way that J. S. Blackton, Emile Cohl, and McCay had toyed with the characters they had created, Max Fleischer and Bud Fisher would joke about the capriciousness of their characters and their resistance (or contribution) to unfair working conditions, as if there were no animators, tracers, in-betweeners, inkers, camerapeople, and cel washers involved in creating those characters. Finally, the animated creatures themselves—Felix, Ko-Ko, Pete the Pup, and others—became increasingly aggressive in their efforts to trade the cartoon world for the real, as if signaling an exponential increase in the condensed and displaced energy provided them through increased staffing and a greater division of labor.[4]

This preindustrial moment within which McCay performed was relatively brief, lasting only from around 1900 to 1913, and is represented by a relative handful of films. American animation industrialized in the incredibly short span of a few years, roughly between 1913 and 1919, and as such forms an ideal locus for considering whether and how that process of rationalization was encountered by animators, exhibitors, and audiences. This entails understanding rationalization and efficiency not merely as industrial practices, but also as lived experience. In their immensely popular and influential sociological study *Middletown* (1929), Helen and Robert Lynd, describing the previous forty years of technological and social change, reported that the "shift from a system in which length of service, craftsmanship, and authority in the shop and social prestige among one's peers tended to go together to one which, in the main, demands little of a worker's personality save rapid, habitual reactions and an ability to submerge himself in the performance of a few routinized easily learned movements seems to have wiped out many of the satisfactions that formerly accompanied the job." Renaming the prosaic landscape of Muncie, Indiana, as "Middletown, USA," the Lynds attempted to delineate the transfer of economic and social power from craft-based industries to newer, rationalized, Fordist enterprises at the turn of the twentieth century. "Inventions and technology," they argued, "continue rapidly to supplant muscle and the cunning hand of the master craftsman by batteries

FIG. 2.2 GM autoworkers attach tires to cars, c. 1922. Courtesy of Bentley Historical Library, University of Michigan, Frank Angelo papers.

FIG. 2.3 The Sullivan Studios animation department, c. 1922. Courtesy of Donald Crafton.

of tireless iron men doing narrowly specialized things over and over and merely 'operated" or 'tended' in their orderly clangorous repetitive processes by the human worker."[5]

As the Lynds' survey of the effects of industrialization on the social organization of middle America in the teens and twenties suggests, the changes in labor practices animation underwent between 1913 and the early 1920s were endemic. Unlike the automobiles or canning jars about which the Lynds wrote, which were themselves mute, cartoons could chronicle the transformation of the means of their own production, obliquely rendering the cultural and material landscape into which they emerged. Animation's rapid industrialization occurred in the midst of a much broader enthusiasm for regimes of efficiency, popularly called "scientific management." Crafton has noted that early patents by Earl Hurd and J. R. Bray used a self-conscious language of industrial efficiency, which he links to the pioneering work of "stopwatch" expert F. W. Taylor. More recently, Yuriko Furuhata has suggested that the plasticity of Disney animation in the 1930s and 1940s, which so fascinated cultural critics such as Sergei Eisenstein and Walter Benjamin and disturbed Max Horkheimer and Theodor Adorno, is a visual expression of the imposition of Fordist production on animation workers—the plasticity of characters akin to the adaptability of any given worker to a task, and to the predominance of the task over the individual worker.[6] Technical innovations to the process of animation in the late teens, even as they helped to increase fluidity of movement or the stability of backgrounds, also contributed to the division and regimentation of the drawing process. Relatively simple innovations, such as the standardization of registration pegs (the posts on which individual drawings were placed while being worked on, traced, inked, or photographed) and the switch from rice paper to celluloid, were cumulative advances that led toward the more (cinematically) lifelike animation for which Disney became famous in the 1930s. At the same time, these technical innovations contributed to an economy of actions that permitted the subdivision of tasks and the interchangeability of workers engaged in them.

In the teens and early twenties, though, before Disney had fully arrived on the scene, practitioners in the emergent discourses of efficiency and scientific management viewed workers as the source of raw data and as the primary beneficiaries of its analysis. Just as animators would observe the actions and behaviors of people and animals, management experts, such as F. W. Taylor, or Lillian and Frank Gilbreth, studied workers' movements in the workplace in an effort to locate the "one best way" to complete any task—and celebrated that process in widely circulating books and magazine articles.[7] For the Gilbreths in particular, those studies were meant to resolve the conflict between workers' need for a relaxed and healthy work environment and the repetitive and tedious work that automated production increasingly required them to do. More than simply abstruse research intended to train a growing managerial class, though, scientific management found a crossover audience in popular magazines of the day and in how-to manuals for applying its principles to the home.[8] If a factory could more efficiently produce widgets, there was no reason one could not apply the same logic to washing dishes and beating rugs. In a pop-cultural mise en abyme, popular discourse about streamlining labor celebrated its observation and its reduction to its smallest component movements in every aspect of daily life, collapsing the distinction between laboring and living—between an autonomous self and the self as repository of labor power—and lionizing management as the application of brain power to the brute tasks of an emerging industrial society, converting them into more civilized and perhaps humane activities.

Those regimes were applied in varying degrees to the new industry of animation, whose business was *itself* the observation and reduction of physical movement into its component parts.[9] So, where McCay had performed animation as a relatively solitary operation—and had actually been reluctant to share the job with his assistants—Bray, Raoul Barré, Sullivan, and other early animation industrialists studied how best to break up the tasks of animation into component parts whose specificity allowed for their more rapid completion and whose standardization permitted one worker to take up or finish the task of another.[10] A strange hybrid of a fading craft system and a new industrial one, animation in the late teens and early twenties—both as process and as product—formed an object in which those changes in social and material practices found visible expression on the screen. To give but one example, the complex interplanar relations in the performance of lightning-sketches described in chapter 1, dependent as they were on the interaction of a performer, audience, and camera, were largely replaced within a few years by narrative cartoon shorts that were comparatively flat, and that had, for expediency's sake, backgrounds that were often represented by little more than a few lines. These backgrounds, which were more easily mass-reproduced

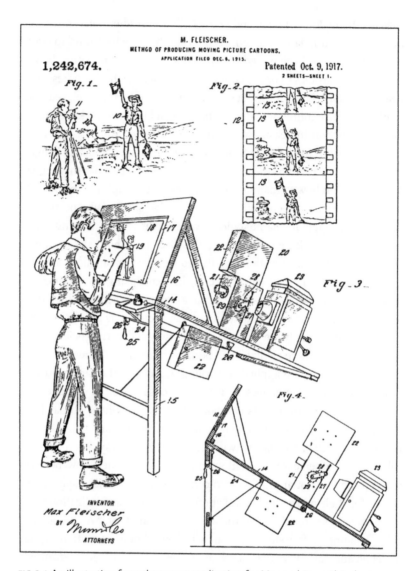

FIG. 2.4 An illustration from the patent application for Max and Dave Fleischer's rotoscope, c. 1915, demonstrates a concern in the industry for methods of efficiently producing lifelike characters.

than the more complex ones featured in a film like *Gertie*, became simple backdrops in front of which the more character-centric actions of emergent animated "stars" would unfold.[11]

This fascination with standardization was epitomized, perhaps, by Max and Dave Fleischer's 1915 patent for the rotoscope, a device that used the cinematic recording of motion as an aid in the drawing process, with the aim of creating more fluid and lifelike movement in animated characters. The rotoscope operator filmed a live actor, then animators traced over that film record frame by frame to create animated characters with much more fluid and lifelike movements. According to Max's son Richard, the Fleischers' development of this process (which initially and often made use of Dave in a clown costume) gave birth to their first popular trademark character, Ko-Ko the Clown.[12] The Fleischers not only rotoscoped Ko-Ko on a regular basis, they also celebrated the rotoscope in the public relations for their Out of the Inkwell series (1919–1929). As the series name implies, the Out of the Inkwell shorts featured the material base of animation: the ink, pen, and paper (not celluloid) of it. But the Fleischers also celebrated the systematic efficiency of rotoscoping—as a mechanical means by which to produce more lifelike images—elaborating on their fantasy of automating production through mechanical processes, embodied by characters who drew themselves and their own backgrounds.

In part, this was extradiegetic showmanship: working for Bray during World War I, Max had produced military training films; he had also worked as the art editor for *Popular Science Monthly*. In press releases, the Fleischer brothers (there were actually five in all) depicted themselves as a family of inventors and mechanical tinkerers and their animation studios as their laboratory.[13] Yet in spite of the Fleischers' well-documented fascination with regimes of efficiency and automation, in their Ko-Ko cartoons they chose to frame their on-screen performances as ones in which Max and Dave were lone craftsmen, working without the aid of technical apparati and absent the highly rationalized and regulated division of labor that was actually the industry standard after 1915.[14] For the inkwell out of which Ko-Ko sprang was filmed, not drawn, and the world where the trickster clown regularly sowed chaos was a cinematic representation of the Fleischers' animation studios. Yet, like Winsor McCay's vaudeville fantasy of giant bales of paper and barrels of ink, the studio where Ko-Ko capered was depicted as little more than a small, plain office where Max and Dave seemed to work, each at a desk all by himself. When Ko-Ko came to life, it was from a few spare lines drawn at one of these desks, or from a spot of

FIG. 2.5 In *Ko-Ko Needles the Boss* (1927), a rotoscoped Dave Fleischer as Ko-Ko the Clown does battle with Ko-Ko's putative creator, Max Fleischer.

ink spilled on the floor. This was an inside joke: even as their public relations celebrated the brothers' part in the rationalization of the animation industry, their films pretended that their animated minstrel was virtually a product of spontaneous generation, an expression of forces inherent in the black ink and plain white paper from which he sprang.

There is a certain historical logic to this. As Mark Langer has pointed out, prior to 1923 the Fleischers did a great deal of their animating themselves, and their studios got by on around ten workers.[15] According to Langer, though, it was the Fleischers who created the role of the in-betweener, an animator-in-training who learned on the job by filling in the intermediary movements between in and out figures drawn by a lead animator—as was the case, for instance, when Art Davis learned the trade working under Dick Huemer.[16] In spite of this, the Fleischers maintained the performative conceit of their small, simple, two-man office throughout the run of the Out of the Inkwell series, long after the studio had greatly expanded its staff. There, as elsewhere, a tension existed between the increasingly rationalized production of animation and its public performance.

Beyond spoofs of animation itself, such as the Fleischers' *Cartoon Fac-*

tory (1924) and Van Beuren's *Making 'Em Move* (1931), commercial animation in its early years regularly called into question a harmonious relationship between life as lived and life as drawn. That is, like the live slapstick shorts also popular in the early twentieth century, cartoons thrived on the comic portrayal of struggle, conflict, and animosity, what Rob King has called the (nontransformative) "liberatory pleasures . . . of slapstick."[17] Yet unlike live shorts, fewer of which called into question their actors' ontological status, many cartoons portrayed that conflict as deriving from the cartoon character's troubled existence in and relationship to a world that was clearly *drawn* by *somebody*. Continuing cartoon characters appeared autonomous, rebellious, and determined to alter the conditions of their existence—but they were created under conditions of increasing regimentation and regulation by workers who remained relatively anonymous. In retrospective interviews, veteran animators have described workplace tensions between artists and managers—between process and product, innovation and regimentation—as a constant. Felix the Cat creator Otto Messmer, who served as both manager and animator at Sullivan Studios, in the late teens described a piecework system in which the going rate for finished film animation was a dollar a foot, studios turned out a cartoon every one to two weeks, and the studio's lawyer once jokingly referred to Sullivan's animators as his "slaves."[18] Yet at the same time as it demanded much of its workers, animation's performative conventions celebrated the intense labor of making drawings move; cartoon production as struggle, while certainly not animation's only topic, remained a constant theme. The nascent American animation industry often celebrated a fantasy of its labor, if not its reality; yet the rebellion of the animated character often took the form of an escape from the drawn world (oppressive for unknown reasons) into that same reality. That contradiction begs some detailed consideration.

A TRADE OR AN INDUSTRY?

Even in animation's simplest industrial form, each animator had defined tasks, a relatively solitary laborer contributing to a larger collective effort. In spite of this, accounts of the business from its beginning in the teens to the present are thick with tales of playful camaraderie and collaborative education between senior and up-and-coming animators. As a craft, American animation was at its best fraternal and supportive. Yet in its early days it was also a fiercely competitive industry grafting rationalization onto an increasingly anachronistic craft model and in which competition between studios took precedence over the fellow feeling and cooperation between animators that existed both within a given studio and between studios. Animators could profess and practice comradery; animation was an extremely competitive and very contradictory industry. Yet even as that industry participated in a larger trend toward rationalization and efficiency, this move existed in tension with its historical connections to the vaudeville stage and the graphic arts. Alongside its performative traditions, animation's roots in the relatively solitary practices of newspaper and magazine cartooning and advertising attenuated its regimentation. Likewise, while the tradition of animation's public performance as an act of solo bravura and legerdemain required the elision of the collective nature of its backstage artistic production, it retained elements of a craft model. Otto Messmer recalls the craft of animation in the days prior to its industrialization: "In those days everybody did their own cartoons in their homes or in a small studio of their own. They'd have to bring it [to a film studio] to be photographed."[19] This was the one-room studio that McCay had depicted and that became a retrospective fantasy for the Fleischers—a true cottage industry, if short-lived.

A significant portion of the industry's division of labor was built around an in-service training model that developed and used apprentices, journeymen, and craftsmen (and they were mostly men)—even as that craft model operated within a larger industrial system. A good example of this is Dick Huemer's description of his first job as an animator, at Raoul Barré's studios, in 1916:

> Actually, I was not yet an Animator. It took a whole month before I graduated to that elevated station. They were indeed hard up for recruits in this toddling business. At first I was . . . a TRACER, one who followed up the animator and traced in the parts he left out that didn't change in the action. This was an archaic process entirely different from the present day CEL system. . . . The best that can be said for it is that it was fun. We animators inked directly on paper, which afforded us a lot of creative freedom and the opportunity to express our own techniques and individuality. . . . It never occurred to us that uniformity in appearance was a desirable thing. But this is something that the cel system later accomplished automatically.[20]

Disney animator Frank Thomas describes a similar trajectory: "The normal process, if a fella shows promise, is to start him through production down at the bottom. It's kind of tedious, but we've found it takes one solid year of doing inbetweens before the fundamentals of animation begin to click. You can teach everything you know in a matter of weeks, then it's a matter of saying it over and over and over. And one day, bing! A little light will go on, he's beginning to catch on. That's just to grasp the fundamentals."[21] Of course, commercial animation required a great deal of uniformity in order to maintain stable product lines. Characters had to appear consistent from shot to shot and cartoon to cartoon; ideally, motion was to be fluid and continuous; backgrounds had to remain still and consistent. (Disrupting these fundamental norms became a joke unto itself in later shorts such as *Duck Amuck* [1953].)

While much of the education of animators happened on the job, that training also became standardized over time. The first substantial manual for animators was Edwin Lutz's *Animated Cartoons: How They Are Made, Their Origin and Development* (1920). As several animation historians have noted, this how-to manual was an essential text for many second-generation animators and producers, including Ub Iwerks, Walt Disney, and Friz Freleng.[22] In keeping with regimes of efficiency popular when he published it, Lutz's book systematically broke down the history of animation and the means by which one could become an effective industrial animator. Its first chapters are titled "The Beginning of Animated Drawings" and "The Genesis of Motion Pictures," and by midbook it moves on to drier topics with titles such as "On Movement in the Human Figure," "Notes on Animal Locomotion," and "Inanimate Things in Movement"; chapters follow on photography, emplotment, and the educational value of cartoons. In keeping with the tenor of the times, Lutz encouraged systematic observation and the decomposition of movement and bodily systems, declaring that an "understanding of the principles underlying locomotion in man—walking or running—is an important matter to consider in this art. When an artist knows the basic facts of movement in the human figure, he will more readily comprehend animal locomotion and all other movements in general."[23]

Animation in its first stages of industrialization, then, operated in a constant tension between creative individuality and standardized regimes of efficiency, and these impulses were seen as complementary, not contradictory. As Lutz put it, describing labor- and time-saving shortcuts, "The true artist, in keeping with his talent for creative work, will be disposed to devise helpful contrivances or expedients to lighten irksome and monotonous details arising in his art. . . . He must be quick in deciding on the

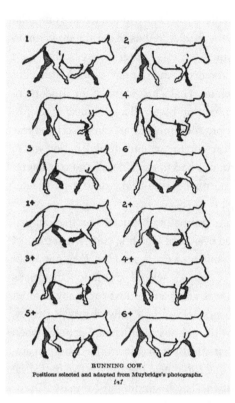

FIG. 2.6 A page from Lutz's *Animated Cartoons* adapts the photos of Eadweard Muybridge to demonstrate the mechanics of animal locomotion. Other pages offered illustrations of the work of Etienne-Jules Marey.

RUNNING COW.
Positions selected and adapted from Muybridge's photographs.
{a}

best means of economizing on his labor, so that he can spend more time where thorough drawing is needed."[24] This advice imagines the animator as an autonomous worker, setting his own pace and determining his own tasks. Yet, as Langer points out, the Fleischers also later developed an in-house manual that further standardized these sorts of animation practices, providing a reference document through which producers and lead animators could both train and regulate their journeymen employees. Following a contentious and costly strike by Fleischer workers in 1937, the manual was developed by Seymour Kneitel and Isidore Sparber and promulgated in 1940 after the Fleischer Studios had moved from New York to Florida (a right-to-work state) in 1938. This "Bible" was meant to streamline management, reduce labor costs, and undermine further union organizing through improved regulation of the workplace. As Langer notes, the manual was "designed as a guide to artistic practice, but also to institutional practice."[25]

One can easily point to other examples of procedural streamlining in American animation as essential to both its history and its aesthetic development. Walt Disney Productions has been credited with systematizing story development in cartoons in the early 1930s; Leonard Maltin credits Disney with developing the storyboard, and histories of the studio make note of its "sweatboxes," screening conferences in which animators had work in progress critiqued by producers and other animators.[26] Thomas and Johnston also maintain that even as Disney pushed rationalization, it encouraged a quasi-familial, journeyman atmosphere, as when director Ben Sharpsteen "gave drawing problems to all the assistants and in-betweeners, not so much as a competition, but so they could learn to talk over the difficulties and observe the variety of solutions."[27] Animation, as a truly industrial art, framed standardization and rationalization as means through which creativity could be most effectively exploited. Since animation was not as monotonous or ubiquitous as bricklaying or auto assembly, it did not lend itself to the sort of particularized analysis of time and motion in which the Gilbreths or Taylor engaged. But because it nonetheless required a highly uniform product, studios developed systems that standardized and regulated in-house production practices, which employees were required to learn and follow.[28] At the same time, however, many (excluding inkers, painters, tracers, and others with more rote jobs) were encouraged to experiment and to learn from one another . . . even as they were taught standardized methods for reproducing characters, backgrounds, and the like to the exacting specifications of a given studio. And a tradition existed in the industry of supplying art classes to animators, both apprentice and senior, as Dick Huemer learned when he worked for Barré, who "organised art classes for after-hours studies, where the animators could improve their skills by drawing from the live models which he supplied free of charge. This is something which Disney also did so many years later," through in-house sessions and at the Chouinard Art Institute. Animation was (and is) a form of rationalized craft.[29]

So, from its very inception as an industry animation operated in a tension between creative activity and its standardization in a piecework system—and that tension found an imperfect and indirect outlet in the onscreen performances of animator-producers, such as Max Fleischer and Walter Lantz, and in story lines that featured characters who rebelled against regimentation and restriction.[30] This was a convention that found its origins in the relatively flat management structure of early animation studios, in which a producer or director (if there was a director) was also likely to be an animator and in which animators were given a fair amount of leeway in structuring gags and plot points. While the Bray organization, for instance, was relatively highly structured, in smaller studios such as the early Fleischer operations, Barré's studio, or Terry's, there was significant overlap between animators and administrators, and crushing production schedules often meant that cartoons scanted on plot to focus on individual gags.[31] In this environment, the convention of a cartoon character able to do fantastic things, to challenge the conditions of its environment and its making—in particular to challenge the hand of its maker— became a visual expression of the admixture of freedom and restraint that the rapidly industrializing field required. For example, Chuck Jones claimed that Daffy Duck—who was regularly tormented on-screen and as much as any other Warners character aired his complaints (to no avail) in asides to the audience—was the embodiment of his producer, Leon Schlesinger, whose commitment to producing low-cost (hence higher-profit) animation was reportedly equaled by his indifference to the content of those cartoons: "We were grossly underpaid, but we still did what we wanted to do. Daffy's voice and Sylvester's voice, which are the same voice, really, except that Daffy's is speeded up a little, are really very similar to Leon Schlesinger's voice, because Leon too lisped when he talked."[32]

These tropes circulated widely, not simply because animators watched each other's work in theaters—Otto Messmer, for instance, remembers seeing McCay's work as a child, as did Dick Huemer—but because in animation's early days there were so few animators, and the business was so unstable, that they moved regularly from one studio to the next in search of better working conditions and better pay.[33] Although he started slightly later than many second-generation animators, Jones's experience in the early 1930s, when he started working for Ub Iwerks, is representative:

> The first time I was [at Iwerks] was probably for not more than a year. ... I started out as a painter, as everybody else did. Then I graduated to cel-washing, and inking, and then, eventually, to in-betweening. Then I went to Walter Lantz for a short time; these periods were all very brief, the whole time period that embraced my tenure at Ub's and then Universal and Oswald with Bill Nolan and Walter Lantz was less than two years. Then I worked for Charlie Mintz [Screen Gems] for a short time. ... In 1933, I went to Warner's as an assistant, and spent the next twenty-eight years there.[34]

Just as Thomas and Huemer had, Jones describes an apprentice-journeyman-master craft system embedded in rationalized industrial operations. This mode of professional/industrial development necessarily balanced individual talent against a willingness to engage in repetitive menial tasks as training, and an ability to faithfully imitate the work and working styles of others. The industrial craft of animation operated in a state of tension between personal initiative and talent and its sublimation in repetition and rote imitation and did so within an extremely demanding work schedule.

The performances of the labor and craft of animation that Winsor McCay made famous in his early films, and that became conventions repeated in large and small ways in later cartoons, are important for understanding how the business of cartooning publicly celebrated and fetishized the *work* of cartooning. Yet beyond those self-reflexive performative gestures and what they say about the iconography and metaphysics of animation, the actual labor of drawing and American animation's incredibly rapid development from a craft model to a rationalized industrial adjunct to Hollywood also have much to tell about how cartoon conventions developed, circulated, and stabilized. For in a fledgling industry, crushing production schedules and the fluidity and rapid circulation of labor between studios could quickly transform a convention from the province of one animator or studio into an industry standard. As Crafton has noted, Warner Bros., in their in-house newsletter, even joked about turnover: "The comings and goings listed in *The Exposure Sheet* [suggest] a factory with a very high worker turnover. . . . There was also the spurious announcement that, to spare employees 'the embarrassment, not to mention the inconvenience of leaving here for Fleischer's only to return in a few weeks,' Schlesinger 'has just purchased Fleischer's with certain plans in mind. An underground tunnel will be built with a moving platform, enabling everyone to hop on or off at will.'"[35] Playing on the interchangeability of animation workers, the joke also points to the means by which regimes of efficiency contributed to practices of marginal differentiation and to economizing conventions. Simply put, standard practices such as drawing four-fingered hands, covering them in gloves to reduce detail, or (in the business's early days) using dashed lines to indicate sightlines (thus reducing the need for extra drawings to produce eyeline match cuts) all had their origins in the meeting of aesthetic conventions and work routines. Tom Sito has argued that the illusion of the animation studio as playground was just that, and that in "the 1930s everybody worked a forty-six hour, six-day workweek: 9:00 A.M. to 6 P.M., Monday through Friday, and 9:00 A.M. to 1:00 P.M. on Saturday."[36] In the 1920s, because the industry was still in formation, the hours could be even longer and less predictable. The demanding nature of commercial animation—producers often negotiated unreasonably short turnarounds with distributors, which resulted in brutally long hours—led to the animation "sausage mill" that Shamus Culhane recalled from his early days in the field.[37] Dick Huemer suggested that Fred Quimby (of MGM) and Leon Schlesinger (of Warner Bros.) both "loved to see everybody working at their boards as if in a sweatshop."[38] At the same time, collegiality among animators also meant that workers moved from one company to another frequently on invitations or recommendations from coworkers, encouraging both innovation (to stand out) and stylistic conformity (to plug into existing character lines).

Likewise, the movement of animators from one studio to the next, with relatively few animators staying with one company for any length of time, encouraged the dissemination of techniques and styles across product lines, and the very rapid stabilization of the look and performative meaning of cartoon characters during the first few decades of American commercial animation. Younger animators by necessity emulated more senior colleagues when they did the in-betweening for segments, and the legibility of characters—their appearance, attitude, movement, and signature gestures—required a deft hand at reproducing the styles of others. Grim Natwick provides one example of this tension. Widely credited as the creator of Betty Boop, Natwick started at the Fleischer Studios shortly after Dick Huemer had left and not only greatly admired Huemer's work but also had to reliably reproduce it when he drew characters such as Ko-Ko and Bimbo.[39] While those characters could and did change gradually over the course of several cartoons—likewise, Betty evolved into a human being from what was either a very human dog or a very canine human—they still had to be recognizable to distributors, exhibitors, and audiences, regardless of who drew them. This sort of incrementalism encouraged the conservation of convention, including those conventions linked to blackface minstrelsy. Thus, innovation was always tempered by the requirements of the job, of the reigning popular character, and of the current conventions. Yet at the same time, branding demanded that any convention—the wide mouth or eyes, bodily elasticity, the gloves—vary enough to mark a trademark character as the output of a specific studio. (There were plenty of generic characters, or animated extras, in the form of dogs, cats, hippos, and even elephants, that could have been produced at and for any studio.) When asked whether animators carried styles and techniques from one studio to another, Huemer answered yes they did, but "even though you retained a little; you couldn't help doing things certain ways" (i.e., the way the new studio required).⁴⁰

This tension between the rationalization of animation and its roots in craft practice is central to the fundamental activity of animate bodies in space. As animation studios became content suppliers to major Hollywood studios, an emergent class of producers—Bray, Sullivan, Fleischer, Disney, and others—worked to produce legible, competitive brands centered around popular characters, developing and promoting trademark characters and creating an easily recognizable look for their product lines. As in other industries, this translated into the strategic practice of marginal differentiation, building characters and backgrounds based on those already popular with audiences, but different enough to create a sense of novelty and avoid claims of copyright or trademark infringement. So competing trademark characters tended to resemble each other, which led to a veritable plague of dogs (Pete, Fitz, Bimbo), cats (Julius, Krazy, Felix), rabbits (Oswald, Bugs), and mice (Mickey, Jerry, Mighty). Add to this practice of marginal differentiation the circulation of animators between studios, working on one dog at one moment and another later, and aesthetic conventions became sedimented in the form through practice.

This conventional shorthand extended beyond backgrounds and sight lines to the characters themselves. The stereotypical depiction of Jews, Latinos, Asians, Scots, the Irish, Germans, and African Americans, borrowing both from well-established graphic traditions and from minstrelsy, variety shows, and vaudeville, also traded on an economy of efficiency in which characters immediately telegraphed their seemingly inherent natures and from that their place in the gag. For example, when the *Publix Opinion*, an in-house paper for Paramount/Publix exhibitors, described the central character of the Fleischers' *Swing You Sinners!* (1930) as "a poor creature that attempted to steal a chicken," exhibitors and audiences already familiar with the hit blues song would know what sort of short to expect and that the character was meant to read as black and poor and by his very nature a chicken thief.⁴¹ The representational efficiency that governed backgrounds had its corollary in the legibility of characters, and that legibility was not unfreighted by race's commodity form (see chapter 4).

Like the wires that ran from Max's desk into Ko-Ko's body in *The Cartoon Factory*, a circuit connected the social and material relations of the animation industry to its products, embodying in them its attractions and frustrations, its contradictions. The rationalization of techniques and their promulgation through patenting and licensing tells part of this story: certain production norms, such as the use of standardized equipment for the registration of images or of specific materials (types of pens, ink, paper, celluloid sheets) or methods of creating movement against a background (e.g., "slash and tear") were learned at one studio and carried to the next, with variations and modifications driven by a desire to innovate and to avoid license fees and restrictions (imposed primarily by the predatory Bray organization).[42] Likewise, material continuity joined process and product, with pen and ink and the hand that wielded them signifying the mystical force of labor power that animated seemingly inert materials. Even as the intruding animator's hand recalled trademark characters' production from the stuff of animation—ink, paper, celluloid—'toons made much of their fluidity, of being malleable material objects, albeit living ones. These self-aware commodities—Felix, Ko-Ko, Julius—bit, poked, and slipped between the hands of their makers. Yet at the end of every episode each was tamed: Felix's tail was reattached to his body, Julius and Alice went their separate ways, and Ko-Ko was sealed firmly back in his ink bottle.

In fact, the repeating trope of the inkwell as primordial soup celebrated the very specific materiality for animated characters: lest we forgot, they were made of ink. Fluid, flexible, and mercurial, ink was represented as the essence of their being and of the blackness of their material base. Like the burnt cork and shoe polish of the blackface minstrel, ink was a distillation of the qualities of an ideal blackness that began formless, took shape as a trickster and rebellious commodity, and finally returned to the bottle from whence it had poured. In their repetitive resistance to their passive commodity status, these characters seemed to do Marx one better, apparently able to reverse their transformation from raw stuffs into sociable forms. Recall that Marx said of the making of a commodity, in this case a table: "The form of wood is altered . . . if a table is made out of it. Nevertheless the table continues to be wood, an ordinary, sensuous thing. But as soon as it emerges as a commodity, it changes into a thing which transcends seriousness. It not only stands with its feet on the ground, but, in

FIG. 2.7 Toward the end of Walter Lantz's *Voodoo in Harlem* (1938), savage characters return to the inkwell from whence they sprang.

relation to all other commodities, it stands on its head, and evolves out of its wooden brain grotesque ideas, far more wonderful than if it were to begin dancing of its own free will."[43] Marx's tongue-in-cheek description of commodity fetishism performs the very elision it describes: by imagining the table itself as the author of its transformation, it erases the laboring bodies that actually produced it. A product of sensuous labor, the continuing cartoon character, like the table, is animated by all the social and material relations that inhere in its form. Like the table, which simultaneously stands on its feet and its head (performing an eccentric dance like Eddie Leonard), the 'toon outdoes the table when it expresses its contradictory character: deriving from inanimate materials, given life by skill and labor, it doesn't just dance; it turns on the hand of its maker. Drawn and sometimes able to redraw itself and its surroundings, the cartoon minstrel escapes the bounds of the conditions of its making, only to ultimately encounter the punishing hand of its maker and to take refuge in its originary form, ink. While Marx's imaginary table betrayed its maker by escaping into the marketplace and there continuing to perform its semiotic inanity, flaunting fantasies seemingly of its own making but actually of those who abetted its escape, when the continuing cartoon character fled the bounds of the drawn world only to be corralled by its maker, it was herded back toward the page and stopped up in the ink bottle, forcibly reminded of its subordinate materiality.

Of course, *free* will is the key term here. Seemingly autonomous, ani-

FIG. 2.8 In *Ko-Ko in 1999* (1927), Ko-Ko the Clown draws himself while Max's pen hovers, ready to assist or to stymie him.

mated minstrels often performed with their putative creators a compulsive ritual of rebellion and its suppression. Like the chattel slaves from whom they ostensibly sprang, they were granted free will as a necessary fiction: they appeared to act and be acted upon of their own accord, but only to demonstrate the ultimate constraint placed on that seeming free will, its conscription into the master's self-congratulatory narrative.[44] There is hardly a better model for alienated labor: faced with depersonalization within emerging industrial modes of production, yet clinging to a craft model of production, animators created a commodity that appeared to speak back to its creators and assert its independence from the social and material order of its making . . . only inevitably to be put in its place. In an industry renowned for its highly idiosyncratic and creative employees yet increasingly dependent on rationalization in its production regimes, the recurrence of characters who rebelled against their containment within their drawn universe becomes legible as (among other things) the displacement of the social relations of production onto the field of the product.[45] That these figures proliferated under animator-cum-managers such as Max Fleischer, Walter Lantz, and Walt Disney, or under animator-directors such as Dave Fleischer and Ub Iwerks, makes of the animator (or his disembodied hand) a creature less fantastic than his creator but no less tinged with regret.

There were, of course, many cartoon shorts in which the minstrel figure did not dominate, or was absent altogether. Series such as Dreamy

Dud, Bobby Bumps, and the Katzenjammer Kids, for instance, opted for young, white rapscallions as repeating characters. While the visual iconography of these cartoons avoided blackface, some of their performative conventions—indirect resistance to authority, indifference to normative social behavior, disruption of the drawn environment—fell within minstrelsy's performative register. However, series such as these—often derived from popular Sunday comics—were produced alongside more directly minstrel-inflected cartoons. (Bobby Bumps was produced at Bray at the same time as the Fleischers made their Ko-Ko shorts there.) The minstrel-inflected continuing character was not an absolute, either obviously present or completely absent. Rather, its conventional characteristics existed on a continuum of visual and performative tropes. Nonetheless, the enduring and most popular animated characters did reproduce the blackface minstrel's rebellious relationship to the conditions of her/his making.

CONVENTIONAL LOCATIONS

These social and material conditions of production had their aesthetic correlates, not just in terms of popular continuing characters but also in the formulation of animate space. For example, in the teens and early twenties, the relationship between the fore-, middle-, and background in cartoons was usually kept simple, and much of the animation turned out at this time shared a reliance on strong, clean lines that very schematically described the performative space of animation.[46]

As Crafton has pointed out, most cartoons of the late teens and early twenties favored this schematic layout. In a passage otherwise devoted to a genealogy of character body types, he notes that "with industrialized techniques, series production was not simply made feasible; it became economically mandatory, and this affected the structure of the image. Specifically, generalized backgrounds were designed for reuse in several films. A horizon line with a few rocks and trees sufficed for 'outdoors.' Three converging lines denoted an interior corner of a room. . . . Repeated gestures and compositions implied film-to-film consistency and encouraged the spectator to place the character in his fictive universe."[47]

Although individual studios worked to establish *stylistic* differences— and much more so in their characters than in their backgrounds—*formally*, the animated realms that different houses produced described a relatively uniform cartoon universe.[48] The landscapes in which characters dwelt re-

FIG. 2.9 A still from *Felix Dopes It Out* (1924) demonstrates the schematic simplicity by which a few lines can represent an outdoor scene.

FIG. 2.10 A frame from *Felix Out of Luck* (1924) shows how few lines are required to create an indoor scene, efficiency reprising the basic iconography of the vaudeville backdrop.

mained remarkably consistent across different product lines, which were limited not only by technical and material constraints but also by a fluid and interchangeable community of practice that circulated between the major studios.[49] It was as if there really were a single "toon town" such as the one Robert Zemeckis created for *Who Framed Roger Rabbit?* (1988): the conventional backgrounds of different cartoons came to suggest a unitary geography, located elsewhere, yet nearby. "Animation" increasingly formed a coherent set of practices, a shared set of representational tropes, and a collation of ideas and jokes that spanned individual production facilities and producers, initiated by those early practitioners and in turn reproducing those tropes and practices in subsequent generations.[50]

With the coming of sound to film exhibition in the late 1920s, the larger cartoon studios developed more distinctive backgrounds — Disney tending ever toward (cinematic) "realism" and depth; Warner Bros. most often relying on a generic pastoral backdrop that MGM's cartoons also eventually used; the Fleischers alternating between a vaudeville drop-curtain style and the more elaborate backgrounds of later Betty Boop, Popeye (1936–1942/1957), and Superman (1941–1943) cartoons, while their 1930s Color Classics tried to outdo Disney in orotund cuteness. Yet the spatial relations between background, middle ground, and foreground in commercial animation remained extremely consistent. Even as Disney and the Fleischers competed over modeling three dimensions, and as Disney strove to emulate the look and feel of live cinema, the long-standing tropes and conventions of the cartoon short self-reflexively pointed away from that notion of real cinematic space and toward its own repeated deconstruction and reconstruction.[51]

American animation was also from its beginnings indebted to the comic strip for the simplicity of its graphic organization. At a fundamental level of intermediality, popular daily and weekly comics of the early twentieth century often were made into cartoons, as newspaper publishers such as Hearst or Pulitzer and the distributors that served them sought to cash in on the popularity of series such as *The Newlyweds* (1904–1916), the *Katzenjammer Kids* (1897–present), *Krazy Kat* (1910–1944), and *Mutt and Jeff* (1907–1982). Beyond that commonplace connection, however, for newspaper cartoons the pressures of a regular production schedule in the service of a mass product favored an economy of form and an indexical style of representation in which both space and character were indicated through the hieroglyphic of stereotype and the schematic form of the simple line. (In this regard, the baroque detail of McCay's *Little Nemo* and early *Dreams* cartoons are exceptions to the rule.) A range of scholars, from Crafton to David Carrier and to Scott McCloud, Scott Bukatman, and Drew Morton, have argued as to whether and how comics and cartoons demonstrate a relationship between serial graphic media and live film aesthetics.[52] Yet ongoing debates about the vectors of influence aside, newspaper cartoons and animation shared a set of production practices and stylistic gestures borne of and contributing to their shared conventions. Weekly panel comics had but a few frames in which to produce any given story, just as the cartoon short had roughly seven minutes in which to create the minimal plotline on which it hung its gags. Both forms, then, depended on a spare economy of conventional gestures, as well as on an audience properly schooled in reading those conventions.

This seemingly contiguous animate space—a world apart of 'toons— was a visual correlate for the emergence of a fluid community of practice, one simultaneously competitive and collaborative. Yet there are other ways to understand this relationship between labor practices and aesthetics. The foreshortening of a scene's fore-, middle and background into a narrowly confined space, though efficient, also visually echoed the backdrop or scrim in front of which a variety act unfolded, recalling animation's origins in, and indebtedness to, vaudeville. It reproduced the aesthetics of the vaudeville stage, on which simple backdrops were often used to signal the location of a bit, with a common understanding that they didn't signal realism but were gestural. Faced with a two-dimensional backdrop depicting a street corner, a parlor, or a police station, audiences weren't meant to suspend disbelief and locate the performers at those places; rather they understood that the backdrops were another example of vaudeville's iconic shorthand, its sparse economy of signification. Extended to cartoons, this simple approach favored a metaphysics of animation in which often rebellious or mischievous continuing characters such as Felix or Ko-Ko could easily puncture the frame, rearrange the landscape, or even transform one object into something utterly different. Owing no debt to the reality or even to the depth of the scene in which they cavorted, the characters could remind viewers of the materiality of the backdrop or the frame in the same way that a vaudeville performer could whack a backdrop and make it shudder to emphasize the artificiality of the situation.

The animated character's wink to the camera is also of a piece with what Jenkins has called this "vaudeville aesthetic" invoking the self-referentiality of the lightning-sketch.[53] Like other vaudeville acts, the lightning-sketcher acknowledged her or his audience by turning to laugh,

FIG. 2.11 In *The Enchanted Drawing* (1900), James Stuart
Blackton mugs for the camera, acknowledging his audience.

wink, and comment, or by having a character do the same. It was a performative gesture that implicated viewers, locating them in an apparently
coherent spatial continuum that included the theater's house, its stage,
and metaphysically more remote spaces within the drawing pad and beyond its margins. This suggested a collapsing of the distance between
organized layers of space and a bond between the audience, the character, and—on increasingly rarer occasions—the animator (see chapter 3).[54]
While chapter 1 described this organization of space in early animation as
a performative gesture, here the cartoon character in animated space becomes a visual corollary of the labor that produces it and its relationship
to the viewers who consume it. Rather than asking the viewer to forget its
constructed nature, hence the person(s) involved in making it, the cartoon
invokes the process of production through its seeming self-awareness, its
aggressive relationship not only to the animator but to an environment
with which it shares its material basis. The rebellious cartoon becomes
the very material embodiment of the labor that produced it, insisting that
it is both of and more than the material from whence it derived, obstinately refusing to occlude the labor and materials through which it came
into being.

Cartoons that consciously invoked the lightning-sketch, or in which a
continuing character such as Ko-Ko or Felix interfered with the hand of
the animator or reorganized the drawn space in which they dwelt, were
a subset of a much larger number of cartoons in which the struggle with
the producing or constraining hand seemed absent. Yet even in those

more mundane cartoons—such as Carlson's Dreamy Dud (1915–1920) or Hurd's Bobby Bumps (1915–1925) series—conventions such as a dashed line of sight or the not infrequent double take are examples of a self-reflexive acknowledgment of an audience. (In some later Bobby Bumps outings, Walter Lantz interacted with and attempted to control Bobby.) Regardless of the degree to which a given cartoon was self-reflexive, the "self" in that equation was not the cartoon as a made object unto itself but the cartoon as an intermediary between (working) animators and their audience, one that acknowledged the presence of both.

SOUND AND THE METAPHYSICS OF LABOR

This desire to either celebrate or mourn the labor and the materiality of making cartoons is a hallmark of American silent animation in the late teens and twenties. With the coming of sound to film during the 1920s and 1930s, the division of labor in animation changed (as it did in film generally), and with it the representation of the relationship of that labor to its products—animated characters—also changed. Accelerating a trend toward a more refined division of labor in cinematic production, the transition to sound led to the addition of whole departments for the recording, editing, and design of film sound. The transition also significantly changed technologies and practices in other parts of the process. Cameras and lights were changed, as was the architecture of the movie lot itself. Vocal talent and regional accents had to be taken into account alongside looks and physical types.[55] In terms of live cinema, this history has been well rehearsed and debated; less so for animation.

One would expect animation's transition to sound to have been simpler than that of live cinema. With much smaller budgets than their live counterparts, most animation houses made little initial effort to achieve voice synchronization. Instead, they minimized dialogue and played up sound effects and music. Although voice talent would become important by the middle of the 1930s, initially it was not. Even when voices became significant in animation, the relationship between the "performer" and its voice remained arbitrary. (Any photograph of Mel Blanc will confirm that he looked like neither a duck, a canary, a cat, a rabbit, nor a stunted, hyperactive ginger cowboy.)[56] Soundstages were unnecessary, as was the elaborate soundproofing for cameras, lights, and so on that had contributed to the increasing division of labor in live cinema. While early sound cartoons had few of these problems, the established conventions of the form were already a self-reflexive reminder of their status as made objects. Thus, as live cinema moved away from the vaudeville aesthetics of its first sound shorts and toward a cinematic aesthetic that worked to obscure (rather than celebrate) the conditions of its making, the relatively asynchronous quality of early sound cartoons further revealed their seams. Every time a voice spoke from a mouth that did not move, or vice versa, viewers were reminded that the object they watched was (poorly) assembled. Better synchronization would eliminate that particular inadvertent indexical marker of production/performance in favor of a coherence internal to the text and contiguous with the emerging realism of the live cinematic texts with which it shared the screen; but that would not happen until later in the 1930s.

Still, the transition to sound did bring about fundamental changes in American animation. Throughout the 1920s, as the form became more thoroughly integrated into the moviegoing package of shorts, live acts, and features (and then helped to supplant live acts), the favored cartoon was the gag-oriented situational short. Ongoing cartoon series such as Bray's Colonel Heeza Liar (1913–1924) or Terry's Aesop's Fables (1921–1933) opted for a format similar to that of live comedy shorts: a succession of simple gags organized along a slim narrative spine. The same was true of cartoons based on Sunday comic strips, which were already episodic and situational in nature. But the backgrounds for these shorts, the aesthetics of the spatial orientation between fore-, middle-, and background, remained fundamentally those of the vaudeville stage: the action unfolded within a shallow space more presentational than representational, indexically as much backdrop as a signifier of genuine three-dimensional space. Even the aesthetically sophisticated Felix the Cat series, which occasionally used live footage or photographic backgrounds, relied largely on a simple, flat format that favored the character and gag over a more richly detailed environment. Regardless of the complexity of the narrative, though, animated characters in the 1920s capered in a realm that did not pretend to the real: it was space that was understood as produced, not extant. It was nowhere and everywhere, ephemeral and immanent—it was, indexically, "drawn."

Walt Disney Productions' *Steamboat Willie* (1928) looms large in this history, and in film history generally, as *the* landmark for the introduction of synchronous sound into the animation industry, and for Disney's rise to an almost monolithic preeminence in the field. So great is the gravitational pull of that one short film that it was reasonable that Crafton named his landmark history of early animation *Before Mickey* (1982) in an effort to reclaim that history from the centripetal force of what Richard Schickel once called the "Disney version" of events.[57] Yet even as an easy landmark, *Steamboat Willie* is misleading: tales of its import (and corrections to those tales) usually center on the technological advances the film heralded (or claimed for itself) or on the business savvy of Walt Disney himself.

All well and good. Yet *Steamboat Willie* is also important as a marker of the increasing division of labor in animation—for example, as a harbinger of Disney's creation of a story department and a "sweatbox" to test new animation in the 1930s, following from the inevitable divisions of labor that attended adding synchronous sound to images—and in the occlusion of that labor.[58] For it was through (the ballyhoo around) *Steamboat Willie* that in its public relations Disney began in earnest to efface the image of the on-screen working animator and replace it with that of the animation producer. Far more successfully than Max Fleischer before him (or J. R. Bray before *him*), Walt Disney came to stand in as the maker of the magic of animation, a force distinct from, and in control of, the material base of its creation. Throughout the 1930s, the company celebrated Disney's industrial acumen, so much so that by 1937, *Time* apotheosized Disney's management skills, claiming: "Walt Disney has not drawn his own pictures for nine years. To turn out the mass production issued nowadays under his name, he would have to have 650 hands. And 650 hands he has. With slim, 36-year-old Walt Disney as the guiding intelligence, his smooth-working cinema factory produces an average of twelve *Mickey Mouse* films and six *Silly Symphonies* every year."[59] Yet if Disney came to epitomize this refinement in the organization and representation of animation labor, the company was not alone. This change wasn't solely a matter of marketing strategy. The conventions of the sound era, in order to foreground the synchronization of sound, gradually eschewed vaudeville aesthetics in favor of those that suggested an enclosed cinematic space, one that admitted no world outside itself, including the world of the performatively laboring animator at war with his creations.

For this reason alone, it is important to move past the hype around *Steamboat Willie* and to consider the effect of sound on the social, spatial, and material relations of animation. With the coming of sound, American commercial animation turned even more toward a set of graphic and performative practices that elided the (performed) working animator and the (cinematic) real world in which he dwelt, in favor of a contained realm

FIG. 2.12 Sound did not technically preclude the animator's presence in the frame. In *Betty Boop's Rise to Fame* (1934), Betty rides "Uncle Max's" pen into her next scene with him.

created and governed by what Klein has called "full animation"—a set of techniques and conventions that added volume to characters, gravity to movement, and depth to animate space, enclosing it as a realm wholly discontinuous from the (cinematic) reality of the performing animator.[60] If *Steamboat Willie* is a harbinger of any change, it is of this enclosure of animate space and the labor of its creation and the concomitant shift to a performative public relations in which Walt Disney was made to embody and mobilize an entire workforce that, unlike its animated counterparts, seemed not to resist that control.

The reasons for this foreclosure of space were not entirely practical—at least not in the sense that the maintenance of older tropes became impracticable or technically impossible with the coming of sound. Newer practices that mitigated against the performance of animation (as opposed to animated performances) were as much about labor and commerce as they were about evolving aesthetics. As Rudy Ising's colloquy with Bosko during his premiere in *Bosko the Talk-Ink Kid* (1929) or Max Fleischer's introduction of Betty Boop to a curious "reporter" in *Betty Boop's Rise to Fame* (1934) suggest, as sound became the norm in commercial cinema, it was still reasonable for an animator (or producer) to share the screen with a talking character. So, the motive force behind the enclosure of animate space in the early sound era was not so much practical as it was conventional: the performing animator as marker of industrial labor needed to disappear. Yet neither Ising nor Fleischer were really performers (though Fleischer was far better in that regard than Ising). Unlike Winsor McCay, who conceived of animation as an integrated part of his vaudeville show and designed characters such as Gertie to be performers in that show, Fleischer and Ising were not acting talent, and it showed: in terms of fluidity and ease, their animate creations were more at home in front of an audience than they were. The increasing division of labor that had begun with the industrialization of animation intensified with the coming of sound—the silent-era performing producer's lack of an actor's physicality now multiplied by a lack of vocal training—and the distance between the shop floor, the back office, and the screen increased.

All of which is to say that animation, which had at that point a long-standing conventional history of celebrating its own performativity, and of repetitively performing the labor of creation (and destruction), made the transition to sound by slowly disavowing its vaudevillian roots and by obscuring the actual labor of cartooning. Even though Hollywood's transition to sound depended heavily on vaudeville and on Broadway for its short subjects in its initial stages, as the 1930s progressed, vaudevillian self-reflexivity increasingly gave way to the narrative enclosure of a cinematic space encapsulated within a classical Hollywood style that many followers of André Bazin have fetishized as an evolutionary step toward an increasingly adept articulation of a necessary cinematic realism.[61] As the film industry refined synchronous sound, it celebrated that technology through narratives that offered a self-contained world untroubled by spaces or noises outside a stable matrix of the cinematic real. That is, with relatively few exceptions, conventional practice in Hollywood filmmaking after the transition to sound increasingly eschewed techniques that called attention to the means of production, to the construction of a film as taking place outside the narrative space represented on screen, or to characters as performed (as opposed to living).[62] Although this shift is usually understood as driven by technological change, with aesthetic and economic implications, it is also important to consider it as a change in the relationship between audiences, performers, and producers, between whom film acted as a medium of communication. The conventions that consolidated around synchronous sound in animation directed the attention of the audience away from traditions of performativity and of celebrating the tortured relationship between the animator and the fruits of his labor. And with that shift, those qualities that had identified the continuing character as a form of the blackface minstrel became vestigial—

still present but far less frequently remarked on. The "self" to which self-reflexive cartoons had once referred ceased, with the coming of sound, to be either the animator as worker or a performer on a vaudeville stage.

In that aesthetic shift, those who drew and the very act of drawing continued a gradual fade from the self-reflexive world of the silent popular cartoon into the more self-referential sound cartoons of the late 1920s and early 1930s. Earlier animation had often invoked the materials and means of its making, while the "self" toward which these later cartoons pointed was more likely a world populated with knowing caricatures of Hollywood celebrities. A trademark character might occasionally acknowledge that it was being drawn by an unseen and unnamed hand, but that hand remained unseen, and rarely led back to the real, working animator.[63] Even when they gestured toward it, these cartoons excluded the silent-era struggle between the animator and his creation that had played out at the boundary between the drawn world and the real. The removal of the animator-as-interlocutor positioned the viewer as spatially and socially more distant from the world of the cartoon, from the cartoon as an object, and from the animator as creator. Viewers became separated by an ontological gap formerly inhabited by the stage and by a performer on that stage who was present either literally in the live performance of animation or, later, figuratively in a cinematic reprise of that performance. The fabled self-referentiality that emerged in the output of virtually every major animation studio of the 1930s and 1940s became one centered more on animation's place in an imagined "Hollywood" than on its modes of production.[64] Animation in the late teens and into the twenties had made jokes about its own constructed nature, in which animators and their creations battled for control of the screen space; in the sound era the animation industry repositioned itself more often as a jester in the court royal of Hollywood celebrity.

This approach was not entirely new. For instance, Felix the Cat creator Otto Messmer had joined in the Chaplin craze in the late teens, when he and Pat Sullivan produced a number of Chaplin cartoons.[65] Of this effort, Messmer recalled: "Chaplin sent us at least thirty photographs of himself in different poses. He was delighted because this helped the propagation of his pictures. He encouraged us . . . and we copied every little movement that he did. . . . Chaplin had a great influence on us."[66] As Felix became a star in his own right, Chaplin's gestural economy would make it into his repertoire, and Buster Keaton also chose to underwrite the cat's walk, paying Sullivan studios so that Felix adopted trademark gestures from Keaton; the comedian returned the favor by using the cat's characteristic gait.[67] However, these were the exceptions to the rule, and with the coming of sound the referential mix shifted more drastically toward the movie industry. In *Hollywood Goes Krazy* (Columbia, 1932), Krazy Kat tries to break into the business by disguising himself as Charlie Chaplin and Groucho Marx while his girlfriend discovers the horrors of the casting couch. In *Toyland Premier* (Universal, 1934), animated versions of Eddie Cantor, Bing Crosby, and Laurel and Hardy help Santa premier new toys. In *Hollywood Capers* (Warner Bros., 1935), Beans (an ultimately unsuccessful continuing character) reprises Krazy Kat's backstage performance. *Hollywood Bowl* (Universal, 1938) uses the popular newsreel format to offer up visual and auditory caricatures of popular stars, and foreshadows Disney's *Fantasia* (1940) with Leopold Stokowski conducting an orchestra of disembodied minstrel gloves. In *You Ought to Be in Pictures* (Warner Bros., 1940) Porky Pig convinces Leon Schlesinger to let him out of his contract so that he can try to make it in live cinema. And in *Swooner Crooner* (Warner Bros., 1944), rooster versions of Bing Crosby and Frank Sinatra use their dreamy voices to spur on wartime egg production on Porky's chicken farm. Even Disney, which usually tried to distance itself from the excesses of Hollywood and of its relatively uncontrollable live stars, got into the act with *Mother Goose Goes Hollywood* (1938), in which the Marx Brothers play fiddle for Old King Cole and Humpty Dumpty is W. C. Fields.[68] A good example of the change from a self based in labor and performance to one based around celebrity is Warner Bros.' *Thugs with Dirty Mugs* (1939), in which the villain, who admits to the audience that he is modeled on Edward G. Robinson, is turned in to the cops by an audience member who has seen the cartoon before. In short, then, the "self" of the self-referential cartoon of the 1930s became less that of a product conscious of the conditions of its making and more that of a commodity fully enclosed in the apparently autonomous realm of other performing commodities (i.e., stars), aware at best of their generic unreality but not of their makers. The cartoon as space in which knowing creatures challenged the conditions of their making and the scope of a known animate world was shrinking.

FIG. 2.13 In *Hollywood Goes Krazy* (1932), Groucho Marx dances with a befuddled stage guard.

FIG. 2.14 In *Hollywood Bowl* (1938), Groucho pursues Greta Garbo, who has very large feet.

FIG. 2.15 In *Thugs with Dirty Mugs* (1939), a bulldog version of Edward G. Robinson threatens an audience member.

What, then, of the minstrel in the midst of these changes? As the animation industry matured, the rapid standardization of its practices created an
environment in which successful conventions and tropes circulated and
stabilized equally rapidly. The gloved hands, the wide, painted-on mouth,
and the morphological similarities between mice, cats, dogs, and rabbits
whose bodies all were black with white highlights became widespread
so quickly because the industry's practical environment facilitated their
quick condensation into standards. The same was true regarding the use
of other ethnic and racial stereotypes: they succeeded because they were
legible to audiences of the day but also because they made efficient use of
the limited narrative structure of the gag cartoon. With only seven minutes to win or lose an audience, the easy legibility (not to mention popularity) of stereotypes was of a piece with other moves toward greater efficiency. In the argot of vernacular social Darwinism, stereotypes reduced
complex cultural characteristics to simple and amusing character tics,
ones the American Dream promised could be erased through assimilation . . . for some. In that process of condensation, more nuanced notions
of the minstrel as a figuration of labor's rebellion against its impressment
became sublimated into regimes of production.[69] As the body and hand of
the performing animator faded, with it went direct references to the labor
it represented, and the rebellion of the cartoon minstrel became detached
from that against which it had once taken shape.

Yet because of that rapid rationalization, the structures and flows of
labor in the formation of American commercial animation also offer a
useful avenue for understanding how the figure of the blackface minstrel
became so prevalent and so important to early American cartoons. Even
as the earliest practitioners of the form—J. S. Blackton, Winsor McCay,
John and Margaret Bray, and others—incorporated the performative
norms and conventions of vaudeville and minstrelsy into their products,
the generation of animators they trained or employed, and who trained
the generations after them, also normalized a set of labor practices (and
management–labor relations) that facilitated the movement of animators
between studios on a regular basis. From that movement followed the
circulation of norms and ideas about characters, backgrounds, story, and
animate space itself, within which the minstrel figure quickly became a
standard, and almost as quickly became detached from the performative
racial regimes in which it had developed. In the relationship between the

labor practices of animators and the sorts of stories and characters they produced, the practical and the conventional intersected. The minstrelsy of trademark and continuing characters—which would become vestigial with the coming of sound—derived from and constituted participation in a long-standing performative and representative tradition that had produced the minstrel as an embodiment of white fantasies of labor's rebellion against its impressment into the service of capital.[70] Likewise, the minstrel's conventional status as outside of, and commenting on, polite society informed the cartoon minstrel character's playful resistance to the conditions of its making.

How animators in the early twentieth century did their jobs encouraged the standardization of continuing characters as minstrels—usually with white gloves, black and plasmatic bodies, mobile and voracious mouths, wide eyes, and willful and capricious personalities—and the often onerous conditions under which those characters were produced lent an affective charge to their rebellious behavior. As fetishes for the labor of animating, minstrel characters such as Felix, Bimbo, Ko-Ko, or Mickey expressed the contradictory nature of the form: they were made by animators to resist the conditions of their making, turning back on themselves, on their world, and—often enough to be notable as a trope—on the very hand that made them.[71] For these reasons, the labor of animation is incredibly important as work whose product is actually a visual and auditory commentary on itself.

In *The Poetics of Slumberland* (2012), Bukatman zeroes in on the central role that the depiction of labor plays in the pivotal tropes of early twentieth-century animation. He suggests that "animation as an *idea* speaks to life, autonomy, movement, freedom, while animation as a *mode of production* speaks to division of labor, precision of control, abundances of preplanning, the preclusion of the random.... And at the intersection of all of this stands the animator.... The presence of the animator, or more accurately, the animator's *hand*, figures in early animation as an image both of work and its erasure."[72] Discussing some of the earliest cartoon characters in American animation, such as Flip and Impy in McCay's *Nemo*, Bukatman also notes that in the animated figure, race and ethnicity sometimes intersected in an expression of the struggle between (white) animating forces and the things they animated.[73] Yet the nexus of minstrelsy and labor for Bukatman becomes a spur for a virtuosic analysis of the echt forces animating print and film culture in the early twentieth century—from the high of Picasso paintings to the low of R. F. Outcault's comic strip *Hogan's*

Alley—and remains primarily organized around the analysis of visual experience. No doubt. Yet beyond the visual experience of texts is an encounter with the practical and performative, such as that which Donald Crafton outlines in *Shadow of a Mouse*. Bukatman quite eloquently marks the relationship between Eisensteinian plasmaticness, racial ambivalence, and labor in the service of the organization of a visual culture that spans the high and the low. Yet commercial animation in the United States of the early twentieth century did more than simply depict those relations; it also performed them, both on-screen and in the press. In doing so, the animation industry helped to give substance to racially inflected fantasies about the proper relationship between labor, management, and production—and it also contributed to discourse around those fundamental categories. The practical and hierarchical relationships that developed in the animation industry, as they changed over time, drew from and contributed to the visual and performative economies of the time, serving as an expression of those relations. Within this matrix, the minstrel was a given, the fantastic *prima materia* and conventional substrate informing the seemingly generic plasmatics of the continuing cartoon character. Beyond their poetics, these gestures toward the material substances and productive practices made the evocation of labor and its creations an embodied political economy of emerging popular entertainment industries.

CONCLUSION: THE METAPHYSICS OF ANIMATE SPACE REVISITED

Walt Disney's rambling, Spanish studio in Hollywood, California, is a factory for making myths. A factory, because there the technical problem of producing the 10,000 or so separate drawings that go into a one-reel animated cartoon (some eight minutes of entertainment) is solved with the utmost speed and efficiency which modern industrial methods will permit. . . . In Disney's studio a twentieth-century miracle is achieved: by a system as truly of the machine age as Henry Ford's plant at Dearborn, true art is produced.
—"The Big Bad Wolf," *Fortune* (1934)

The intimate association between animation and labor is not something hidden that has to be dug out of archives or discovered through careful frame-by-frame analysis.[74] In the early twentieth century, Winsor McCay celebrated his own labor in the film versions of his stage shows because he was proud of his hard work and the magic it seemed to produce. Twenty-odd years later, Walt Disney Productions offered reporters tours of its Hyperion Avenue facilities (and soon afterward its new Burbank studios) and pumped them with information that mimicked in numerical form McCay's cinematic celebration of his own labor. The difference was, of course, that McCay did his own drawing and proudly performed it on-screen, while Walt Disney did not. By the time that *Fortune* celebrated Disney's cinematic rationalism, Walt had not animated in over five years.[75] By the end of the 1930s, Disney proudly publicized that Walt was no longer an animator but that as a producer he had, like an industrial Shiva, multiplied his hands manifold times, the godlike manager of a Fordist animation factory.

Yet while Disney had specific reasons for touting its industrial acumen, the (celebration of) the labor of animation was by no means its sole domain. *New York Times* film critic Bosley Crowther, surveying the field in 1938, reported that the Fleischers employed, like Disney's legion of laborers, "a staff of about 250 artists and technicians who work like a hive of bees . . . laboriously drawing the little pictures which go to make up a full cartoon" and that Paul Terry also employed sixty workers in his facilities in New Rochelle, New York.[76] It was a common trope in the public relations of American commercial animation to remind readers that it was an *industry*. Cartooning was no longer the folksy stage show that Winsor McCay had made of it, nor was it a cottage industry; it was an integral part of the movie *business*.

Another way to understand this, though, is that the performance of the labor of animation did not cease at all: as Eric Smoodin has pointed out, it shifted from the stage and the screen to the popular press.[77] A shorthand interpretation of this move might be that with "casts" of workers that now numbered in the hundreds, the only forum for this performance was the press. Consider how the *New York Times Magazine* made sense of the industry in 1931:

> Watching the precise processes by which magic is created, you can well believe that it would take one man two years to make all the drawings for one seven-minute picture. But behind the screen Mickey and Minnie are too abstract for me; the concrete picture I carry away from the Disney studio is one of the "effect men," in the orchestra . . . earnestly emitting the riotous noises of the sound cartoon. If those squeals and whizzes sound funny from clowning animals and vocal hatracks, imagine how they sound from oldish, serious men. Up in the music room, a

young woman scores a symphony. Sitting beside her, plump, dapper, a trifle pompous, a young man is barking heartily like a terrier.[78]

An inverse of Van Beuren's *Making 'Em Move* (1931), this is still labor as entertainment; it's just shifted from the screen to the page. And it is entertainment in the service of the commodity rather than the commodity in the service of entertainment. And, like the dwarfs in *Snow White and the Seven Dwarfs* (1937), these workers seem to care little about the final product, so swept up are they in the joy of working.

With the aesthetic, economic, and technical demands of sound cinema, the space in which animate characters dwelt gradually became foreclosed to animators, and to depictions of the labor of animation itself. If audience penetration into the (representational) space of an imagined production process were still possible (as in *Making 'Em Move*), it wasn't through the theater; instead, one got "backstage" glimpses in the mode of a fan on a press agent's guided tour. This foreclosure of animate space was further hastened by the "naturalistic" animation increasingly favored by Disney, as the company eschewed the relatively shallow vaudevillian organization of space for a well-rounded realism consonant with an ever more codified classical Hollywood cinema. (What is "naturalistic" about *Snow White* [1937], for instance, is its mimicry of contemporary live cinematic conventions, not its attempts to faithfully render a real world.) Even Warner Bros. and MGM, as they developed what Norman Klein refers to as the "zip-crash" school of animation—which retained some vaudevillian modes of staging and performance—increasingly shifted their cartoons' self-reflexive address from the relationship between the vaudeville stage and its audience to screened entertainment and its audience, a move that effaced the animator altogether.[79] The same was true at Universal (first under Mintz, then Lantz) and Columbia (Mintz and Screen Gems). At least until 1934, when they began their Color Classics, the Fleischer Studios clung to vaudevillian self-reflexivity more aggressively than the other studios did, but during the 1930s even the Fleischers phased out the performance of the animator interacting with his creations.[80] This became especially true with the studio's highly acclaimed and short-lived Superman series (1941–1943). As vaudeville became a thing nostalgically reprised on radio and then TV, in cartoons the vaudevillian performance of the struggle between animator and animated ended. A unified cinematic space—an idea that the worlds depicted in movies were located *elsewhere* than in the theater—demanded obscuring the means and social relations of production. The "fourth wall" of the screen slammed shut, and the spaces off, the places into and out of which the morphing cartoon character moved, became dissociated from the performative present with which they once had been linked. In a metaphysical realm that valorized realism, how could an animated character escape into the real without suggesting its own manufacture? And how could the animator escape the real into the drawn? At best, there were guest appearances: in *Betty Boop's Rise to Fame* (1934) Betty visits Max and performs a retrospective for a "reporter"; in *Anchors Aweigh* (Sidney, 1945) Jerry of Tom and Jerry does a dance routine with Gene Kelly; in 1955 Mickey joins Walt Disney on the small screen to inaugurate "Disneyland" (both the park and the television program). In those anomalies, the contention and struggle between commodities and their makers that had once been a hallmark of such meetings between 'toons and real folk were replaced with diplomatic graces that suggested letters of passage. The producers reigned triumphant; the animators and their commodity avatars had been contained.[81]

In an unpublished fragment from 1931, Walter Benjamin elliptically and enigmatically comments: "Property relations in Mickey Mouse cartoons: here we see for the first time that it is possible to have one's own arm, even one's own body, stolen. . . . The route taken by a file in an office is more like that taken by Mickey Mouse than that taken by a marathon runner."[82] What begins as an observation about the separability of the cartoon character's body (if not of everything within the frame) swerves suddenly into a discussion of . . . what? The route of a file in an office is direct. Having been updated, affirmed, adjusted, it travels only from the desk where it is amended to the cabinet where it is filed, becoming the physical instantiation of the action that moves it, the file being filed. What Mickey is not, it would seem, in the realm of property relations, is something that goes the distance, that endures and overcomes hardship and demonstrates its own autonomous worth in the end. He lives, yet he is fungible.

Five years later, in "The Work of Art in the Age of Its Technological Reproducibility," the apparent trepidation of these delphic statements transforms into a seeming celebration of the mouse's antics: "The ancient truth expressed by Heraclitus, that those who are awake have a world in common while each sleeper has a world of his own, has been invalidated by film—and less by depicting the dream world itself than by creating figures of [a] collective dream, such as the globe-encircling Mickey Mouse."[83] Striding across and through the "optical unconscious," Benjamin's version of Mickey seems to operate well beyond the relatively bounded distance and direction of the marathon runner: he is nothing less than the "trigger [of] a therapeutic release of unconscious energies" that might ward off the mass psychosis of fascism.[84] In a footnote to that encomium, however, Benjamin immediately adds doubts:

> Of course, a comprehensive analysis of these films should not overlook their double meaning. It should start from the ambiguity of situations which have both a comic and a horrifying effect. . . . Some recent Mickey Mouse films offer situations in which such a question seems justified. (Their gloomy and sinister fire-magic, made technically possible by color film, highlights a feature which up to now has been present only covertly, and shows how easily fascism takes over "revolutionary" innovations in this field, too.) What is revealed in recent Disney films was latent in some of the earlier ones: the cozy acceptance of bestiality and violence as inevitable concomitants of existence.[85]

Although in this essay Benjamin harnessed Mickey to a larger project—a historical meditation on art, technology, and the constitution of social and political subjects—he did so at the expense of his own earlier, more elliptical yet succinct assessment of the rodent. Mickey's celebrity and Disney's promotional skills made of the mouse a synecdoche, one that seemed poised to overshadow not only any other cartoon character of the era but also the craft and industry as a whole. The earlier Benjamin had for a moment seemed aware of the labor and materiality of animation, even as represented in a rapidly rising Mickey. By 1936 Mickey straddled the globe like a colossus, lambent with the crystalline desire of the masses yet for Benjamin casting a long shadow of doubt. Ironically, what the critic noted with fear was nothing more than a set of traditions long at play in animation—the violence of deformation and metamorphosis and an emphasis on carnality—intensified by the occlusion of the performing and the working animator as creator and target of at least some of that violence, and by the enclosure of animate space as separate from the social and performative spaces from whence it sprang.[86]

In 1927 the American animation industry was small but relatively diverse, not only in the types of cartoons it produced but in its geography and its relationship to a rapidly consolidating Hollywood studio system. New York was still the geographic center of the industry, home to the Fleischer Studios, Terrytoons, Van Beuren, and Charles Mintz's operation. A decade later, the Fleischers would move to Florida to try to avoid a labor dispute, only to be taken over by Paramount, and Van Beuren would

FIG. 2.16 This pencil sketch from *Mickey's Man Friday* (1935) offers a performance of Disney's global reach, as Walt's minstrel avatar battles cannibals in a colonial adventure. Courtesy of AnimationResources.org.

be gone. In California, Disney would reign as the preeminent studio, and MGM, Columbia, Universal, and Warner Bros. would all have established their own cartoon divisions or begun distributing the work of major producers, such as Disney, Iwerks, Harman and Ising, and Lantz. New York, which had fostered minstrelsy, burlesque, vaudeville, and the nascent film industry, gave way to Los Angeles as the primary nexus of popular entertainment. Radio remained centered in New York, and on radio (and later in variety television) the vaudeville aesthetic lingered a little longer than it had in film. But in the visual, aural, and narrative logic of Hollywood following the transition to sound, commercial animation turned away from the playful self-reflexivity of the variety stage in favor of a self that found its origins in the mythic spaces of Hollywood soundstages, not on the worn boards of vaudeville houses.

Even Disney—with its roots in Kansas City and its operations in Los Angeles the least vaudevillian of the major studios of the late 1920s and early 1930s—demonstrated that shift in the development of the visual style of its Silly Symphonies. *Skeleton Dance* (1929), drawn by Ub Iwerks with music by Carl Stalling, considered one of Disney's best early efforts, features the face-forward (or in this case, skull-forward) and loose-limbed style of a vaudevillian or a minstrel "eccentric dancer." Made only a few years later, *Egyptian Melodies* (1931), with uncredited direction by Wilfred Jackson and drawing by Ben Sharpsteen and Rudy Zamora, largely eschews the presentational style of *Skeleton Dance* (or for that matter the Zip Coon minstrelsy of *Steamboat Willie* [1928]) in order to play with much more "cinematic" depth effects and to mock animation's two-dimensionality in a hieroglyphic dance sequence that takes place on and off of a frieze. Yet at key moments the film's spider protagonist still makes asides to an imagined audience, indicating a trace of porousness between worlds.[87] Finally, in 1935 *The Band Concert*—also with uncredited direction by Jackson and uncredited drawing by a host of animators—offers up middlebrow nostalgia for a performance of the *William Tell* Overture in a public park, with Mickey as conductor. Deploying neither the self-conscious play with depth of *Egyptian Melodies* nor the face-forward style of *Skeleton Dance*, *The Band Concert* is contained within a well-defined cinematic space. Donald Duck's vaudevillian intrusion into that space, playing "Old Zip Coon" on a fife, so disrupts Mickey's conducting that it seems to spawn a cyclone that threatens to tear the place apart, yet which is of course ultimately contained. (Even Donald's winks to the camera are framed as directed toward the drawn audience of the concert.) In each instance, the cartoon demonstrates the early sound era's reliance on music to sell the new technology. Yet each also demonstrates the recession of cartoon action into an increasingly distant animated cinematic space.

Donald's insistent and unwanted intrusion into the concert, playing the minstrel song that had launched Mickey's career, speaks to the ongoing vestigial presence of the blackface minstrel in American commercial animation and to an attendant need to disavow that disruptive figure. Like Ko-Ko before him, Donald is more a minstrel in the performative register than in the visual. Which is to say, bluntly, that he appears very white but remains a mischievous, lascivious trickster. When he intrudes here it is to play a classic minstrel song and to trouble a very white nostalgia for a very nineteenth-century brass band concert. According to Disney's public relations, the company developed Donald in the mid-1930s because Mickey Mouse's popularity had denatured him. An essay celebrating Mickey's twenty-first birthday, in 1949, had Walt Disney explain why Donald came to replace Mickey: "The Mouse's private life isn't especially colorful. He's never been the type that would go in for swimming pools and night club;

FIGS. 2.17-2.18 The Silly Symphonies *Skeleton Dance* (1929) and *Egyptian Melodies* (1931) offer a capsule view of Disney's move away from the vaudevillian style of the 1920s and toward an animated version of cinematic realism in the 1930s.

more the simple country boy at heart. Lives on a quiet residential street, has occasional dates with his girlfriend, Minnie, doesn't drink or smoke, likes the movies and band concerts, things like that."[88] That's what Mickey had become by 1949. Disney's conceit, of course, was to treat Mickey not as a drawn character but as Walt's son reaching his age of majority, and as an actor and employee of the studio. That gag dates back to the earliest days of animation, but in this instance it had been updated to suggest that however wild Mickey might once have been and however much he might still look like a minstrel, he had been neutered. The same article complained that during the 1930s, so much expectation of good behavior had accrued to Mickey—both in his cartoons and extratextually in his multitudinous PR appearances—that he was not allowed to drink, smoke, or act too violently and that the company had created Donald as an outlet for the pent-up creative energies of its animators. Thus, in cartoons that increasingly failed to credit the laborers who made them, Disney performed an elaborate disavowal of American animation's indebtedness to the blackface minstrel, and an act of displacement that distanced continuing cartoon characters such as Mickey from those minstrel roots while maintaining minstrelsy as a vestigial element stripped of its explicit connotations.

It is no accident that in the late 1930s and early 1940s, when animators at the major studios went out on strike (including at Disney in 1941) one of their demands was for greater screen credit and visibility. Exiled to a space off, their labor had been replaced with the "magic" of management, through which they were made *less* real than their own creations. The moment when the animator had shared the stage with his creation—had defended the stage from his creation—was brief but important. Its history is nothing less than the performance of the alienation of labor from its products, and when the commodity finally spoke, in the end it was only to peek its head out from behind a referential curtain and stammer, "That's All, Folks" as if there were nothing more to see.

slaves don't benefit from the fruit of their labor.

SPACE

If space is a product, our knowledge of it must be expected to reproduce and expound the process of reproduction. The "object" of interest must be expected to shift from things in space to the actual production of space. . . . Yet this space is always . . . a present space, given as an immediate whole, complete with its associations and connections in their actuality. Thus the production process and the product present themselves as two inseparable aspects, not as two separable ideas.
— Henri Lefebvre, *The Production of Space* (1974)

In May 1928, the Paramount Publix corporation announced to its affiliated exhibitors that it was joining the ballyhoo and getting into talking films. Even as it touted the coming of sound, though, the company's in-house paper, the *Publix Opinion*, warned that "films made by 'Yankee' voices may not be natural in Dixie, and visa versa. At any rate, the universality of films is apparently at an end, or else they will make the whole world learn to speak the same language."[1] Sound film promised to end a utopian cinematic harmony, or to force upon the United States (if not the world) a monotonous totalitarian linguistic uniformity. Implicit in that threat was the emergence of a more geographically contiguous and perhaps less autonomous world, one that would require careful negotiation by producers, exhibitors, and audiences.

Animation played a significant role in making that changing cinematic geography legible and desirable. The shift to sound movies in the United States of the late 1920s contributed to a wide range of changes to social and material relations surrounding cinema production, distribution, exhibition, and reception. Cartoons, however small they were as film texts, played an important part in those changes. Yet actually, in terms of technology, performance, labor, and the racial dynamics implicit in the announcement, cartoons had already been intimately involved in that process for almost a decade. Whether in its conventional history of combining live and filmed performance or in its experiments with new sound technologies in the early 1920s, American commercial animation had long been involved in playing with the place of movies in an emergent mass culture. As a subsidiary industry and a complex of practices, animation became useful to the movie industry in the 1920s and early 1930s as it experimented with exhibition models that combined live performance and films, and later helped to replace those live performances (and performers) with filmed ones. Animation's conventional history of performing the porousness of boundaries between life as lived, as represented, and as performed proved very useful in the reorganization of the economic, cultural, and social spaces of moviemaking and moviegoing in the early sound era, and cartoons offer a record of struggles over the shifting spatial ontologies occasioned by those changes in its presentation and public relations. Key to animation's role in the changes that surrounded the transition to sound film was its ongoing history of calling into question the metaphysical relationship between the real spaces in which films were made, the representational spaces they created, and the theatrical spaces in which they were received. At the same time, this change in spatial ontologies would play a significant role in repositioning the cartoon minstrel as vestigial, rather than as overt; this chapter examines how that shift in racial formation related to the complex negotiations around real and imagined space that the movie industry in general, and animation in particular, navigated in the transition to sound.

As the epigraph to this section indicates, the (ostensibly white) movie industry, as it negotiated the transition to sound, faced issues such as regional linguistic biases and in regions where racial segregation was an important part of daily life (sometimes reduced to "the South") the careful reinscription of the color bar. Once characters began to speak, understandings of place and self that were located in the shifting interstices between the world on the screen and the world in the seats were called into question. In 1930, for example, Paramount Publix offered tips on how to sell the MGM all-black musical *Hallelujah!* (Vidor, 1929) through the example of an exhibitor in Knoxville, Tennessee, who overcame white racist hostility (referred to in the article as "local tradition") and the fear

SALES SLANT CORRECT!

"Selling "Hallelujah" as a quality production, and playing up the colored cast despite local tradition to the contrary, Manager J. C. Cartledge of the Strand, Knoxville, Tenn., devised this elaborate front to let the folks know that the 'cotton was on de stalks.'

Laurence Dukes, artist, and the entire staff worked on the exhibit. The quality campaign on the picture proved so successful that after a run of a week the picture was held over for three additional days.

FIG. 3.1 A featurette in a 1930 issue of *Publix Opinion* offers an example of how one Tennessee exhibitor sold King Vidor's *Hallelujah!* (1929) by constructing a cotton field in his lobby.

of virtual miscegenation through intimate contact with on-screen African Americans by setting up a cotton field in his lobby.[2] Even as King Vidor and MGM attempted (and largely failed) to create a movie that sympathetically overcame stereotypes, this exhibitor resorted to the plantation, a central trope in the iconography of blackface minstrelsy, to create a safe conceptual enclosure for the film, and Paramount affirmed that choice as appropriate. If Publix theaters were to feature the intimate (yet stereotyped) lives of colored folk on the screen, exhibitors could still put white audiences at ease (and perhaps keep audiences of color in line) by reasserting relations of domination and submission in the lobby, as they did in the theater's segregated house.[3] Anticipating the Production Code's ban on miscegenation, this type of display might serve as prophylactic against a sense of any space, real or imagined, becoming equally shared.

These two examples concerning dialect and display, coming just two years apart, indicate some of the issues that attended the emergence of sound cinema—in this case, the real and imagined role of film production, distribution, and exhibition in the production and regulation of social and cultural boundaries during the Great Depression. The latter example in particular points to the powerful role that place—both actual and representational—played in regulating ideas about the relationship of blackness to whiteness as a public, social practice. The Knoxville exhibitor's reductive response to an attempt to present a more nuanced and sympathetic portrayal of African American life and Paramount's performance of fears that sound film might eliminate regional dialects describe anxious tensions around the perceived penetration of a mass medium into local life.[4] The Tennessee exhibitor grasped at a stereotype to frame *Hallelujah!* for his audience because the stereotype was an economical and succinct way to suggest a proper racial dynamic. Stereotyping had been a mainstay of the seven-minute cartoon since its beginning for the same reason: it served as a shorthand signal to audiences about how they were to understand its characters as types in relation to each other.[5] Stereotypes served as social hieroglyphics, embodying tensions between social groups while expressing dominant (mis)understandings of subordinate cultures. Similarly, just as Paramount/Publix anticipatorily raised the fear of a unitary dialect in order to influence discourse around the introduction of sound film, the film industry more generally sought to sell sound to audiences by creating and managing relationships between past and present practices. It did so not just through feature films but also by using short subjects, of which cartoons were a key component, and evenings that combined filmed with live performances as a means of downplaying the strangeness of the new technology.

The shift to sound film production and exhibition is most often celebrated through signpost films such as *Don Juan* (Crosland, 1926), *The Jazz Singer* (Crosland, 1927), and *Steamboat Willie* (Iwerks/Disney, 1928). Shift the focus from landmark texts to production processes and the transition also becomes about changes in the use and meaning of labor: the introduction of sound film and the passing of vaudeville marked a struggle between a nationalizing film industry, the fading mass medium of vaudeville, and the local and regional performance communities that sound film was supplanting. With the rise of motion picture palaces in the late teens and early twenties, the relatively distinct mass entertainments of movies and live performance found increasingly common ground in lavish extravaganzas called "presentations" or "combination shows." By the end of the 1920s, major movie producers would film stage talent as a means of introducing audiences to sound technologies. Even as performers from Broadway and vaudeville helped to demonstrate this new technology, they contributed to the diminution of their own industry, demonstrating through their filmed performances their own approaching obsolescence. Alongside these live performance shorts, cartoons also played a significant role in that change. Because animation could create visual correlates for abstractions, it worked out issues around the transition to sound, not just through the bodies of its cartoon characters but in the way it organized, represented, and played with spatial relations.

Whether in live cinema or in cartoons, the transition to sound was a contest in spatialized practices, one that had a racial dimension more or less evident at any given moment.[6] In addition to replacing live acts that employed local performers of different races and ethnicities, in the transition from live to recorded amusements, cartoons also promulgated and stabilized fantasies of the body in ways that live performance, however stereotypical, never could. Not only did American animation repeatedly play on some of the same ethnic and racial stereotypes deployed on the vaudeville stage and in some short-subject films but many cartoons also replayed the struggle between a racialized performing object (the trademark character as minstrel) and its creator, a tense battle between the maker and the thing made. A detailed examination of the changing relationship between cartoons, live performance, and the film program in the 1920s and 1930s, then, offers further perspective on how the transition to sound was negotiated on the ground. Given animation's long conventional history of embodying struggles over the meaning of labor, of ethnicity and race, of gender, and of more fundamental ontological questions about boundaries between the human and the commodity, cartoons become useful objects for considering just how the transition to sound was realized in changing regimes of production, distribution, exhibition, and representation. Finally, the details of that process also offer a plausible explanation as to why, as the 1930s progressed, the cartoon minstrel became vestigial, edged aside by more virulent racist caricatures of the swing era.

TRANSITIONAL SPACES

Cartoons figured in the transition to sound not just as adjuncts to feature films but also as integral components in short-subject catalogues, alongside newsreels, slapstick two-reelers, and varieties. As Hank Sartin has suggested, short subjects, including cartoons, were key to the introduction of sound film and to the gradual elimination of live performance in movie theaters.[7] During the late 1920s, exhibitors began replacing hybrid slates that had combined live local or regional performers with all-film programs produced for national and international markets. As such, short subjects in general, and cartoons in particular, were important in the gradual overlaying of more localized formations of space and place with a more national and international popular geography, and were integral in the gradual diminishment of local performance networks by mass-produced entertainments such as movies and nationally broadcast radio programming. In that this required negotiation around changing standards of performance and interaction—for example, around how voices were to sound or how certain types of people should be represented—short subjects in general and cartoons in particular offer a window into how Depression-era mass media worked through problems of how common spaces, whether in the theater or on the screen, were to be regulated and understood.

Vaudeville would play a significant role in this process. In that vaudeville had long been a mass medium in which issues of class, race, and gender had been playfully performed, that's not surprising. The shift in entertainment from local performances that combined live and filmed entertainment to mass-market all-film programs in the age of Jim Crow sometimes required a negotiation of the meaning of racialized bodies and the spaces they occupied, and vaudeville, as a transitional form between live and filmed performance, proved useful for producing new understandings of bodies in space. Donald Crafton, writing about animation in particular, argues that even after "vaudeville was no longer a significant component of popular entertainment, it was still useful to cartoonists as an idea. It became historical fiction. . . . Vaudeville provided a ready-made world, available to be shared as memory by filmmakers and their audiences."[8] Even after vaudeville began to lose ground to the movies as a mass entertainment, its construction as a space within which audiences and performers alike engaged in the rough-and-tumble performance of democratic similarity and difference remained an object of nostalgic affection for animation producers and audiences alike.[9]

Hugh Harman and Rudy Ising's 1929 cartoon *Bosko the Talk-Ink Kid* is a good example of how this racial organization of space played out in animation's performance of the new technology of sound film. The short features Rudy Ising and the newly minted Bosko in a routine typical both of the interplay of animator and character and of the minstrel show's interlocutor and end man. Ising begins by drawing Bosko on a sketch pad, from which the character speaks to him in the broad dialect of the minstrel, demonstrates his racial range by dancing the horah to "Khosn, Kale Mazl Tov," a silent-era musical cue for stereotypical Yiddishness, then re-

FIG. 3.2 In *Bosko the Talk-Ink Kid* (1929), Rudy Ising meets Bosko, whom he has just drawn.

turning to "black" vernacular.[10] Turning toward the camera, Bosko asks Ising who the audience is. Ising explains, then asks whether Bosko can make them (us) laugh. Provided by Ising with a piano, Bosko launches into Al Jolson's minstrel hit "Sonny Boy" (1928). Yet where Jolson (or even a less well known minstrel) could perform fantastic blackness only through makeup, dialect, and conventionalized song and dance, Bosko's body twists and contorts in ways impossible for any human actor, demonstrating a monstrous flexibility. When Bosko finally sings a horrible clinker, Ising sucks him off the page with his fountain pen and deposits him back in the inkwell. (Popping out at the last second, Bosko bids us farewell and blows a raspberry at Ising, unbowed.) Clearly operating in the registers of minstrelsy and vaudeville, and playing between the flatness of the drawing pad and the depth of animate space, the cartoon demonstrates the fantastic possibilities of the animate character, the fluid spatial relations of minstrel shows, vaudeville and cartoons, and Bosko's resistance and near-absolute submission to Ising. The short, with its nostalgic use of vaudeville heightened by the sentimentalism of Jolson's song, blends novelty and familiarity, the live and the drawn, to perform and contain the shifting social and spatial relations occasioned by the new technology — all refracted through the prism of race.

It is not surprising that when Harman and Ising sought to move into sound film, they chose a blackface minstrel as their trademark character. Minstrelsy is important to this moment because of its place in 1920s vaudeville and because it informed the very beginnings of American animation, profoundly influencing the look and performance aesthetics of early trademark cartoon characters such as Ko-Ko, Felix, and Mickey Mouse.[11] (Although Ko-Ko was a clown in whiteface, his behaviors, physical plasticity, relationship to his ostensible creator, Max, and frequent violations of the film frame boundary clearly marked him as *performatively* a minstrel, even if his face was not blacked up.) Yet the coming of sound would pose problems for other animation producers: how should their trademark continuing characters, who had up to this point signified through their bodies and behaviors, sound? A *direct* relationship between the blackface minstrel and the continuing cartoon character was more apparent in animation's early silent days. By the time sound film was fully established in the 1930s, that connection began to be overshadowed by more overt and aggressive racist caricatures that linked fantastic and grotesque animated black bodies to the swing music in vogue at the time.[12] In this, Bosko's broad minstrel dialect proved an exception to the rule: when they finally spoke, many trademark characters who had in their behavior and morphology long appeared to be minstrels seemed less so in comparison to the broader racist caricatures with which they now shared the screen. In either the cartoon minstrel or the overt racist caricature, however, American animation studios made tangible white fantasies about the meaning of black bodies and culture, crystallizing in those imaginary bodies a complex of fear and desire about overt carnality and its suppression in a modernizing society. The blackface minstrel embodied racist fantasies of the rebellious slave or the overreaching northern "free Negro" in a nostalgic register; racist jazz caricatures imagined black libidinal excess unleashed by music and dance, unfettered by that nostalgic sentimentality. Changes wrought to and by cartoons during the 1920s and 1930s describe a mutually constitutive relationship between the political economy of technological change and the aesthetics and social relations cohering around that change, a chain of being extending from the ideal to the material and back again. Having secured a place in emergent all-film programs, cartoons created further distance between themselves and the live minstrel show, and that is why, when Mickey plays "Zip Coon" on livestock as he sails upriver in *Steamboat Willie*, most audiences today hear it as "Turkey in the Straw."

From its inception, American commercial animation not only produced lifelike and memorable characters, it also experimented with the spaces they inhabited. Long before the swooping and wheeling virtual cameras of CGI, hand-drawn animation could make light of the limitations that early live cinema technology placed on the representation of movement in and through space. As Crafton has pointed out, for practical/economic reasons, much of the cartoon output of the teens and twenties represented narrative spaces minimally, confining much of their action to the middle ground of narrowly defined spaces that used a line or two to represent a horizon, or in interiors three converging lines to represent a corner, thus a room.[13] Yet at the same time this more pedestrian fare was being produced, there were occasional examples of inventive play with motion in seemingly three-dimensional space, and with decidedly cinematic concepts of depth of field and planes of action. Winsor McCay's 1911 *Little Nemo* features Nemo contorting fellow characters Flip and Impy as if they were trapped in the curved plane of a Coney Island funhouse mirror.[14] His *Gertie* (1914) has Gertie flinging a troublesome mastodon far into the background, dramatically demonstrating McCay's fabled mastery over perspective. And an intertitle in *The Flying House* (1921) proudly announces, in the style of a traveling scientific lecturer: "To teachers and Students—Special attention is to be called to the remarkable piece of animation that follows. The earth and moon revolving in their orbits in the firmament, drawn true to astronomical calculations, with the beautiful constellation 'Orion' in the background." The cartoon delivers on that promise, performing scale, perspective, and motion masterfully as the house rises from a rotating Earth, the orbiting moon grows in relation to both, and the "camera" gradually pulls back to take in the dance of house and spheres. Roughly a decade later, Ub Iwerks would become known for his signature move (soon copied by others), in shorts such as *The Skeleton Dance* (1929) and *Egyptian Melodies* (1931), of characters looming from the middle ground toward an imagined camera, then diving back into the action.

These cartoons express a tension found in a number of shorts from the first two decades of American commercial animation. On the one hand animators sometimes playfully explored and manipulated the dynamics of cinematic space, toying with emerging conventions around its organization and legibility, in some cases producing visual effects that exceeded those available to live cinema producers of the day.[15] On the other, cartoons generally maintained the conceits of the direct form of address and intertextual play with other popular amusements that signaled animation's ongoing relationship with the vaudeville stage. Even as they demonstrated a greater facility with representing and manipulating cinematic space, they did so in service of the cartoon as an attraction rather than an integrated narrative whole. Complex play with depth, scale, and motion had less to do with creating stable regimes of cinematic realism and more to do with extending animation's performance of mastery beyond cartoon bodies to the very spaces they inhabited.

What of the minstrel in this process? Even though blackface minstrel Eddie Leonard claimed in 1914 that "high-class vaudeville killed the minstrel show," a more syncretic take would be that beginning in the early 1900s, vaudeville absorbed minstrelsy into its diverse and catholic offerings, and from there blackface made its way onto the screen.[16] In the 1920s, vaudeville, Broadway, and the movie industry had a relationship that was sometimes collaborative and sometimes competitive, and in which conventions and traditions from the stage sometimes migrated onto the screen. With the coming of sound, vaudeville served as a facilitator in its own demise, providing the on-screen talent and variety format that would help to make more costly, complicated, and sometimes unreliable live performances appear relatively unpalatable to Depression-era exhibitors. Cartoons, with their easy manipulation of space and place, would also play a key role in that transition. And, as they were deeply imbricated in the racial formations of the day, they would also serve to secure minstrelsy's important place in the selling of sound to moviegoing publics of the 1920s and 1930s. Cartoons helped to sever the immediate relationship between the stage minstrel and its animated counterpart in the same way that high-class vaudeville "killed" the minstrel show: by absorbing its conventions and distancing itself from minstrelsy's historical referents in the search for broader audiences.

PROLOGUES, PRESENTATIONS, AND EPILOGUES

Yet early American animation's debt to vaudeville for many of its conventions is not simply an origin story. Commonly considered the medium that killed vaudeville (after it killed minstrelsy), in the 1920s movies sometimes helped to keep that business alive. Beginning in the early 1920s and continuing until sound cinema was well established in the early 1930s, major movie palaces and some smaller venues staged live shows and reviews—variably called prologues, presentations, or combination shows—as part of an evening's bill of fare. Some of these shows had little overall thematic coherence but featured the best talent available from "legitimate" and vaudeville stages. Others built elaborate reviews around the theme or story of an evening's feature film, and some actually interwove live and filmed performances throughout a single evening.[17] Whether elaborate or simple, these hybrids created the possibility of complex relationships between the space within the screen, the stage over which it hung, and the house in which the audience sat and watched. And even as animators played with spatial relations within the confines of the screen proper, they also participated in this live review phenomenon by constructing their own elaborate confections. Producing interactive cartoons that encouraged the audience to participate in a live performance, or elaborate spectacles built around an individual cartoon, they also found ways to reimagine and mass-produce the playful relationship between the live and the drawn that Winsor McCay had developed a decade earlier.

While different animation houses participated in the presentation trend to varying degrees, one of the hybrid exhibition form's most enthusiastic participants was the Fleischer Studios.[18] Not only did the Fleischers often make direct and indirect reference to vaudeville performance in their cartoons, they also contributed to combination shows and pursued technical innovations for the staging of cartoons that helped to usher in sound cinema. In this regard, the Fleischers offer a condensed example of the exploration of spatial dynamics at which animation already excelled and which the formal experimentation with exhibition encouraged. Fleischer cartoons made during the 1920s and early 1930s epitomize animation's exploration of notions of cinematic space and its relation to exhibition space, offering a primer on how those experiments foregrounded changing dynamics between producers, exhibitors, and audience members. The arrival of sound at the end of the decade led to significant and long-lasting changes in the metaphysics and practical representation of space in cinema; the decade leading up to that transition offers a glimpse of the working out of those choices. Animation, especially though not exclusively as practiced by the Fleischers, became a site where the changing social and material relations occasioned by the introduction of sound were made manifest by cartoons' ability to bring relations between the real and ideal into sharp relief.

Around 1924, as the presentation trend grew around live cinema and

FIG. 3.3 At the opening of the Fleischers' *Vaudeville* (1924), an unknown hand draws the outline of Ko-Ko the Clown, who then waits impatiently until the details of his location are drawn and he is filled in.

some animation producers experimented with new ways of combining live performance and animation, the Fleischers began producing the Song Car-Tunes (1924–1927), some of which made use of sound technology several years before Disney's much-touted *Steamboat Willie*. Yet even before they made these sing-along cartoons, the Fleischers already engaged in the performative tradition of the animator sparring with his creation that the likes of McCay and James Stuart Blackton had worked into their stage shows and shorts: many of the Fleischers' Out of the Inkwell cartoons (1919–1929) featured their star, Ko-Ko the Clown, escaping the two-dimensional world to spar with Max and Dave and create havoc in three dimensions, and a brief consideration of one will better frame the studio's choice to produce and market sing-along cartoons.

Vaudeville (1924) makes literal many of the performative tropes the Fleischers borrowed from the vaudeville stage.[19] The short opens with a (photograph of a) hand quickly sketching an outline of Ko-Ko on a white background. Once drawn, he comes to life as the hand continues to trace a desk, drawing board, and man (Max) while the clown's outline fidgets and looks on. The hand paints in a photographic background, and in a quick cut Max is alive and Ko-Ko has been transposed from the desktop to a drawing board. Dipping his pen into the inkwell, Max fills in Ko-Ko's outline, but the clown tries to move before the ink has dried, and he and his black substance are separated. Max takes a pen-knife and pries the ink from the page. Ko-Ko then shimmies into the outline and after a few hi-jinks is made whole; he celebrates by climbing out of the page onto Max's arm, and then back into it. Max then places the clown in front of a vaude-ville theater. When Ko-Ko tries to enter, though, the door comes to life and bars his way; eventually Max intervenes and places him in the box office; in that instant he has gone from a potential audience member to a worker.

Ko-Ko soon appears onstage as the emcee, introducing an imitation of Will Rogers, whom he brings on by dragging a movie screen with a cartoon cowboy on it onto the stage, creating a cartoon-within-a-cartoon. He then introduces an equestrian act, and there is a cut to Max applauding as he drags another cartoon onstage. An overweight equestrienne is met with yawns while Ko-Ko plays all of the instruments in the orchestra pit. Next are trained seals, also in a cartoon. Max applauds that act, and then Ko-Ko seems to pull on another screen, but it turns out to be a pole rather than the screen's leading edge. Max yells at Ko-Ko to get off the stage, calling him a "HAM" (a term associated with the ham fat used to remove blackface). Ko-Ko refuses, instead launching into a corny and unconvincing magic act. The scene cuts to an alternately bored and excited audience and then to Max, who shouts at the clown that he's no magician. Max then proceeds to mount his own magic act, using a handkerchief to hide his face as he transforms himself through quick cuts into a Native American man, a white woman, a black man, a white man with a monocle, a Hasid, and then finally back into himself. He shouts at the page, via intertitle, "Now, let's see you top THAT!"[20] In response, Ko-Ko squeezes the ink out of his own outline, creating a shadow version of himself, which then proceeds to unravel that outline. Max responds by swallowing the ink from the inkwell, which then spews from his mouth, converting him into a frightening ink blob creature that melts down and leaps onto the page and into the vaudeville theater. The blob of ink then absorbs the shadow Ko-Ko and erases the proscenium arch of the theater before spinning itself into an ink cyclone that pours off the page and onto the desktop. The scene cuts to the inkwell furiously boiling over as the screen fades to black.

This cartoon short is rife with gags and imagery that speak to expectations about the conventions of vaudeville, to the use of race and ethnicity as signifiers of transformation and its resistance, and to the evolving relationship between film and live performance in the 1920s. The short begins with an unnamed hand that draws Ko-Ko first and then Max as his animator—begging the question, whose moving hand started it all? Then, Ko-Ko's trouble with his outline plays on his character as a troubled fusion of black and white: as if it architecturally embodies the color bar, the vaudeville theater refuses him entry. How does he gain entrance? Only when Max's hand turns him into a worker in the theater. Yet as emcee, Ko-Ko doesn't bring live acts to the stage; instead he uses the stereotypical

FIGS. 3.4–3.5 In *Vaudeville* (1924), Max Fleischer performs a quick-change act, becoming in succession a Native American man, a white woman, an African American man, a dandy in a monocle, and finally a Hasidic man, proving to Ko-Ko that he is the better magician.

vaudeville hook to drag on a screen on which cartoon versions of each act appear, neatly encapsulating the 1920s' gradual replacement of live vaudeville or theater acts with their filmed counterparts. Max only objects to Ko-Ko's performance when he fails to bring the screen back on and tries instead to act as a live performer. At that point, after making what could be an oblique reference to Ko-Ko's status as a minstrel (calling him a ham), Max, an ostensibly "live" performer, takes over the performance, showing the clown what real magic looks like. What does it look like? The ability to transform one's self into any race or gender (really, any stereotype) and back again.[21] Ko-Ko's response is to once again separate his white self from the black, and to have the black (which would seem to hold his agency) disassemble the white. In an escalation, like Dr. Jekyll Max swallows ink and becomes the substance itself, which, once animated (but now lacking an animator), has the ability not only to consume Ko-Ko but to erase the theater itself. The animator, distilled to the essence of his ink, seems to destroy vaudeville (or at least a theater), and the image the audience is left with is of the inkwell itself, boiling furiously, barely able to contain all that it has consumed.

This short is representative of the scores of cartoons that the Fleischers put out in the 1920s whose central gag was consistent and even repetitive: Max drew Ko-Ko, who would then escape the page to wreak havoc on the real world until he was finally contained in an inkwell. The novelty of each cartoon was in the inventiveness with which the studio varied this basic shtick. Utilizing the standard vaudeville trope of theme and variation/elaboration, the Fleischer Studio put its energy into imagining wild scenarios into which Ko-Ko would stumble once he entered the real world.[22] Yet beneath the repetitiveness, the gag of Ko-Ko's intrusion into that world referred to the performative tradition of the animator's ability to produce a living being (one with enough free will to cause trouble for that same creator), in the process causing a breach in the boundary between real and ideal worlds.[23] Almost every Ko-Ko cartoon was about that breach and repair: in them, the representation of space was both practical and metaphysical, a claim to be able to manipulate and control the boundaries between a drawn world and a real (albeit fictional and cinematic) one through drawing. Even as the cartoons made visual jokes about the relative translatability of two dimensions into three, they also participated in a larger joke about the proper boundaries of that three-dimensional world. The boundary between the drawn and live worlds, also the boundary between the world of the commodity and that of its maker/owner, reciprocated social boundaries that defined identity and proper social location. The Fleischers were not the only animators to indulge in this conceit, though. Otto Messmer had Felix the Cat interact with the real world in shorts such as *Felix Saves the Day* (1922) and *Comicalamities* (1928). In its Alice series (1923–1927), Disney blended the real and drawn in the duo of Alice, a live little girl, and her cartoon cat, Julius. While working for Bray, Walter Lantz appeared on-screen often with Dinky Doodle in shorts such as *Dinky Doodle's Bedtime Story* (1926) and *Dinky Doodle in Uncle Tom's Cabin*, and with Pete the Pup in shorts such as *Petering Out* (1927) or *The Lunch Hound* (1927). Yet throughout the 1920s, the Fleischers made this gag their signature.[24]

MY OLD KENTUCKY HOME, OR LET'S ALL SING ABOUT RACISM

Most of the Fleischer Out of the Inkwell cartoons were silent and designed to be accompanied by live music and sound effects. Attempting to enlist audiences in their performances (and sometimes using innovative sound technology), the Fleischer Song Car-Tunes were meant to do more than that: they offered audiences an opportunity to join with animated characters in an evening of music-hall singing.[25] Each cartoon was a sing-along in which the audience followed lyrics on the screen with the help of animated characters and/or a bouncing ball. (As early as 1924, the Fleischers experimented with producing some of these with a soundtrack, using the DeForest Phonofilm process, but this venture failed when exhibitors refused to spring for the equipment necessary to screen them.)[26]

The Fleischers put out between thirty and forty Song Car-Tunes between 1924 and 1927. These cartoons were almost always sentimental and nostalgic, and many dealt either with race or ethnicity. Of these, nine (roughly a quarter) were minstrel tunes, including *Dixie* (1925), *Old Black Joe* (1925), and *Swanee River* (1925). Another six took up ethnic themes, such as *Has Anyone Here Seen Kelly?* (1926), *The Sidewalks of New York* (1925), and *My Bonnie Lies Over the Ocean* (1925). The rest might best be described as rousing and/or sentimental, from wartime songs such as *Pack Up Your Troubles* (1925) to tearjerkers such as Irving Berlin's *When I Lost You* (1926) or *When I Leave This World Behind* (1926). Approximately half of the Song Car-Tunes were issued with sound, as were all of their 1930s successors, the Screen Songs (1929–1938), which continued the tradition of the sing-along and of playing on themes of race, ethnicity, and sentimentality.[27] While not as well remembered as the Fleischer Betty

Boop, Popeye, or Superman shorts, these novelties went over well with audiences raised on vaudeville and music-hall traditions of singing along with the Tin Pan Alley hits of the day.

The Fleischers' preference for sentimental favorites had practical as well as social purposes. In narrow economic terms, their song choices were often drawn from the public domain or from the Paramount catalogue, so they could save on rights costs—and of course, knowing the words to popular songs was a must for singing along. But the practical intersected with the social and cultural in that their cartoons joined audiences in an act of common performance, often around words and images that invoked racial and ethnic stereotypes. Rogin has argued that sentimental performances of race and ethnicity, and of blackface in particular, were a means by which Jewish writers, performers, and producers (such as the Fleischers) in the early twentieth century could ease themselves out of ethnicity and into a whiteness more legible and acceptable to middle-class Christian elites.[28] According to Rogin, it was as if blackface's nostalgia for simpler times and clearer racialized relations of power, epitomized by Al Jolson's sentimental minstrelsy, defused tensions and resistances that ethnic immigrants felt as they tried to assimilate, as well as displacing nostalgia for their originary cultures. The Fleischer Song Car-Tunes offered the possibility of extending this operation by conceiving of audiences not as relatively passive observers of sentimental performances such as Jolson's but as active members in a sentimental chorus.

The Song Car-Tunes, then, redoubled the nostalgic tenor of minstrelsy by linking it to the sentimental practice of the sing-along. Writing about nineteenth-century literary and theatrical performances of sentimentality, Saidiya Hartman has suggested that they were an essential means by which those who identified as white—whether abolitionist, indifferent, or slave-owning—practiced a subjectivity relatively superior to the object status of the black bodies they either possessed, competed with, or wanted to rescue.[29] For Hartman, the sentimentality of minstrelsy, regardless of its secondary effects, reduced the horrors of the slave ship and the plantation to abstractions, evoking at best pity and at worst a longing for the clarity of times past or the renewal of chattel slavery. The Song Car-Tune attempted to amplify that inherent sentimentality through affective bonding, to create within the movie theater a community based in shared performance.

Sing-along cartoons aside, the discourse of sentimentality also applies more broadly to blackface minstrelsy in animation. (Consider the senti-

FIG. 3.6 The Fleischer Song Car-Tune *My Old Kentucky Home*
(1924) blends Stephen Foster's racist lyrics with the pleasure
of a group sing-along, linking the segregation of public space
to nostalgia and sentimentality.

mental and nostalgic register of many Mickey Mouse cartoons, for instance.) Yet in the case of these mixed-media sing-alongs, sentimentality
provided a further affective frame for the inherent nostalgia of the minstrel. These combinations of filmic and live entertainment offered a space
within which to participate in a collective nostalgic performance that
simultaneously engaged in new technologies—whether the simplicity of
an animated bouncing ball or the startling novelty of sound film. The
themes of race and ethnicity circulating through many of these films were
further inflected by this collective expression of nostalgia and sentimentality—one likely performed/experienced in a segregated theater. Cartoons such as *My Old Kentucky Home* (1924) and later Fleischer offerings
such as *I've Got Rings on My Fingers* (1929) or *When It's Sleepy Time Down
South* (1932) were racist in their lyrics and images—and one need not add
the caveat "by today's standards." Yet their potential for producing effective (or affective) racial formations becomes more apparent when they
are understood as imbricated in other sentimental social practices. Put
simply, in the back-and-forth of audience interplay that marked vaudeville
and early animation, performances of race and ethnicity in these cartoons
were interwoven with the sentimentality and the fun of the sing-along,
offering ostensibly white audiences an affectively positive experience of
collective and distributed racism.

If one credits reviews and the Fleischers' own public relations and
memoirs, these cartoons were very popular. *Film Daily*, which reviewed
the Song Car-Tunes on a regular basis, found some better than others, but

its overall tone was positive. Likewise, *Moving Picture World*, in its take on *Dolly Gray* (1926), claimed: "There is good snap to this war song of years ago and the handling of the chorus is a pippin. . . . Even if your patrons do not remember the song they will roar at the way the chorus is handled."[30] An anonymous reviewer in the *New York Times*, describing a Saturday matinee program, reported that a "charming feature of these Saturday mornings are the 'Ko-Ko-Cartunes,' [sic] wherein the words of well-known songs are flashed upon the screen while the organ plays the air. . . . The youngsters join lustily in the singing, showing none of the shyness that restrains their elders."[31] Accounts such as these portray younger audiences exuberantly following the on-screen bouncing ball, singing along to popular tunes of yesteryear. Older crowds, while reticent, appeared to have joined in with a little encouragement. In one instance, *Film Daily* reported that projectionists at a test screening began singing without any musical accompaniment.[32]

RETURNING ANIMATION TO THE STAGE

The Song Car-Tunes had their antecedents in vaudeville, of course, but also in performances mounted in and around movies more generally.[33] Since audience participation was a tradition well established in vaudeville (if officially discouraged in the "better" houses) it wasn't a huge leap to convince moviegoing audiences to chime in.[34] In at least one case, *Moving Picture World* reported, the cartoons' popularity led a theater owner to expand one Song Car-Tune into an entire evening's entertainment. H. M. S. Kendrick, the manager of the Mosque Theatre in Newark, New Jersey, staged the Fleischer cartoon short *My Bonnie Lies Over the Ocean* "precisely as though it were a feature," with the theater's fifty-piece orchestra playing an introduction:

> And the film was on, with the audience joining in the song. At the first chorus, a male quartet off-stage joined in and sang to the end. . . . As the Car-Tune ended, the lights went up on a Scotch mountain scene. . . . The sound of bagpipers, playing "My Bonnie," grows clearer and clearer, until they enter together with twenty Scotch lassies. The troupe . . . played some Scotch melodies, while the girls, the Mosque ballet, did the Highland Fling. Several solo songs and dances, and then the pipes begin again, to be taken up by the orchestra. The curtain came down amidst a veritable tumult of applause.[35]

This "epilogue," as the author called it, was more an exception than the rule. More common were "presentations," which mixed vaudeville or theatrical performances with films and were themed to support an evening's feature film, or "prologues," performances that set up the cartoons or the main attraction. Director Richard Fleischer, son of animation producer Max, writing about elaborate presentations at Manhattan's Rivoli, Rialto, and Criterion theaters during the 1920s, fondly recalls that each venue offered a different feature, and each "was preceded by a huge theatrical production: dozens of elaborately costumed dancers; a full symphony orchestra; enormous sets. These productions were based on the theme of the picture and acted as a sort of mood-setting introduction to the feature that was to follow."[36]

According to Douglas Gomery, presentations were the invention of New York exhibitors such as Sam "Roxy" Rothafle—who had on occasion actually inserted performances into the middle of films—and the Chicago theater owners Balaban and Katz, whose shows "opened with an overture, usually 8 to 10 minutes long, followed by a presentation of 15 to 20 minutes, then a newsreel of 7 minutes, a short of ten minutes, and then a feature [that] filled the remaining two-hour period." While Los Angeles exhibitor Sid Grauman championed the prologue over the presentation, "Roxy offered the alternative variety show in which several highly [paid?] vaudeville acts filled the twenty minutes. . . . Smaller theaters tried to copy these strategies whenever possible. Most usually followed Roxy's plan, using the cheapest available vaudeville acts."[37] This last point is important: while high-end presentations such as those by New York impresario Hugo Riesenfeld might have employed relatively well known performers, other, smaller presentations provided employment to lesser vaudevillians at a time when the vaudeville stage was contracting.

These presentations were mounted in major movie palaces in the early 1920s and in smaller venues that could afford them. *Wid's Daily* and its successor *Film Daily* featured regular, thorough reviews of the biggest of these presentation shows, under the heading "At Broadway Theaters."[38] For example, in 1920, *Wid's* reviewed a Riesenfeld production at the Criterion Theatre, describing the evening as "a pretentious program" whose highlight was a prologue, "the setting for which was designed by Joseph Urban, who also had much to do with the settings of the picture." After an overture, the second and major number, called "A Melody of Flowers," offered "six musical compositions of varying popularity, all of which are named after or contain the name of a flower. The prologue and feature follow[ed] with a Mutt and Jeff cartoon, the 'Merry Cafe,' concluding the program."[39]

These presentations were not a flash in the pan. On April 16, 1925, *Film Daily* reported on an elaborate show at the Capitol, describing an orchestra overture featuring Mascagni's "Intermezzo" from "Cavalleria Rusticana" and the song "'Come See the Place Where Jesus Lay,' sung by William Robyn, Douglas Stanbury, and the Capitol Singers," which was accompanied by a tableau and a filmed travelogue. The show's fourth act featured a solo performance of "The Blue Danube Waltz," and then, "after the news weekly is screened, Mlle. Gambarelli offers a novel number titled 'A Bit of Bric a Brac.' The seventh offering on the program is titled: 'Impressions of the Sultan of Sulu,' with a large cast of singers and dancers. 'Proud Flesh' is the feature, after which is presented 'Swanee River,' a 'Ko-Ko Song Cartune,' and 'Big Chief Ko-Ko,' an Out-of-the-Inkwell reel, both Red Seal Pictures. The organ closes with a solo."[40] Nor were these shows limited to New York. In July 1925, for example, *Film Daily* reported that the Keith-Albee vaudeville chain would combine movies and vaudeville in their new Cleveland palace, with eight features by Fox moving through on a weekly basis, along with "six acts of Keith vaudeville." The trade sheet further promised that if "the picture-vaudeville policy proves successful, it is quite likely it will be continued."[41] This expansion by Keith-Albee into film exhibition suggests a healthy market for intermedial entertainments in the years leading up to the talkies.[42] Yet it wasn't the fading popularity of presentations that helped to usher in sound film. On October 9, 1927, three days after the premiere of *The Jazz Singer* (though a few months before its general release), *Film Daily* reported on an elaborate Riesenfeld presentation at the Colony Theater in Manhattan, ending its detailed report by stating that the "entire program was tastefully presented without hitting extremes of jazz or 'arty' production. . . . Riesenfeld is introducing a new brand of entertainment to Broadway that will bear watching."[43]

Richard Fleischer's nostalgic reminiscence about those presentations in his memoir served as a prelude to describing how his father and Riesenfeld, the musical director of the Rialto, created a prologue for a Song Cartune, probably in late 1925.[44] In 1926 *Moving Picture World* detailed the techniques used to create that prologue, also suggesting that the Fleischers had intentionally engineered their cartoons to be integrated into stage shows.[45] The scenario offered detailed instructions for other exhibitors and was designed to imply a fluid boundary between stage and screen. To signal the Fleischers' current studio, Red Seal, the instructions

FIG. 3.7 Three panels from a 1926 article in *Moving Picture World* illustrate instructions for the exhibitor who wants to mount a live show with a Song Car-Tune featuring Ko-Ko the Clown.

proposed hanging two red seals on either side of the proscenium, with a "strip of canvas painted to represent a strip of motion-picture film" attached to wires that would also hold the seals in place. The seal on the left was to "have a scrim covered center. . . . so that the face of a singer may be discerned in the center of the seal during the running of the subject," the whole purpose of which was to introduce "a character made up as 'Ko-Ko' or either a straight [man?] to lead the audience in the singing which is bound to result when a Cartune Song [sic] is presented. The singer gets the song off to an early start, and overcomes audience timidity . . . until the song is sold."[46] These instructions, even as they demonstrate the elision of strict boundaries between screen and stage, also suggest that however popular the Song Car-Tunes might have been, some needed a bit of a boost to be "sold." To reinforce the bond between audience and stage, the article further suggested building a set of cardboard cutouts called "the 'Ko-Ko Quartette.' . . . These figures should be life size. . . . An oval cut-out should be made in the face of each poster so that the singer's face may be seen. . . . The arms should be attached to the body so that . . . the singer back of the poster may operate them in a 'mechanical gesture' during the song."[47] In addition to a singer in the wings, then, a "quartette" of apparently life-size cartoon characters would also accompany the film, moving "mechanically," as if they were less than human, and more like (poorly) animated characters. (The effect was not unlike that used roughly seven years later in Disney's *Mickey's Mellerdrammer* [1933].)[48] In addition, even if timid audiences sometimes required coaxing to sing along, *Moving Picture World* assured its readers that "every subject is a live one, [and] the song-cartunes [sic] are the best song films we know of in the matter of synchronization."[49]

Given his connection to the Song Car-Tunes, Ko-Ko may have been a natural for the stage, but he wasn't the only cartoon character to tread the boards. In October 1925, *Moving Picture World* also reported that Felix would be available in January 1926, or "Short Subject Month." The trade journal offered a two-page primer on how to stage a prologue for Felix cartoons, building them around an actor in a Felix costume doing one of three scripted pantomimes. To make sure that the actor playing Felix could pull it off, the article offered visual examples of Felix's trademark gestures and promised that what had already proven good for features would work for cartoon shorts as well: "Prologues and presentations for short subjects have . . . become a striking reality to showmen, as will be illustrated by the suggested novelty along this line now available to exhibitors presenting 'Felix, the Cat Cartoons' [sic]. . . . With prologues rapidly being devised for all manner of lengthy features, it was merely a matter of time before the little features would be accorded a pre-screening presentation."[50]

Whether called prologues, presentations, or epilogues, these popular mixed-media events created a continuum between the performers on the screen and those onstage (and in the orchestra pit). While not necessarily always as explicitly scripted as in these examples, they created thematic links between stage and screen. As sing-alongs, the Fleischer Song Car-Tunes and subsequent Screen Songs extended that continuum to the amateurs in the audience. But even without the encouragement to sing along, the presentations and combination shows of the mid-1920s describe a film culture that—at the risk of stating the obvious—was neither truly silent nor necessarily limited to the confines of the screen.

While this was true for both live film and cartoons, animation in particular had a performative and conventional relationship with the vaudeville stage that admitted the blurring of boundaries between stage, screen, and audience. From the sparring of animators and animated characters to the hand of the maker interfering with that which he made, and to Ko-Ko or Felix escaping from animated into cinematic space, Alice leaving the "real" world for animated space, and presentations, prologues, and epilogues, animation had a conventional history of puncturing the otherwise stable boundaries between screen space, stage space, and the world beyond. That the appearance and behaviors that defined trademark characters such as Felix, Krazy, Mickey, and Ko-Ko were drawn from a minstrel tradition that itself consciously joined the actual space of performance to the imaginary southern plantations from which it claimed to borrow, then to the house and the audience with whom characters communicated, only heightened this conventional complication of the spatial practices of filmgoing.

There were countervailing social, economic, and aesthetic forces at play in the transition to sound in cinema that trademark cartoon characters had to negotiate. On the one hand emerging conventions regarding narrative coherence demanded a concordance of sound and image as occupying the same spatial location.[51] On the other hand exhibition conventions in the 1920s—including those that foregrounded sound as a new technology—militated *against* that singular location and *for* a porous boundary between audience, stage, screen, and narrative space. These conventions ran counter to practices cohering around the enclosed cine-

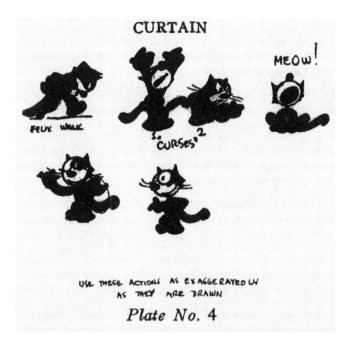

FIG. 3.8 A detail from a 1925 article in *Moving Picture World* provides instructions to the costumed actor in a live performance to accompany a Felix the Cat cartoon.

matic space of sound film. In efforts to sell sound cinema to its audiences, "the talkies" were first offered up both as attractions and as vehicles for enhanced narrative. The cartoons and variety shorts that did so much to sell sound cinema at the end of the 1920s, like combination shows and sing-alongs, used familiar social and performative tropes to introduce audiences to the new technology—a technology that eventually obviated the need for those very social and performative practices, and for the performers who provided them.

CARTOONS AND THE REGULATION
OF (RACE IN) CINEMATIC SPACE

Cartoons, then, were involved in instances in which film exhibition encouraged, rather than inhibited, live performance, yet they also became part of the all-film programs that eventually ended those practices. Criticizing Donald Crafton's claim that the transition to sound in the film industry was chaotic and unstable, Douglas Gomery has suggested that different players in the movie industry acted in a rational, orderly, and strategic fashion during the uneven introduction of sound.[52] Favoring an emphasis on industrial practices, he faults Crafton for focusing too much on audiences and reception. A more rounded look at the transition to sound, though, one that takes into account both the industry's efforts to convert and audience reactions to that conversion, suggests a situation that was both chaotic *and* orderly, in which those engaged in the seemingly steady progress of implementing and standardizing sound, including animation studios, used instabilities in networks of practice and performance to their own rational advantage. Reading that transition from the vantage of animation's playful manipulation of space suggests instabilities and shifts in the spatial ontologies of producers, exhibitors, and audiences at that moment. In the conversion to sound cinema, there were changes in the representation of cinematic space that had corollaries in the reorganization of actual exhibition spaces, and practical discussions about that transition delineate a landscape contested by producers, performers, exhibitors, and audiences. Animation, with its traditional relationship to vaudeville and its trademark characters that operated simultaneously as commodities and performers, was one place where that contest was made visible. In that those continuing characters were with few exceptions blackface minstrels, those cartoon corollaries for the changes wrought by the transition to sound also made visible (and audible) racial formations as lived in the 1920s and 1930s and contributed to changing them. Though expressed primarily through bodies, the conventions and regimes of blackface minstrelsy also expressed a spatial ontology, and it also contributed to and was altered by the transition to sound in film.

This focus on the black/white binary in animation is not a claim that less binary formations of racial difference were not also at play in either live film or cartoons.[53] As already noted, for instance, the Fleischers offered a number of ethnically stereotyped numbers in their Song Car-Tunes and Screen Songs, and they were far from unique in that regard. Drawing on conventions from vaudeville and the graphic arts, all of the animation studios in this period depicted wily Chinamen, lazy Mexicans, simpering Jews, drunken Irishmen, and so on, either in human or thinly veiled animal form.[54] Discussing vaudeville's relationship to animation, Crafton suggests that vaudeville's "cheap tickets brought immigrants and their cultures in contact with American 'natives' throughout the nation. On the one hand this fostered international awareness and promoted assimilation. On the other, vaudeville also spotlighted differences through its inevitable spreading of stereotypes and prejudices based on gender, race, and ethnicity."⁵⁵ Deploying an economy of stereotype, vaudeville performers and bookers billed their acts by (performed) race and ethnicity, and individual performers were summarily judged on their ability to make familiar material new through unique timing and improvisation. (The same was true for animated shorts, in which racial and ethnic stereotypes were seen as efficient, because an audience could read a character at a glance and then appreciate a gag according to how well it was pulled off.) When the mass entertainment market eventually shifted and vaudeville declined, changes in the representation of race and ethnicity were reflected in employment: fewer live shows meant fewer ethnic and racial acts. Animation had a distinct advantage over live performance, though, in that the inclusion or elimination of any particular character was of no consequence to the character itself (or even to the people drawing it). As J. R. Bray had pointed out at the dawn of the industry, any cartoon character could be easily replaced (see chapter 2).

Yet even as animation studios adjusted their use of stereotypes according to audience standards, their repetitive use of the black/white binary continued to evoke cartoons' fixation on labor and its regulation. The visual and performative minstrelsy of continuing trademark characters such as Felix, Oswald, Bosko, and Bimbo remained central to the form even as they appeared alongside other stereotypes. A case in point is the MGM short *Chinaman's Chance* (1933), by Ub Iwerks. After leaving Disney in 1930, Iwerks developed Flip the Frog in an attempt to create his own trademark character in the minstrel mode. Looking more like a mouse than a frog, Flip was, like other cartoon minstrels, resourceful, mischievous, and able to manipulate his environment to suit his purposes. In this short, Flip plays a cop tasked with bringing in a criminal "chinaman," whose name, Chop Suey, adds insult to injury. The short is rife with verbal and visual puns: Flip and his canine companion track the villain to the Ob Long Chin Laundry, where the villain battles them with a hot iron, gets his pigtail caught in the rafters, traps Flip in an alligator pit, evades him in an opium den (where Flip hallucinates him as a "dragon lady"), and tries to dispose of Flip by tying him to a giant firework. In the midst of all of this, Flip bops along to a jazzy beat and manipulates the drawn environment to suit his purposes, tying a snake around the snout of an attacking alligator, passing unharmed through a laundry mangle, and flying while high on opium by merely flapping his arms. In the end, Flip the minstrel figure defeats Chop Suey the racial stereotype, a gesture that coats American

FIG. 3.9 In *Chinaman's Chance* (1933), Ub Iwerks's Flip the Frog performs as the animate minstrel opposite a shorthand racist caricature of a "chinaman."

nativism in an extra layer of complexion. As in many other early sound cartoons, dialogue and action are delivered on the short's slightly jazzy beat, securing the space of the cartoon against an alien intruder through rhythm.

But as a sound cartoon *Chinaman's Chance* was somewhat exceptional. Although American cartoons from the late 1920s and early 1930s offered many examples of ethnic stereotyping, as film's move to sound progressed, cartoons began to move away from many broad stereotypes, favoring trademark minstrel characters and more pointed and racist caricatures of African Americans. (Propaganda cartoons made during World War II, especially those made by Warner Bros., expanded the range of racist stereotyping to include vicious depictions of the Japanese in particular.) Stereotyping continued, but its inflection changed. In the live vaudeville varieties that shared the shorts program with cartoons, a similar phenomenon occurred. While vaudeville stages of the early twentieth century had no shortage of huffy "Dutchmen" (Germans), voluble and pompous Frenchmen, drunken Irishmen, tight-fisted Scotsmen, and so on, the live vaudeville shorts of the early sound era tended to eschew ethnic acts in favor of (generically white) comedians, dancers, musicians,

FIG. 3.10 In the Vitaphone short *Pie, Pie Blackbird* (1932), jazz star Nina Mae McKinney is required to perform as Mammy to the Nicholas Brothers and to sing about her "Massah."

and novelty acts.[56] A few "Oriental" acts and fan dances made their way onto film, along with some minstrels, yet live sound film varieties increasingly avoided the thornier precincts of race and ethnicity altogether.

That relatively fewer filmed acts were performing stereotyped exoticism contributed to a segregated cinematic imaginary in which African American performers appeared in what seemed to be an all-black cinematic cosmos that operated alongside a largely white one. Often performing in the register of minstrelsy, African American singers, dancers, and comics found work in "black vaudeville" shorts, in which the color bar extended into film production, distribution, and exhibition. Popular black vaudeville acts that crossed over from the stage to the screen, such as Nina Mae McKinney or Miller and Lyles, often had to trade in racial stereotypes in order to gain exposure: narratives depicting them as mammies, bellhops, and busboys were the seemingly obligatory frames for their considerable performing talents, which nonetheless reproduced the racial binary as a central social fact.[57] Their characters stepped out of black worlds to serve whites and then returned to a separate, and quite cartoonish, all-black existence. In the musical short *Pie, Pie Blackbird* (1932), for instance, McKinney plays a mammy in a kitchen, preparing a pie for an absent "massa," while the young dancers Fayard and Harold Nicholas pepper her with childish questions. When the pie is cooked, it magically opens to reveal Eubie Blake, Noble Sissle, and a small swing band in chef costumes, the "blackbirds" baked into it. As the song progresses, McKinney appears in evening wear on a pie-bound piano, and the Nicholas Brothers dance wearing miniature chef costumes. The entire live short operates in the metamorphic register of the cartoon: McKinney's performance of her considerable talents as a singer and the Nicholas Brothers' phenomenal skills as tappers are carefully contained within a narrative that first places them in massa's kitchen, then whisks them inside the pie McKinney has just baked for him, where they join Blake and Sissle, who for no clear reason are dressed as servants. The force that moves them from one stereotypical location to another is the same one that requires their containment: fantastic blackness and its attendant anxieties. As Crafton points out, while talkies encouraged a brief fascination with jazz-era black culture, that culture only appeared in caricature, and only in caricatures that would not offend delicate white, middle-class sensibilities.[58] Segregated labor policies and stereotypical representational regimes intersected in shorts like this, in which a desire to labor for (and perhaps as) one's self was limited by a requirement that one occupy a stereotype to do so.

The repressive stereotyping of major African American talent, though, occurred as part of a larger shift in employment practices of emerging mass-entertainment industries. In the rapidly foreclosing combination-show circuit, opportunities for live performers, regardless of race, declined.[59] Name acts of color, such as the black minstrels Glenn and Jenkins, who had once found work with larger exhibition chains such as Publix, faded into obscurity as theater chains moved away from touring regional combination shows to all-film programs; regional entertainers without name billing, such as those who had been featured in Publix shows like the "Florida Revels" and "Chinese Fantasy," also faced reduced opportunities. That live race and ethnic acts became a casualty of the transition from combination shows to all-film programs in the early sound era begins to describe a facet of the changing exhibition landscape of the time, but only touches on the alterations to performative practices and labor relations that the transition engendered. As Gomery has pointed out, as combination shows caught on, major exhibition chains such as Paramount-Publix and Loews developed their own touring circuits in which traveling presentation troupes worked different movie palaces in succession.[60] This shift necessarily limited the access of regional vaudeville performers to those major venues, intensified competition for audiences, and encouraged the migration of vaudeville talent to major cities, especially New York and Los Angeles. Yet for a time this change also encouraged independent theaters to mount their own more modest presentations and prologues and, though limited in their resources, to hire lesser talent when they could.

Sometimes, though, the burden of paying for live performers was too great. An anonymous Warner Bros. corporate history created in 1940 argued that prior to sound, the larger "exhibitor attempted to protect his investment in his theatres by adding to the screen show, vaudeville and stage show presentations, with elaborate orchestras." Smaller exhibitors, Warners suggested, could afford second-run features but "could not afford the price of the orchestra or stage show. As competition among first-run houses became greater . . . [second-run] exhibitors suffered in greater proportion from the competition of the deluxe first-runs."[61] This retrospective imagined Warner Bros.' Vitaphone Varieties as a boon to those smaller exhibitors trying to compete against first-run houses that could afford better live talent, rather than as a means by which exhibitors large and small could avoid hiring live performers at all. According to Crafton, though, "Warner Bros. saw the presentation fad as a double opportunity. The exhibitor who wanted one could have it, but filmed, not live." Small exhibitors' efforts to compete with the majors suggested to Warner Bros. that it could use its Varieties to take advantage of an unstable market, offering a means by which the "showman who wanted to get rid of the expense of the presentation could substitute much cheaper Vitaphone 'virtual' versions. From the producers' point of view, filmed presentations could help drive away live competitors."[62]

Presentations were a significant element in exhibition practices throughout the 1920s, so to call a ten-year trend a "fad" seems a bit unreasonable. The introduction of sound shorts, including cartoons, accelerated what the presentations had begun. Even as the sound shorts momentarily revived vaudeville, they intensified the use of talent from major metropolitan centers in the traveling companies of the major chains. With the coming of sound, those traveling companies were themselves gradually replaced by short-subject catalogues, such as the Warner Bros. Vitaphone Varieties and MGM's Movietone series, which featured vaudeville (and sometimes Broadway) stars from those same metropolitan areas.

A glance at a short-subject distribution schedule from the 1929 MGM *Distributor*, a new-release guide for exhibitors, gives a snapshot of those changing labor practices.[63] Its schedule of short films leads off with the white singer Cliff Edwards (eventually the voice of Jiminy Cricket in *Pinocchio* [1940] and of Jim Crow in *Dumbo* [1941]) appearing in blackface; two weeks later come the dialect comedians Van and Schenck; two weeks after

METRO MOVIETONE ACTS
Descriptive Schedule of Second Series (A-27 to A-52)

NO.	REELS	FILM OR DISC	ARTISTS	TYPES OF ACTS	TITLES AND DESCRIPTIONS
A-27	1	Film	UKELELE IKE	Cliff Edwards in a blackface act which he has made famous in years of successful entertaining. Lots of pep.	(a) "What A Night For Spooning." (b) "Oh Baby, Don't We Get Along."
A-28	1	Disc	GUS EDWARDS Song Revue	A tabloid review, done entirely in Technicolor, and introducing a dazzling array of singers and dancers.	Dramatizations by special companies of Gus Edwards most famous song hits.
A-29	1	Disc	BERNARDO DE PACE	"The Wizard of the Mandolin." A familiar figure in his clown costume wherever good vaudeville is shown.	(a) "Thais." (b) "Ramona." (c) "Morning, Noon and Night."
A-30	2	Disc	ROBERT AMES CARROLL NYE CHRISTIANE YVES YVONNE STARK	One-act drama by Kenyon Nicholson, dealing with a tragedy of the World War. An outstanding sound production. In big demand.	This is CONFESSION, the playlet which has set new standards in short feature sound production. Directed by LIONEL BARRYMORE.
A-31	1	Film	Gus Joe VAN and SCHENCK	One of the highest-priced teams on the vaudeville stage. Singers whose renown is world wide. B. O. value.	(a) "Pasta Vazoola." (b) "Hungry Women."
A-32	2	Film	LOWELL SHERMAN CYRIL CHADWICK BETTY FRANCISCO	One-act comedy by Stanley Houghton, concerning the domestic troubles of a British peer and his extravagant wife. An artistic production.	Entitled NEARLY DIVORCED. Subtle humor which gets a steady stream of laughs. Directed by LOWELL SHERMAN.
A-33	2	Film	METRO MOVIETONE REVUE Number Three	FRANCES WHITE in kiddie costume; the PONCE SISTERS; the REYNOLDS SISTERS; JOSEPH REGAN, tenor; JACK PEPPER, Master of Ceremonies. Big show.	(a) "Monkey in the Zoo." (b) Snappy dance number. (c) A sentimental ballad. (d) Monologue and songs.
A-34	1	Film	MARION HARRIS	Famous musical comedy, film and recording artist whose voice is considered among the best for sound reproduction. Accompanied by Jack Gordon.	(a) "He's All Mine." (b) "Ten Little Miles From Town."
A-35	1	Disc	SONG OF THE ROSES By Gus Edwards	Song and dance revue. In Technicolor throughout. Beautifully combining sound, color, picture and entertainment. A $6.60 show.	A complete show in itself. Patterned after the successful Broadway revues. Lots of pep and action, with one snappy musical theme predominating.
A-36	1	Disc	George Dewey WASHINGTON	Sensational baritone, dressed in his famous tramp costume, the setting being a tenement section alley. One of best sound subjects yet produced. Will stop the show.	(a) "Lonely Little Bluebird." (b) "There's a Rainbow Round My Shoulder." (c) "Sonny Boy."
A-37	1	Disc	GEORGE LYONS	Singing harpist. Photographically, a most unusual subject. Interesting close-ups of hands as they play the harp. Real motion picture technique with exceptional sound quality. An unusual subject.	(a) "Mother of Mine." (b) "Bouquet of Memories." (c) "King For a Day." (d) "Happy Days, Lonely Nights."
A-38	1	Disc	Jan GARBER'S BAND	Very elaborate set. Each member of the band is a soloist and is shown in close-ups. Two of the numbers are sung by a tenor.	(a) "Blue Shadows." (b) "Memories of France." (c) "Tiger Rag."
A-39	1	Disc	VINCENT LOPEZ (Himself)	World famous artist in evening dress is shown broadcasting a group of piano solos. The picture is entitled "On the Air." A big time act.	(a) "Flapperette." (b) "Twelfth Street Rag." (c) "Canadian Capers."
A-40	2	Film	Flournoy Aubrey MILLER and LYLES	A snappy comedy act, with jazz orchestra, singing, cabaret girls and a whirlwind dancing contest between the principals. Lots of action.	General title "Jimtown Cabaret." Several orchestra numbers and singing by the famous "Snuffle Along Four."

FIG. 3.11 A slate of available short-subject films in a 1929 issue of the MGM *Distributor* offers a blending of blackface, ethnic, and unmarked acts, indicating the ongoing importance of racialized vaudeville to emergent sound film exhibition practices. Courtesy of the Academy of Motion Picture Arts and Sciences.

that the African American singer George Dewey Washington appears in a tenement setting; and two weeks after that the schedule closes its offerings with the African American blackface minstrels Miller and Lyles. On the one hand this slate is balanced between seemingly generic acts and those that feature race and ethnicity; on the other, all of the latter play on stereotype.[64] Prior to their film work, each of these performers had appeared on the vaudeville stage in either the major or minor circuits, their acts supported by lesser regional acts. With the coming of sound film, each could appear in multiple venues simultaneously, reducing the need for live performers. Yet as important as that change was to labor practices, by transposing the familiar terrain of the vaudeville stage, with its carefully calibrated expressions of race and ethnicity (and their attendant geographies) to the screen, these films also served as valuable transitional objects, primers on the continuities and discontinuities between one technosocial formation and another.

An article in the *Exhibitor's Herald* makes clear that these changes in exhibition practices were understood as a struggle between local and national interests. Writing in 1929, editor Martin Quigley commented that well before sound, Educational Pictures "had some 13,500 theatres on their list," which "meant a lively demand for short comedies," but that the studio lost clients when first-run theaters in larger cities began dropping shorts "to make room for presentation acts. Smaller theatres in smaller cities began to follow suit." With the coming of sound, however, "the short features came promptly back into their own. . . . Big theatres which dropped the short comedies for acrobats and singers, orchestras and masters of ceremonies, have come back to short features. Comedies are back in style. The shrinking list is on the mend."[65] The contraction of live performances of "acrobats, singers, and orchestras" meant an increase in short films, including cartoons, that could reproduce those performances at a fraction of the (labor) cost. This was just business: film producers had an interest in promoting movies over live shows. Yet it was also a power struggle: the less dependent exhibitors were on live performers, the more dependent on producers they became. Later in 1929, the *Exhibitor's Herald* noted that shorts (both comedy featurettes and varieties) allowed exhibitors to "change their presentation policies radically" and that "the public in many localities has tired of stage acts and is going for the talking two and one reel pictures with tremendous enthusiasm."[66] The unsigned article went on to suggest that part of the appeal of sound shorts was that "many names are being presented in these pictures which were formerly feature picture names only."[67] Paramount Publix echoed this sentiment in early 1930, when director of theater management D. J. Chatkin argued to exhibitors that "all-sound programs proved superior in drawing power in almost every instance, and indicated a very receptive attitude on the part of patrons towards straight sound programs. . . . [This] makes it possible for us to plan programs which do not require stage units to make them attractive in a superlative degree."[68]

So a change in technology that was presented as a means of meeting nascent audience desires and of changing their relationship to the stage and the screen also contributed to an economic struggle between performers, bookers, and exhibitors. As Jack White of Jack White Talking Comedies put it, "In the first place, take the millions of dollars which it will save for exhibitors all over the country. No more red tape and no more trouble with unions. . . . The day of the act is over, both on and off the screen. . . . We have seen the trend. And the exhibitor who is out to do a little budget slashing and at the same time keep up the standard of his performance sees it, too."[69] For White, talking shorts were cost-cutting measures and a means of eliminating labor strife, particularly with musicians' unions.[70] Setting aside White's obvious bias, though, his cavalier dismissal of both live acts and filmed versions of vaudeville in favor of comedy shorts suggests a significant change in attitude in a very short time. Only a year earlier, the head of the Butterfield Circuit had suggested in the *Exhibitor's Herald* that sound shorts were actually a useful complement to presentations and that showing a two-reel comedy "not only gets the audience in a good frame of mind for the acts and feature, but also serves a useful purpose in pleasing the performers of the acts, who thus do not have to go on 'cold.' As a rule, the comedy can hold its own in the opening spot very nicely, and the people working in the deluxe acts are cheering this style of arranging the show."[71] For this transition-era exhibitor, at least, there was room on the stage for the live performer, the filmed act, and the comedy short, and this arrangement seemed to suit audiences, performers, and exhibitors alike. Of course, the one constituency this arrangement served least well were producers, who continued to have to give up a percentage of profit (and attention) to live performers. Live performance also offered independent exhibitors a margin of control over their schedules, which became limited once they signed on with film distributors for an entire day's programming. Perhaps describing cautious calculation, this article hints at the gradual weaning of audiences away from live presentations rather than describing a sudden loss of interest in them. Filmed varieties themselves would last only a few years, giving way to more narrative shorts, particularly comedies. The exceptions to this trend were, of course, newsreels and cartoons. Eliminating live acts permitted exhibitors to stabilize and reduce labor costs and allowed producers and distributors to offer enhanced product packages. It also shifted the balance of power in the movie industry, for a time giving exhibitors limited power over the few remaining live acts they did book, and producers and distributors more power over exhibitors, who became more dependent on them for a greater portion of an evening's content. In smaller markets, this resulted in some independent exhibitors going under, unable to compete with the large chains then associated with the studios.

The more that live talent was supplanted by all-film programs, the fewer possibilities there were for vaudeville performers to find work, regardless of race. But as opportunities became increasingly constrained, performers of color had both fewer and more stereotypical options for work, as the representational spaces and roles in which they appeared were subject to the color bar. Hence major talents, such as Bill "Bojangles" Robinson, Ethel Waters, and Nina Mae McKinney, made the transition to the screen performing as house slaves, country bumpkins, and mammies. While more well-established black stars, such as the Nicholas Brothers, Robinson, and Miller and Lyles, made the transition to sound film, on radio, the other major medium for vaudeville performers no longer able to easily get stage bookings, there was less use for African American performers other than singers. While popular jazz acts were featured on radio, "black" voices could be covered by white performers—the most prominent example being Freeman Gosden and Charles Correll's *Amos 'n' Andy*, which premiered in 1928. And radio, of course, had little use for visually oriented song and dance routines or for novelty acts featuring black performers.

The human costs of this shift in representational practices were not simply measured by a body count in representational space, nor were they only about the number of performers able to find work. Also at stake was the social and material reinforcement of a segregated racial regime. For example, a trade ad for the 1929 film *Why Bring That Up?*, starring popular white blackface performers Moran and Mack, promised exhibitors tie-ins that linked the duo's radio performances to trucks with ads, window signs, and handbills, all of which were meant to create mass coverage for the film. At one level this was simply another marketing blitz. At another, though, it was the aggressive public dissemination of a pervasive and hos-

FIG. 3.12 An ad for Philco radios features Charley Mack of the blackface duo Moran and Mack hawking their stage show, radio program, and feature film, signaling the transition of these minstrels from combination shows to all-film programs and hinting at how radio could do without African American vocal performers.

tile racial imaginary, a linking of public space (including radio airwaves) to the private space of the theater (and of homes with radios) and to the representational spaces of the film itself. In simple terms, such a marketing campaign, which focused on a majority-white audience, was also an aggressive public performance of Jim Crow—of the implicitly violent inscription of racism through minstrelsy. Similarly, the promotional ballyhoo for Al Jolson's 1930 production of *Mammy* ("a joyous Jolson Jubilee of Jokes, Jazz, and Jollity") called for a parade of minstrels to take to the streets of New York.[72] Nor was this a one-off idea: the *Publix Opinion* (which shared local exhibitors' promotional ideas nationally) also offered a photograph of a recent *Mammy* parade in Boston, complete with a motorcycle police escort, implying the presence and approval of the state in the regulation of its racial imaginary.

These two examples concern live feature films, but this logic also applied to short subjects such as the Fleischer Song Car-Tunes, which were regularly reviewed alongside live racial shorts in the *Publix Opinion*. The

PROMOTE PARADES FOR FREE BALLY!

This minstrel parade on "Mammy" passed along the Boston A. A. Marathon Course the day the picture opened at the Olympia and Uptown Theatres, preceding the annual marathon race by 20 minutes. Plenty of crowds the whole distance! Parade climaxed an intense campaign on the re-opening of the Olympia after renovations and re-seating. It included a 35-piece band and 15 bannered cars, promoted by H. F. Kayes, publicity director, and sixty marchers recruited from service staffs of Boston theatres. George Laby, manager of the Olympia, and Al Fowler, of the Uptown, swung the permit to precede the marathon, and got a motorcycle escort as well. That's taking advantage of made-to-order opportunity.

FIG. 3.13 Public-relations tips for Al Jolson's *Mammy* (1930) suggest staging a parade of minstrels, thus bringing the racializing practice off the stage and into the street as a public demonstration. Here, a parade for *Mammy* in Boston featured a motorcycle escort, suggesting state support for the public performance of racial masquerade.

racial short formed a segregated whole, distinct and separate from the other elements on the bill. Like the cartoon, it presented African American life as existing in a physical and metaphysical realm in which the stereotypical markers of fear and desire, love and theft (to put it in Eric Lott's terms), not only tagged the body but actually delimited the geography of day-to-day life. Complicity in the American apartheid of the 1930s did not always require an explicitly articulated racial ideology to support the maintenance of segregation, nor did it require self-avowed racial separatists or race-baiters. Instead, the color line could be reinforced through discourses and practices that produced links between the representational world of filmed entertainment, its fantastic idealization in the cartoon, its public celebration in marketing, and finally, at the end of the chain of signification, the experience of segregated theaters, their lobbies, and the streets onto which their doors opened. The fantastic spaces that appeared, even as they were other to the real places where they were per-

"SWING YOU SINNERS," Talkartoon (8 min.) Synopsis: As an example of clever drawing and originality this one is notable. Subject is reminiscent of a nightmare with its strange figures, ghosts, ghouls, etcetera, rising to haunt the poor creature that attempted to steal a chicken. "Sing You Sinners" is used as the basis for the music. (The lyrics have been changed slightly to fit). There has been nothing just like this before in cartoons and it must be seen to be appreciated.

Criticism: Absorbing cartoon, fast moving and funny. Will appeal especially to better type audiences.

Booking-Routining: Avoid playing with mystery feaures and do not use on the same program with "HER FUTURE" which also uses "SING YOU SINNERS." Spot on prominent position on program. Suggest it be placed immediately ahead of feature.

Exploitation: Suggest it be mentioned as a new and radical idea in cartooning.

EDUCATIONAL

"SI, SI, SENOR," with Tom Patricola, Joe Philips (19 min.) Story: As the scene opens the two boys are being pushed over the Arizona boundary line into Mexico by an irate sheriff. They start on a long hike over the desert and coming upon two Spaniards who are bathing in a pool, they steal their clothes and run. Later entering town they are mistaken for the two Spaniards

FIGS. 3.14–3.15 An issue of *Publix Opinion* combines a review of the live racial short *Si, Si, Senor* with that of the Fleischer Talkartoon *Swing You Sinners!* (1930), which trades on minstrel stereotypes.

formed, affirmed segregation as a metaphysical as well as a physical fact, a confirmation of the consonance between imagined and real geographies.

And, in spite of a shift toward all-film programs during the transition to sound and the foreclosure of cinematic space that this shift engendered, the Fleischer Studios continued to produce sing-along cartoons for Paramount well into the 1930s, only giving them up completely at the end of the decade. This suggests not only a significant exhibition market for the sing-along format but also an ongoing desire by at least one major producer-exhibitor to include these films (and their hybrid audience experience) in its repertoire. Cartoons in general were a reliable staple: they had served in presentations and feature film prologues and rounded out the shorts catalogues of the late 1920s and early 1930s as well.[73] The Fleischer Song Car-Tunes and Screen Songs allowed Paramount and its exhibitors to have it both ways, providing transitional audiences with stage interaction without the inconvenience of live performers. At the same time, however, they offered a link between filmed entertainments and the cultural trends of the day, especially music and dance. In terms of the racial/spatial logic of the moment, they epitomized that bridge between the segregated imaginary of filmed entertainments and the Jim Crow world in which movies were exhibited and consumed.

WANNA BE A MEMBER? SPACES OF INCLUSION AND EXCLUSION

The process of converting from silent to sound movies was as much a matter of political economy as of technology. The 1920s were a moment of intense research and development for many animation studios, each of which worked to differentiate its products as superior in their use of sound, and eventually (in the case of Disney and the Fleischers) in their ability to present two-dimensional space as 3-D.[74] As with any other moment in the history of American animation, changes in the representation of narrative space were accompanied by alterations in production practices, and with them in understandings of the social and cultural geographies that those fictional spaces were meant to represent.[75] Technological and aesthetic innovations that were developed in the jockeying for market share in animation during this period correlate to shifts in the spaces being represented on screen, but they also point to changes in how producers, exhibitors, and audiences understood the theatrical spaces in which cartoons appeared. Yet unlike prior moments of flux in animation's brief history, the transition to sound signaled transformations that were more than visual, adding the incorporation of recorded voice, music, and effects into what was understood as primarily a viewing experience.[76] If previously cartoons had been presented *accompanied* by sound (as were other filmed entertainments), in the late 1920s and 1930s they were increasingly presented as *containing* that sound. This meant changes in understanding the theatrical experience that had to be promulgated and regulated by exhibitors and learned and practiced by audiences. Chief of these was that the exclusive focal point of attention was now a space internal to the screen, the cinematic space of the text, which did not abut or include the space of a stage once shared by filmed and live entertainments. In short, at the moment of transition to sound cinema there was a change in the relationship of the representation of space to the spaces in which that representation took place.

Although the first sound films were popularly called talkies, when it came to speech, the first sound cartoons were actually fairly inarticulate, as poor recording technology and techniques often muffled speaking voices. Rhythmic and repetitive songs were a simple solution to this problem: popular songs, with words that were already well known, softened popular judgments about the fidelity of early recording technologies, and music and rhythm helped to place early sound animation even more firmly within the playful performative precincts of vaudeville. At the same time, however, the introduction of sound served as an invitation to work through how the new medium might reorder spatial relations on the screen and in the world beyond. Early sound cartoons broke down into fairly stable categories: musical revue numbers that used a strong vaudeville presentational style; comedy shorts that relied heavily on visual humor; children's stories and fairy tales; and, as swing music became more popular, reinterpretations of popular jazz tunes. Cartoon interpretations of swing tunes were in effect "soundies," forerunners of music videos, promoting popular songs through fantastic visual interpretations of their lyrics.[77] Animation could render the lyrics of any song in spectacular form and could easily create a visual complement to the tempo and mood of the music itself. In their Song Car-Tunes, for instance, the Fleischers maintained vaudeville's direct address when they encouraged the audience to sing and then visually presented and interpreted the lyrics of each song. Their Screen Songs, which succeeded the Song Car-Tunes, generally alternated between live shots of performers, some of whom spoke directly to the audience, minimally animated shots of the lyrics, and more elaborately animated interludes. (When jazz greats such as Cab Calloway,

Louis Armstrong, and Don Redman made guest appearances in Betty Boop shorts, however, they were subsumed into the diegetic landscape of the cartoon.) Other animation houses also produced musical shorts, such as Walter Lantz's Oswald comedy *Amature Nite* (1929) and Disney's *The Opry House* (1929), that used the narrative frame of a theatrical review, talent show, or amateur night to showcase animated "acts" that mugged and played to the camera.

Within a few years, though, these sorts of face-forward performances were greatly reduced, and direct address to the audience took the form of an aside at most, a bracketing of diegetically contained action. As animation followed the trend away from variety formats, developing more substantial, but still minimal, narratives and moved toward producing a cinematic space distinct from that of the theater where the cartoon screened, as vaudevillian direct address began to fade, cartoons' performative conventions of interactivity and of puncturing the frame and screen boundary came to be wholly contained within a diegetic world created by the pen of an animator who had left the stage.

Two cartoon shorts capture the enthusiastic and confusing interplay of music and image that the move to sound engendered in animation: Van Beuren Studios' *Making 'Em Move* (1931) and the Fleischer short *Bimbo's Initiation* (1931). Although many cartoons in the transition years played with changing spatial dynamics, each of these films in its own way highlights the warping and disruption of space that animating in the jazz idiom seemed to encourage. The plot of *Bimbo's Initiation* has already been described elsewhere as a tale of immigrant anxiety about ethnic assimilation into a mainstream white, Protestant, middle-class society.[78] It represents that anxiety in very spatial terms, as a chaotic pastiche of sound and image, alternately appealing and foreboding. The cartoon opens with a college fight song sung over the Fleischer logo, after which Bimbo appears. A Mickey Mouse knockoff based on Fitz, Ko-Ko's 1920s sidekick, Bimbo is walking happily down the street of a slum when he is suddenly swallowed by a manhole and locked underground by an evil version of Mickey. Digested by the city, Bimbo emerges inside a haunted tenement where neither the laws of physics nor those of polite society seem to apply. Confronted by a cult of robed figures with deformed black faces who are backed by a musical pastiche that includes snippets of jazz, orchestral arrangements, and vaudeville and minstrel standards (including "Zip Coon"), Bimbo flees in a panic, but the building refuses to let him go. Windows and walls move at will. Floors become elevators. Doors open on doors, and strange contraptions threaten him with everything from death by spikes and knives to an eternal spanking powered by his own frantic pedaling on a stationary bicycle. All of this happens on the beat, and Bimbo's screams are punctuated by a single question chanted by the cult—"Wanna be a member? Wanna be a member?"—to which Bimbo repeatedly and resolutely yells, "NO!" Eventually, after many torments, a cult member sheds its skin to reveal Betty Boop beneath—and on seeing her Bimbo instantly relents and joins. On his "Yeeesss!" the walls of the tenement are revealed as mere backdrops, and all the other cult members strip away their disguises to form a chorus of Betties, all of whom surround an ecstatic Bimbo to sing and dance as the camera irises out to black.

Bimbo's Initiation is of a piece with and yet distinct from the practices of silent-era animation. The seemingly random mixing of a college fight song, classical orchestral arrangements, and jazz riffs recalls the silent-era use of fake books by piano accompanists or pit orchestras to thematically reinforce the visual imagery of cartoons.[79] While the cartoon shares much with its presynchronized predecessors, though, it departs from them in the way it treats the space through which Bimbo moves. Many of the Fleischer Out of the Inkwell cartoons of the 1920s played with the relationship between drawn animate space and the "real" space of a stripped-down, movie-set version of an animation studio, and their Song Car-Tunes often encouraged audiences to sing with characters on the screen. Yet both Fleischer products treated animated cinematic space itself as inherently flat, and most movement in that space happened in a horizontal plane, either from right to left or from left to right. In this sync-sound cartoon, however, space warps and bends, and the song propels Bimbo into interior spaces that suggest life beyond a predetermined x/y axis. Yet at the same time, where earlier Fleischer offerings imagined cartoons as unfolding across spatial boundaries, *Bimbo's Initiation* traps Bimbo in only *one* place—until the ending reveals that the building's walls are nothing more than drop curtains, the tenement building merely a fantasy created on a vaudeville stage. The cartoon represents cinematic space as stable up to a point, yet still malleable, and in the end as an illusion that yields to its own performativity. While it is an ambivalent text that admits various readings, one that seems apt here is that *Bimbo's Initiation* not only speaks to an immigrant's struggle to navigate between traditional, mass, and dominant cultures but also addresses (and tries to resist) the foreclosure of cinematic space in the early sound era. The cartoon tries and fails to settle into its diegetic space, and in the end what Bimbo joins is nothing

FIG. 3.16 *Making 'Em Move* (1931) offers a fantasy of cartoon production in which human labor has been replaced by that of the characters themselves, some of whom are machines.

more than a performance, a celebration of the (now absent) extradiegetic space of the theater.[80]

Making 'Em Move performs a producer's fantasy of the industrial process of animation production.[81] This cartoon has achieved minor cult status because of its vertiginous and self-reflexive take on cartoon production and its intimate (if fantastic) relationship to live performance. A buxom young woman (also a minstrel) passes the front door of an animation studio. Curious, she convinces the guard to let her see how cartoons are made. He walks her down a hallway that distends inward as they progress, until finally she falls into a vortex of paper.[82] When the pages settle she is gone, and we are in an animation sweatshop populated by cartoon animals, each at a drawing table, churning out product. In a play on what would soon be known as Mickey Mousing—timing the beat of an action to the downbeat of the music—an animated orchestra keeps time for the workers, who work at a manic pace, tearing drawings off their pads and handing them on to the next line-worker for further embellishment. As they work, an anthropomorphic camera dances through the room, pausing to record each worker's output. The camera then attaches himself to a gramophone needle, which, in a fusion of Phonofilm and Vitaphone technologies, records the orchestra directly onto the film, adding sound to image.

The cartoon then moves abruptly from a fantasy of production into one of exhibition. The film that we just saw made—a hackneyed cartoon melo-drama within this cartoon comedy—is screened in the open air of a vacant lot, its cartoon audience sitting on crude wooden benches. As the audi-ence screams at the villain and cheers the hero to his rescue, it becomes clear that the primary difference between one remove and the other is that the melodramatic characters on the screen within our screen are bare stick figures while the "live" audience (like the animators before them) appear to have weight and volume. In a confusing nod to its vaudeville roots, the last image in the cartoon within the cartoon is of an asbestos fire curtain lowering and raising and the melodrama's characters taking a bow as if they were on a stage rather than a screen. When the villain takes his bow, one audience member reprises Edwin S. Porter's *Uncle Josh at the Picture Show* (1902) and attacks the screen, tearing it to the ground. The rest of the crowd joins him in a tumult that visually reprises the cyclone of paper that started the cartoon, which now fades to black.

While it is tempting to read this cartoon symptomatically—as the angry output of underpaid and overworked animators in an industry in transition—*Making 'Em Move* is more interesting for the means by which it struggles to locate itself in a rapidly reorganizing cinematic space.[83] In its first half, the cartoon suggests what Crafton has called a hermeti-cally contained, parthenogenetic world in which workers who are them-selves already cartoon characters reduce their live, performing models to schematic versions of themselves—drawings rendering other drawings as stick figures—in a frenzy of production driven by a "live" soundtrack at what appears to be a merciless pace. In its second half, comedy becomes a parody of melodramatic cinema as those stick figures act out a stereo-typical tied-to-the-railroad-tracks chase and rescue. Yet in the end, those very stick figures seem to develop the agency of live performers, acknowl-edging an audience that seems just as confused about the relationship between the live and the cinematic as they are, and a film marked by vio-lence and oppression in its depiction of production erupts into violence at the ruptured boundary between "stage" and "screen." In *Bimbo's Initiation*, racially ambiguous characters threaten and punish the central minstrel character, only to reveal themselves as apparently white women, hence attractive and potentially forbidden objects of desire. In *Making 'Em Move*, a factory is staffed by minstrels who produce debased versions of them-selves, who in turn move other minstrel characters to violence against each other and against the screen itself. In their seeming confusion, these cartoon shorts offer an anxious performance of a representational regime in transition, one in which practical concerns find expression in their cartoon correlates.

In "The Voice in the Cinema" (1980), an analysis of the phenomenological and sociopolitical consequences of the coming of sound to the organization of cinematic space, Mary Ann Doane argues that the incorporation of sound into the cinematic image always "carries with it the potential risk of exposing the material heterogeneity of the medium."[84] A moment of asynchrony between sound and image may alienate the viewer, detach the image from of its narrative continuum, and direct attention toward its material and nondiegetic base.[85] Likewise, a voice-over not properly linked to a known character or narrator can puncture the diegetic uniformity of the narrative, as can a voice off not properly located through a match cut to a known space or body. Synchronous sound, then, offers the viewer a fragile compact: in exchange for a promise that the conventions of continuity will always make clear whose voice is connected to whose body and that the technologies of synchronization will perfectly match a spoken word to the mouth that purportedly speaks it, the viewer will accept all of the action she witnesses as taking place in a cinematic space wholly discontinuous from the "real" place she occupies.[86]

At the risk of stating the obvious, animation's history is rife with examples of the willful exposure of the medium's material heterogeneity. From its inception, animation was inherently self-reflexive, with that "self" grounded in an uneasy relationship between its maker and its material base. The tools of its making, the pens, ink, and paper/cels, frequently figured in cartoon narratives, as did the synecdochal hand of the animator. Even in those cartoons in which the animator (or his hand) did not appear, convention—a set of agreements between producer, exhibitor, and audience—permitted the disruption of the narrative flow by appearing to corrupt the material base of the film: characters such as Felix, Ko-Ko, or Julius sometimes tore at their background, shredded the frame, or escaped the drawn world for that of the cinematic real. Although the basic rules of continuity and the organization of narrative space and time were applied to animated as to live cinema, for animation the pleasure of viewing existed as much in their violation as in their maintenance.[87] Sometimes reveling in and revealing the cartoon's means of its production and its status as a made object, the convention invoked a set of spatial relations that suggested contiguity between the space of the cartoon's making and the space of its reception, paradoxically reminding viewers of their place in the theater—not alone, but watching with others like them.

The coming of synchronous sound contributed to the ongoing alteration of the metaphysical organization of this animated space. The need to spatialize sound, to link voices to bodies and to respect sound's inherent directionality, imposed limitations on what space would be permitted to do and to signify.[88] As the sound cartoon developed from an attraction to an important element in all-film programs, the convention of the interceding animator's hand, which violated these new compacts of cinematic space, necessarily faded from view.[89] The same was true for the animated space off, the metaphysical elsewhere of a cartoon. If a cartoon background still sometimes signified the vaudeville backdrop, as it often did for Warner Bros. in the 1930s, tearing at it would not bring the character closer to the (cinematic) real but only to another backdrop, as if the animated world it had once occupied were now only a virtual sound stage. This enclosure of cinematic space in animation constituted a significant disruption of long-standing conventional relationships between the animator and the animated, and between the animated character and the cinematic real occupied by the animator. As minstrel figures, trademark characters had performatively punctured the bounds between animated space and the putative space of the animator in acts of rebellion; inserting their hand into the frame, animators had repressed that rebellion (which they also had created). Thus, in addition to fraying the associative links between the trademark character and the live minstrel, the coming of sound also disrupted the circuits of ritual violence that those conventions had permitted. It was in this moment of enclosure that the often violent racist caricatures of the swing era emerged, as the whipping boy (or girl) of a workforce denied even the minimal pleasure of the performative gesture.

Yet this rise in racist caricatures alongside cartoon minstrels did not simply happen because when the space of animation became foreclosed to animators they took out their frustrations by creating a new class of characters to abuse. The animator-as-performer was itself a nostalgic trope, a backward gesture to the vaudeville performances of the likes of Winsor McCay or James Stuart Blackton. Yet the persistent use of this gesture by producers and directors, on-screen and in their public relations, indicates the ongoing significance of the labor of animation and its connection to the magic of bringing inanimate objects to life. Animation continued to be a performance of the magic of labor, the mystery of the living commodity and its ability to intercede (if ineffectively) in social and material relations. Thus, there is a correlation between changes in the racial formation of cartoons and the organization of space in animation. Crafton argues that animation studios, especially Disney, reorganized animated space to better locate more fully embodied and emotionally naturalistic characters in an equally (cinematically) real space, that "the transformations of the 1930s were driven pragmatically by the studios, which were retooling the simplified space of the 1920s Tooniverse to better accommodate the increasingly complex characterizations of toons."[90] For Crafton, this pragmatism centered on marginal differentiation and competitive innovation, representing the aesthetic outcome of technical explorations into how to better achieve through ink and paint effects that emulated contemporary notions of liveness. As such, this choice also signaled a response to radical revisions of social relations in space. Attempts to emulate or accommodate the spatial relations of live narrative cinema by cartoons meant the diminution of the vaudevillian and the minstrel, the gradual reorganization of cartoons' representative imaginary to better harmonize with that of the live films they supported.

To be sure, of the hundreds of cartoons made during this period, many made no direct reference to the reorganization of cinematic space. Still, the crossover popularity of swing music among white audiences and its promotion through cartoons led to an increase in broad racist caricatures that overlapped in their stereotyping with the traditions of blackface minstrelsy yet were distinct from minstrelsy's performative and iconic traditions.[91] Those broader racist caricatures invoked the jungle, the plantation, and the ghetto and had a more immediate referential relationship to contemporary white fantasies of blackness than did the increasingly nostalgic figure of the minstrel. As a result, the associational links that joined cartoon minstrels such as Bimbo, Mickey, or Krazy Kat to that earlier form of fantastic blackness became increasingly attenuated, and their minstrelsy became vestigial, still evident in behaviors and appearances but less directly linked to nostalgic fantasies of African American life and culture. This may be why, as the 1930s progressed, American audiences could see oddly redundant cartoons such as Krazy Kat's *The Minstrel Show* (1932) and *Mickey's Mellerdrammer* (1933) in which characters who were already minstrels blacked up yet again.

The gradual collective abandonment in the sound era of conventions that worked to maintain relationships between audiences, live performers, and screen texts did not simply make room for newer spatial relations in sound cinema, nor did it produce a racial formation wholly discontinuous from that which had produced the minstrel characters of stage and screen. Instead, the regulation of the representation of space that sound film required—the visual, auditory, and narrative reminders that the space on the screen was necessarily discontinuous from that of the stage where the screen appeared and from the audience—facilitated the production of a racial imaginary that deepened imagined links between Africa, the South, and black urban ghettoes as a spatial continuum parallel to, yet separate from, that of an equally imagined white cosmos. In this universe, the metaphysics of Jim Crow were complete in ways they never could be in the real world. Unlike Rudy Ising and Bosko's minstrel-and-interlocutor performance of 1929, in films such as *Wonder Bar* (Warner Bros., 1934) or its cartoon parody, *Goin' to Heaven on a Mule* (Warner Bros., 1934), or *Clean Pastures* (Warner Bros., 1937), the cartoon parody of *The Green Pastures* (Warner Bros., 1936), African Americans were contained in representational ghettoes that were wholly separate from the white imaginary.

VESTIGIAL MINSTRELS AND RACIST CARICATURES

Whether in *Clean Pastures* or in MGM's *Cabin in the Sky* (Minnelli, 1943), as far as Hollywood in the early sound era was concerned, the color bar extended from the depths of hell through our earthly precincts and right up into heaven. Yet the conventional history of animation, with its tradition of presenting offscreen space as metaphysically contiguous with, yet sometimes in opposition to, the spaces of the animation studio or the stage, positioned cartoons as particularly apt for delineating a fantastic alternate universe of blackness, one that might intersect with an imaginary white world yet remain distinct from it. Within the emerging narrative enclosure of the early sound era, swing cartoons, while related to the more blackface-inflected animation that preceded them, converted the nostalgia and sentimentality of the minstrel stage into more explicitly brutal and extreme racist caricatures. Mischievous but good-natured minstrel figures such as Mickey, Bimbo, and Bosko were joined by a growing horde of cartoon cannibals, chicken thieves, and cotton pickers, all acting to the beat of the new "jungle music." The plausible deniability of the cartoon minstrel, the creation of a trickster rebel and its punishment by the hand that made it, began to be occluded by the ostensibly extreme libidinous excess of jazz.[92]

As Daniel Goldmark has made clear, American animation and jazz have a long and intimate history. Even before the coming of sound movies, the need for accompanists provided work for up-and-coming jazz musicians. Jazz legends Fats Waller and Count Basie both accompanied silent films, and Waller also provided intermission music at the Vendome theater in Chicago. Storied early composers for sound cartoons, such as Frank Churchill, Carl Stalling, and Scott Bradley, got their start accompanying silent films, where they refined the art of weaving together popular tunes with iconic motifs—the musical stereotyping that signified attacking cannibals, Jewish merchants, or Chinese villains (for example)—into seemingly impromptu film scores. They later adapted the same techniques for cartoon soundtracks.[93]

This historical juncture, then, describes a definite yet shifting relationship between the technologies used in motion picture exhibition, labor practices in film studios and in the theaters where movies appeared, and the representational conventions that dictated the organization and understanding of those performative, social, and productive spaces. Although vaudeville had played an integral role in the formation of combination shows and in providing labor for the film varieties that replaced them, its practical and symbolic associations with the local, with past or passing conventions and attitudes, as well as with the immediate experience of live performance, were eventually at odds with the practices and conventions of an increasingly national film industry. Vaudeville was gradually superseded by narrative films, radio, and to a lesser extent a more spectacular musical theater.[94] Since vaudeville had been the main venue for minstrelsy as a performance art in the twentieth century, blackface also began to recede, and when it did, so did its immediate links to trademark characters such as Mickey and Felix. While their gloves, painted smiles and eyes, ill-fitting costumes, and trickster performances continued to produce minstrelsy in drawn form, the real-world referents for those tropes began to disappear. Although minstrelsy continued for a time in venues such as Moran and Mack's radio appearances as "Two Black Crows" (1928–1933) or the Amos 'n' Andy radio and television series (1928–1960; 1951–1953) and in popular 1930s films by Al Jolson and Eddie Cantor, by the end of the 1930s, the popular imaginary increasingly located minstrelsy in a receding past, treating it as a nostalgic relic from bygone days, as in films such as *Babes in Arms* (Berkeley, 1939), *Holiday Inn* (Sandrich, 1942), and *The Minstrel Man* (Lewis, 1944).[95]

This dissolution of the bonds between the cartoon minstrel and its real-world referents begins to explain, then, how popular characters such as Mickey, Felix, or Bugs could continue to visually and gesturally act as minstrels but over time lose a direct association with blackface itself. The tropes of the animated trickster were well enough established that their original referent, the live blackface minstrel, could depart the stage without diminishing the power of her/his replacements in the drawn world. Likewise, with the exception of Bosko in his early outings, most continuing trademark characters, when they began to speak, eschewed the broad dialect of the minstrel, ceding that particular stereotypical gesture to the racist caricatures arising around swing music. These caricatures also appeared in cartoons with titles such as *Swing Wedding* (1937), *Uncle Tom's Bungalow* (1937), or *Coal Black and de Sebben Dwarfs* (1943), which not only offered patently offensive visual and verbal characterizations but also visited incredible violence on ostensibly African American bodies (see chapter 4). In MGM's *Swing Wedding*, for instance, famous African American performers such as Louis Armstrong, Fats Waller, and Cab Calloway are depicted as big-lipped frogs in a swamp and at the climax of the cartoon are whipped into such a frenzy by the jazz they are playing that they begin assaulting their respective musical instruments, and assaulting each other with those instruments, as well as treating each other as instruments to alternately play and assault. Tambo and Bones—themselves characters synonymous with the instruments they played, tambourine and bones—return in the guise of anthropomorphic, cartoon jazz musicians. This extreme violence offered a cartoon fantasy of African American "savagery" operating in an imaginary continuum that linked Africa, the South, and Harlem and took as its soundtrack the syncopated beat of swing.[96] The invocation of Africa and the South that had validated blackface minstrelsy consisted no longer merely of claims made on a playbill or verbal gestures by a white interlocutor; they were literalized in the locations and actions of cartoon characters.

This was not simply and immediately a linear evolutionary process. The fading of the live performance of minstrelsy and the concomitant loss of an immediate link between the blackface minstrel and his animated replacement did not directly give rise to the more aggressive racist caricatures of golden age cartoons. Rather, one was a permutation of the other, a visual realization of changing social and historical attitudes and circumstances. Many of the men who created these cartoons were attracted to African American culture, particularly swing music and dance.[97] Just as the minstrel figure had represented to white animators and their audiences both the constraint of free labor and its rebellion against the conditions of that restraint, the jazz caricatures of the early sound years seemed to pay homage to an imagined libidinous freedom of swing music and culture and to immediately offer up guilty punishment for taking pleasure in its apparent excesses.

Cartoons such as *Swing Wedding* or *Uncle Tom's Bungalow* are more than simply an indication that some animators of the early sound era, many of whom were young men steeped in popular culture, were jazz fans. These cartoons also gave shape to how they imagined their audiences' desires and fantasies. As Crafton would have it, "Animators embody not only their characters but also their future viewers, since the goal of their conditional performance—the entire artistic and commercial point—is to entertain their customers. . . . Viewers' and animators' embodiments are thus reciprocal, which is not to suggest that their intentions and interpretations are the same."[98] The images that animation studios associated with swing circulated in and supported a larger representational matrix in which black cultural production was understood as emanating from a physical (and metaphysical) realm different from and elsewhere than that of an ostensibly white world. Swing music was, in the press and on the lips of radio announcers and nightclub emcees, "jungle music," a backbeat for unrestrained native passions. When it didn't issue from the jungles of darkest Africa it wended its way up the Old Muddy from New Orleans or from "Darktown," aka Harlem, Chicago's South Side, or Eighteenth and Vine in Kansas City. These cartoons imagined jazz music as the product of American urban ghettoes, themselves fantastic portals to Africa and the Old South. Embodying white fantasies about black life in their characters, they also reproduced dominant black/white dynamics as a set of spatial relations organized and stabilized in a circuit of discourse that operated between primary white producers, distributors, and segregated audiences. They gave shape and voice and home to a dominant racial organization of space, engaging in a mutually constitutive production of Jim Crow between local and national producers, articulating a productive relationship between the representation *of* space and social practices *in* space.[99]

OUT OF AFRICA—OR THEREABOUTS

The conventional minstrel show had long taken as a central conceit a few distinct degrees of separation between its performers, the plantation, and via that plantation, Africa. The interlocutor, often in whiteface and always well spoken, was the go-between for the minstrels and their audience. Minstrels performed purportedly authentic artifacts of plantation life—the songs, dances, wordplay, and banter that described the means by which slaves, through their native wit, had supposedly made their captivity not only bearable but resistant to their masters' demands.[100] This was a fantasy of a constrained yet resistant labor, a convention that informed the animated minstrel and that gradually diminished with the coming of sound and the fading of vaudeville and live blackface minstrelsy. Yet sound animation continued to promulgate a fantastic continuum centered not so much on minstrel traditions as on physically and spatially locating the origins and meanings of swing music. And animation, with its ability to render the abstract tangible, produced a number of cartoons that made explicit a geographic continuum starting in Africa, extending to the plantation, and continuing into the urban ghettoes of modern black life—as if these were all part of one vast metaphysical realm of blackness. In the place of the minstrel narrowly defined was the black jazz musician or enthusiast, rendered in a variety of fantastic forms but contained within a universe largely segregated from that of his or her white audience. Cartoon depictions of swing pointed to the baldest stereotyped notions of blackness: indolence, stupidity, voracious gustatory and sexual appetite, and so on. Yet while these stereotypical elements were of course located in representations of the black body, cartoons from this period also created an ideal geography of race, as when *Clean Pastures* cartographically located Harlem on the African continent and the 1938 Walter Lantz short *Voodoo in Harlem* fused that New York neighborhood to Haiti and to the African continent, in what the cartoon called a "black rendezvous."

At first blush, *Voodoo in Harlem* seems an exception to the trend of enclosing cinematic space in order to produce a more fantastic racial geography. Like the more performative cartoons of the 1920s, this one begins with a live prologue in which Lantz sits at a desk, drawing successive images of a cute kitten. The performing animator, it would seem, has returned. Except that this cartoon opens with the title card "Oswald Rabbit Presents": instead of the animator introducing his trademark character to the world, it's the other way around. And Lantz never actually acknowledges the camera; he draws his sketches, yawns, then leaves his well-appointed office for the night. The live prologue continues with shots of moonlit skies (accompanied by Beethoven's Piano Sonata 14, the "Moonlight Sonata") and of the wind rising in the trees. A breeze blowing through an open window tosses the drawings around and upsets an inkwell. The ink spills onto a page on the floor, pooling there. From that pool of ink four caricatured African natives emerge and begin to sing the

FIGS. 3.17–3.18 Two examples of the swing-era animation practice of conflating the ghetto, plantation, and jungle. In *Clean Pastures* (1937), Harlem is located in Africa. *Voodoo in Harlem* (1938) literalizes that connection through song and image.

title song, "Voodoo in Harlem," straight to the camera. As the lyrics confuse Harlem's Lenox Avenue with Haiti and gospel prayer with opium and voodoo rituals, these standard cannibal types cavort through the storm-tossed sketches, singing and dancing the Lindy Hop and the shimmy. The performance is done in the style of a black vaudeville number, with the singer-dancers facing the camera and directing their song to an imaginary audience. This production number takes place before a background of photographic stills of an office that is richly appointed in art deco furnishings and books, looking more like an executive suite than an animation studio. The song continues until the cock crows, at which point the savages dive headfirst into the ink, vanishing moments before an African American maid enters and begins to clean up the mess, asking herself what the black blob of ink might possibly mean. (A cultural Rorschach test, perhaps?) She throws all of the pages into an incinerator, the page with the inkblot last, and the cartoon ends with an ominous shot of the chimney from which its ashes will emerge.

What makes this cartoon different from any number of Max Fleischer's earlier run-ins with Ko-Ko (or a younger Lantz dueling with Pete the Pup) is not simply that the character introduces the animator, instead of vice versa. Instead, it is that Lantz barely performs his role as animator, neither facing nor acknowledging the camera before leaving the scene; his presence is perfunctory and indexical. Not only does he not create a trademark character, he never meets, let alone spars with, the creatures that emerge from his spilled ink. Nor do those animated Ubangis ever challenge the boundary between the drawn and the real. Instead they use the real-world office as a theatrical backdrop, in front of which they stage a black-and-tan review that suggests that the ink they sprang from is a conduit to a fantastic black realm that spans Africa, Haiti, and Harlem. The final shot of the chimney suggests both the momentary containment of that imaginary and its ongoing threat.

In this fantasy a segregated and coherent black world existed alongside that of a white one. Its metaphysical geography made of Africa, the Deep South, and black urban ghettoes (particularly Harlem) a contiguous and legible world, whose soundtrack was jazz and whose main diet was bathtub gin, watermelon, and fried chicken. (The chicken, of course, stolen, as in the gag in the middle of the Terrytoon *Mississippi Swing* [1941]—a parody of *Show Boat* [Pollard, 1929; Whale, 1936]—in which three black minstrels finish a song only to have chickens pour from their frock coats and top hats.) This fantastic space was metonymic, standing in for both

FIG. 3.19 A later entry in the use of racist caricature, Terrytoon's *Mississippi Swing* (1941), features minstrelized black men who are naturally compulsive chicken thieves.

the reality of black urban life and white fantasies of the seductive danger-ousness of the racial Other. In the hands of cartoonists, both became lit-eral. The Fleischers in particular favored depicting jazz as arising from an underworld that signified both death and African American culture, giving substance to the double meaning of the derogatory term "spook." In their broader racist caricatures, relative latecomers Warner Bros. and the animation houses that supplied Columbia, Universal, and MGM all represented swing as originating either in the back alleys of Harlem or in America's closest thing to darkest Africa: the Deep South. In shorts like *Scrub Me Mama with a Boogie Beat* (Universal, 1941) and *Clean Pastures* (Warner Bros., 1937), these studios linked the hotness of jazz to the hu-midity of the swamp and the torpidity of the plantation Negro.

The minstrelsy and caricature pervasive within the conventions and traditions of American animation, and their links to fantasies of the jungle and more generally of a space of black primitivism, are slightly dif-ferent from the high-culture "Africanism" that James Naremore outlines in his discussion of the all-black musical *Cabin in the Sky*.[101] That African-ism derived, Naremore claims, from high-cultural precincts such as the

FIG. 3.20 The Fleischers' *Snow-White* (1933) features Cab Calloway as Ko-Ko as a "spook" who dances in front of a ghastly backdrop associated with jazz and the ghetto.

FIG. 3.21 Walter Lantz's *Scrub Me Mama with a Boogie Beat* (1941) features a southern backwater, Lazytown, only somewhat shaken out of its torpor by the rhythms of Harlem.

WPA Writers Project folklorism of the mid-1930s—typified by such quasi-Africanist output as Orson Welles and John Housman's 1936 "voodoo" production of *Macbeth* at Harlem's Lafayette Theatre—and by modernist art that celebrated African primitivism. While this idea of related African and African American cultural authenticity may have informed the making and critiques of *Cabin in the Sky* or any number of black cast or native-themed films, its high-culture fantasy of the redemptive power of raw primitivism was not what informed the racial inflection of American popular cartoons of that era. The minstrelsy and racist caricature that mark the golden age of American animation derive from much humbler roots, ones grounded in primitivism as spectacle rather than as source. (Or perhaps it would be more accurate to say source *as* spectacle.) This derivation, evident in the pseudo-anthropological conceit informing the origins of minstrelsy, is from the popular native habitat exhibitions at the world fairs and expos of the late nineteenth and early twentieth centuries and from the many popular African-themed and plantation-inspired reviews of the first decades of the twentieth century—what Duke Ellington would later describe as a "black-and-tan fantasy." In other words, this continuum linking Africa, the Deep South, and Harlem did not derive from a white, elite intellectual desire for authenticity but arose within a long-standing history of attractions designed by and for working- and middle-class sensibilities. Such entertainments, up to and including swing-era cartoons, were not meant to edify or to produce—as the Roosevelt administration might have hoped—a heightened appreciation for African American contributions to a uniquely American culture. Indeed, given the offensiveness of some of the images produced for wartime consumption, either live or animated, it is hard to understand how they might have contributed to the hoped-for sense of national unity and purpose that drove many WPA projects.[102]

This fantastic geography was made explicit in *Porky in Wackyland* (Warner Bros., 1938), in which Porky Pig plays a great white hunter in search of a dodo bird. Porky flies a plane to Africa, which is subdivided on the globe over which he soars into territories marked Dark, Darker, and Darkest (at the heart of which is a question mark). Arriving at the darkest part of Africa, he finds Wackyland, whose border is announced by a sign and an ominous voice-over, both declaring that "It Can Happen Here" (a send-up of the 1935 Sinclair Lewis novel *It Can't Happen Here*). The landscape of Wackyland is animated by a hot swing soundtrack, to which insane and impossibly Dalí-esque denizens bop along (including a couple

GEORGE WALKER as the Cannibal King
singing "It's hard to find a king like me," in "ABYSSINIA."
Photograph by White, New York.

FIG. 3.22 George Walker as a cannibal king in *Abyssinia* (1906) exemplifies the early twentieth century's mass-cultural fascination with spectacular African-ness. Courtesy of the Billy Rose Theatre Division, The New York Public Library for the Performing Arts, Astor, Lenox and Tilden Foundations.

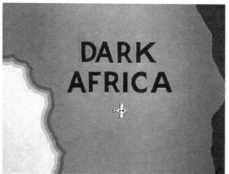

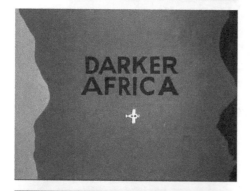

FIGS. 3.23–3.26 In *Porky in Wackyland* (1938), Porky descends into the heart of darkness in search of the mythical last dodo bird.

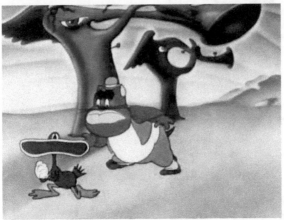

FIGS. 3.27–3.28 In *Tin Pan Alley Cats* (1943), Warner Bros. repurposed material from *Porky in Wackyland* (1938), replacing Porky with a racist caricature of Fats Waller.

of minstrel ducks, one of whom imitates Jolson's cry of "Mammy!"). The spatial logic of Wackyland is confusing, with doors and windows appearing in thin air and opening into other dimensions, landscapes becoming vaudeville backdrops, and vice versa. The dodo leads Porky on a merry chase with the jazz cry "bo dodee oh do," at one point even hiding behind the WB logo.

Four years later, Warner Bros. shifted along this continuum, moving through time and space from Africa to Harlem. Merrie Melodies animators reused much of the Wackyland sequence and its blending of surrealism, swing, and implicit and explicit blackness in *Tin Pan Alley Cats* (1943), which transposes the landscape of the 1938 cartoon from Africa to an urban waterfront and replaces Porky with a cat who looks and sounds like Fats Waller. Walking along the docks, he is confronted by a mission band, which tries to save his soul. Opting instead for the juke joint next door, he steps in, sits down at the piano and plays the popular tune "Nagasaki" (Warren/Dixon, 1928), which gets the crowd dancing. Asking a trumpeter to send him "outta this world," he is blown upward by successively higher notes right into a slightly updated (and now Technicolor) version of the surreal heart of darkness from *Porky in Wackyland*. After an exchange with a floating set of giant lips, in which he utters one of Waller's trademark phrases, "Who dat?," the cat wanders past the same Dali-esque creatures, who now parade in front of slightly different backgrounds (including a giant slice of watermelon). The main deviation in the sequence, though, is the addition of grossly caricatured Hitler and Hirohito figures, who do a rumba, whose time is marked by the bumping of their distended, rubbery butts against each other. The Wackyland dodo is replaced by a grossly caricatured black elevator operator, and Wackyland's door to nowhere becomes an elevator that leaves without the cat. As Stalin Cossack-kicks Hitler in the rear, the cat screams into the camera, "Get me outta here!" and is delivered back to earth, where he races to join the mission band in what is likely only temporary repentance.

The other world of *Tin Pan Alley Cats* is a place of abjection and objection, of intense violence and humiliation, all of which are visited on the cat and then on Hitler and Hirohito, who have landed in a place where they will literally have their asses kicked by Stalin. In the case of the Fats Waller–esque cat, transported there through the ecstasies of swing, violence extends beyond the abstract cruelty of exclusion and separation that is Jim Crow and into a relatively concrete space in which the humiliation of alien bodies derives from the orgiastically charged landscape itself. Yet even these two cartoons are spectacular in their racist caricatures, it is not that animation *itself* is inherently racist, and therefore violent. Rather, the inherent violence of animation seems particularly well suited to the expression of both racist and jingoistic violence.

The racist caricatures of the sound era, then, extended from cartoon bodies to a landscape that was understood as the realization of a fantastic realm of blackness that joined Africa to the Deep South and to northern urban ghettos and jazz nightlife. There, the seemingly chthonic forces of black subculture, the voracious and the violent—in scenes crowded with watermelons, dice, and razors—enacted the libidinal attractions of that subculture even as they punished its denizens for their unbridled animal passions. Swing music delivered viewers to the surreal Wackyland of the unconscious, where a revolt against repression was met with celebration and punishment, all made visible through the magic of plasmaticity. From the cotton fields in a lobby display for *Hallelujah!* (1929) that opened this chapter to the all-black heaven in *Wonder Bar* (1934) or *Clean Pastures* (1937) to the happy cartoon darkies in Terrytoons' *Mississippi Swing* (1941), the color line required and regulated bodies, but extended beyond them, from this world into the next.

CONCLUSION

As the composer Alvin Lucier wryly demonstrated in *I Am Sitting in a Room* (1969), in sound you hear space. Lucier, who stuttered, recorded his speaking voice in a specific room. He then rerecorded that recording again and again until his words were reduced by the room's resonant frequencies to inarticulate, harmonically beautiful tones, creating a piece of music that brilliantly demonstrated the importance of different spaces to recording and to listening, to making what is heard.[103] The shape of a space, the materials of which it is made, its relation to other spaces all color what we hear. Sound is a profoundly spatial phenomenon, one often taken for granted, though entertainment companies of the 1920s and 1930s did not.

Changes made to the organization of movie palaces in the 1920s and 1930s to accommodate new sound technologies did not just require the addition of new electrical and electronic equipment; they also ushered in a reorganization of social and material relations for everyone having business in those spaces. As Michel Foucault pointed out in "Of Other Spaces," understanding different institutional spaces as engaged in and

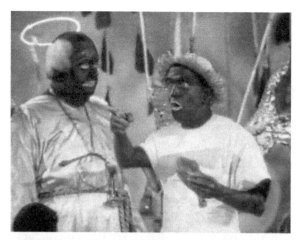

FIGS. 3.29–3.30 The perverse version of the black fantastic in the coming of sound film: Al Jolson samples the fruit of a pork-chop tree in an all-black heaven in *Wonder Bar* (1934), while cartoon darkies joyfully pick cotton in *Mississippi Swing* (1941).

producing different discursive and social effects allows us to better analyze their potential for reinforcing or disrupting dominant narratives that gloss over the production, regulation, and suppression of difference.[104] In *The Production of Space*, Henri Lefebvre critiqued approaches such as Foucault's as relatively unsystematic and as not grounded in real relations of production. Lefebvre argued for a more systematic analysis of space as a set of distinct relations between social spaces, representations of space, and the spaces in which representation takes place.[105] Certainly, movie theaters are social spaces where spatialized representations take place; but in historical discussions of their organization they also become representations of space. Motion picture houses, then, are material arguments about the social organization of space.[106] Considering such material arguments, Homi Bhabha, in *The Location of Culture*, takes up and critiques Jameson's notion of a "third space"—as well as the implicit centripetal force of Foucault's genealogical approach to history—to argue for something that, in the end, sounds (to good purpose) like Marxist standpoint theory extended beyond the precincts of class and outside the march of teleology. Providing an escape from tacit assumptions about the transit of power to and from the metropole, Bhabha's analytics encourage a reading of spaces as mutually contingent and hybrid rather than as unitary in how they are occupied, used, and contested.[107] While these arguments about relationships between space, subjectivity, political will, and agency diverge in various ways, they share a common understanding that notions of identity, subjectivity, and difference—or the production of knowledge systems and discourse—find their central locus not solely in bodies but in complexes of meaning that form between those bodies, the spaces within which they operate, and the conventions that govern those relations themselves.

In this instance, understanding how race manifests in animation may begin with a discussion of how race is represented through continuing cartoon characters—whether, for instance, 'toons are minstrels or racist caricatures—but it cannot end there. It must also extend to the representational spaces where those bodies are or were located, and to the presentational spaces where the cartoons in which they caper appeared. Even more than that, a full reading of animation's role in the production and regulation of racial formations must take into account how ideas of space and of being in space were articulated in their circulation between the diegetic space of a given cartoon, the stage space within which it was screened, and the theater that housed that stage, screen, and audience—

how that circulation produced and regulated the fantasmatic relation between racializing bodies and spaces, both real and imagined.

In American commercial animation's earliest days, these relations were often expressed through an antagonistic relationship between the animator and the continuing character (a living trademark, as it were), a blackface minstrel and rebellious commodity whose primary purpose was to challenge the confining boundaries of the screen and to disrupt stable relations between the real and the imagined. Created for this very purpose, that same living commodity was punished for doing its job, for fulfilling its purpose, and that punishment was a punch line. In the hands of animators during the transition to sound, the "hotness" of jazz and its real and imagined connections to African American culture structured anxious images of sexuality and violence and through them a fantasy of redemption from the strictures of an ostensibly white middle-class society. In doing so, these images offered that generation an imagined ludic space within which to confront the violence of a changing symbolic order with their own violence, to speak back to culture in a rough voice. While the blackface minstrel had previously served as scapegoat, in the transition to sound it shared the stage with more direct and virulent racist stereotypes. The requisites of synchronized sound slowly sealed the porous boundaries between screen and stage, banishing the live performer, and reduced the performing animator to the role of at most a studio tour guide. As cartoons became further contained, further partitioned from other social and representational spaces, the associative links between minstrels onstage and on-screen were attenuated, and the fantastic violence visited on caricatured jazz musicians redoubled that which had been visited on the rebellious minstrel. American animation in the transition to sound, from its more obvious manifestations in the Jim Crow segregation of movie audiences to its production of a contiguous African American imaginary stretching from Africa to the plantation, to Harlem (in a perverse recapitulation of the movement from the Middle Passage to the Great Migration), and to its gradual dissociation of live from drawn minstrels, became a place where the symbolic violence of race was made manifest in deed and in practice.

This is important for several reasons. First, the transition created tensions between animation's performative history (starting with the likes of Blackton and McCay and continuing with producers such as Fleischer and Lantz) and its place on stages where live performance was seen as an adjunct to cinematic offerings. Second, the introduction of sound, as it encouraged an understanding of cinematic space as wholly distinct from the exhibition space where it was received, also helped to generate a contiguous associative animated space that located black and blackface characters in a realm that seemed to link Africa to the Deep South and to the black urban ghettoes of the North, especially Harlem. Which is to say that the transition to sound film produced a reinforcement of lived Jim Crow on the screen, one that cartoons reproduced in a graphic and violent manner. In this way, shifts in production and labor practices were intimately related to changes in aesthetics and in viewing practices, and these in turn helped to generate a racialized continuum to and from which animated characters seemed able to come and go but into which live performers did not venture. This regime produced a racialized and racializing space that anthropologist John Jackson, in his study of the ongoing gentrification of Harlem, has described as alternating between the real and the ideal, taking shape in the repeating yet modulating period of that oscillation. It also describes the creation of a space that Fred Moten, in his study of the blues, might call one of "objection." Moten takes that word to have a double meaning. On the one hand it refers to the objection raised, the cry of protest. On the other, it refers to the inarticulate sound that the subject-made-object (the commodified slave in this case) makes as it is rent from the already unstable terrain of agency.[108] This takes place in a space of violence both real and represented, in the ordering of space as an institutionalization of violence (see chapter 4).

In his meditations on Mickey Mouse, Sergei Eisenstein referred to the metamorphic abilities of cartoon characters (and their worlds) as "plasmaticness," animation's capacity to reveal beneath the seemingly stable commodity form—such as a recognizable shape like Mickey—a fundamental substance that precedes reification and promises an endless potential for productive change.[109] This stuff—the stuff of convention and formal practice—can as easily make Mickey as Mussolini (or can make Mickey into Mussolini), and can subject either to the same torments, depending on who manipulates it. The violence of Wackyland is not just expressed through the cutting, stretching, and smashing of bodies; it also operates by forcing the raw plasmatic substance of the animated world into recognizable commodity forms. Because those forms, encapsulations of the social and material relations of their moment, can become legible only at the expense of possibilities left unrealized, this is an absolutely necessary violence.[110] American animation from its outset favored the use of anthropomorphic animals as its continuing characters, and that act of anthropomorphizing immediately imbricated those animals in the social and material networks of the humans they were meant to represent, networks with socially and historically specific relations of race, class, gender, and sexuality.[111] American animation's recurrent violence, its celebration of abjection and objection, flows out of a history of creating and manipulating implicitly and explicitly racialized bodies, of creatures who (like slaves) were wholly the possession of their producers yet were understood as imbued with a life force that made them inherently resistant to those masters and creators. With the coming of sound film, racist swing cartoons, in particular, made that violence explicit and contained it within a sealed diegetic world. Where the animator's hand once delivered the violence against the animated minstrel, in the sound era the disappearance of that hand, and the body to which it had once been attached, meant that the violence and subjugation inherent in animation appeared to be a motive force deriving from the landscape itself, part of the natural order of things.

RACE

HUMOR AND VIOLENCE

We shall best understand the origin of the pleasure derived from humor if we consider the process which takes place in the mind of anyone listening to another man's jest. He sees this other person in a situation which leads him to anticipate that the victim will show signs of some affect; he will get angry, complain, manifest pain, fear, horror, possibly even despair. The person who is watching or listening is prepared to follow his lead, and to call up the same emotions. But his anticipations are deceived; the other man does not display any affect—he makes a joke. It is from the saving of expenditure in feeling that the hearer derives the humorous satisfaction.
—Sigmund Freud, "Humor" (1928)

When it comes to cartoons, Sigmund Freud's description of humor as the invocation of affect and its diversion speaks well to the existential horror we call the gag. Especially in the short subjects that defined American animation until 1937 and still thereafter provided its bread and butter, life is an eternal cavalcade of pain.[1] Bodies twist, stretch, explode, melt; they are crushed by anvils, pianos, giant mallets, whole buildings; they are sliced and diced by razors and knives—and through it all we laugh. Why is it that, faced with such horrific violence and fierce torment, we are amused, tickled, jollified? And why have cartoons in particular linked that mayhem to other, more specific acts of degradation—inflected by race, gender, sexuality, ethnicity—happily harmonizing social and physical violence?

Of the rude shocks that 'toons have delivered and taken on our behalf, the brutality of racism is among the worst. Although the earliest days of American animation were relatively equal-opportunity in their stereo-

FIG. 4.1 Violence is a fact of life in the cartoon world. In *Rabbit Fire* (1951), Daffy Duck seems merely annoyed that a bullet has ripped his scalp from his skull.

typing of race, gender, and ethnicity—caricaturing with gusto Africans, African Americans, the Chinese, Mexicans, Scots, Jews, the Irish, Germans, and so on—parodies of Africans and African Americans, tied as they were to the vicious histories of slavery and segregation, offered a particularly virulent insult to human dignity and to the human bodies with which they were associated. In theory, European immigrants could expect to eventually assimilate into a generic American whiteness, while immigrants of Asian descent were sometimes afforded an uneasy accommodation as hardworking, clever, and inscrutable—therefore nearly on a par with whites—in the eugenic hierarchies of the day (which has sadly continued to be the case in more recent quasi-scientific racial fantasies).[2] Other ethnic and racial stereotypes were subsumed slowly, in a process of grudging inclusion, and this only added further insult to the ongoing injury of white-black racism.[3] This is a difference not of degree but of kind, and cartoons have continued to be a place where the cruelty of the unredeemable stereotype of blackness has found fertile ground for the ongoing expression of that distinction.[4] Fantastic African American 'toons, whether as minstrels or as racist caricatures, have performed a repetitive dream about the libidinous power of black bodies, and the desires and anxieties that attend that dream make those characters the targets of anxious violence—even as their very morphology constitutes an expression of the inherent violence of stereotyping itself.

The cartoon minstrel and its relative the swing-era racist caricature served as avatars for the displaced affect of industrial-era workers
(whether in the studio or in the audience), racialized embodiments of the
aggressive regulation of labor and of social desire. Perhaps, then, examin-
ing the often racialized violence of animation may offer a productive avenue through which to understand the relationship between laughter and
violence generally, as well as an insight into why that violence was often
expressed in specifically racist terms. The operation of the racial binary at
the dawn of the American animation industry, articulated within a contemporary logic of "separate but equal," attaches to the imaginary black
body of the (cartoon) character an implicit and ongoing social violence of
separation ("separate") as well as of a hierarchy invoked and disavowed
("but equal"). As avatars for the lost freedom of "wage slaves," cartoon
minstrels were made to perform resistance to control and to be immediately punished for that performance. Likewise, their descendants, swing-
era racist caricatures, gave shape and voice to a Depression-era fantasy
of African American life as rooted in a nature that bracketed a faltering
dominant culture. The inherent violence of animation, deeply imbricated
within its racialized origins, gave form to these historical moments of normative and operationalized social and economic violence, and that form
was first the minstrel then the racist caricature. Laughing at the implicit
and explicit violence that surrounded these characters has offered ostensibly white audiences an opportunity to externalize the violence to the
self that is daily life in the capitalist fantasy of a free society. Far more an
explanation than an expiation, a reading of the means by which this has
been accomplished opens the heart of darkness from which the minstrel
as comic figure has been taken.

The Betty Boop short *I'll Be Glad When You're Dead You Rascal, You*
(Fleischer, 1932) offers an example of this carefully articulated fantastic
racial violence. This short doesn't open with the iconic flapper or with
her sidekicks Bimbo and Ko-Ko. Like many of the animated shorts the
Fleischers produced with popular musicians of the early 1930s, it starts
with live footage—here of Louis Armstrong fronting a small big band.[5]
After Armstrong and the band get rolling, the short's animated section
begins. Betty, Bimbo, and Ko-Ko are explorers in the jungle, set upon by
the generic cannibals common to the racist imaginary of early twentieth-
century America.[6] Betty is of course kidnapped by these savages, and of
course Bimbo and Ko-Ko attempt a rescue. After a bit of business they
all break free and flee the cannibal village. Yet one native in particular is

FIGS. 4.2–4.3 In *I'll Be Glad When You're Dead You Rascal You* (1932), Louis Armstrong's joyous singing in the style of the dirty blues is transformed into the ravenous slavering of a cannibal.

dogged in his pursuit, and soon his body morphs into a giant flying cannibal head that, as it chases Bimbo and Ko-Ko, is intercut with a close-up of Armstrong's disembodied head, and both sing the title song, "(I'll Be Glad When You're Dead) You Rascal, You." Although Armstrong is dressed in a suit in the opening sequence and is carrying a trumpet and his trademark handkerchief, in the close-up he wears a black turtleneck and his shoulders are matted out of the frame. He sings with obvious pleasure and gusto. After a few verses, the image morphs him back into the voracious cannibal head, which so terrifies Bimbo that he sweats himself away to nothing (an obvious phallic joke). The cannibal then so scares Ko-Ko that a speedometer emerges from his ass; when it passes 120 mph it reads, in Hebrew, "Kosher."[7] In the end, the protagonists (of whom Armstrong is obviously not one) vanquish the natives and go free.

The short is so obviously racist that it barely seems worth the ink to say so. In his compendium on racist imagery in American cartoons, Henry Sampson classed this type of film as an "Animated Safari" and said of its sort: "Even if these cartoons did not directly incite bigotry, they certainly encouraged disrespect for people of African descent and therefore tended to reinforce the justification of the continued colonization of Africa by Europeans in the minds of the movie going public."[8] The core of this assessment—that this sort of film was racist and colonialist—is quite reasonable. Yet *how* it is racist is also important: how it achieved its humor through its racism, and how it mobilized its racism through its humor. Armstrong was one of the greatest musicians and performers of the twentieth century and was noted for the enthusiasm and joy he brought to his performances (which were sometimes criticized as Uncle-Tomming).[9] That pleasure in performance is evident here: Armstrong savors the lyrics (which imagine someone cursing out a man who has slept with his wife), at moments performing as if his rival were right in front of him. In the hands of one of the premier animation houses of the time, that relish becomes voraciousness, literalized as a cannibal head—all lips, tongue, and eyes—slavering after his white victims, and Armstrong's pleasure in singing is transformed into a desire to consume the errant explorers. That Bimbo melts into puddle of sweat and Ko-Ko's terror causes him to sprout a Hebraic speedometer from his butt—as the cartoon mocks their inadequate masculinity—only casts the racial binary in stronger relief: Armstrong's/the cannibal's voracious sensuality is that which reveals Bimbo's impotence and Ko-Ko's anxious (and incomplete) white masculinity.[10]

For all that, though, the Fleischer cartoon is at moments funny, and it is well made. The music is vital and exciting, and the drawing is inventive, lively, and unpredictable. The cartoon is full of the sorts of transformations that Norman Klein has described as the stuff of "nightmarish humor [and] drunken hallucinations."[11] It is alternately funny *and* racist, startling in its monstrousness. Its humor, or at least the affect behind that humor, is inextricably interwoven with its racism, its demeaning and derogatory portrayal of a great (African American) man. *I'll Be Glad* is charged with a blend of fear and desire—the fear of Louis Armstrong as a desirable object as much as a desiring subject—that threatens the film's protagonists, emasculating and whitening them at the same time. Bifurcating Armstrong between an ostensibly real self-contained and self-contented man and an idealized fantasy of uncivilized hunger, the film points up the relationship between the two, between the real and the ideal.

While the cartoon does this, though, it also performs the reinscriptive process by which the Fleischer trademark characters' strong associations with minstrelsy were obscured by the more potent and direct racism embodied by its stereotypical savages. By this point relegated to the status of sidekicks to the popular Betty Boop, Ko-Ko and Bimbo had each in his own moment been created as a continuing trademark character. Ko-Ko, in whiteface but performatively a minstrel nonetheless, had been the studio's mainstay from the late teens through most of the 1920s, the central character in struggles for control of the screen. As his popularity faded, the studio developed Bimbo—who more clearly carried the visual markers of the minstrel—as a potential replacement. Both of these trickster characters, however, lost their more direct associations with blackface minstrelsy when confronted by figures like the cannibals in *I'll Be Glad* or the ghetto underworld of *Snow-White* (1933).

A rereading of cartoons such as this should not understand this shift in the expression of racial formations in animation, in which swing-era racist caricatures joined trademark minstrels on the screen, as an unfortunate turn in an otherwise benign and childlike medium. The problem of understanding racism in American commercial animation is like that of discussing violence in cartoons more broadly. Generally, criticism of cartoon violence attempts to bracket it from the form itself, as if cartoons could simply be less violent and still be vital and interesting. This attitude ignores something that children and adults alike know and celebrate: animation, with its stretching, squashing, and metamorphosis of bodies, relies on a certain abstract violence as an essential demonstration of its distinct formal properties, of what it does best and differently from live cinema, if not life itself. Likewise, the idea that cartoons could easily be evacuated of their racial overtones fails to attend to how fundamental those overtones have been to the social and cultural circumstances within which animation took form, to its understanding of the metaphysics of everyday life. And, finally, the blending of such racial and racist fantasies with animation's propensity for staging physically violent interactions with the human (or anthropomorphic) form itself isn't merely additive: racial stereotyping is a form of social violence that was often made literal through the visual iconography of animation. Cartoons have had a conventional history of featuring misbehaving characters that beg to be disciplined by someone—if not by their creator then by another character standing in for him—then to perform their unpleasure in the face of that discipline. In short, the (troubling) vibrancy associated with the cartoons of this period depends on a sadomasochistic racial fantasy of encounter and resistance that foregrounds the metamorphic qualities of the form, one that is played out again and again.

Following Freud's logic, the humor of such racist cartoons, based on turning toward and then away from this history of horrible violence, should be hysterical. It sometimes is. Whether in the antics of Bosko the Talk-Ink Kid (1929–1938) or in the swamp-bound parody of Harlem night-life Swing Wedding (1937), again and again brutality is visited on ostensibly black bodies, whether they are physically assaulted or merely suffer the symbolic violence of grotesque caricature. And yet this racialized violence is performed in the service of a laugh, and in their manic pacing, jokes, and visual ingenuity these cartoons may evoke laughter. The racist stereotypes that inform these sorts of cartoons emerged from a specific iconographic lexicon and have circulated in animation as commonplace expressions of contempt that dismiss the harm they express as ultimately harmless: in cartoons no one bleeds and no one dies. It's all good fun, and it's not really real. The intense affect of racism, instead of evincing either vicious malice or utter horror, is reduced to a joke, a double take, a gag, a disavowal.

Those gags, as they have fed into larger systems of structural and institutional racism, have contributed to human suffering. According to Freud, though, the intense affect that informs them, however brutal, may be converted to relatively more felicitous laughter. Yet most agree that this laughter is still inappropriate and that this sort of conversion does nothing to blunt the racism itself. A historical understanding of race—if not common decency—requires that good people decry racist humor and censure their own laughter if they are in any way amused. Yet since many different people, even the intended objects of these jokes, sometimes find them funny, we are left with a nagging question: can good people see these cartoons as simultaneously racist *and* humorous? Ostensibly good people—people who did not think of themselves as racist—made these cartoons. Ostensibly good people have watched them and laughed. It is quite possible to watch today and laugh: in their pacing, language, and visual creativity, many of these cartoons are funny in their gags even as they are racist in their stereotypes. In the circuit between their production and their reception (and back again), even as they reproduce stereotypes and violence, they simultaneously convert the venomous horror of racist discourse into something laughable. The impulse to turn away too quickly from racist routines, to censor them, to disavow their humor as nothing more than viciousness made commonplace, marks an unwillingness to unflinchingly consider what that laughter might tell us about the feeling experience of participating in racist discourse. Arthur Knight, in his study of real and imagined African American culture in American musical films, argues that if "scholars and critics permit discomfort and distaste to dominate (as oppose to inform) history writing and interpretation, then we risk reifying past practices and, consequently, reproducing the worst aspects of those practices as their opposites."[12]

Is there a way, then, out of this either/or bind? Freud's notion of humor depends on a notion of the universal experience of suffering—the endless rude shock of human existence. We all suffer, and one common response is to laugh. But racist humor is *specific*: on its surface at least it depends on specific hurts to particular people. In this regard, though, the racist cartoon, as much as it contributes to this formulation, may offer an oblique way out. If the problem lies in the either/or, then the ambiguous ontological status of these animated characters—made yet alive, objects yet with an independent subjectivity—may crack open the affective bind that racist cartoons present. They become a useful correlate for how black bodies were imagined by American popular and legal discourse at the beginning of the last century. Like the animated character, perched on the border between the living and the inert, the minstrel, predicated on a fantasy of plantation life, has long suggested a transit point from the object status of chattel slavery toward a fully universal subjectivity—a point that, in the age of "separate but equal," one could always approach but at which one might never arrive.[13] This is decidedly not to analogize all African American historical experience with cartoons. It is, however, to point out the utility of animated characters for expressing and exploring this contradictory tension between subject and object—as well as the threat to the subject status of nonblack bodies that this tension represented.[14]

That is, there is a history in the United States of predicating subjectivity on a hierarchical continuum extending backward from an ideal and fully autonomous white (male) subject to the black chattel slave as living object, with varied intersections of race, gender, ethnicity, and subjectivity operating between the two poles—and where and how one is located on that continuum becomes important for organizing one's affective response to this humor. Put more simply, one's perceived or actual place on that continuum of subjectivity may determine whether one responds to racist humor with censure, with empathy, or with sympathy. Censure indicates an unwillingness to engage, a full disavowal of the object: it is a bad thing and we will not speak of it. In an empathic response, one understands oneself as of a kind with the butt of the joke (in this instance); in a sympathetic response, one need only recognize and acknowledge (yet not share) the feelings that the joke's object might experience. Parsing those different encounters with sympathy and empathy, a necessary tension between a subject and an embodied object emerges. In this chain of being, does one act as a fellow subject, as a subject among objects, or as a subjective object among fellow objects?

If one acts as the latter, in the moment of recognition and empathy racist parodies become simultaneously injurious *and* funny. They are injurious because they participate in practices designed to inflict real injury and insult on specific people and to implicate others in inflicting that injury. They may be funny when we view them, not in the sadistic model that Freud elaborated in his earlier work on humor but from the vantage of his later work on empathy and shared affect.[15] In this view, the racist cartoons of the early to mid-twentieth century continue to be funny, not because today's audiences necessarily choose to continue to practice or suffer the active, overt racism that informed their making (though that may sometimes be true), but because the social and material struggles that underpin that racism are still very much alive.

When approaching early American animation and its necessary involvement in contemporary racial formations, as well as its participation in overt racism—that is, through its use of both the subtler codings of race that shaped enduring minstrel characters such as Krazy Kat or Mickey Mouse and of broader racist caricatures—delineating animation's varied uses of stereotype becomes a useful way to productively engage with this tension. This requires once more revisiting the performative and visual traditions of blackface minstrelsy popular at the birth of American animation, this time from the perspective of violence and humor. For while more virulent and direct racist caricatures came to the fore in American animation's embrace of swing music in the late 1920s and early 1930s, the vestiges of blackface minstrelsy—the white gloves, wide eyes, voracious mouth, and tricksterish resistance—had already informed animation's most popular characters and lived on long after the racist excesses of animation's golden age seemed to pass.[16] Contemplating the similarities and shared histories of those forms, as well as their significant differences, in the light of the distance between sympathy and empathy may offer, if not solace, at least perspective.

GENTLEMEN, PLEASE BE SEATED

To rewrite the concept of a management of desire in social terms now allows us to think repression and wish-fulfillment together within the unity of a single mechanism, which . . . strategically arouses fantasy content within careful symbolic containment structures which defuse it, gratifying intolerable, unrealizable, properly imperishable desires only to the degree to which they can be momentarily stilled.
—Fredric Jameson, *Signatures of the Visible* (1992)

While a variety of racial and ethnic stereotypes facilitated the efficient shorthand of the gag in the early studio animation era, the metaphysics of the form favored rather particular stereotypes of blackness. More plainly put, the fantastic and resistant form of the blackface minstrel was an embodied corollary to the plasmatic substance, the metamorphic form of the cartoon character, a being that could alter itself or its environment seemingly at will (and certainly at the will of its creator). While live minstrels lacked this total transformative power, their transgressive nature and willful resistance to the conditions of their making resonated with the metamorphic and disruptive qualities of the cartoon. The same racial formations that had positioned black bodies as in transit from the object status of slavery to (near) personhood—or as occupying both of those contradictory positions simultaneously—informed a logic of animation that saw in fantastic blackness a means to express the permeable boundary between the real and the ideal. The live blackface minstrel and the trademark cartoon character were cognates: both had the ability to cross boundaries—whether social or physical—if not to rewrite them altogether.

FIG. 4.4 Judy Garland in blackface with Mr. Interlocutor in the minstrel show in *Babes in Arms* (1939).

Yet animated minstrels did not simply replace their live counterparts. Blackface played a (subsidiary) part in vaudeville well into the 1920s, fading as vaudeville gave way to radio and the movies, but it experienced a brief renaissance in the late 1920s and early 1930s with the rise of popular two-man minstrel acts such as Miller and Lyles, Moran and Mack, and Gosden and Correll's Amos 'n' Andy. Yet none of blackface's mediated forms—the minstrel show, vaudeville act, cartoon, live film, radio program—simply replaced its predecessor. Their years of popularity overlapped, and one or more of these attractions could occupy the same stage in the same week—if not the same night. Vaudeville's famous comedic two-man acts (such as Abbott and Costello, Hope and Crosby, and Burns and Allen) followed the same conventional principles as Tambo, Bones, and the interlocutor, and animation in return borrowed from both.[17] To recall: in minstrelsy the interlocutor served as the conduit between the audience and the minstrels. He addressed the audience directly and often as an equal and interrogated the minstrels in a quasi-ethnographic fashion about their friends, their families, and the current events of the day. The interlocutor was the instigator and butt of the minstrels' mangling of meaning, and his frequent inability to make them understand his simple questions performed the limits of race, education, and class superiority in the face of natural turpitude. Operating at the border between nature and culture, the interlocutor attempted an always failing regulation of the minstrels' fantastic minds and bodies. Vaudeville comedians (or the writers who supplied their material) would compress this triadic relation by folding the interlocutor into the duo of Tambo and Bones, making one

comic in the "two act" more intelligent and "civilized" while the other remained ignorant and resistant. Just as the interlocutor could not make the
end men make sense, Bud Abbott failed to contain the childlike Lou Costello and George Burns failed to make Gracie Allen see reason: they were
the conduits of *nonsense*.[18]

Like those end men before them, animated minstrel characters—Felix,
Mickey, Bugs—were tricksters and interlopers at the boundary between
the screen and the real, arising from a tradition of interplay with their
creators and expressing a desire to escape the bounds of two dimensions
for the real world of their animators.[19] This was more than a matter of homology: the white gloves, big smile, and wide eyes that sat on an ostensibly racially ambiguous or unmarked body (usually that of an animal)
were the markers of minstrelsy. Likewise, the animated minstrels' behaviors—their resistance to both the animator-interlocutor who created
them and to the physical strictures of animate space—underpinned both
the fundamental gag structure of many an early animated short and the
basic template of the trademarked continuing character. And like their
live counterparts, animated minstrels performed a desirable and humorous irrationality that begged both admiration and punishment.

Eric Lott has described the minstrel's performance of imagined fantastic black characteristics as an act of "love and theft," similar to what Stuart
Hall calls the "ambivalence of stereotype."[20] This performance expressed
(and expresses) a desire for an imagined liberation from social norms,
a liberation perversely located in subjugated bodies, a desire alloyed with
a fear of the raw sensual power of those same bodies. Based as it was on a
notion of the indolent and shifty slave, minstrelsy replicated a white fantasy of plantation life, of lazy African Americans wallowing in a sensual
torpor, almost devoid of higher mental and moral functions yet possess-
ing an innate natural intelligence that made them crafty and sly. (Likewise, the rakish yet absurd figure of the black urban dandy, such as Zip
Coon or Jim Dandy, spoke both to a desire for fashion and style and for the
incommensurate possibility of black cultural equality.) Torture, rape, and
forced labor—and all the institutions they supported and that supported
them—were occluded in minstrelsy, leaving the rustic domesticity of the
slave cabin. Saidiya Hartman has suggested that minstrelsy's playful show
of resistance titillated precisely because of the threat of recriminatory violence at which it hinted: "Certainly, the disciplinary vengeance of farce ex-
ercised in minstrelsy reproduced black subjection, albeit accompanied by
laughter. On the minstrel stage, the comic inversions, bawdy humor, and

lampooning of class hierarchies nonetheless operated within the confines of the tolerable, particularly since this transgression of order occurred by reproducing the abject status of blackness."[21] On the minstrel stage, then, blackness was not only abject but was also resistant, and these qualities were inextricably linked. In cartoons, that resistance was created for the purpose of its regulation. Christopher Lehman argues that following a revision to the Production Code, in animation "slave figures receive[d] a more humane depiction . . . and no cartoon produced after 1934 showed the whipping of slaves."[22] This generous gesture, of course, did not apply to the violence inflicted on or by vestigial minstrel characters or to the implicit violence of the stereotypes themselves. The slave represented the nadir of labor's enthrallment to capital in an era when contract labor was called "wage slavery" to signify its subordinate status. The minstrel, once removed from the slave, stood in for labor unchained: s/he was the slave who talked back, who resisted work in favor of carnal pleasure, whose very laziness was work wasted, a passive revolt.[23] The whip may have been removed, but the convention of animated characters violently disciplined for their rebelliousness had not. And, whether vestigial minstrel or racist caricature, cartoon characters in the 1930s encountered and engaged in increasing levels of violence—enthusiastic, exuberant violence—suffering incredible torments yet remaining, in the end, unscathed.

Yet as with the slapstick vaudeville routine or film short, this did not engender identification *with* a protagonist but identification *of* the situation and its referents. If the viewer in the classical cinematic apparatus, the one who gazed and was sutured into the narrative, was an individual whose interpellation occurred through the repetitive yielding of her or his self to the story, the vaudeville spectator was also meant to experience a subordination of the self—not to a subjectivity produced in concert with the image, but to a collective appreciation, to the crowd looking up at the stage or screen.[24] Rather than withdrawing the viewer from his or her immediate surroundings and into a dream world of (dis)embodied fantasy, the spectatorial practices of vaudeville, minstrelsy, and animation proffered the wink and the nudge, a collective experience in the here and now, located not in a cinematic imaginary but in the theater itself. There, the pleasure was not in seeing one's self in the protagonist but in witnessing the virtuosity with which the performers executed their acts.

In terms of an identificatory model based in empathy rather than on sympathy, this difference is essential. To identify with(in) the crowd is to locate oneself in a community of practice, and the experience of identification is first with one's fellow audience members and then with the performer onstage (rather than with the character or abstracted cinematic gaze). Even in those instances when an audience rejects a given performance and boos a performer (for instance), the community of practice (audience and performers) remains whole, bound up by shared convention.[25] The empathic reaction that may come from watching a member of one's own (even provisional) community (succeed or) fail—and suffer—is possible, even as one perhaps makes a contribution to that suffering (by, say, booing). Sympathy, on the other hand, requires only that the viewer feel *for* (rather than *with*) the performer or character.[26] Like pity, not only does it not invoke an equal emotional investment in the other, it actually depends on emotional distance: sympathy requires the narcissistic investment of identification, the conventional fantasy of replacing (rather than aligning) one's self with a character, which paradoxically reinforces a sense of one's self as powerful enough to assume the role of protagonist and then return to the safety of one's self at film's end.

Conversely, and oddly, an empathic reaction to a performance does not necessarily require that defense of self. Conventionally, empathy is premised on one person's affective response to another's condition as *shared*: what happens to one's self could just as easily happen to another. In the case of minstrelsy—whether live or animated—empathy is in this light an emotion shared between human commodities, between those whose labor has been expropriated, whether under the voluntary pretense of freedom of contract or violently through enslavement. But unlike cinematic suture, whose investments depend on the requirements of the unconscious, this sort of identification may be consciously *chosen*: there is no always already interpellated subject, no yielding against one's will to unconscious urges amplified by an implacable apparatus. Instead there is a division of the subject between theater seat and stage or screen.[27] In empathy, one may laugh because the shared markers of experience, the very divided consciousness to which Freud refers at the beginning of his 1928 essay on humor—when he describes a condemned man cracking a joke on the gallows—are performed not as threats to the integrity of the threatened ego but as embodiments of its protective ideal, creatures who provide necessary ruptures in the tidy frame of reality.[28] The minstrel, whether live or animated, is always a creature divided. In the minstrel's live incarnation, the greasepaint sits uneasily on the face: an ideal of blackness atop a raced performer.[29] In the cartoon, the animated minstrel performs a similar duality—that of a seeming autonomy entirely controlled

by its maker. Viewing either (racist) performance, one may laugh and ending that laughter say, "Well, that's not right." In empathy both expressions
are felt and both feelings legitimate.[30]

Or perhaps it would be better to say that both sets of feelings may
be legitimate, depending on whether one has done work to find a common ground from which to view those cartoons. To understand the transit
and transformation of stereotypes, of racist caricatures, and to appreciate
them at a feeling level, one must attempt to situate one's self, and them,
in the same historical frame. Performances of race and racial stereotype
in American commercial animation have a distinct genealogy. Commercial animation at the beginning of the twentieth century turned to the
minstrel stage to produce enduring continuing characters such as Felix,
Krazy, and Mickey. During the swing era, American cartooning looked to
blackface's founding conceits, imagining the blackness of the minstrel as
one link in an associative chain that stretched backward from the urban
ghetto, through minstrelsy's fantastic plantation, and on to an originary
African jungle. When cartoons took up jazz they rendered an invisible
world of (imagined) black culture visible, depicting jazz not just as a
musical form but as a force able to produce an amalgamated embodiment of those three locations—the jungle, the plantation, and the ghetto—a force that animated everyone and everything that dwelt there. For
ostensibly white audiences, then, cartoons offered access to a forbidden
territory of fear and desire, and the laughter they were meant to invoke is
better understood, though not absolved, through a careful survey of that
landscape.

TRADER MICKEY: THE MINSTREL IN THE HEART OF DARKNESS

The 1932 Disney short *Trader Mickey* performs this racialized geography
explicitly. The cartoon follows a fairly standard format for early sound
efforts: a minimal plot and a centerpiece musical production number
highlight the wonders of the still relatively new technology of sync sound,
and popular melodies and dance numbers play on the trends of the day.
The story here is that Mickey Mouse and his dog, Pluto, are captured by
cannibals and dance their way to freedom by playing on the natives' innate susceptibility to jazz rhythms. The film is significant not only for its
inflection of the popular swing-era trope of jazz as "jungle music" but also
because Mickey's capture at the hands of these animated cannibals offers
an instance of cultural contact between a blackface minstrel (Mickey) and

the less oblique racist stereotypes that historically had informed the minstrel's libidinous, animalistic, and uncivilized appeal. Reading a seemingly innocuous cartoon short, then, offers a shorthand look at the complex of race, violence, and desire that charged fantasies of blackness in the early twentieth-century United States. It also provides an avenue for understanding how the figure of the minstrel became so embedded in animation during its silent era that by the time of Mickey's arrival in 1928, a direct association between trademark cartoon characters and blackface minstrels was fading into a set of conventions that maintained a less direct relationship to (an imagined) blackness. Trademark cartoon characters such as Mickey were becoming *vestigial minstrels*, carrying all (or many) of the markers of minstrelsy while rarely referring directly to the tradition itself.[31] Live performances of blackface minstrelsy were waning along with vaudeville, and minstrels' place in live cinema limited to serving as a marker of bygone performance styles and simpler times. Increasingly robbed of direct referents, minstrels in animation became more deeply embedded in the visual, auditory, and performative traditions of the cartoon, and less immediately understood as engaged in the performative acts of blackface minstrelsy.[32]

Reinscribing Mickey and his fellow cartoon tricksters as minstrels, however, is not a mere act of (empty and symbolic) reparation; it is an effort to place the often marginalized but always extremely popular form of the animated cartoon short more firmly into a historically specific racial matrix that included the vaudeville stage, the minstrel show, the world's fair midway native village, and the black-and-tan review—all of which, within a complex, varied, and sometimes contradictory fabric of discourse, produced, contested, and regulated race relations on the ground.[33] Beyond revealing the racial (and racist) foundations of beloved animated characters, the point of understanding those characters as minstrels is, first, to witness how stereotypical ideas that were considered increasingly unacceptable in one forum could pass relatively unnoticed in another. Yet beyond that, seeing Mickey, Bugs, and Daffy as minstrels permits a more nuanced and detailed picture of animation as a fantastic, violent, and excessive popular art form.

Framed by that history, *Trader Mickey* is an interstitial object that brings the conventions of blackface minstrelsy undergirding American animation into conversation with the violent and excessive racist caricatures that crowded the jazz-inflected cartoons of early sound cinema. So, witnessing the difference between the minstrel and the racist caricature

FIG. 4.5 A frame grab from the video game *Epic Mickey* (2010) reveals a darker, less wholesome side of Mickey Mouse than his previous incarnations.

in this cartoon may serve to alienate a few of the practices we have come to see as natural in animation—particularly its tendency toward excessive yet seemingly inconsequential violence. For although *Trader Mickey* is not the most vicious of the cartoons of the early sound era, even it is rife with violence threatened and enacted, and Mickey Mouse, who is so deeply associated with sweetness and light that Disney had to briefly mount a PR campaign to reintroduce his "edge" for the video game *Epic Mickey* (2010), is no exception.[34] *Trader Mickey* describes the difference between the animate minstrel and racist caricature, and the cartoon illustrates how the minstrel's intimate associations with voice, silence, and violence made it an appropriate avatar for the artisan animator increasingly constrained within an industrializing art form.

The very term "Mickey Mouse," with all of its various connotations, speaks to the character's semiotic weight. To describe something as "Mickey Mouse" is to call it trivial. Why? Already extremely famous when *Trader Mickey* premiered in 1932, Mickey was widely and enthusiastically praised by critics and by Disney's public and was a merchandizing juggernaut available in myriad forms, well on his way to becoming a ubiquitous household object.[35] Critics such as Walter Benjamin and Sergei Eisenstein carefully bracketed Disney's enthusiasm for capitalism while they celebrated the mouse, and in 1934 Cole Porter in "You're the Top" suggested that the object of his affection was as good as Mickey Mouse— that is, well, "the top." Yet it was his very ubiquity that contributed to the

FIG. 4.6 The opening of *Trader Mickey* (1932) finds Mickey and Pluto making their way upriver in a paddle-wheel boat.

rodent's triviality. Mickey Mouse was simultaneously a beloved cartoon character and a trademark icon on every bit of gimcrackery one could imagine, from watches and water glasses, to toothbrushes and notebooks, to frocks and flatware. So, to become "Mickey Mouse" was and is to be cheapened through excessive commodification. Often figured as Walt Disney's progeny, Mickey was also the company's trademark and mascot yet was also presented as an autonomous being whose impish ways, although increasingly tamed as the 1930s progressed, spoke of a minstrel's tricksterish, resistant behavior.[36] Made by hand yet acting as if he were autonomous, Mickey Mouse was the exemplar of the animate commodity: a living thing that signified itself and more.[37] In the midst of the Great Depression and its anxious celebration of Algeresque fantasies of self-making (for which Walt Disney was hailed in the press), Mickey seemed, as a living being, to produce his own value but to hold none of it.[38] The figure of Mickey was (and is) contradictory: important in its triviality; handmade yet living; capricious and willful yet ultimately good-natured and obedient; and, of course, simultaneously racially coded as both black and white. It is through this dense and self-refractory complex of meaning that we encounter the mouse in *Trader Mickey*, and through which we may approach the sadomasochistic complex that informs both the trademark animated character and the blackface minstrels who informed it.

Trader Mickey opens on Mickey and Pluto cruising upriver in a ramshackle paddle-wheel steamer loaded with cargo, passing hippos and crocodiles, their mouths agape. Mickey is perched atop his cargo, merrily plucking away at a banjo. Within a few shots, this seemingly harmless cartoon confection has presented us with a wealth of information. Making his way into the heart of darkness a year after *Trader Horn* (1931), in the same year as Frank Buck's *Bring 'Em Back Alive* (1932), and several years before the onset of the tropical kitsch of Trader Vic, Mickey plays a trader in Africa like a vaudevillian donning a loosely fitting costume.[39] A trader of what? His makeshift boat is loaded with some sort of goods, but we are not sure for what (or whom) he expects to trade them before he heads home on his return voyage. The paddle wheel on his boat could just as easily signal the old South as a colonial adventure in an African rain forest. To be blunt: at best Mickey plays a dry-goods merchant working the byways of some colonial interzone; at worst he is slave-trader Mickey, and his trade is in the savage bodies he is soon to encounter. As a minstrel he is neither fully white nor fully black; as an anthropomorphic mouse, neither fully animal nor human: he is a liminal figure in a liminal zone.

In *Trader Mickey*, Africa, the originary locus of the black slave body, collapses into the putative site of its eventual forced labor, the South. This is not so much an act of pentimento as the generation of a continuous alternative space of subjugation: one of a number of representations that imagined the Old South as symbolically contiguous with Africa (and in the jazz age, with Harlem), the film posits (or accepts) a fantastic geography based on race. Blackness simultaneously signifies the plantation and the jungle. This repeats one of the foundational conceits of minstrelsy. Early minstrel performers often framed their shows as anthropological reports: visiting the plantation they had witnessed the primitive dances of enslaved Africans (barely removed from the jungle) and were pleased and privileged to reproduce them for audiences distanced by geographical location and/or cosmopolitanism from their meanings.[40] Black or white, but always in blackface, minstrel performers were sometimes called "delineators," as if what they performed were less a representation and more a re-presentation. The wooly wigs, burnt cork, and greasepaint that delineated the head, eyes, and mouth of the minstrel were only the beginning, as were the gloves that increasingly became a trademark of the form as the nineteenth century progressed.

What were delineated as well were dances, songs, speech patterns, and the jumbled and confused thoughts of a primitive savage attempting to communicate in the tongue of his master—the mangling of which revealed both the limited intellect of the minstrel and the social and political contradictions inhabiting the common sense of the day. Lampooning the pretentions of the "civilized" set, the banter between interlocutor and end men and the stump speech reveled in contradiction, performing through playful inversions a coded ressentiment.[41] For example, the routine "Free Translations," pasted into George Christy's journal and dated December 1850, offers this lampoon of the nineteenth-century bourgeois notion of an education built on "small Latin and less Greek":

A: Well, now, you've been to college two years, I suppos [sic] you
   can translate Latin some, can't you?
B: Yes, I can translate anything.
A: Can you? Well, what does this mean—*Poeta nascitur non fit?*
B: Oh! That means, a nasty poet is not fit![42]

(A more accurate translation would be "A poet is born, not made.") Likewise, a stump speech attributed to J. Martin and delivered in March 1861 makes light of and hints at the tensions surrounding the looming Civil War:

Look at the patriots ob dis country. Talk 'bout Kossuth and Garibaldi; ain't we got Henry Ward Beecher, Horace Greeley, Wendell Phillips, and W. L. Yancey? Talk 'bout Garibaldi consolidatin' Italy. Why *dem* fellers is goin' to make any quantity of countries out ob dese United States, dem's de fellers dat tinks E Pluribus Unum sounds vulgar, so dey're goin' to changer it to E Unibus Plurium. Dat's what's de matter. . . . In de year Aunty Dominix, 1776, how was dis country bounded. I'll tell you—it was bounded on de Norf by dat celebrated female Sara-toga. . . . It was bounded on the de Souf by Gin'ral Jackson and de Cotton Bales. On de East by Moll Pitcher de Salem Witchcraft and de Boston Tea Party. An' on de West by—by—a howlin' wilderness. Now how is it bounded? Its bounded on de Norf by eberytin' dat's good to eat and drink; its bounded on de Souf by Secession; its bounded on de East by New Jersey, Harper's Ferry, and de Great Eastern. . . . Dat's what's de matter.[43]

In both of these instances, the minstrel's apparent guilelessness, a condition of his exclusion from polite society and of his native inability to grasp the finer points of language, ideology, social norms, or historical fact, allows him to send up the pretensions of the dominant classes, but it also provides a fantastic outsider's view of an emergent history of which he is seen as an object rather than a subject. The blackface minstrel, as stand-in for the chattel slave (or for his northern counterpart, the free but not fully assimilated black man), embodies the outside: as an object he is outside the flow of history; paradoxically his containment on the plantation places him outside free society. He exists on the margins of cognition, speech, and action, yet that seems to be a privileged vantage point from which he converts institutional and immediate violence on his body into violence against common sense. Likewise, Mickey Mouse, as a made object granted a sentience and agency constantly in danger of being limited, doubles that liminal condition as a minstrel: he is doubly dislocated. In its verbal form, blackface minstrelsy performed the deformation and metamorphosis of language that cartoons would render visually in silent, "plasmatic" form for their first fifteen years; with the coming of sound they would also admit the fast-paced patter of Bugs Bunny or Daffy Duck.

But more than just (dis)location connects *Trader Mickey* to minstrelsy. As he chugs upriver, Mickey is happily strumming a raggedy tune on his banjo, and this isn't the first time he has played music specifically associated with the minstrel stage. In his first outing in sync sound, *Steamboat Willie* (1928), Mickey played the minstrel standard "Old Zip Coon" (also known as "Turkey in the Straw") on the bodies of various farm animals as *that* steamboat made its way upriver.[44] Although *Steamboat Willie* is often erroneously celebrated as the first sound cartoon, rarely do those accolades mention its indebtedness to the minstrel stage for its sonic performance.[45] So in *Trader Mickey* the mouse is, quite simply and quite reasonably, a minstrel traveling steadily toward the headwaters of the tradition that spawned him. It is not just the happy strumming that signals him as such, though: Mickey sports the uniform of white gloves, black face, exaggerated mouth, and wide eyes that marked both the popular animated characters of the day and their progenitor, the blackface minstrel. But beyond those obvious physical markers, he also performs the minstrel's traditional role of the trickster, the imp who operates on the margins of social and material convention and who embodies significant destructive and productive powers. He is a force of disruption—albeit one somewhat tamed by an emerging Disney aesthetic that increasingly eschewed extremes in favor of a performed moderate wholesomeness. Yet as that force he exists in a world of hurt, an animated cosmos in which incredible vio-

FIG. 4.7 As Mickey Mouse heads toward the cannibal village in *Trader Mickey* (1932), he strums the minstrel tune "Old Zip Coon" on his banjo, reprising his first sound performance in *Steamboat Willie* (1928).

lence circulates through seemingly indestructible bodies, visiting itself on hero and villain alike.

Here and elsewhere, Mickey is more than just a trickster, a lord of misrule. As a minstrel, he is an indexical marker, a gesture toward the Old South, the plantation, and slavery. Epitomized by minstrelsy's end men, Tambo and Bones, the minstrel did more than signify a generic African American body; s/he even invoked more than an enslaved African American. The body to which the minstrel referred and which informed the trickster figure of the trademark cartoon character—Mickey, Felix, Ko-Ko, Oswald, and so on—was one that recalled the recalcitrant slave who, through an artful combination of stereotyped laziness, cunning, and the performance of a studied ignorance, attempted to avoid the forced labor and regimes of punishment that were the lot of chattel slavery. For the central tropes of minstrelsy—the singing and dancing, the stump speech, good-naturedly misdirecting the interlocutor—all derived from the necessary fantasy of the slave as a creature closer in the natural chain of being to the (equally stubborn) mule or the cunning Br'er Rabbit.[46] This figure purportedly felt less pain than her/his white counterpart and was natu-

FIGS. 4.8–4.9 Like Jim Crow, in his dress, his makeup, and his gestural repertoire, Mickey Mouse is not like a minstrel, he is a minstrel. Jim Crow courtesy of the Library of Congress. *Trader Mickey* (1932).

rally inclined to hard physical labor in the open air. As Childs has described it in relation to the chain gangs that were contemporary with the cartoon minstrel: "The physical branding that slaves received upon their kidnapping onto the coffle and slave ship [was] coupled with their epistemic branding as animalistic, infantile, and lazy; as such the forebears of the plantation 'darky' [were] incapable of feeling the pain of internment, of recognizing the enormity of their dispossession, or of performing industrious labor without the spur of punishment. For those humans branded as savage 'monkeys,' terror and collective disappearance are an occasion for joviality, merriment, and song."[47] By the time of those chain gangs, and of the beginnings of the American cartoon, that rhetoric was very much operative. For instance, Lichtenstein reports that in 1912 the assistant director of the U.S. Office of Public Roads, arguing in favor of chain-gang labor, argued that the "negro is accustomed to outdoor occupations . . . [and is] experienced in manual labor . . . [and] does not possess the same aversion to working in public . . . as is characteristic of the white race."[48]

For Hartman, this fantasy marks slave and minstrel bodies alike as provisional subjects, as lacking full autonomy and available for appropriation by others: "The bound black body, permanently affixed in its place, engenders pleasure not only ensuant to the buffoonery and grotesqueries of Cuff, Sambo, and Zip Coon but above all deriving from the very mechanisms of this coercive placement; it is a pleasure obtained from the security of place and order and predicated upon chattel slavery."[49] It was not just the capering of Tambo, Bones, or Mickey that afforded audiences pleasure, then, but the very association of those characters, however attenuated, with the enslaved body, the system of chattel slavery, and the larger racial hierarchy it embodied. This pleasure could be described as sadistic, deriving from the forced subjection of others. At the same time, though, according to Hartman, it was in witnessing minstrelsy's systematic and distanced performance of the institution of slavery that the black body became sensible as fixed in a natural order, an order through which one's own humanity might be affirmed if one were (able) to identify as white. Blackface minstrelsy celebrated the black body as outside of and resistant to (white) civilization. Through that body's very necessary subjugation and its subsequent defiance of that civilization the minstrel delineated polite society's very humorous foibles and failings.

That in blackface minstrelsy this performance was often offered by a white man in blackface only added to its frisson. One could, watching this performance, participate in the subjugation and exchange of another person at a distance, visiting that economic and social control on a body simultaneously white and black. Like a sadomasochistic act, this pleasure combined the performance of subjection with the fantasy that its objects willingly entered into it, that the subjection was as pleasurable in its own right to the masochist as it was to the sadist. In those not infrequent cases of black performers blacking up in order to gain access to the stage (and a livelihood), the pleasure of witnessing subjugation and an engagement in that system of domination was asserted even over ostensibly free black bodies. The black performer seemed to willingly yield to a system of signification that made reference to his or her own (potential) enslavement, in order to perform that enslavement as the positive condition of the happy darky. "In this regard," Hartman argues, "the donning of blackface restaged the seizure and possession of the black body for the other's use and enjoyment. The culture of cross-racial identification facilitated in minstrelsy cannot be extricated from the relations of chattel slavery."[50]

As far as the animated minstrel was concerned, this was no less true. The continuing cartoon character carried the physical markers of the minstrel—the white gloves, the black face (or, in the case of Ko-Ko, white but still painted on) and exaggerated eyes and mouth—as well as the bodily elasticity, the propensity to dance (and, with the coming of sound, to sing), and a willfully disobedient character.[51] But it was particularly in the interplay between the character and its animator in cartoons of the early silent era that this subjugation made itself most evident. Characters such as Felix the Cat, Pete the Pup, or Ko-Ko the Clown frequently interacted with their audience or tested the bounds of the screen itself, and (especially in Ko-Ko's case) were often punished for asserting themselves. As with the live minstrel created by whites to be subjugated by whites, the early animated character was created and disciplined by the same animator/audience.[52] Donald Crafton has suggested that this convention demonstrates "the propensity of animators and the complicity of audiences to construct timescapes, that is, worlds imagined in the likeness of a particular time, place, and significance in history that are convincing in their details but patently fictional. Animation's preservation of minstrelsy and its insistence on highlighting bodily performance are examples of cultural timescapes that cartoons perpetuated."[53] By the time Disney made *Trader Mickey*, the trope of the intruding hand of the animator had largely disappeared, but the animate minstrel remained nonetheless subject to constraint and punishment, if not by hostile figures such as the cartoon's cannibal king then by the environment itself; animated characters by their nature were the victims of torture—for the sake of amusement.

INSTRUMENTAL INTERLUDE

Yet these shared conventions only begin to tell the tale of why the black-face minstrel might figure significantly in the emerging cosmos of American animation, and why the violence sublimated in the song-and-dance of the minstrel stage would reemerge with a vengeance in the cartoon world. For the "security of place" about which Hartman speaks refers to the plantation in either its literal or figurative form—as a brutally codified, hierarchical social order. But it also organizes the North and the South into fantastic realms of free and unfree labor. To return to the cartoon, when Trader Mickey sets foot on the riverbank and slaps his feet on the mud of the Mississippi/Congo, he is met by a tribe of ravening cannibals, led by a buffoonish king who can't stop laughing.[54] Mouse and dog are seized, and Mickey is thrown into a pot and prepped for cooking, while the king and his tribesmen sort through the items he has brought to trade with them.

Oddly, they find that much of Mickey's stock consists of trumpets, trombones, tubas, and the like—the instruments for a jazz band. Mystified, the grotesquely caricatured cannibals try to play them and end up only injuring the instruments, themselves, and others. But from this moment on the cartoon performs a continuum of animate being. Although the instruments are inanimate, they still strike back at the cannibals when abused. Similarly, in later scenes the natives will play not only the instruments but each other. In other words, both cannibals and trombones are relatively animate instruments. Plastic beyond the usual bounds of their being, their interaction reveals a mutual instrumentality, a common primitive bond. More tool than human, they share a certain happy deformability, and while each is instrument to the other, all are instruments to those above them.

But this gets ahead of the story. Just when it seems that all is lost, the chef who is preparing Mickey tries to use an alto saxophone as a ladle. Mickey gets hold of it and begins playing, and of course the natives can't help but dance. That dance will bond the trader and cannibals under the sign of rhythm, which the fantastic black body, true to stereotype, cannot possibly resist. The tune Mickey belts out sets off a medley of standards that signify both the Harlem demimonde and the Old South, including "St. James Infirmary Blues" and "Darktown Strutters Ball." Suddenly, even

FIGS. 4.10–4.12 In *Trader Mickey* (1932), the cannibal chef trades a ladle for a saxophone before Mickey grabs it and triggers the natives' rhythm genes. Some break into his stores and wrestle with instruments they do not understand but on which they manage to play jazz music perfectly.

though the cannibals continue to play their instruments incorrectly, the tune is clear, and the audience witnesses a full-blown production number with Mickey and the savage king as its costars. This production number, which is the centerpiece of the cartoon, literalizes the fantasy of jazz as "jungle music," replete with the thrills of cannibalism, upriver crossed with uptown. As a number of critics have noted, this implicit message, carried forward from the minstrel stage, was often made literal, as in the announcement in Paul Whiteman's *King of Jazz* (Anderson, 1930) that "jazz was born in the African jungle to the beating of voodoo drums."[55] Discussing the Fleischers' use of otherworldly motifs in their live/animated jazz series, three of which featured Cab Calloway, Goldmark suggests that early American animation repeatedly invoked the jungle and plantation to signal the primal roots of African American culture: "The dark jungles represent jazz's supposed primeval origins, while the caves that appear in all three Calloway cartoons work as metaphors for the urban source of jazz, Harlem nightclubs. The portrayal of these exotic locales in cartoons provided white audiences with a safe outing to a strange and unusual world, much like a visit to the Harlem clubs."[56] But Africa, Harlem, and the South are not the only realms invoked in the Disney production number. Mickey and his captors blithely make use of the copious human bones that litter the village. They play them like percussion instruments, they use them to adorn ad hoc costumes, they dance atop piles of skulls: mass death is everywhere in the frame, even as everyone happily rollicks their way through the Black Bottom and the Charleston. Like the Fleischers' contemporaneous Betty Boop shorts, which featured jazz greats such as Calloway and Armstrong live and then imagined as animated creatures, this visual iconography also placed African American social and cultural life in an underworld teeming with death and violence, fusing the seemingly innate joyousness of the natives to their ever-present chthonic threat.

CHAINS OF BEING

Trader Mickey takes the case a little further. As the natives dance and play, small details flit across the screen. Many of the cannibals wear bracelets and anklets, some of which have an odd extra ring attached to them, as if they are shackles. It is a fleeting and random image, equally suggestive of an escape from bondage as of being ready for chains. The chronology matters little; the gesture is toward the association (the linking) of the osten-

FIG. 4.13 Like the underworldly figures in Fleischer jazz cartoons, the natives in *Trader Mickey* (1932) link jazz to death and decay.

FIGS. 4.14–4.15 In *Minnie the Moocher* (1932), Betty Boop and Bimbo cower in fear at the underworldly "spooks" engendered by Cab Calloway's singing.

FIG. 4.16 Mickey dances with the natives, who for some reason wear shackles, in *Trader Mickey* (1932).

FIG. 4.17 Both Mickey and the Cannibal King (wearing a girdle for a crown and spats over bare feet) signify through the markers of the minstrel that they are more evolved than the other natives.

sibly black body with the condition of slavery, of being both subject and chattel. As if this offhand gesture weren't enough, chains or no, some of the natives dance and play their instruments upright while others play on all fours as if they were prehuman missing links. Here the much-noted anthropomorphism of the classic cartoon takes on a more subtle gradation: while somehow Mickey, an oversized mouse, is the most civilized creature present, the apparently African natives, who are meant to read as human, gambol apelike, playing their jazz instruments with equal ease with either their hands or feet.

Yet even within the social order of the cannibals there are necessary gradations of humanity. At the high end of the spectrum, both the king and the chef, like Mickey, wear the white gloves of the minstrel. A chain of being presents itself in the dance number, which, like a minstrel show, is performed face-forward, and in many of the shots the characters clearly acknowledge their audience. This performance describes a developmental timeline that begins at the protohuman—the cannibals not yet upright—continues to natives on two legs and then on to those who have donned the minstrel gloves but are still savage, and ends at Mickey, an anthropomorphic minstrel mouse who dances for his life—and toward a civilization he will never fully occupy.

It would be enough to point out that this voracious dance of life, death, and dirty blues produces a sadomasochistic fantasy in which ostensibly black bodies are so steeped in their own physicality, their own animal nature, that they revel in a world in which pain is an unremarkable part of a celebration of a sensual yet inherently incoherent life. It would be enough to point out that this particular cartoon hints at that primal fantasy about which Hartman speaks, one that traces the minstrel body back to the quasi-animal realm of the African native, and that it further implicates that minstrel figure in the slave trade. (For, again, what do the natives have that Mickey would want?) It isn't hard to read the cartoon as another in a long line of cinematic and performative fantasies in which the very nature of blackness masochistically invites its own torment.

But noting one more node in a matrix of fantasies about the African or African American body as a missing link between a white modern humanity and its roots among the apes does not tell the whole tale; nor does it fully account for the anxious violence that attends the cartoon minstrel. In addition to recapitulating a fantastic primate taxonomy, *Trader Mickey* also illustrates the minstrel's relationship to the slave as chattel, object, and tool. What the landscape of the cannibal village reveals (and this is also true of animation in general) is that no body, no thing, is completely human or completely an autonomous subject. Because they are animated, and because they are located on a taxonomic continuum from the ape to the minstrel, every thing and person in the cartoon, up to and including Mickey, has the potential to be a useful object for anyone else in the cartoon. Of course, Mickey, being more civilized, is more likely to use than to be used, but this becomes assured only after he has deployed jazz to sublimate the brute force of the cannibals into song and dance.

As with its live counterpart, then, the animated minstrel stands as a fetish for a set of relations that are present but not fully nameable. He is a fetish in the sense that he is a commodity, a "social hieroglyphic," a crystallization of the social and material relations that obtain around his creation that occludes those relations through its production as a social object.[57] He is also a fetish in the psychoanalytic sense, in that his apparent condition as a living being is a disavowal of the hand of the maker behind him and of the violent appropriation of the labor that went into his making. He is at one and the same time a subject and an object, or at the very least an object masquerading as a subject.[58] In this instance, the animated cannibals that threaten Mickey serve to underscore that disavowal: they, too, are alive, yet they seem unable to completely demonstrate their humanity. Mickey, too, seems to behave like a human, but he is also a mouse. Mickey is anthropomorphic; the cannibals are zoomorphic; together they offer a visual treatise on the racial underpinnings of subject–object relations, circa 1932.

This is the fetishistic magic of animation: any object in an animated world has the potential to come to life, and any living thing or even one of its body parts may be reduced to an object. Subjectivity is ephemeral and uncertain, granted by external circumstances and revocable. Thus, while *Trader Mickey* allows for the neat turn of providing a primer on the fantastic relationship between the savage and the minstrel, a compressed history of minstrelsy's anthropological conceit, Mickey would still be a minstrel, his subject status still contingent, regardless of whether he were threatened by cannibals. He was a minstrel before and after this particular cartoon. What this scenario permits is a study in contrasts: the cannibals are classic racist caricatures, but they are not minstrels. They do not obtain the status of pretenders to civilization because they have not yet bought into (or, more accurately, been sold into) relations of exchange. Mickey, on the other hand, as a trader in goods (and perhaps people), has. As a minstrel, Mickey embodies the animator's alienated labor: like the blackface minstrel who enacts the imperfect resistance of the recalcitrant slave, he may take pleasure in his rebellion, but he will never fully realize its fruits.[59] As a commodity that lives and works, Mickey enacts the fantastic relationship between property and labor, and in this, of never being fully the owner of his own self or his labor power. Minstrelsy is instrumentalism illustrated: the end men Tambo and Bones are both characters put on by their performers and the personification of the instruments they play, the tambourine and the bones: they are essentially instruments playing instruments.[60]

By 1932, four short years after Mickey's creation, his minstrelsy was already becoming vestigial, sharing the screen with other swing-era racial formations. Columbia Pictures' *Swing Monkey Swing* (1937) offers up an example of American animation's use of more overt racist caricatures to express the shifting boundary between object and subject, figure and ground.[61] Playing off of a popular "desert isle" theme, the film opens on a cabal of chimpanzee-like monkeys dancing in a circle to a big-band number reminiscent of Cab Calloway's "Minnie the Moocher" (1930). Sporting a derby like that of Fats Waller, the monkey most immediately in the foreground swings close to the (imaginary) camera and intones a single scat phrase. After his appearance, the monkeys invoke Calloway more directly by scatting "hidey hidey hi, hidey hidey hey" as another monkey swings in front of the camera, singing the song's bass line. The scene then cuts to a quartet of monkeys singing in the style of the Mills Brothers (who were famous for performing vocally all the instrumental parts of a jazz quartet). From the get-go the cartoon has invoked jazz as "jungle music" and rendered famous jazz musicians as singing simians. Yet a careful look reveals that the background to this jungle scene is a circle of huts, hinting at a human presence. That human presence is never fully realized. Or it might be as accurate to say that the presence is never fully realized as human: the huts belong to the monkeys, who logically, then, must be missing links, falling somewhere in the primate world between chimpanzees and humans. And they're missing links who swing, hard.

In fact, they swing so hard that soon the whole island rises up out of the waves and dances to the beat, as even the ocean slaps at the shore in time to the music. Jazz infuses and informs the landscape itself: it blurs the line between human and animal, between animate and inanimate. When the chimps play their clarinets and trumpets, the horns wail so hard that their bells become mouths—or the chimps' mouths travel through the horns, joining instrumental bodies to embodied instruments. Likewise, in a brief Afro-Caribbean segment, the monkeys' teeth take the place of castanets. Later, a monkey blows such hot licks on his clarinet that he starts a fire for everyone to dance around. Suddenly, the African jungle mixes with the Pampas, and with the ghettoes of the United States: some monkeys are dressed as gauchos but dance to the tune "St. Louis Blues." As the cartoon builds to a crescendo the cutting accelerates, and the red of the fire and the shadows of dancing bodies dominate the scene. After that dance, a male monkey sings a trumpet part while a female takes the vocals, performing a parody of juke-joint shouters like Ethel Waters or Bessie Smith. In the short's final production number, which consists only of different chimps rapidly repeating the song's chorus ("Got the St. Louis Blues / just as blue as blue can be"), the entire image shifts through primary colors—red, yellow, blue—as if the music were disrupting even the cartoon's color registration itself. This is an expression of race in a very different register from the minstrel antics of Mickey, Bosko, and Bugs: swing-era jazz cartoons made explicit the implicit racial formations that had helped shape trademark continuing characters, and in the process helped to occlude those minstrel origins with their brash, broad racist caricatures.

In the world into which this cartoon and *Trader Mickey* were projected, the free laborer maintained a real fiction of self-possession, of being able to divorce one's own body from its products in the act of exchange. This required, of course, a notion of surplus labor: the free laborer was understood to enter into negotiation with an employer to determine the value of her or his labor, the tacit understanding being that the employer would realize a profit from whatever excess value the laborer was forced to give up in order to complete the contract. (This, as Marx points out, is how the commodity-relation operates. The employer imagines profit as deriving from the commodity itself when it is sold; the worker understands profit as deriving from her or his inability to realize the total value of her or his labor when *that* is sold.)[62] It was a necessarily unequal operation, an unfriendly transaction masquerading as a friendly one, a hiving off and selling of a portion of one's self in order to maintain the rest. Artists who went to work for cartoon studios in the formative years of the American animation industry did so freely, and in doing so they agreed to perform extremely creative work under often onerous working conditions. Animation production at that time was not unlike other piecework industries, with journeyman animators churning out up to thousands of drawings in a day. Recall Bray's boast in 1917 that in his studio twenty workers turned out sixteen thousand drawings in one week; in a six-day week that would amount to almost three thousand drawings a day. In that regard, Van Beuren's *Making 'Em Move* (1931) was not far off.

Even beyond the particulars of work in the animation industry itself, the cartoon minstrel as resistant trickster speaks to and of a culture moving from nineteenth-century craft modes of production to twentieth-century rationalized mass production. Read in this light, Mickey and his ilk would be examples of what Fredric Jameson has called "a kind of homeopathic strategy whereby the scandalous and intolerable external irritant is drawn into the aesthetic process itself and thereby systematically worked over, 'acted out,' and symbolically neutralized."[63] Jameson was reading the impulse toward repetition and the use of mass cultural icons in modernist avant-garde production; extending that model to mass-cultural workers of the same period suggests only that the shock of the modern was felt by more than simply those of relatively more delicate and refined sensibilities.[64]

There is no doubt that Mickey and his ilk existed for the pleasure of others, and that the excessive violence visited by and on them, in a form often associated with childish joy and innocence, has long been a puzzle. In his critique of Hartman's analysis of the relationship between subjectivity and subjugation, and of the violence lurking in sentimentality, Fred Moten has noted that Hartman stops short of considering all the implications of the relationship of the slave (real or imagined) as subject and as *object*.[65] Specifically, Moten asks us to consider the slave as a fantastic object—the commodity that speaks. More than speaking, though, this commodity cries out in the pain of being both property and labor, of never being the owner of its self or—in the case of the commodified body (real or imagined)—of its own labor power. Wracked with the physical pains of torture, imprisonment, and forced labor, the slave also suffers from an internal division: as property, the person who is enslaved lacks the legal and ontological foundation to argue for her or his very personhood. How can a possession argue for its own independent existence? To do so would be to attempt to appropriate the property of one's self for one's self—for the slave, in effect stealing one's self from one's master. A necessary exception, the slave in its abjection serves to prefigure the constellation of labor in emergent industrial capitalism: "In the transition from slave labor to free labor, the site or force of occasion of value is transferred from labor to labor power. This is to say that value is extracted from the ground of intrinsic worth . . . and becomes *the potential to produce value*."[66] The slave body may, once harnessed, produce labor for the master, but even prior to that labor that body itself has discrete value. Thus, the slave is both the site and producer of value but never the possessor of either.[67] The free laborer, on the other hand, maintains the real fiction of self-possession, of being able to divorce one's own body from its products: "This transference and transformation is also a dematerialization—again, a transition from the body, more fully the person, of the laborer to a potential that operates in excess of the body, in the body's eclipse, in the disappearance of a certain responsibility for the body."[68] A paradox seems at play here. The slave (or minstrel or cartoon minstrel), by virtue of her status as object and property, is more fully embodied as a thing, useful for labor. The free worker, by contrast, is divided between her condition as the holder of labor power and her ability to dispense with that labor power as she sees fit. In this, the free laborer is abstracted, divided, pitted against herself.

According to Moten, this implicitly violent transaction will "crystallize, later, in the impossible figure that is essential to that possessive and dispossessed modality of subjectivity that Marx calls alienation. . . . Now the commodity is rematerialized in the body of the worker just as the worker's body is rematerialized as the speaking, shrieking, sounding commodity."[69] Which part of the worker is alienated from which? Which is figure, and which ground? An exception necessary for the rule, the slave in its vocal and physical abjection seems to give a perverse voice to the mute cries of the supposedly free worker's body as s/he has her/his labor wrested from her/him during a seemingly voluntary participation in the labor market. The performance of this abject black body, engaged in what Corin Willis describes as "overdetermined signification"—for the minstrel, expressed in everything from the verbal excess of the stump speech to the sartorial excess of wide cuffs and collars and white gloves, to the bodily excess of an oversized mouth and eyes, and even of jumping Jim Crow—articulates and delineates the mute cry of the alienated worker parted from her/himself.[70]

The animated minstrel, who progressed from the silent and self-manipulating Felix to the logorrheic hijinks of Bugs or Daffy, became over time the yet more fantastic embodiment of that cry, the displacement of the violence of the separation of one's labor from one's self (if not one's self from one's self).[71] A figure representing the descendant of the recalcitrant slave, this character was created as willful and resistant by the animator, made to be punished for resisting its own subjection, its own

FIG. 4.18 Sound made tangible: in the Disney short *Alice the Whaler* (1927), when the music of a jig made visible floats by, a parrot plucks a note from the air and eats it.

abjection. Hence one aspect of the primal, repressed, incredible violence of cartoons.

For Moten, this cry of *objection*, the sound of value rematerializing in the object body of the slave, is necessarily inarticulate: the subject's formation in and through language—the ability to speak of and for one's self—being something simultaneously inherent in the subject's coming to being and withheld from the slave-as-property. Integrated into a symbolic order that will override one's status as a speaking subject in favor of one's value as an object, the objecting slave will declare her/himself as an objection to that regime. If the very language that you would use to defend yourself names you as an object and not a subject, then it has betrayed you. Moten reads this necessary inarticulation as underpinning black radical performance in the twentieth century—the blues, jazz, poetry— as an act of refusal to acquiesce to regimes of commodification that cannot transcend race yet are not wholly defined by it either. To be a wage slave, after all—at least that part of one's self that must earn—is to be kin to the slave, and to freely give up one's labor, one must speak, must agree, must concede. The contradiction between subject and object embodied in both slave and minstrel is attenuated (alienated?) in the emancipated laboring body, but it is decidedly not gone.

This problem of the speaking commodity makes animation's transition to sound worth parsing carefully one more time. The continuing characters of the silent era, such as Felix, Ko-Ko, or even Disney's live Alice and her drawn companion Julius, lacking the power of speech, visually marked and remarked on their made environment, of which they were an uneasy part, using it against itself, sometimes even attempting to escape its bounds, into which they had been forcibly placed. Truly formed as an objection, apparently autonomous yet without free will, these continuing characters were forced to appear to resist the conditions of their making, then to submit to their masters for punishment for that very act of manufactured refusal.

THE ALIENATED LABOR OF ANIMATION

The animated minstrel, then, embodied a protest at the conditions of its own making and begged punishment for that very protest. This performance of condensation and displacement was the mechanism by which the animated cartoon was so easily integrated into blackface minstrelsy.[72] Only fifteen years passed between the industrialization of animation in the United States and its transition to sound. In that time, a robust but relatively insular cartoon business arose, based on a journeyman-apprentice system that trained up artists to be industrial workers and within which workers often shifted from one company to another in search of better wages, working conditions, advancement, and recognition. This system engaged entry-level workers in repetitive task work such as washing cels, erasing pencil lines, and (eventually) "in-betweening"—drawing the motion of characters between one gesture and another—over and over. Even lead animators, who were charged with character and story development, had that pleasure tempered by repetitive task work and long hours.

The cartoon minstrel was an embodiment of this rapid rationalization, an avatar of alienation. In this milieu conventions not only cohered quickly, they also spread from company to company through migrating workers. Popular characters were imitated, with only enough marginal differentiation to avoid litigation. Likewise, as in vaudeville and the silent live comedies of the period, gags that worked were lifted and repeated, creating a stable repertoire of repeating themes across product lines. In this creative labor environment animated minstrels—Felix, Ko-Ko, Oswald, Bimbo, Mickey, and others—representing the rebellious products of creative talent channeled into mass production, propagated incredibly rapidly. These animate minstrels, certainly not the sum total of the panoply of animated

characters of the time but equally certainly the most popular and enduring, embodied a commodified objection.

Another inflection of the cry of objection, the cartoon minstrel was
simultaneously made and yet seemingly autonomous, existing in a world
bounded by a frame within which it attempted to exert its will and within
which that will was thwarted. During the silent era, one of the signature
themes in cartoons was that of confinement and escape: cartoon characters regularly remade themselves or their drawn environment in order
to assert their will, to escape the bounds of the frame, or to fend off the
attention of the animator. Although the trickster of the swing-era sound
cartoon—Mickey, Bugs, Daffy, and others—became increasingly more articulate, its world also became more bounded as it became imbued with
an articulate speaking voice. Located in a world more distinctly separate
from that of the animator or the audience, the character shifted its violent
opposition to the conditions of its existence from the cartoon's frame to its
contents and denizens. Gone were the sing-alongs that signaled a world
outside the frame, and gone was the (hand of) the animator entering into
it to interfere with the character's autonomy and with the continuity of an
increasingly cinematic animated space. The Mickey of *Steamboat Willie* or
even of *Trader Mickey* could barely make more than an inarticulate squeak.
Yet compared to the more articulate Mickey soon to emerge, let alone the
loquacious Bugs or Daffy, he had more freedom to challenge the fundamental conditions of his making, more opportunity to acknowledge his
own existence as a made object—if somewhat less than his silent precur-
sors. There was, to put it in Moten's terms, in silence a lack of voice yet
also a lack of *being* voiced; as cartoon characters gained that voice (the
voice of another), they ceased to autonomously challenge the conditions
of their own making and regulation.

To see in something as seemingly trivial and ephemeral as a cartoon
short the expression of labor's protest against its own impressment may
seem absurd. Likewise, to associate the incredible and real history of violence against the bodies of slaves—confinement, torture, and rape—with
sadomasochistic performance (and also with cartoon characters) may
seem a grotesque trivialization of a horrible inhumanity. It is. And it has
been so in American popular culture for generations. Long before Winsor McCay capered with his animated creations, blackface minstrelsy was
very concerned with issues of labor, freedom, and desire; it still is.[73] Nor
is the association of sadomasochism with working through issues of labor

FIG. 4.19 In *On Strike* (1920), the cartoon characters Mutt and Jeff negotiate with their creator, Bud Fisher, over their hours and percentages on net profits from each film.

and power a gesture of petty homology for the sake of mere titillation.[74] For all that Leopold Sacher-Masoch's Severin does to protest the involuntary nature of his desires, he also necessarily performs a *willing* subjection.[75] At the risk of stating the obvious, unlike Severin, the slave is not free. The fantasy of the slave's (un)willing participation in chattel slavery as being rooted in a core animal self is inflected in the masochist's performative gesture of yielding to his master's will—and serves as a root act of the primal violence that charges sadomasochistic fantasy: the masochist uses his will to tame his will, to willingly become the slave. An actual chattel slave, on the other hand, is (imagined to be) a slave because his (or her) animal urges outpace his will and betray him to his captors. Yet as *Venus in Furs* makes clear, without the figure and fantasy of the slave, the sadist and masochist can find no ground on which to build their mutual fantasy, which is entirely taken up with exploring the limits of subjection and free will. Likewise, for the minstrel, animate or otherwise: her/his comic denial of the horror of slavery depends on that very horror.

Why would this be so in something as seemingly trivial as early American animation? For the animator of the early twentieth century, minstrelsy—a fading popular performance form—offered a ready-made fantasy of the rebellion of forced labor. In an art that went from an artisanal mode to a full-blown industry in the blink of an eye, the minstrel stood in for the animator as artist-for-hire, a creator become fabricator on spec.

Animators at the dawn of cartooning's industrial age were expected to be skilled artists and draftsmen and able to readily reproduce characters created by others. Continuing characters such as Ko-Ko or Felix became avatars of that impressment, simultaneously thwarted and assaulted and rebelliously and deviously fighting back against the conditions of their existence. More masochists than slaves—that is, performing a pantomime of "freedom of contract" in which both employer and employee pretend to meet as equals though they are not—early animators were willing subjects in an emerging industrial system, subjugating that will and their talents in order to participate, and to get paid. In the process, they made a commodity of their labor power—and displaced and embodied that act in the characters they made then compulsively punished.

The conventional marking of the continuing character as a blackface minstrel points to a complex interaction between animation studios and their audiences. Both animators and critics of animation have noted the form's indebtedness to minstrelsy, and the persistent popularity of minstrel characters in a commercial art form constrained by tight profit margins and highly sensitive to taste and preference indicates that the choice resonated with moviegoers. The animated minstrel, then, served as a touchstone in the changing racial formations of the early twentieth century. That these uses of the minstrel were not widely named as racist at the time, and that the direct associative links between the minstrel and the continuing cartoon character have been occluded over time, are both indications that in any cultural regime, dominant or otherwise, racial formations are not stable or consistent, and it is as much in tracing their alterations as in outlining their forms that the operations and applications of race become clearer.

With the coming of sound and films such as *Trader Mickey*, racist caricatures such as the cannibal king—themselves stand-ins for the profound matrix of desire and fear engendered in polite white society by the efflorescence of African American culture in the early twentieth century—joined the minstrel trickster on the screen.[76] In the process the more explicit links between the continuing cartoon character and the stage minstrel were subsumed in that emergent swing-era racial formation—not replaced but complicated and obscured. While the animator ostensibly freely sold his marketable skills and labor power to cartoon producers, his creations violently enacted a fantasy of enslaved labor unchained, rebellious and duly punished for a rebellion instigated by their creator. Whether for the creator or the created, a fantasy of consent was predicate to the violence that was sure to follow, and it guaranteed never to fully redeem a contract made in bad faith. Mickey Mouse may have been ubiquitous, but he was in the end "Mickey Mouse"—a cheap object repeated endlessly, made valuable through his own repetition, rising above his conditions only through the subjection of others.

IMITATION IS NOT THE SINCEREST FORM OF FLATTERY

Since his creation in 1928, Walt Disney Productions has suggested in its public relations that Mickey, far more than just a mouse, was actually Walt Disney's child. The studio even went so far as to build a tiny garage for his imaginary car on its Burbank campus. However, Mickey was not alone in his ambiguous ontological status: since James Stuart Blackton's back-and-forth with his lightning-sketches in the first decade of the 1900s, animators have played with the notion that cartoon characters, though they are made, are (semi) autonomous beings. What marks animation as a substantial expressive form, a place of contentious pleasure, is that at its best it maintains this tension between the ideal and the real. More so than live cinema, animation is produced and regulated as an other to what is real. Its alterity, its uncanniness, is contained in its very name: to animate is to enliven that which is not alive.[77] Animation produces an other that lives but doesn't, an object that perpetually threatens to become a subject.

Animated characters have never been cut from the same cloth as those of us who live in the real world. They are homunculi, distillations of behaviors, attitudes, beliefs, and prejudices; they are condensations of displaced desires and fears. For the sake of expediency and efficiency, animation has a tradition of drawing on stereotypes for its characters: in the seven-minute cartoon the stereotype was efficient because it allowed for the rapid recognition of a social hieroglyphic through character type, thence the easy designation of its proper social status. Scotsmen were cheap. The Chinese were hardworking and either excitable or inscrutable. The Irish were lovable but irascible drunks. Mexicans were lazy. And so on. Just as vaudeville performers found utility in stereotypes for their short bits, so did cartoonists. Where longer narrative forms permitted the emergence of characters over time, the vaudevillian gag used stereotyping to transmit a dense packet of social and cultural information in a short period of time. Stereotypes—the perversely ideal inflections of the real—were brutally efficient.

In this sense, the stereotype is itself a form of commodity fetish, a

FIG. 4.20 Predating and setting the stage for the practices of ethnic stereotyping in early animation, an ad for Larkin soap from 1881 depicts Irish immigrants as finely dressed apes in the style of Zip Coon.

crystallization of social and material relations, a way to effectively and efficiently sell a gag. At the same time, like a Freudian fetish, it is built around a disavowal: it is the aggressive refusal to acknowledge an object of fear and desire for what it is, and an act of replacing it with a substitute container for the affect of that desire and its repression.[78] The stereotype, even as it draws on the necessary social and corporeal substance of persons, is a disavowal of their basic humanity in favor of grossly exaggerated features that represent characteristics both feared and desired by an imagined dominant audience. And nowhere is this operation clearer than in the figure of the "darky" or minstrel, based as it is on the bodies of subjected persons denied their basic humanity. In this figure, and in stereotypes more generally, the real is necessary as ground and is necessarily repressed in the service of a functional and efficient ideal: the fetish is a shorthand for an experience simultaneously acknowledged and denied. In animation this has been all the more true because the artist puts pen to paper (or now stylus to pad) and feelingly produces the stereotype as totem, a sign for relations effaced then immediately made present in its tormented body. The conjuring trick that fueled this difference was, first and foremost, located in the hand that made the animated character that resisted it, a hand that asserted its own dubious reality in relation to what it had made, and that audiences accepted as their own avatar in this struggle.

THE HAND

Aggressivity is the correlative of a mode of identification that we call narcissistic, and which determines the formal structure of man's ego and of the register of entities characteristic of his world.

—Jacques Lacan, "Aggressivity in Psychoanalysis" (1948)

In early animation, the animator's hand (or a photograph of it) imparted life to an image of the Other, and then attempted to control it. Like the stereotype, this was a gesture of delineation, of creating clarity and with it control. Just as the disavowal at the heart of the Freudian fetish is a not-so-secret gesture toward one's own fragile integrity (isn't the same true for Marx?), so the mimetic gesture of the comic stereotype—the claim to know the essence of another—speaks of the struggle between sympathy and empathy. If it is hostile, this gesture is an attempt to deny any close relation with its object, to fend off the substantial affective reality of the Other, the threat of an independent being lurking outside the range of narcissistic projection. If it is merely sympathetic, this gesture is an equally narcissistic nod toward affinity through the acknowledgment of an intimate (mis)understanding of similarity *and* difference that assimilates the experiences of the Other into one's own.[79] Both bespeak an intensity of affect through disavowal, the incredible energy that informs that bizarre social gesture, which itself hovers between voluntary and involuntary, known as laughter. The hand of the animator, whether tracing an overt stereotype or producing the animated minstrel, serves as a metonymic interlocutor, feelingly producing a totemic body that stands in for his or her divided self, performing an aggressive act of self-preservation that knows itself as doomed yet cannot help but continue, compulsively, to repeat the act.

FIG. 4.21 Flip in *Little Nemo* (1911) seems to demand the attention of the viewer.

It is for this reason that the trope of the drawing hand is so important to early animation: the hand that draws the lines that appear alive is an appendage as important to animation as the eye that witnesses the illusion of motion and calls it life. If live-action cinema is the celebration of the abstracted eye and its refinement in realism our conventional entraining in scopic passivity (or, if you like, a fantasy of aggressive activity), then animation as a trade and a set of practices celebrates the moving hand, the hand that imparts motion. Like a child clamoring for its mother's attention, Winsor McCay's first animation, *Winsor McCay, the Famous Cartoonist of the N.Y. Herald and His Moving Comics* (1911), begins with the plaintive imperative "Watch Me Move." Yet the short film features McCay's hand as much as its animated products. The repeating trope of the intruding animator's hand in early animation was a gesture in two contradictory directions: one pointed to the lightning-sketch, a performative tradition in which the live *performance* of animation centered on the animator's deft hand as the locus of skill and transformation.[80] Yet if this one hand gestured toward tradition, skill, and craft, the other, which became in practice little more than a photographed cutout of a hand, pointed toward a paradoxical tradition of transgression. Having created the illusion of a separate and whole animate world, the hand intrudes into that world to remind us that that world is a fantasy and that it is *handmade*. The intruding hand tears at the seams of coherence and spatial contiguity, playfully pulling at the loose threads of suspended disbelief. It reminds the viewer of the film's status as a made object, of the incorporeal qualities of the bodies on the screen, of being a *viewer*. And it gestures to (at) the animated character both as living and as made.

FIGS. 4.22–4.23 Bugs Bunny intentionally destroys the film he occupies in *Rabbit Punch* (1948).

This convention is fundamental to animation's alterity: the animated character's insistence on its ontological status as a made object (or the animator's insistence on a place in the frame as its maker) creates a relationship between producer, text, and viewer that is fundamentally different from that offered in live-action cinema. We are reminded that what we watch was made "by hand," and in that awareness we acknowledge a difference. The animator and historian John Canemaker summed this up recently when he suggested, "I'm not that fond of literalism in any form of animation: I think the interpretation of the artist is the important thing, and how the hand and mind are seen in the product."[81] The things we watch on the screen, be they abstract lines and dots, rabbits and ducks, humanoids, or giant talking lemon candies, are alive yet unfree, tied always to the hands of their makers but made to strain at the leash. With live-action cinema, though, we grant agency and autonomy to the fantasmatic bodies that appear before us, indexically linked as they are to ostensibly living persons in an ontological realm that we presumably share with them. We believe that Brad Pitt and Angelina Jolie exist more or less as we do. On the other hand, in the world we inhabit, Mickey Mouse is at best a giant plush costume that houses a sweating, slightly nauseous "cast member" of indeterminate age, race, gender, and sexuality who stands in for the hand that animates the mouse.[82] The conjuring trick in animation is in the hand that makes the animated character that resists it, that asserts its own dubious reality only in relation to what it has made. Animation occupies an ontological realm adjacent to that of live cinema, and this proximity—and the many years of theoretical and production practices that have worked to keep the two apart—is part of what has delivered the promise of realism in live cinema.

WHO DAT SAY WHO DAT?

This hand, fading with the development of animation from a presence, to an indexical marker, to an implied presence, gestured not merely toward the abstracted process of making a cartoon; it also invoked in each iteration a landscape charged with the fantastic presence of labor and its appropriation. Whether in its performance of animated blackface minstrelsy or in producing racist caricatures, the hand feelingly constructed a geography that became coextensive with the world in which it was made and through which it circulated. American commercial animation contributed to the broader circulation of racial formations in both the nostalgic trope of the blackface minstrel and its more virulent cousin the racist caricature. An example of this circuit—discussed briefly in chapter 3—is the movement of the blackface duo Moran and Mack ("Two Black Crows"), whose stage show was also featured on radio and made into films such as *Why Bring That Up?* (1929) and *Anybody's War* (1930). One of their trademark routines eventually found its way into a 1936 MGM Happy Harmony cartoon called *The Early Bird and the Worm*, which features two crows who not only shun work in typical minstrel fashion but also borrow their dialogue directly from Moran and Mack:

MACK: You wouldn't be broke if you'd go to work.

MORAN: I would work, if I could find any pleasure in it.

MACK: I don't know anything about pleasure, but always remember
    it's the early bird that catches the worm!

MORAN: Uh, the early bird catches *what* worm?

MACK: Why, any worm!

MORAN: Well, what of it, what about it?

MACK: He catches it, that's all!

MORAN: Well, what's the worm's idea in being there?

[Continued argument.]

MORAN: Who wants a worm, anyhow?[83]

In the circuits that traced from this routine from the stage to the radio and to its eventual expression in a cartoon, the more explicit lines of racist caricature were absent—the blackness of the characters referred to obliquely through their depiction as (Jim) crows—but the vestigial markers of the minstrel remained for those who knew the referent in the original routine.

What was the difference, then, between the cartoon minstrel and subsequent racist caricatures? Associated with the native wit of the young "pickaninny" to which Otto Messmer referred in his description of Felix the Cat's origins (see chapter 1), trademark characters such as Felix, Mickey, or Bugs partook of the minstrel's fantastic blackness and redemptive disregard for the bonds of either social convention or physical reality. While the blackface minstrel was a *form* of racist caricature, it alloyed a fear of blackness with a desire for the freedoms imagined to derive from it, especially around the rebellion of unfree labor.[84] With the coming of both radio and sound film—and with them broader and more explicit expressions of an autonomous black culture, especially in jazz music—the more explicitly *negative* qualities associated with fantastic blackness

FIGS. 4.24–4.25 Intermediality in the early sound era: the blackface minstrels Moran and Mack circulate between the stage, radio, and the screen (and between the live and the animated) as the vestiges of the minstrel show and vaudeville stage are subsumed into newer forms of mass entertainment.

FIG. 4.26 In *Swing Wedding* (1937), jazz whips the frog musicians into such a frenzy that they destroy their instruments; one injects himself with music from a trumpet valve.

(fear, violence, lust, stupidity, etc.) were increasingly assigned to clearly marked racist stereotypes in animation, and increasingly detached from figures of rebellion and resistance. These more vituperative stereotypes found their expression in figures such as the jazz maniacs of *Scrub Me Mama with a Boogie Beat* (Universal, 1937) or *Tin Pan Alley Cats* (Warner Bros., 1943), who existed in a purely segregated world. Grotesquely exaggerated physiognomy, a simple matter in animation, and the admixture of fear and desire that charged popular reception of swing music and dance, for instance, were combined in these cartoons to produce caricatures that, while they shared a history with vestigial minstrels such as Ko-Ko or Bugs, differed in their direct, hostile, and far less ambiguous depictions of blackness. While continuing characters referred back to the minstrel—ostensibly a white or black man playing a nostalgic ideal of blackness—these caricatures simply and directly referred to raw racist stereotypes. Reading the MGM Happy Harmony cartoon *Swing Wedding* (1937), Lehman notes that "Harman-Ising turned the hip, urban Cotton Club musicians into unsophisticated rural blacks. The studio also caricatured them as frogs; former studio animator Mel Shaw recalled that because of their large mouths, frogs were considered suitable animals to depict as African Americans."[85] There were exceptions to the rule, however, as when Cab Calloway played opposite Betty Boop, an ostensibly white character. Even as his voice and dance moves remained unmistakable, he could be made "white" (as in *Old Man of the Mountain* [1933]) or roto-scoped onto an ambiguous minstrel character such as Ko-Ko (*Snow-White* [1933]) or a ghostly dancing walrus (*Minnie the Moocher* [1932]). More respectful only by comparison, these shorts made more explicit the chain of signification between the minstrel and the inchoate and anxious desire for black culture that it represented.

Another way to understand the relationship between the vestigial minstrel and racist caricature is through their ideal relationship to their audiences. A common tumult of reappropriated ressentiment associated with the slights related to assimilation and the struggles around nascent working-class movements offered early vaudeville and film audiences a communal performative space in which to experience/express similarity and difference, and the pleasure of that common experience was to come from the conversion of the expected sting of oppression into humor.[86] More simply put, stereotypical representations of ethnicity on the vaudeville stage and on-screen converted nativist hostility into a shared joke, a common experience of resistance. This was the vaudeville turn, the production of unexpected differentiation, the defamiliarization of the all-too-familiar realities of class and ethnic inequality.[87] Burlesque and early vaudeville had the potential to invert operations of power in a carnivalesque celebration of the underdog, and in doing so could offer an imagined reply to those structures; later, "big" vaudeville sanitized that performance somewhat for an imagined white, middle-class audience. In blackface, a minstrel such as Tambo or Bones referred to the plantation fantasy of the recalcitrant slave who resisted oppression through a combination of inherent jubilation and native cunning. In that carnivalesque turn, blackness served as a fundamental ground for difference, a place apart from those operations and, according to Rogin, a performance (by nonblack performers) that pointed to the possibility of transformation of ethnic others from tinged into white.[88]

Yet, again, the very power of the minstrel as trickster and as protest against power depended on the very inescapability of the real oppression that informed it. Because at the end of the day, when the house lights came up, as the minstrels wiped the cork from their faces or the screen flashed "The End," audiences likely left through different doors marked

FIG. 4.27 In *Ko-Ko the Barber* (1925), Max Fleischer is tricked into blacking up when Ko-Ko slips ink into his shaving cream.

"Black" and "White," if they even shared the same theater to begin with. Then a different sort of recognition set in, one of enforced and immutable difference, not of commonality. Yet even leaving through those different exits, the crowd dispersed into the same discursive matrix, within which metamorphosis and immutability remained inextricably intertwined. The animated minstrel expressed the power of transformation, and of escaping the confines of the animated space, precisely because the real people on which the minstrel was based could not escape larger institutional logics of race. Like his brother on the stage, the cartoon minstrel embodied the guarantee of the melting pot, the promise of changing one's circumstances, only because he was invested with the immutable charge of blackness, the racial alterity that came from alloying the subject with the object, the commodity with itself. Created by the animator and standing in for him, the animate minstrel enacted a rebellion against its commodity nature that was designed to fail. Circumscribed and legally delimited as other and elsewhere, blackness was powerful only in that commodity nature, in its distillation of the social and material relations that regulated the intercourse between subjects and objects.

The Fleischers, for instance, built this dynamic into the many gags in which their trademark character Ko-Ko used the ink from which he was made to foil Max—as when Ko-Ko would splash ink onto Max's white shirt or mix it into his shaving cream, causing him to inadvertently black up.[89] The animate character was a made object actively resisting the hand of its maker, with the added twist that the maker also created that resistance. While the Fleischers revisited this trope more often than most studios, it was a recurring trope in American animation—from Winsor McCay's struggles with Gertie, through Col. Heeza Liar's frequent winks at his audience, to Felix's deconstruction of the cartoon frame, Bosko's raspberry blown in the face of Rudy Ising, and Daffy Duck's desperate plea for order in *Duck Amuck* (1953). The cartoon character's disruption of the animated world of which it was a part marked the commodity's conventional and compulsive underlining (or delineation) and undermining of its own commodity status, the always failing fantasy of its autonomy. In the context of this compulsive convention, the stereotypical blackness of the minstrel reads as a shorthand marker for the worker resisting his or her own commodity status, a status imposed on him or her by the seemingly free choice of entering a virtually compulsory labor market.

VIADUCT? WHY NOT A CHICKEN?

Is such a historical and instrumental explanation of the genealogy of the racist practices in animation that led from the minstrel to the more racist caricatures of the sound era exculpatory? No, and that's not the point. The point might be the specific historical relationship between racist stereotypes and the humor that some people found or find in them. According to Dave Fleischer, Cab Calloway fell to his knees and rolled on the ground in hysterics when he saw the Fleischers' rotoscoped rendition of him singing "Minnie the Moocher" as a ghostly walrus.[90] But Calloway's purported willingness to laugh at himself being reproduced as a "spook" is not an absolution, any more than the widespread popular African American acceptance of *Amos 'n' Andy* in the late 1920s and 1930s is an indication of the accuracy or goodwill of the program's depiction of African American life.[91]

Nor does blacking up indicate, in and of itself, a performer's individual affinity with or hostility to African Americans. For example, it was possible for Bert Williams to black up, to complain of racist discrimination at the hands of a white dressing-room attendant, and yet to state, categorically, "The white men who have interpreted our race in this manner [of blackface] have done us no discredit; they have given apt expression to our humor and sentiment."[92] In such unresolved contradictions lurks the intense affect that charges racist laughter—an affect that policing does not undo. Veteran animator Dick Huemer, confronted with the suggestion that the crows he had a hand in animating for *Dumbo* (1941), one of which was actually named Jim Crow, were racist caricatures, was shocked, and responded that the "colored" choir that had voiced most of them "liked it very much and enjoyed doing it hugely. They even offered suggestions, and we used some of their ideas, lines of dialogue or words, little touches. . . . I don't think the crow sequence is derogatory. In fact, when someone mentioned the possibility to me, I was quite taken aback."[93]

The important and meaningful discursive work in instances such as this—with their focus on the words or acts of individuals—draws on a commonplace confusion between personal and institutional racism. Eddie Cantor, for example, was a brilliant comedian who made a name for himself as a blackface minstrel (among other talents), not because he created or even regulated minstrelsy but because he found in it one means for expressing his considerable talents. The same may be said for his friend Bert Williams, who, as Louis Chude-Sokei has pointed out, was a West Indian immigrant who blacked up to create African American characters—racist stereotypes through which he could create geographical, cultural, and political distance from a contemporary African American culture with which he was sometimes uneasy.[94] The intentions of the individuals in each of these instances are not as important as the discursive racial matrix in which those intentions and acts became legible. Their acts were racist, *and* they were funny to many. That humor gained some of its affective charge not in spite of that racism but *because* of it. As Dutch, Hebrew, or Irish acts used offensive stereotypes to take advantage of their transgressive qualities, so did minstrelsy. As with the absolutely necessary yet seemingly endless debate around the uses of the word "nigger," the purposes and effects of deploying stereotypes depended very much on circumstances, intents, and practices: within the moment of a stereotypical performance the weight of institutional racism could be manifested, felt, and dealt with in terms momentarily concrete and immediate. The damage didn't happen only onstage or on-screen; it happened within and in relation to a world in which African American audiences in front of those stages and screens were required to come and go through separate entrances, or to patronize black-only theaters, and watch seated separately, with "their own kind." The racial matrix, and the affective charge behind the associated humor, happened in the gap between the real and the ideal.

Yet the impulse to situate this work in relation to race, and sometimes to rationalize it, has been no less true in animation than elsewhere. Art Spiegelman, intentionally drawing on animation's uneasy racial history, has recounted how in developing the graphic novel *Maus* (1986), he drew the inspiration for his depiction of Nazis and Jews as cats and mice from racial caricatures in early cartoons.[95] In conversation, some animation collectors and historians have readily agreed that the white gloves, broad mouths, and overly large eyes that are standard for many animated characters derive from blackface minstrelsy.[96] Yet, a breath later, they have insisted that early animators' adoption of minstrelsy became sedimented in famous continuing characters for purely *practical* reasons: First, there was an issue of *contrast*: in the early days of animation, when the quality of film stock, cels, and lighting was uneven, black bodies were easier to register than white ones. (To fully accept this answer, we have to overlook all of the early "white" continuing characters, such as Heeza Liar, Bobby Bumps, and Dreamy Dud, who are somehow less well remembered today than their minstrel counterparts.) Second, *economy*: white gloves on a four-fingered hand meant less repetitive detail to draw, since hands were hard to render well. (This, of course, contradicts the argument for contrast, even as it appeals to efficiency.) Third, *clarity*: the large eyes and mouths and broad gestures were more emotionally expressive, which was important in the short form. Somehow, these technical limitations required recourse to blackface minstrelsy.

So, yes, indeed and yes, but: one explanation does not contradict another. Exploring a forbidden terrain where images and gags might be racist *and* funny, it becomes possible to understand that these sorts of practical explanations are all at least historically valid, *and* that the practices they explain (away) were still grounded in racist institutions and discourses. They are historically reasonable in that they may have served as rational explanations given by animators at the time their cartoons were made. But even if that were true, and even if we grant that those animators had far greater technical facility and a far better understanding of the shortcuts and tools that made for efficient and effective animation, it would not exempt them from the racial formations within which they lived and made their choices. That animators from the early twentieth century may have lacked the critical discourses available to animators today

FIG. 4.28 At the end of *Uncle Tom's Bungalow* (1937), Uncle Tom's gloved hand reaches through an iris-out to reclaim the pair of dice that he used to gamble his Social Security benefits into a stake for Eliza, Topsy, and Eva's life.

(i.e., that "they didn't think of what they were doing as racist") does not immediately mean that the choices they made were not of a piece with racial and racist discourses of the time.

But it is sometimes difficult to raise this point, that racist attitudes were the coin of the realm for ostensibly white artists and audiences of the day, because it seems to suggest a maliciously racist intentionality (or duplicity) on the part of the discursive founders of animation and their patrons. And if that were so, it would require good people to disavow those cartoons as wrong, and not at all entertaining. It would certainly be enough to argue that broad racist caricatures and the use of the vestigial elements of minstrelsy point to black stereotyping as underpinning early animation practices. Accepting this, it becomes more valuable to read the presence of racial and racist formations in the emergence of American animation in discursive, institutional, or structural terms rather than in personal ones. Whether any specific animator was or was not intentionally racist, the practices that animators by necessity entered into were, and that is worth noting. But it becomes a more significant exercise to explore how racial animus in animation was important to the joke itself, how the "ambivalence of stereotype," the imbrication of intense fear and desire in the same derisive image, alloyed fear of racial difference with desire for that difference.[97]

Humor is not resigned; it is rebellious. It signifies the triumph not only of the ego, but also of the pleasure principle, which is strong enough to assert itself . . . in the face of . . . adverse real circumstances. . . . By its repudiation of the possibility of suffering, it takes its place in the great series of methods devised by the mind of man for evading the compulsion to suffer—a series which begins with neurosis and culminates in delusions, and includes intoxication, self-induced states of abstraction and ecstasy.

—Sigmund Freud, "Humor" (1928)

In a 1928 essay on humor, Sigmund Freud revisited the psychology of what was funny at exactly the historical moment when the animated sound cartoon—with all of its very troubling dynamics of race, class, gender, and sexuality—was exuberantly bursting onto the scene as a popular form of short entertainment. Yet Freud, in describing humor as a violent rebellion in service (or perhaps honor) of the pleasure principle, knew the genteel, white society of Vienna, where he had dwelt for most of his life, far better than the raucous districts of the swing-era cartoon. This was the same Vienna that, also in 1928, attempted to bar the scandalously sexual and nonwhite Josephine Baker and her "heathen dances" from its streets and stages for fear of cultural pollution.[98] The former vaudevillian's "danse sauvage" and its associations with the jungle and the American ghetto, with "self-induced states of abstraction and ecstasy," titillated European audiences enough to make her enticing, hence a threat. Jazz, the mongrel music of America, had become a worldwide phenomenon, and in Europe the (sometimes celebrated, sometimes abhorred) eruption of the "jungle" into polite, white civilization threatened/promised to disrupt/accelerate its tidy march into modernity. For ostensibly white audiences—whether in the United States or Europe—blackness stood, in the guise of jazz, the minstrel, and the racist caricature of the lazy coon, as a rebellion against the strictures of white, Protestant, middle-class life and in favor of the pleasure principle.

In the United States, the brashness of movies, jazz, vaudeville, and minstrelsy sparked elite anxiety and a reformist impulse to shore up "civilized" behavior in a rapidly urbanizing public landscape increasingly crowded with uncivilized immigrants, migrants, and rubes straight off the farm.[99] For black audiences, of course, the psychic violence of the "civilizing" force could signify quite differently from the way it did for rural migrants and ethnic immigrants undergoing Americanization and urbanization. At the beginning of the Great Migration of African Americans from the South to the North, in the time of the coal wars and the Scottsboro trials, violence against black bodies was neither abstract (nor abstracting) nor necessarily, as Freud might have had it, simply internalized. The simultaneous performance in cartoons of blackness as primally powerful yet as pitifully abject seems more fruitfully understood in terms of identification than of internalization, hence through the interrogation of (one's own) laughter. In the fantasy of blackness that underpinned both racist caricature and the vestigial minstrel, cartoons offered up not a model for behavior as much as a test of affinity. In the case of laughter, they begged the question: which kind? What Freud outlines in the epigraph to this section is the difference, in brief, between laughing *at* (which he covered in detail in earlier work) and laughing *with*.[100] Or, more properly, he encourages one to consider the fine distinction between whom one chooses to laugh at, or to laugh with—the choice between the side of the subject or that of the object. Is it possible to laugh, not in sympathy with the violence visited on others, but with empathy for all on whom that violence falls (including, perhaps, one's self)? Maybe one meeting ground, one place where sympathy may reasonably give way to empathy, is in one's relationship to the commodity self—a relationship that the (performed) animator demonstrated so well in creating a commodified character designed to resist the conditions of its making and to suffer for that resistance.

Here the distinction between the animated minstrel and the broader racist caricatures of animation's "golden age" remains important. The trademark–minstrel character offered the image of a safe but violent rebellion against normative social mores and the strictures of rationalization, one in which the character's race was masked by the plausible deniability of its being an anthropomorphic animal or a clown. The race made literal in the racist caricatures presented the flip side of that desire, the fear that the symbolic and carnivalesque revolt of the minstrel would shade into actual rebellion, the disruption of a racialized social order by a vibrant, emergent African American popular culture. What had been in early animation a pantomime of the creature's rebellion against its creator, and its inevitable failure and discipline, became in the early sound era the literalization of post-Emancipation blackness as rebellious excess and its necessary and violent repression. The MGM short *Lucky Ducky* (1948), directed by Tex Avery, provides an example of a standard swing-era gag that compressed this cycle of displacement into a single series of actions: a

FIG. 4.29 An exploding shotgun shell transforms two witless hunters into pickaninnies in *Lucky Ducky* (1948).

seemingly vulnerable trickster character, in this case a mischievous duckling, chased by an enraged attacker, suddenly turns and savages that attacker by shooting him or blowing him up. Yet rather than being reduced to the carnage that reality would require, the attacker is instead blown into racist black(face) caricature, and becoming unwillingly "black" expresses his abject humiliation at the hands of the animate minstrel trickster.

In the aborted chase at the center of this gag, the motive force of the trickster/minstrel is made manifest: its potency derives from its very desirable blackness, and in that moment of violence the complex interplay between appropriation and subjection becomes literalized in the blackening of the desiring pursuer: be careful what you wish for. The gag articulates the danger in the amalgam of fear and desire that is the stereotype: an attempt to fully possess the raw power of the minstrelized object (such as Lucky or Bugs) may blast you into abjection. (Compare this to *Mickey's Mellerdrammer* [1933], in which the mouse intentionally blows himself into blackface in order to play Uncle Tom.)

The joke literalizes an omnipresent threat: do not desire too much, and do not identify too much, either. It is the color bar violently maintained all the way down to the ground, even in cartoons. The "compulsion to suffer" about which Freud speaks (to and from a certain neurotic subject position) could vary both in the degree of its interiority and in its objects. The compulsion to conform to white middle-class norms of socialization, itself internalized from within a larger set of social and material relations, was that which Rogin described as an avenue to whiteness for Depression-era ethnic Americans.[101] As has been well remarked for generations, for African Americans that internalization was a path to double consciousness, a potential act of violence against one's self, the internalization of oppression, and offered no guarantee of social acceptance or advancement.[102] Thus, the laughter that the joke might elicit is inflected differently by experience and by circumstance. As Glenda Carpio puts it, discussing the work of the late comic Richard Pryor: "In this and other performances . . . black folk 'see themselves as whites see them,' in the tradition of double consciousness articulated by W. E. B. Du Bois, 'but they like what they see,' and whites 'now see themselves from the outside as well; but they are content, for the length of the occasion, to lend their mechanical bodies to the comic machinery.' Blacks and whites 'laugh from different positions that go in and out of symmetry . . .' but 'they all laugh.'"[103]

Even for those making the transition from ethnicity to whiteness, that internalization carried with it the requirement of the repudiation of the object, and positioned real empathy as a gesture of historical self-immolation. Yet even careful distinctions between the forms and objects of the social (and sometimes material) relations from which shared laughter erupts leave only the uncertain possibility of a collective empathy overtaking a necessarily failed liberal sympathy.[104] Imagine a segregated audience—whites in the orchestra, blacks in the balcony—laughing together at the same animated caricature or minstrel. Except in the most compassionate and detached abstraction that sees such an audience as a unified whole, all sharing in the victimhood of racism's violence (in which an injury to one is an injury to all), the meaning of that laughter is not uniform, any more than is the fabric of struggle and violence that informs it. The investments of the various audience members are too diverse, as are their locations in the racial formation of the moment. To the potentially included, the threat of empathy in the context of the racist cartoon is that it may rob one of a precarious subject status. That is, to feel for others—to imagine feeling *as* another—carries with it the risk of becoming as partial and divided as those who are the objects of ridicule. Sympathy, on the other hand, is a safer choice that permits the illusion of subjective unity, denying the freedom to laugh *with*, leaving only the possibilities of censoriously not laughing, or of unsympathetically laughing *at*.[105] In all of this, the cartoon character, whether vestigial minstrel or racist character, serves as fetish, as a simultaneous embodiment and disavowal of these belabored social relations.

But there is, in the end, still laughter. This is where Marx's gloss on the fetish meets Freud's.[106] Both build their notion on a romantic anthropological conceit that has its roots in a fantasy of an African Other—a superstitious believer in the animate power of an inanimate object—as that which stands in materially for a larger set of historical forces whose open avowal would fatally disrupt the social order. (And both assume that fetish is the embodiment of an almost willful misconception of those forces.) For Marx, the history invoked in this operation is social and material/oppositional; for Freud, it is cultural and personal/integrative. Usually, Freud is read as describing the production of the fetish as a refusal to acknowledge the sexual difference produced through the violence of (imagined) castration. Yet that disavowal is also a refusal to accept the incommensurable tension between difference and similarity. In Freud's example, the boy witnesses in his mother and cannot face the threat of paternal castration that she seems to represent. He disavows her difference, replacing it first with a scarred similarity so horrible that it, too, must be denied, then with an object charged with the affect behind that disavowal. The situation is similar with blackness in cartoons. The tension that informs the animate minstrel (or the racist caricature) is twofold: it requires witnessing blackness as human—but as necessarily and simultaneously less so than whiteness (primitive, not in possession of one's self and one's labor, subjugated) and more so (naturally carefree and free from the bondage of labor and of civilized decorum)—and seeing the animated creature as living yet handmade. To paraphrase Marx, it addresses an audience that is hailed as selfmade but knows (and needs to forget) that it has lost the tools of its own making.[107] And so there is violence. And so there is laughter, the raucous screams of the (perpetually disavowed and disavowing) commodity.

CONCLUSION

In his study of American animation, *7 Minutes*, Norman Klein suggests: "Blacks in musical comedy had so powerful a meaning in American entertainment, and they were so often played by whites themselves, they almost transcended the issue of race itself. *Almost*, but certainly never entirely.

To say 'almost' merely captures the sense of how important 'blackface' was to the cartoon form."[108] While Klein admits to the centrality of African American music and dance, and of blackface minstrelsy, in the development of cartoons in the United States, he does not actually explore exactly why race and minstrelsy so deeply informed the art and craft of animation. Nor does he quite explain the incredible tension in his amazing claim—the tension that is concentrated in the word "almost." Perhaps the beginning of an explanation is in the strange ambiguity hiding in the use of "they" in the same passage. At first, it seems that Klein is speaking of the incredible influence of actual African Americans on the development of an (implicitly white) American entertainment. Yet as his thought unwinds, we discover that some of these influential blacks were actually whites in blackface, and that being authentically black seems to be not about race but about performance. As with the fetish, that performance is rooted in the material world, indeed requires it, but leads inexorably away from it. And one direction it leads is toward the hand that draws the animated minstrel who must turn on that hand, but only because it has been made to do so—by that very same hand. The cartoon minstrel was almost real, almost uncontainable in its contradiction. The white hand of the animator created in that animated minstrel a compulsion to rebel against the conditions of its making, and destined it to fail in that rebellion. And if that makes for laughter, then that laughter is complicated; it is sometimes nervous and hesitant. Other times it is raucous with guilty pleasure. As with its audiences, it is many and various. But it always begs the question of who is laughing, and how.

Yet the ambiguity of the audience and its relation to the minstrel is not the same as that which Klein confronts as he slips from delineating actual black performance into the register of minstrelsy. *That* fantastic blackness, premised as it was (and is) on an anxious white fantasy of rebellion, resistance, and countercultural critique, certainly requires as its ground actual African American life and culture, actual people. Yet only as a point of departure: the minstrel itself always hovers immediately over the body, no further than the distance between skin and greasepaint. In the formative stages of American animation, when blackface minstrelsy hovered between popularity and nostalgic reinvention, the minstrel offered a template for continuing characters in the form of the recalcitrant commodity rising up against the hand of its maker, against the frame, the very stuff of which it and its world were made. That these characters—Felix, Ko-Ko, Bimbo, Oswald, Mickey, Bosko, Bugs—were popular enough to catch the public's eye and imagination suggests that the fantasy, while originating on the drawing board and circulating from studio to studio as convention, found fellow feeling in its publics.[109]

To see in that fellow feeling something empathic is perhaps optimistic. And, parsing the difference between the animated minstrel and the racist caricature of the 1930s and 1940s, that optimistic reading is predicated on a notion of the minstrel as a conduit through which a shared resistance to an (un)equally shared commodity nature was imperfectly expressed— one that depended on the distance between the fantasy of blackness that the minstrel represented and the actual facts of African American life on which it depended. That is, at a moment when African American cultural life expressed something beyond the register of the nostalgic and safely contained rebelliousness, something truly human, the response of the studios was anything but empathic. Even as animation demonstrated a fascination with swing-era music and culture, it punished the avatars of their expression for a presumption of underregulated difference. Given the very distinction between those two modes of figuration—between the minstrel and the racist caricature—the laughter could not help but be different, and in the latter case could not help but be in response to texts that were vital and exciting yet very racist, a reaction to the promise and threat of autonomous African American cultural production. That the cartoon minstrel depended (and depends) for its vitality on the constant collapse of that distinction between figure and fantasy over which many a critic has stumbled over the years argues for a gentle reminder that behind each and every subject lurks a howling object much like ourselves, one that we can laugh with, rather than at.

THE "NEW" BLACKFACE

CARTOONS AND THE NEW BLACKFACE

When we were not working we frequented the playhouses just the same. In those days, black-faced white comedians were numerous and very popular. They billed themselves as "coons." Bert [Williams] and I watched the white "coons" and were often much amused at seeing white men with black cork on their faces trying to imitate black folks. Nothing about these white men's actions was natural, and therefore nothing was as interesting as if black performers had been dancing and singing their own songs in their own way.

—George W. Walker, "The Real 'Coon' on the American Stage" (1906)

This project has taken as its central object continuing cartoon characters, the drawn versions of animals and people behind which animation studios made their individual names, such as Disney's Mickey Mouse, the Fleischer Studios' Ko-Ko the Clown and Bimbo, and Warner Bros.' Bosko, Daffy Duck, and Bugs Bunny. Appearing in cartoon after cartoon, these characters served as living trademarks for their makers, and all were minstrels. These trademark minstrels, these living commodities, have much to say about the political economy of American commercial animation in its formative stages. These 'toons weren't merely modeled after minstrels; they were, rather, performing minstrelsy in a different modality. They were and are one more facet in a much larger matrix of racialized and racist performances that works to situate blackness and whiteness in a fantastic relationship with each other. That matrix has included other blackface performances, such as those by white nineteenth-century minstrels; black blackface minstrels of the late nineteenth and early twentieth centuries, such as the famous and popular blackface star of the stage and silent screen, Bert Williams; famous white minstrels of the vaudeville stage and movies, such as Eddie Cantor, Sophie Tucker, and Al Jolson; radio minstrels, such as Moran and Mack or Gosden and Correll; and alongside them Mickey, Bosko, and Bimbo. Those different performers of minstrelsy were all located within the broader conventions of racialized and racist representation. They were especially situated within visual iconographies of racist caricature and popular fantasies of African savagery, including anthropological model villages at world's fairs and international exhibitions; traveling "Zulu" shows; "native" extravaganzas, such as Williams and Walker's *In Dahomey* (1902) and *Bandana Land* (1907); "black-and-tan" stage shows, such as *Shuffle Along* (1921); and plantation and jungle-themed nightclubs, such as the Cotton Club or the aptly named Plantation. Yet cartoon minstrels, like the live minstrels with whom they shared stage and screen, perform more than the fantastic geography of imagined blackness; they also perform a complex play of interiority and exteriority—of the location of authentic being in the interplay between an exterior that is applied as greasepaint and costume and a body that becomes interior with that application.

To better situate cartoon characters within this matrix, it is important to reiterate that American commercial animation didn't borrow from blackface minstrelsy only its outward conventional tokens, remaining otherwise somehow separate from it. Animation became an active participant in that tradition, lending its own popular imprimatur to varied and different performances of minstrelsy. For that reason, in addition to closely reading and understanding the development of the cartoon minstrel, it has been necessary to spend significant space and time in other precincts of racial performance discussed in earlier chapters. Central to this project is the idea that an episteme, a racial formation, the organization of the means by which ideas can be thought and said, is stabilized in practice, and in its ongoing circulation through media and social locations.[1] The continuing cartoon character is one of several transit points in popular culture through which the blackface minstrel has passed, and out of which its meanings—and associated notions of black life, culture, and performance—have been momentarily stabilized and regulated. This study has centered on the animated blackface minstrel but by necessity has regularly set that cartoon character aside to discuss the production and performance of race at other points in the same racial constellation—themselves inflected and stabilized by the cartoon minstrel as it performed within its fantastic, animate universe. The performance of racial fantasy that is the cartoon minstrel cannot be read in isolation from other contemporary performances of that fantasy, or of the social and material tensions that informed those performances.

If the continuum of blackface performance begins sometime in the early nineteenth century and stretches forward to the present day, then the rise of minstrelsy in the continuing animated character in the first few decades of the twentieth century falls roughly in the middle of that span. The cartoon minstrel appeared during the onrush of the Fordist moment in the Industrial Revolution, with its celebration of mechanization, efficiency, and an increasing division of labor and labor power. It arrived with large-scale, mechanized global warfare, and with competition between the new mass media of vaudeville, motion pictures, and radio. And it came of age within the profoundly contradictory (hence extremely productive[2]) apartheid regimes promulgated under the rubric "separate but equal." It developed alongside and in tension with an increasing popular fascination with the performative, literary, and musical output of actual African Americans, and participating in profoundly contradictory anxieties about the social benefits and losses entailed in enjoying and valorizing that culture. For all of these reasons, the ongoing development of the animated blackface minstrel during the early twentieth century provides a fantastic terrain in which to witness the social and material tensions of an emergent modern mass culture, played out at the vernacular level.

Yet the performative mode in which cartoons met these very dramatic historical developments was not the melodramatic, so popular when animation began, nor was it the psychological realism that became increasingly popular on the dramatic stage and in early feature films. Instead, cartoons inflected the intense pathos of the moment through comedy. As with the live performers with whom they shared the status of "coon," cartoon minstrels embodied a nostalgic desire for a natural authenticity in the interplay between surface and substance, in which the greasepaint and body of the live minstrel became the ink and paper (or celluloid) that composed the 'toon. The minstrel as comic figure was a complex sign for the tensions inherent in that relationship, in which a performance of purportedly authentic blackness rested on and disavowed a whiteness perpetually insecure in its own ontological status. So that is where this study finishes: revisiting the relationship between the racialized regimes of authenticity and fantasy it has already explored and contemplating how that relationship might inform the different values assigned to authenticity in comic and dramatic performance in the early twentieth century. This final chapter will accomplish this by once again initially straying from the precincts of animation, but will return to them at its end to make a case for how and why the cartoon minstrel still provides a useful lens for reading expectations and anxieties around embodied authenticity today, as it did during the previous century. It will accomplish that reading not by rewinding again to the nineteenth-century beginnings of minstrelsy and working forward but by taking a moment to closely read relatively recent performances of blackface and then working back from that reading to the figure of the cartoon minstrel at the center of this project.

As much as it should have long ago, blackface minstrelsy has never really ended, and the likes of Mickey Mouse, Felix the Cat, and Flip the Frog are all merely passing players in its ongoing history. Compare the images in figures c.1 and c.2. The first is a playbill for Christy's Minstrels: it is 1855, and Edward Pearce Christy, having proclaimed himself the inventor of blackface minstrelsy in 1843, is on the verge of retirement. Founding Christy's Minstrels in upstate New York in the early 1840s, Christy helped fuel the craze for minstrel shows that began well before the Civil War and continued until the 1870s, when minstrelsy began to be subsumed first into burlesque, later into vaudeville. When E. P. Christy retired as a performer (he eventually leaped to his death from a hotel window in 1862), his troupe was taken over by his stepson, the minstrel and female impersonator George Christy, whose journal—a compendium of jokes, routines, and ideas for dance numbers he invented or happened to borrow from competing minstrel troupes—is now housed in the Special Collections Research Center of the University of Chicago Library. That journal is in large part a record of and node in a discursive circulatory system, through which the tropes of minstrelsy and its descendant forms have traveled—and continue to move.

The second image is a still from the film *Tropic Thunder* (Stiller, 2008). *Tropic Thunder* is a movie about the making of a Vietnam war movie, the last attempt of fading action star Tugg Speedman (Ben Stiller) to reclaim box office glory after a failed attempt at dramatic acting, as a mentally disabled man in a film called *Simple Jack*. Early on in *Tropic Thunder*, Speedman discusses the nuances of an Oscar-worthy performance with Kirk Lazarus (Robert Downey Jr.), an Australian Method actor in blackface and deep in the character of Sergeant Lincoln Osiris. In a trenchant analysis of performance, authenticity, and identity politics in Hollywood film (delivered in blackface dialect), Lazarus/Osiris tells Speedman exactly why his performance as Simple Jack failed. "Simple Jack thought he was smart," Lazarus/Osiris says, "but rather didn't think he was retarded so you can't afford to play retarded." That is, Speedman had to play his character as unknowing, as not realizing that he was in fact disabled. "Being a smart actor playing a guy who ain't smart but thinks he is," he continues, "that's tricky. . . . It's like workin' wit' mercury. It's high science man, it's an art form. You an artist. . . . Hat's off for going there . . . 'specially knowin' how the Academy is about dat shit. . . . Everybody knows you don't go full retard." That is, Lazarus/Osiris informs Speedman, an actor who wants to win an Oscar for a dramatic role never plays a character wholly defined by his disability. He must somehow seem by dint of a true, un-self-conscious nature, to overcome that disability: "Check it out: Dustin Hoffman, *Rain Man*, looked retarded, act retarded; not retarded . . . autistic, yeah, not retarded. Tom Hanks, *Forest Gump*, slow yes, retarded maybe, but he charmed the pants off Nixon and he won a Ping-Pong competition? That ain't retarded! He was a goddamned war hero. You know any retarded war heroes? You went full retard, man. Never go full retard. You don't buy dat? Ask Sean Penn, 2001, *I Am Sam*. 'Member? Went full retard, went home empty handed." This scene is about authenticity and (perhaps paradoxically) its instrumental uses offscreen. As Stephanie Zacharek put it in *Salon*, "The actors playing actors in 'Tropic Thunder' . . . see themselves as craftsmen striving for authenticity in an artificial world—which is why Stiller's Tugg Speedman, an insecure mess, tried to bring a patina of class to his career by playing that simple-minded farm boy." *Tropic Thunder* manages, according to Zacharek, to lampoon Hollywood's anxious search for an honest emotional performance that still has mass appeal, for a way to create a seemingly genuine character to whom everyone can relate— the result of which is inevitably a performance of nothing more than the actor's own narcissistic, anxious need to appear genuine and to be rewarded for it: "When, in the clips from this fake movie, Simple Jack utters a line like, 'It makes my eyes rain!' the joke isn't on the disabled. Whenever I hear a line like that in a real movie, I think, 'Who writes that crap? Or, more specifically, who has the nerve to think he or she can get away with it? The scene in which Downey's Kirk Lazarus dissects Tugg's 'Simple Jack' performance is the most brilliant excoriation of 'Rain Man'–style acting I've ever seen."[3] After the film's release, its filmmakers and actors engaged with disability rights communities in a healthy dialogue about the uses and meanings of satire. Yet what went relatively unremarked on both sides was the film's disturbing juxtaposition of mental retardation

PROGRAMME
FOR
THIS EVENING,
Friday, May 21st,

CHRISTY'S
Original and Popular Band of
MINSTRELS.

PART FIRST.

Medley Overture ....Full Band
Quartette—Come Darkies Arouse—Parody.......................Company
Happy are we, darkies so gay—Parody from the Opera of " La
    Bayadere,"...E. P. Christy
Cinthia Sue—Original Melody.................................T. Vaughn
Grin for the Oak—Parody.......................................S. A. Wells
Duett—Bones and Violin.......................G. N. Christy & R. Hooley
Lucy Neal—Original...E. P. Christy
Stop that knocking—*Original Operatic Burlesque*......T. Vaughn
Julia is a Hansome Gal...T. Vaughn
Git along home my Yaller Gals—Original...................E. P. Christy

BURLESQUE LECTURE ON PHRENOLOGY,
S. A. Wells, & G. N. Christy

PART SECOND,

Portraying the Peculiarities of the Southern Plantation Negroes
Lynchburg Town—Banjo Melody.................T. Vaughn & E. Pierce
My old Aunt Sally.........Messrs. Wells, Vaughn, Pierce, & G. N. Christy
Rail Road Overture...Full Band
Walk in the Parlor...T. Vaughn
Picayune Butler...E. P. Christy
Sugar Cane Green—Parody....................................S. A. Wells
Git along John—Plantation Melody...........................E. P. Christy
Who's that knocking at the Door ?............................T. Vaughn

DOWN IN CAROLINA
Introducing the Cornshucking or Festival **DANCE,**
G. N. Christy & E. Pierce

After which, an Original and highly amusing Burlesque on the popular SWISS BELL
RINGERS, entitled the

COWBELLOLOGIANS,
Or Virginia Bell Ringers.

VIOLIN SOLO—" Sprig of Shillelah,"—with Variations.....R. HOOLEY
....G. N. CHRISTY
FINALE—Burlesque on the popular and Fashionable
    POLKA ....G. N. CHRISTY & T. VAUGHN

Front Seats reserved for Ladies.

Doors open at Seven—Concert to commence at a quarter past Eight o'clock.
Change of Programme every Evening.

Admission 25 Cents.
Children under Ten Years, accompanied by their Parents or Guardians, HALF PRICE

Appropriate Seats will be reserved for the Accommodation of Ladies & Children.

PARTICULAR NOTICE—Gentlemen are respectfully requested Not to beat the Time with
their feet, as it is a source of annoyance to the audience generally, and confuses the Performers.

FIG. C.2 Ben Stiller and, in blackface, Robert Downey Jr. (son of vocal minstrel Robert Downey Sr.) in *Tropic Thunder* (2008).

and an imagined essential African American experience. Also unarticulated was what it might say about the authenticity of that experience in the United States of George W. Bush—whose post-Katrina behavior even Kanye West had questioned—opening onto the eve of Barack Obama's election as president.[4]

Yet there was more than just Method to the madness that the film sent up. Just as George Christy inherited the craft of blackface from his father and refined it, so had Robert Downey Jr. Blackface is a family thing for the Downeys, too. As was discussed in the introduction to this book, in 1969, while making *Putney Swope* (Downey, 1969), when Robert Downey Sr. decided that Arnold Johnson, the actor playing Swope, didn't sound black enough, he dubbed in Swope's voice himself, apparently assuming that he could render the sound of a real black man better than an African American actor could. In that gap between the body of an African American man and a white fantasy of blackness is a representational space where uneasy tensions between ideals of self and performativity dwell.

Robert Downey Jr. was cast in *Tropic Thunder* as a character as obsessed with racial truth as his father was. Rather than simply donning blackface, Downey's character, Kirk Lazarus, actually undergoes surgery to alter his pigmentation. As the PR for *Tropic Thunder* made clear, Downey was a natural for this role, because like his character he was a Method actor known for his immersive acting techniques, volatile temper, and emotional instability. This observation tended to overshadow the Downey family's apparent belief in blackface minstrelsy as a living performance tradition and family craft. As with any racial performance, when it comes to blackface minstrelsy, the motivations are always complex and the modes and opera-

FIG. C.3 In *Putney Swope* (1969), Arnold Johnson starred in the title role, but Robert Downey Sr. provided Swope's voice.

tions always very historically specific. What E. P. Christy did with black-face in the 1840s was different from what George Christy did with it in the 1850s; what Robert Downey Sr. intended with blackface voice in the 1960s seems far from his son's blackface performance in 2008.

Yet they are all intimately related, sharing a fantasy of an authentic self that resides somewhere in the interstices of racial difference, one that takes its affective vitality from an enduring trope of whiteness as always inauthentic when compared to blackness—a fantasy in which the acknowledgment that race is both real and imagined paradoxically reinforces the relative genuineness of blackness. In fact, even as it depends on the material touchstone of actual African American bodies, the *performance* of fantastic blackness paradoxically becomes an epitome of authenticity *because* it is imagined—as if imagination were an act of condensation in which desired qualities associated with blackness—somatic ease, verbal wit, an inherent resistance to unwarranted authority—are located in an ideal body, one sometimes performed by an African American, at other times by a white person in blackface, and sometimes by a cartoon character. That was true when Robert Downey Sr. gave voice to Swope in 1969; it remained true when Robert Downey Jr. created the character Kirk Lazarus performing in blackface as Sergeant Lincoln Osiris in 2008.

FIG. C.4 Robert Downey Jr. as Kirk Lazarus / Lincoln Osiris regards himself in a mirror in *Tropic Thunder* (2008).

FIG. C.5 Ben Stiller as failing action star Tugg Speedman in the role of the mentally disabled Jack in *Simple Jack*, the movie-within-a-movie in *Tropic Thunder* (2008).

Those notions of racial authenticity are also key to understanding *Tropic Thunder*, but the movie expresses them in terms that would have been confusing in 1969, let alone 1869. When *Tropic Thunder* premiered in 2008 it was met with outrage—but not over its use of blackface. Rather, the most vocal public protests were about the film's gratuitous use of the word "retard" and in its patently offensive portrayal of mental disability in cut-scenes from the imaginary movie-within-a-movie, *Simple Jack*. In the heat of anger over perceived slights to the disabled, the film received relatively little criticism for Downey's blackface performance, which Roger Ebert described as "not merely funny but also very good and sometimes even subtle."[5] And *Entertainment Weekly* claimed of Downey that he "elegantly dispatches the *mishegoss* of Method acting with his double-difficulty feat of playing Kirk Lazarus, an Oscar-loaded Australian artiste who com-

mits to the role of an African-American soldier by undergoing skin pigmentation . . . and speaking in a Shaft-meets-Uncle Ben patois even when
the camera is off."[6]

Part of the reason for a lack of widespread outrage over a white actor
playing a black character in 2008 was that it is deftly internalized within
the film itself, through the character Alpa Chino (Brandon T. Jackson)—
his own name a play on histrionic Method actor Al Pacino—who repeatedly rails against Lazarus for his appropriation, not of genuine African
American culture, but of its minstrelized performance. In one scene,
Lazarus/Osiris reacts to Speedman calling the film's ragtag band of actor/
soldiers "you people" by snapping, "What do you mean 'you people'?" To
which Chino asks Lazarus, "What do *you* mean 'you people'?" In another
scene, Lazarus/Osiris sets Chino off by quoting the theme song from *The
Jeffersons* ("took a whole lotta trying just to get up that hill . . .") as a call
to avoid a politics of division and resist oppression. This maneuver, and
Chino's character more generally—whom *New York Times* critic Manhola Dargis described as "mainly around to mock Kirk's impersonation,
which is the filmmakers' way of having their chocolate cake and eating it
too"—signals a knowingness that is truly of the postracial moment we
purportedly occupy today.[7] Like Jon Stewart's occasional use of black gospel singers as a critical counterpoint to his fictitious news reports, the
film heads critics off at the pass by preemptively raising the criticism during the act of offense, with the hope of making any subsequent complaint
seem redundant and stale.[8] Likewise, the film's repetitious use of multi-
layered self-reflexivity generates around itself something like a gestural
authenticity field: so much seeming knowingness anticipates the censo-
rious as less genuine in their unreflective objections: it isn't the jokes that
are hackneyed or offensive, it's the impulse to criticize them that is. Or,
as Lazarus/Osiris notes when Chino calls him on quoting *The Jeffersons*,
"Man, just 'cause it's a theme song don't make it not true." Which is to say,
yes, exactly. It is not true, not real. Hence more true? To which one might
reply—though one shouldn't—well, that's retarded. But I said I shouldn't,
so it's okay that I did. I'm just keepin' it real.

It would be reasonable to criticize *Tropic Thunder*'s equation of mental disability with racial inferiority as offensive and leave it at that. Reading past the outrage, though, one can better observe the mechanism that
generates it grinding away: the film presents both mental disability and
blackness as epistemologically purer, more authentic, than an implicitly
white higher mental functioning. The term "simple" in the title *Simple*

Jack, or Osiris's bromides borrowed from popular culture, all speak of a shared simplicity of vision, a shared outsider status, a tacit refusal to acknowledge complexity or ambiguity. While Jack and Osiris are both structurally disadvantaged, they are simultaneously privileged in a regime of authenticity by their exclusion from self-doubt and self-denigration. And, lest we forget, both are characters performed by actors playing actors in an already fictitious narrative. This idea is not lurking in a subtle and allusive subtext; it's a nod and a wink away. Lazarus (risen from the dead), deeply immersed in the blackface character of Lincoln Osiris (emancipating god of the dead) counsels the onanistically named Tugg Speedman on the dangers of becoming so immersed in one's character (going "full 'tard") that one loses sight of one's real self. There must always be some indication that the actor who invokes the character waits in the wings, out of sight — like a white man in blackface who is hiding in the open.

This seems a contradiction: authenticity is genuine only when it performs its own self-awareness. This contradiction is key to understanding the importance of Method acting to the plot of *Tropic Thunder*. The Method is traditionally and popularly associated with dramatic performances of universal human truths.[9] Acclaimed dramatic actors such as Meryl Streep or Daniel Day Lewis are routinely praised for finding emotional truth in their roles, for an authenticity grounded in the fusion of their own experience with that of their characters. Comic acting, by comparison, is generally considered more particular, less universal, hence inferior due to its own self-referentiality and intentionally anxious self-awareness. The comic actor never pretends to disappear into a role the way the dramatic actor does. She plays against the Method, finding doubt where the dramatic actor finds surety; where the dramatic character expresses blind and fatal certainty, the comic character performs a knowing uncertainty. A banana peel on the road to Delphi might have spared Oedipus and his family a good deal of grief.

It is in relation to the Method and its prescription for plumbing the actor's emotional life to create a character that Robert Downey Jr.'s biography becomes significant. In its self-referential asides, *Tropic Thunder* makes it clear that there is little distance between Robert Downey Jr. the Method actor playing Kirk Lazarus, and Kirk Lazarus the Method actor playing Lincoln Osiris. Downey has long been notorious for his emotionally turbulent personal life. During the 1990s and early 2000s, he was repeatedly arrested on drug charges and seemed to be not only trying to destroy his career but to take his own life: the film winkingly assigns

FIGS. C.6–C.7 Meryl Streep, in *Sophie's Choice* (1982), and Daniel Day Lewis, in *There Will Be Blood* (2007), are exemplars of the relationship between inner and outer life that marks Stanislavskian Method acting.

that biography to Lazarus. In this performative mise en abyme, each level aspires to yet mocks the notion of absolute authenticity, replacing it with a play of surfaces. In the film, blackness serves as a referent, not to the genuine authenticity of a Method actor but to the performed authenticity of a comic parody of the Method. To quote Lazarus as he is interviewed by *Access Hollywood*, "Being an actor is no different from being a rugby player, a construction worker, save for the fact that my tools are the mechanisms that trigger human emotion."

That's the joke. At the beginning of the previous century, Henri Bergson declared that the "comic . . . appeals to the intelligence, pure and simple; laughter is incompatible with emotion. Depict some fault, however trifling, in such a way as to arouse sympathy, fear, or pity; the mischief is done, it is impossible for us to laugh."[10] If we take Bergson at his word, we can see the humor in Kirk Lazarus's statement: his heartfelt attempts to present an emotional truth (as sophomoric as they might seem to some) appeal to the head rather than to the gut. By comparison, Alpa Chino rapping and hawking his energy drink, Booty Sweat, is somehow more genuine for his lack of trying to be more than he is.

Earlier in the same essay, Bergson makes a serendipitous gesture toward the role of authenticity in the production of the comic. In words that (with a few changes) might well apply to Lincoln Osiris, Bergson asks, "Why do we laugh at a head of hair which has changed from dark to blond? What is there comic about a rubicund nose? And why does one laugh at a negro?" What is it, he asks, about comic performance, about the drunk and the Negro, that makes them inherently funny to an imagined spectator such as himself? "The correct answer was suggested to me," he says, "one day in the street by an ordinary cabby, who applied the expression 'unwashed' to the negro fare he was driving. Unwashed! Does this not mean that the black face, in our imagination, is one daubed over with ink or soot? If so, then a red nose can only be one which has received a coating of vermillion. And so we see that the notion of disguise has passed on something of its comic quality to instances in which there is actually no disguise, though there may be."[11] Why *does* one "laugh at a negro"? Because, in Bergson's estimation, it would seem that the imagination cannot separate the man from the minstrel.[12] Bergson's discourse on the comic potential of blackness ends on a note of anxiety and uncertainty about whether dark skin is hiding something or not. There is no disguise—though there may be. Authenticity seems to dwell not in the depths but in a proper understanding of the relationship between surface and interior.

This uncertain relationship between interior and exterior is important for understanding the comic turn. Reviewing Hegel's take on the operation of the universal in epic, tragic, and comic modes of performance, Alenka Zupancic suggests that dramatic performance (in which the twentieth-century Method has found perhaps its most fruitful expression) hinges on the shared conceit that the dramatic actor embodies her character at the expense of her own subjective presence; but the comic actor—so indebted to physicality and to her own uncertain existence—never wholly disappears into *her* character. Here, the dramatic is the inheritor of the epic: classical Greek actors in the epic mode were ostensibly possessed by their masks—through which gods and characters spoke—and in this way became conduits through which the universal appeared in the world. Likewise, Method actors are understood to offer up genuine performances because they become un-self-conscious, accessing the depths of actual emotional experience in their characters through their own "sense memories," which dwell in the preconscious or perhaps even in the unconscious. Higher mental functions such as self-reflection or self-doubt are to this fragile compact the failings of an erring humanity barring the way to pure, universal emotions that would, in their affective clarity, their animal timelessness, speak like gods through the social masks we place between ourselves and the world.

Are there sense memories, then, for comic actors? For Zupancic, where comedy is concerned, it would seem that the Method is madness. There is no collapse of the actor into the character, and no emergence of universal truth in that collapse. Instead there is a necessary tension between the actor, the character, and the performing subject that the two together represent. In comedy, Zupancic suggests, the distance between the actor and the character is productive; it is where the subject emerges. Comedy depends on dividedness, on a struggle between the actor and her character in which the character, godlike, does not overwhelm the actor, nor the actor merely invoke the character: "This coincidence of the self (the actor) and his character means that the split between the two now moves to and inhabits that character itself (that is, the essence), and it is precisely this inner split that constitutes the place of the subject in the character. This is why, when speaking of comedy, we cannot say that the subject-actor represents a (comic) character for the spectator, but that the subject-actor appears as that gap through which the character relates to itself, 'representing itself.'"[13] For Zupancic, the comic subject-actor performs as the obverse of the dramatic Method actor. In evoking sense memories and emotional truths, the Method actor creates an experience of the universal as immanent and channeled from elsewhere. The comic actor maintains a tension between performer and character, and the spectator must always acknowledge the actor as that "gap through which the character relates to itself." This triadic relationship—actor, character, spectator—signals the presence of what Zupancic refers to as the *concrete universal*.[14] It is a reflexive performance that refers to a self that is neither wholly actor nor character—nor the collapse of one into the other—but an ongoing oscillation between the two, itself witnessed by another.

This difference between the operation of the universal in dramatic versus comic acting is captured in two scenes from *Tropic Thunder*. The first is the speech quoted earlier, in which Lazarus/Osiris schools Speedman regarding his failure in *Simple Jack*. Lazarus/Osiris lays that shortcoming on Speedman's misunderstanding of what audiences expect from the

Method. If, in the Method, Jack is meant to be a refraction of Speedman's own sense memories, then to evoke Jack, at his core Speedman would have to have been at some time mentally disabled, a "full 'tard," which he was not. By definition, disability is not universal, it is specific; therefore, in the logic of the Method, in and of itself it could not be accessible through sense memory. Speedman/Jack's audience was forced to locate in his performance the contradictory condition of a seeming universal disability, a contradiction they could not safely celebrate without implicating themselves in that contradiction. What Speedman reveals in *Simple Jack*, according to Lazarus/Osiris (a white man replacing his own internal inauthenticity with the greater external truth and soul of blackness), is that his emotional core does not harbor the universal but the particular and the damaged. There is no there there. Speedman's disability is his narcissism, his lack of access to any emotion other than anxious self-regard. Had he been able to locate the raw emotional truths that inform that anxiety, he might have generated a more genuine performance of a disabled man with similar emotional issues, who necessarily wouldn't have been a "full 'tard." The only truth his performance as Jack accomplishes is that of Tugg Speedman's own desire to be believed, and through that, to believe himself. In other words, Speedman attempted to translate a partial emotional disability, his insecurity, into a total mental disability, which the fictional audience of the drama *Simple Jack* subsequently rejected on those grounds—but which we, the audience of the comedy *Tropic Thunder*, can accept as an authentic performance of failing authenticity.

All of which is to say, what audiences expect of Method acting is not genuine authenticity but an authentic performance of authenticity. *Tropic Thunder* parodies this expectation by rendering it within a relatively authentic performance of inauthenticity. Jack is Ben Stiller's authentic comic performance of Tugg Speedman's failed attempt to embody disability. The payoff of that joke, the reversal of the universal, comes at the film's climax. Speedman, captured by Vietnamese drug lords and forced to perform as Simple Jack over and over, becomes lost in the role. Gone native like Marlon Brando's Colonel Kurtz in *Apocalypse Now* (Coppola, 1979), he confronts Lazarus/Osiris (who's come with two other actors to rescue him) with Lazarus's *own* tragic flaw: his use of the Method to avoid his own inherent sense of inauthenticity:

LAZARUS/OSIRIS: You better focus up now motherfucker and say it. Say, "It's me, Tugg."

SPEEDMAN [flatly, without affect]: It's me, Tugg.

L/O: That's right! Now, Tugg who?!

S: Tugg who I dunno who are you?

L/O: Me?! I know who I am! I'm the dude playin' the dude disguised as another dude . . . ! You a dude don't know what dude he is!

S: Or are you a dude who has no idea what dude he is and claims to know what dude he is . . . by playing other dudes—

L/O: I know what dude I am!

S: You're scared.

L/O: I ain't scared! Scareda what?!

S: Scared of who?

L/O: Scared of who?!

S [sotto voce, holding up a mirror to L/O]: Scared of you! . . .

L/O [sees his face in mirror and dashes it to the floor, falling to his knees]: He's right you know. I am NOT Sergeant Lincoln Osiris! [pulls Afro wig from his head] . . . [Irish accent] Nor am I . . . Father O'Malley [removes his sideburns and beard] . . . [Texas accent] or Neil Armstrong! [removes brown contact lenses] . . . [Australian accent] I think I might be nobody!

The expression in this scene of what Zupancic calls the concrete universal happens in the performance of the shattering of a performed unity of self for comic rather than dramatic effect. What makes the comic performance more genuine than the dramatic is its embrace of its own inherent inauthenticity: after Lazarus strips away Osiris, Father O'Malley, and Neil Armstrong, he yanks brown contact lenses from his eyes to reveal absurdly blue contact lenses in the eyes of Robert Downey Jr., who whines, in a bad Australian accent, "I think I might be nobody." The audience has been given plenty of cues up to this point to understand that Lazarus is not nobody: he is the character that Robert Downey Jr. is playing—one that draws not on the inner turmoil that nearly took Downey's life, but on its outward manifestation in the tabloids. The truth of that performance resides neither in the pathos of Lazarus's inner lack nor in Downey's but in the irreducible tension between the two.

What Zupancic describes is a general condition, a model of how an unmarked comic performer evokes the concrete universal. Like Sergei Eisenstein's notion of plasmatics, it has the potential to seem contradictory: the undifferentiated stuff of the performance/animated character can only be witnessed in that which has always already become substantial

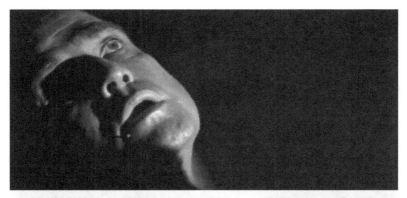

FIGS. C.8–C.9 Marlon Brando as Colonel Kurtz in *Apocalypse Now* (1979), and Ben Stiller as Tugg Speedman/Simple Jack in *Tropic Thunder* (2008).

in its specific and differentiated form. We infer its presence only from its substantial appearance in the phenomenal. This should give some indication of why, with the exception of necessarily problematic performances of Othello by white men, blackface has been reserved largely for comedy. The blackface minstrel—whether performed by a white or a nonwhite actor—is not performing the authenticity of blackness. Nor is she or he necessarily performing the inauthenticity of whiteness. Rather, the performance is of the authenticity of blackness *relative* to whiteness, and of the inauthenticity of whiteness relative to blackness—and always in the terms of the historical moment through which each is invoked.

Some have claimed that following the election of Barack Obama in 2008 the United States has somehow entered a postracial moment. It would be more useful to say that the moment we now occupy is one in which mutually constitutive and often contradictory conceptions of racial difference that have presented themselves in historically specific ways at other moments have come to the fore now as aggressive performances of

FIG. C.10 White Australian comedian Chris Lilley in blackface as the rapper S.mouse in his video *Animal Zoo* (2011).

the struggle over the relative value of authentic identity. In the simultaneous contraction of the American middle class, the ongoing immiseration of its poor, and the concomitant rise of network cultures, claims to authenticity have become increasingly momentary, fraught, and valuable. In this moment, blackface has become a surprisingly popular means by which to mobilize race as critique—for better or worse. Recent instances of this "postracial" performance are too numerous to mention, but a few include the drunken church lady Shirley Q. Liquor (Chuck Knipp); *30 Rock*'s use of blackface to describe failed attempts at postracial and post-feminist behavior (see the introduction to this book); the foolish, narcissistic rapper S.mouse, played by Chris Lilley in *Angry Boys* (ABC, 2011[15]); Ricky Gervais and Stephen Merchant's casting of a purportedly lesbian dwarf in blackface as the epitome of identitarian particularity gone wrong in *Life's Too Short* (BBC, 2011–2013); or Billy Crystal reprising his imitation of Sammy Davis Jr. at the 2012 Academy Awards ceremony. Each of these so-called moments of "new blackface" performs the knowingness of its creators regarding the wrongness of their performance. Authentically inauthentic, they capture the real discomfort of racial difference reduced to the bodies and situations through which it is presented. What remains untouched and always present in these "new blackface" performances—yet which emerges with a vengeance in comments and critiques of them—is how the reduction of racial difference to bodies or to performance leaves relatively untouched the structural and institutional forces that fuel the regimes of difference and of oppression considered so essential to their "truth and soul." Each gesture at knowingness is a performance of that same "postracial" short-circuit by which the self-awareness of the performance itself evokes bigotry for the sake of its disavowal—which therefore can't truly be racist, because what right-thinking person would knowingly be so? The postracial moment in comedy depends on an anxiety about the genuineness of an experience of self in a subjective economy of scarcity in which that authenticity is measured against its perceived proximity to oppression.[16] In this economy, donning blackface is ultimately a tragic gesture toward the failure of meaning, the falling of the concrete universal toward the untidy abstraction of the unreflexive self. As Zupancic has put it, "Comedy knows very well, and puts into practice, the following crucial point: we really encounter nonsense only when and where *a sense surprises us*. What comedy repeats (repeats, not reveals, since revelation is not the business of comedy) in a thousand more or less ingenious ways is the very operation in which sense is produced in a genuinely erratic manner. . . . Sense itself is an error, a product of error; sense has the structure of an error."[17] These performances of "new blackface," meant to signal a freedom from racial hierarchy, fail to the degree that they don't acknowledge that their meaning and affective charge depend on the very same hierarchy. Sense has the structure of an error, in this instance, when it does not acknowledge the lurking contradiction it performs: the desire to be "postracial"—felt very differently depending on who you are—reveals a complex of fears and desires one would have to abandon, the very sense of race, to truly occupy a postracial position. Or, more simply put, if one were truly postracial, why would one perform race at all? Blackface, in these instances, is the performance of race alongside that which masquerades as the unmarked performance of simply being (white). Or, as Tugg Speedman puts it when asked by Lazarus/Osiris if he could stop acting as Simple Jack and simply be himself so they could rescue him (from himself), "I'm a rooster illusion."

Which brings us at last to the domain of Foghorn Leghorn and his ilk: the plasmatic, tricksterish animated material that performs an operation that Zupancic calls "the substance becoming subject." The long-standing traditions of American commercial animation, especially its recourse to the blackface minstrel as a force of misrule embodied in the continuing trademark character, speak to a metaphysics that converts the commodity's performance of willing subjugation into its comic resistance, via its own substance. As a made object, the 'toon's rebellion against its

FIG. C.11 The radical deformation of the body that Eisenstein referred to as plasmaticness, performed in *The Foghorn Leghorn* (1948).

FIG. C.12 A moment of violent transformation in *Snow-White* (1933): the evil stepmother, as dragon, is turned inside out.

own maker forms a resistance that is paradoxically generated by that same maker as the very justification for committing disciplinary violence against it. In the same way that the "new blackface" isn't new, is merely the logical extension of a tradition that has waxed and waned but has never ended, the constitution of American commercial animation around continuing characters that are in varying degrees themselves blackface minstrels is not some historical accident, nor a simple act of appropriation. Whether in Mickey Mouse playing "Zip Coon" on a steamboat in 1928 or in Chuck Knipp's drunken rants as Shirley Q. Liquor, we witness iterations of an anxious and mutually constitutive process through which whiteness leans heavily on a fantastic and hypergenuine blackness for its paradoxically inauthentic superiority. As Zupancic reminds us, comedy does not reveal, it repeats, and in that repetition it enacts the failure of sense that informs the perpetually contradictory nature of the commodity.[18] Reading the field of animation written large through the lens of Disney (personified in Walt), Eisenstein saw that repetition, that nod to non-sense, as "a kind of drop of comfort, an instant of relief, a fleeting touch of lips in the hell of social burdens, injustices and torments, in which the circle of his American viewers is forever trapped."[19] Animation, then, especially via the minstrel, converts the "social burdens, injustices and torments" into humor rendered violently, explosively, yet does so methodically, in the same way any assembly line turns out cars, canning jars, or microchips: again and again, each thing different; each thing exactly the same.[20]

THE REPETITION COMPULSION OF 'TOONS: FALLING HARE AND THERE

Hang time. Wile E. Coyote has once again run off a cliff. Realizing that he is about to fall, he turns to look at us, plaintively, as if there were something we should or could do. The gag is nothing new. We've seen it again and again.[21] Again and again. It enacts what a Freudian would deem a repetition compulsion. In *Beyond the Pleasure Principle* (1920), Freud elaborates on a point that he had made earlier in *Jokes and Their Relation to the Unconscious* (1905): simply, that children have a compulsion to repeat the same action over and over: "Children repeat unpleasurable experiences . . . [so] that they can master a powerful impression far more thoroughly by being active than they could by merely experiencing it passively. Each fresh repetition seems to strengthen the mastery they are in search of. . . . None of this contradicts the pleasure principle; repetition, the re-experiencing of something identical, is clearly in itself a source of pleasure."[22] This compulsion, Freud suggests, derives from the child's struggle to come to terms with the interplay of plenitude and lack, the fleeting nature of pleasure in the face of reality. This leads the child to compulsively engage in unpleasant acts (like tossing away a toy) because it finds that it derives pleasure from learning to master that unpleasure. In his earlier work on jokes, Freud had suggested that this childhood compulsion also lurked behind repetitive humor, marking it as an inherently childish response to an enculturation project that expects the sublimation of that impulse: "The use of moderation and restraint, even in the case of permitted impulses, is a late fruit of education and is acquired by the mutual inhibition of mental activities brought together in a combination. Where such combinations are weakened, as in the unconscious of dreams or in the mono-ideism of psychoneuroses, the child's lack of moderation re-emerges."[23] And in jokes, as well. It is not that the teller of a joke or the person laughing at it is simply being childish. Rather, the inherent nonsense of a joke affronts the subject's investment in sense, stirring that childish admixture of pleasure and unpleasure. For Freud, comic repetition is neither transcendent nor necessarily the expression of a concrete universal; it is a protest against the ongoing process of enculturation, emerging when given an opportunity. And cartoons (particularly cartoon shorts) offer one such opportunity. And that convention of repetitive violence in cartoons also contains a tradition of implicating the viewer—requiring not our action but our inaction. Wile E. Coyote turns to us, pleading, and we do nothing: our sympathy for the victim, or worse yet our empathy, would guarantee the failure of the joke.

Or would it? Animation is inherently violent. Before any 'toon has raised a hand against another, the form itself has committed violence. The very morphology of animated characters allows for squashing, stretching, bending, cutting, reassembling—the severe deformation of the body— what Eisenstein imagined as its "plasmaticness," the primal and revolutionary potential of the stuff of animation to transform not only bodies but the places in which they dwell, to perform through metamorphosis that the stable commodity form is composed of a fundamental substance that defies reification. For Benjamin, writing into the rise of fascism, that metamorphosis was nothing less than the unleashing of the optical unconscious in the face of totalitarian repression: "That those who are awake have a world in common while each sleeper has a world of his own . . .

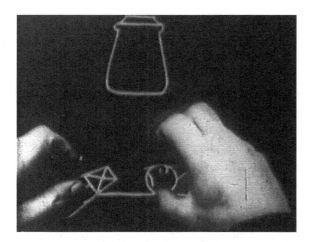

FIG. C.13 Emile Cohl reattaches the head of Pierrot, whom he has decapitated, in *Fantasmagorie* (1908).

has been invalidated by film . . . by creating figures of collective dream, such as the globe-encircling Mickey Mouse. . . . Collective laughter is one such preemptive and healing outbreak of mass psychosis. The countless grotesque events consumed in films are a graphic indication of the dangers threatening mankind from the repressions implicit in civilization. American slapstick films and Disney films trigger a therapeutic release of unconscious energies."[24]

Yet what allows the animated character to morph is not just some quality inherent in the form; the 'toon's malleability is also due to the intervention of the animator's hand, the conventionalized mobilization of his labor. This has been true from the get-go, and it was something that was often literalized in early cartooning, since Emile Cohl cut the head off of his Pierrot and reattached it in *Fantasmagorie* (1908), continuing when Max Fleischer electrocuted Ko-Ko in an attempt to discipline him in *The Cartoon Factory* (1924), or when Rudy Ising forced Bosko back into the inkwell in *Bosko the Talk-Ink Kid* (1929). Early animation is replete with examples of the animator demonstrating the plasticity of his characters by assaulting or deforming them, directly or indirectly. So, it's a small step from the violence of the form itself to the violence that one character visits on another, but a necessary one. Winsor McCay's first performance of animation, his short *Winsor McCay, the Famous Cartoonist of the N.Y. Herald and His Moving Comics* (1911), famously features Little Nemo standing in for McCay, squashing and stretching the characters Flip and Impy.

In *Gertie* (1914), Gertie the dinosaur sends a mastodon hurtling into the background, and McCay disciplines her with a whip. By the time McCay makes *The Pet* (1921), he has vanished from the screen and his title character, untamable, devastates an entire city and has to be destroyed by an army.[25] And so on: whether it was Bray's Colonel Heeza Liar at the bat, or Ko-Ko sparring with Max Fleischer, or Walter Lantz struggling with Pete the Pup, animation in the silent era regularly traded on the gag of the main character submitting to acts of violence that would obliterate a real person, only to return later in the same short, or in the next, in early cartoons at the mercy of the animator, in later ones at the mercy of itself and its fellow 'toons.[26]

Without this inherent mutability and durability of the stuff of animated characters, the violence they visit on each other is at best drawn slapstick. And while cartoon violence is very much related to slapstick (and here the work of Charlie Bowers comes to mind), it is also more.[27] The two don't differ by simply a matter of degree—as in, an animated character can endure more severe punishment than can a live character. Rather, animation favors the violence of slapstick because it is *already* violent in the performance of its own materiality. Animated characters are able to absorb such violence because they are all made of the same stuff: they are expressions of a single plasmaticity divided against itself, constantly attempting an impossible (self-)annihilation. Throughout the silent era and well into the sound era (even in the relatively tame work of Disney), animated creatures performed a contradiction: alive and acting as if they had free will, they demonstrated their inherent thingness, their similarity to the relatively inanimate objects that surrounded them, even as they aggressively individuated themselves. Violence erupted, again and again, framed by the threat of being subsumed into a primordial plasmatic whole, into the inkwell. With the coming of sound, the violence of American animation became more exclusively between characters and less about any sort of expression of mastery over the medium by the animator.[28] Except that—particularly in the output of Warner Bros. and MGM from the 1930s through the 1950s, which Norman Klein has described as a "zip-crash" moment in which new heights of extreme violence were reached—the characters, after they had been most severely violated, looked toward the camera and looked at or spoke to us. Often as not, blasted and mangled, their tone or mien was imploring, as if to ask us why *we* had done to them what the animator used to do.

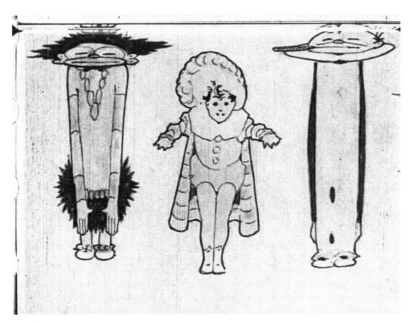

FIG. C.14 In *Winsor McCay, the Famous Cartoonist of the N.Y. Herald and His Moving Comics* (1911), Little Nemo stands in for McCay, deforming Impy and Flip as if they alone were trapped in a funhouse mirror.

FIG. C.15 As too often happens to Daffy Duck, in *Rabbit Seasoning* (1952), his beak is blown off, much to his annoyance.

FIG. C.16 Realizing that he is about to suffer mightily, Elmer Fudd looks imploringly toward his audience in *What's Opera Doc?* (1957).

Of course, we've done nothing to them—nor have we done anything to help them. Klein describes this form of popular cartoon as a "machina versatilis," a Rube Goldberg machine whose gears grind in front of us and for us, leading inevitably either to the violent humiliation of the character or to its own reduction to a cog in that same machine. For Klein, this ritualized performance celebrates the power and the anxiety of the machine age: "The cartoon cannot entirely disown its master or its second master: first the animator, and second the motion picture machine."[29]

There is also a third master, the audience. For Klein, the animated cartoon, particularly of the late 1920s and early 1930s, described an anxious celebration of a mechanism that extended to the motion picture apparatus itself. But it also represented the inhuman, mechanical quality of a relatively newly automated modernity, a drawn version of what Miriam Bratu Hansen has called "vernacular modernism." At the same time, the cartoon graphically delineated the social violence that the celebration of the machine drowned out.[30] Theorists of the comic in the early twentieth century would not have found this efflorescence of repetitive mechanical violence surprising. Bergson, for instance, suggested that a machinic estrangement of the human form was essential to comedy and that "by laughter, society avenges itself for the liberties taken with it. It would fail in its object if it bore the stamp of sympathy or kindness."[31] Wile E. Coyote (or perhaps Chuck Jones) would agree.[32] Which is to say, not only does this versatile machine vengefully and repetitively work its way with its cartoon victims but it does so in a way that leads inevitably to those characters' pleas to their audience for sympathy—pleas that must be denied for the joke to work.[33] The machine must grind on. As Simon Critchley, summing up Bergson, notes, the "comic figure possesses, or better, is possessed by . . . a certain stiffness or inflexibility which is emphasized through an absent-minded, almost unconscious, mechanical repetitiveness . . . [as] in cartoons, where Tom endlessly repeats his pursuit of Jerry, and the Coyote never catches his Road Runner."[34] Yet it is a mistake to locate the comic too literally in the mechanical stiffness of the (cartoon) figure itself. Whether Ko-Ko or Felix or Mickey or the Roadrunner, the 'toon is itself actually far from stiff; it is often fluid, sensual, and sometimes libidinous, quite comfortable in its body. What *are* mechanical, however, are the operations that animate the character, the acts of drawing and photographing, frame by frame, the still images that when aggregated become movement. The machine that generates and torments the animated minstrel is partially made up of humans, and it produces, at least by convention, plasmatic beings: it takes the fluid stuff of ink and renders it corporeal, creating the character in order to torment it, to demonstrate that its subject status is secondary to its existence as an object. The 'toon resists, it cries out (to us), but it knows from whence it came and to where it must return. Critchley, continuing, admits as much as he slides from the animated to the live: "There is a compulsion to repeat in the comic, a repetitiveness that is also endemic to the machinic. . . . At its humorous edges, the human begins to blur with the machine, becoming an inhuman thing that stands over against the human being."[35] Like the animated minstrel created to be punished for a rebellion instigated by its maker, the comic figure, in Critchley's estimation, elicits a laughter tinged with cruelty, with displaced anger at the lurking thought that to be a human subject is not inalienable after all, is perhaps more fungible than one might like to admit.

That this operation is repeated, again and again, in theme and variation, is a suggestion not only of the operation of an implacable machine but also of a compulsion to engage with it. Yet this automation of punishment-as-performance begs a question or two. First, what crimes did a Bimbo or a Daffy commit to suffer our vengeance? And how did that violence against them become a compulsively repetitive act? For Klein, the answer begins in the anxious machine-age excitement epitomized by Max Fleischer—himself an inventor and scientific illustrator so enthusiastic about machine-age modernity that in the early 1920s he actually produced feature-length cartoons explaining Darwinian evolution and Einstein's theory of relativity. At the same time, Fleischer, every bit as much as Walt Disney, depicted himself as a self-made man, an animator who had animated himself first. Right alongside the compulsive violence of cartoons ran a compulsively repeating narrative of self-making, the pervasive early twentieth-century American pop-cultural myth often called the "Horatio Alger story," repeated ad nauseam in pulp fiction and in public relations (including that of Disney and the Fleischers).[36] The routine repetition of the lore of self-making, of so fully embracing the commodification of the self that one becomes its apotheosis, was itself a fantasy about the limits and power of self-will and of the sheer mutability of the commodity self. The animated figure, in all of its plasmatic possibility, represented the very potentiality of that self-making and its constraint in the service of the gag, its processing in the cruel machinery of humor, and its punishment for the hubris of attempting to reach beyond its bounds. The deformation of the cartoon character, which would have been fatal to any (truly) living creature, was a form of necessary proof of its mutability, and a playful testament to the bounds of its identity. That it was often enacted as a struggle between animator and character, or between the character and the stuff of which it was made, simply pointed up the tension between popular formations of creation and self-creation. At the end of the day (or of the short), the cartoon character, pliable enough to assume any form, had to revert to form, first as itself, then (as in the case of Ko-Ko or Bosko) as the ink from whence it sprang. The cartoonist, at the end of a day of repetitive piecework, had created a sort of life, on the page and for himself. The same would happen the next day. And the day after that.

OUTSIDE OF TEXT: THE REPETITION COMPULSION AND VIEWERS

Cartoon and stunt films . . . once . . . allowed justice to be done to the animals and things electrified by their technology by granting the mutilated beings a second life. Today they merely confirm the victory of technological reason over truth. . . . The quantity of organized amusement is converted into the quality of organized cruelty . . . [and cartoons] hammer into every brain the old lesson that continuous attrition, the breaking of all individual resistance, is the condition of life in this society. Donald Duck in the cartoons and the unfortunate victim in real life receive their beatings so that the spectators can accustom themselves to theirs.
—Max Horkheimer and Theodor Adorno, *The Dialectic of Enlightenment* (1975)

For Alenka Zupancic, this violent struggle between form and substance isn't limited just to animation but describes the operation of comedy itself: "Comedy is not the story of the alienation of the subject, it is the story of the alienation of the substance, which has become the subject."[37] Whether speaking about Buster Keaton, Charlie Chaplin, or their avatar, Felix the Cat, this remains true: even as it becomes personified, the comic character never fully escapes its fraught relationship to its material base.[38] In early American animation, performing this distance between the character and its own stuff, the ritual of its subjection, was a necessary station stop on the road to the violent repetition compulsion that marks the golden age cartoons of Warner Bros. or MGM. As if the doctors and nurses had sealed the doors and windows of a madhouse behind them as they left, locking in their inmates, when sound film seemed to demand the spatial enclosure of cinematic space, and the performing animator was gently eased out of the frame, the repetitive performance of rebellion and subjugation that had marked the best of silent animation gave way to the manic mayhem of Bugs, Daffy, and Woody. What had been violence in the service of (always already failed) rebellion became aggression turned inward. If the alienated substance had indeed become subject, the ritual performance of the cycle of its creation and destruction at the hand of the performing animator was a conceit that favored the maker, and one that in that hand's absence suggested a loss of control. The moving finger not only ceased to write, it ceased to exist; the interlocutor had exited, stage left, leaving Tambo and Bones to fend for themselves. Writing in the early days of cinema, before the animator left the stage and the screen, Henri Bergson treated that soon-to-be-untended machine, not necessarily with the enthusiasm of a Max Fleischer, but without the necessary ambivalence that the first mechanized world war and a truly global economic crisis would lend to its implacable grinding, a gentler notion of comedy and bifurcation:

> Let us suppose . . . that our attention is drawn to this material side of the body; that, so far from sharing in the lightness and subtlety of the principle with which it is animated, the body is no more in our eyes than a heavy and cumbersome vesture, a kind of irksome ballast which holds down to earth a soul eager to rise aloft. Then the body will become to the soul what . . . the garment is to the body itself—inert matter dumped down upon living energy. The impression of the comic will be produced as soon as we have a clear apprehension of this putting of one on the other.[39]

FIG. C.17 One of the torments that Tex Avery devises for his protagonist in *Magical Maestro* (1952) is an imaginary hair in the gate of the projector, which flickers distractingly until he finally pulls it out.

For Bergson, the comic form offered a glimpse of transcendence momentarily thwarted, the comic body as the soul tangled up in its material form. And he saw in that body a suggestion of something both human and inhuman, a struggling automaton. This theme of the mechanical construction of the cartoon and its characters repeats on-screen the history of the industrialization of animation itself, making an uneasy joke of the impressment of graphic artists into repetitive piecework.[40] This is a form of social and material violence that found its outlet in the insistent transformation and occasional annihilation of the cartoon body and in the violent, aggressive interplay of the animator and the animated. While its repetition gestured toward its roots on the vaudeville stage—the dance of theme and variation that valued the execution of a gag over the originality of its content—it also enacted the repetitive cycle of creation, freeing, and recapture—Bergson's comedy of failed transcendence.

For Zupancic, though, comedy is an aperture into immanence, not an expression of thwarted transcendence. The complex relationship between the comic actor, her offstage/offscreen self, and her character operates in a state of constant flux and tension, as that "gap through which the character relates to itself, 'representing itself.'"[41] Unlike a performance by a Method actor, through which the character is meant to be made real and whole for the audience, in comedy the "subject-actor" encompasses both the performer and the character, the line between the two is indistinct, and the humor emerges in a struggle, not between body and soul, material and anima, but between a performer anxiously uncertain about her substantial existence and an equally self-doubting character. Zupancic describes a noumenal realm from which the character, as a Hegelian concrete universal, extends itself into our phenomenal space: "Comedy is not the undermining of the universal, but its (own) reversal into the concrete; it is not an objection to the universal, but the concrete labor or work of the universal itself. Or, to put it in a single slogan: *comedy is the universal at work.*"[42] The comic figure, whether animated or live, does not transcend the material world; rather it is made whole in and through that world. It does not become whole but becomes divided, subject and object, in and for itself. In Zupancic's model, the comic actor is herself the gap through which that extension occurs, a conduit. The cartoon character, which so flexibly invokes abstraction in and through itself—but only in relation to itself *as a character*—offers an even better example than the live comic actor. The silent cartoon character replaced the live comic actor's uneasy juxtaposition of subject, actor, and character with that of the triad of animator(s), plasmatic substance, and character. For animation's first two decades, before its entry into sound, whenever the animator's hand or body entered the frame, and when animator/producers were often associated with their characters—Bud Fisher with Mutt and Jeff, Max Fleischer with Ko-Ko, Disney with Mickey, and so on—this relationship between the real and the created appeared on-screen on a regular basis, or was invoked through public relations that foregrounded the metaphysical relationship between the animator and the cartoon character as essential to the experience of enjoying animation. A manufactured object designed to rebel against its maker(s), the minstrel speaking back to the interlocutor, in those moments invoked a fantasy of being made whole, of a commodity attempting to possess itself, yet required by its own nature to fail. That failure, that necessary stumble of transcendence denied and immanence glimpsed but foreclosed, was the stuff of laughter.

With the coming of synchronized sound and the industry's insistence on a unified cinematic space separate from that of the theater, the performing animator grudgingly and gradually departed from animated space. What appears so clearly in the 1930s output of Warner Bros. and MGM, but also in the contemporary work of Disney, Universal, the Fleischers, and others, is that animation's inherent violence doesn't disappear with the body of the animator. Instead it multiplies and turns inward. The

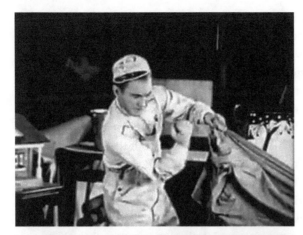

FIGS. C.18–C.19
In *Petering Out*
(1927), Walter Lantz
and Pete the Pup
struggle for control
of the scene.

dyadic form borrowed from vaudeville (itself a distillation of the triad of Tambo, Bones, and the interlocutor) repeats, but now Daffy and Porky joust, and Bugs and Elmer, and Tom and Jerry, instead of Max and Ko-Ko or Walter Lantz and Pete the Pup. Primal forms (who are both animated and animal) engage in a Beckettian struggle that necessarily never resolves. The theme song for the *Itchy and Scratchy Show*, a parodic cartoon short internal to the animated world of *The Simpsons* (Fox, 1989–present), sums this up nicely:

> They fight, they bite,
> They bite and fight and bite,
> Fight fight fight, bite bite bite,
> The Itchy and Scratchy Show!

And really that is all they do, with guaranteed gruesome consequences.[43] The same may be said, yet with less graphic violence, of the popular and long-running Warner Bros. Road Runner series (1948–present). When Wile E. Coyote and the Road Runner fight, it is a Zen inversion of the primal struggle between predator and prey: in each short, the bird needs only get out of the way of the coyote's own self-destructive impulses. The series' running joke is that Wile E. Coyote is his own worst enemy: his ideas for catching the innocent, good-natured Road Runner, instrumentalized and amplified by ACME brand contraptions that almost always misfire, always end up defeating him. He is an expression of a medium seemingly antagonistic to itself. The Road Runner is almost superfluous to this operation, serving only as the necessary cog in Klein's *machina versatilis*, the bait, the one who spurs the coyote to compulsively purchase his machines from ACME—producer, as Crafton has recently discussed, of the cartoon-industry standard animation stand—set them in motion, and then suffer the consequences of his inevitable bad choices. The coyote's pathetically compulsive repetition of self-abjection, and the demonic, indifferent, and implacable force of Fordism that the ACME products represent, play up the force of repetition in acts of self-made (un)pleasure. The cartoon short is an implacable, infernal mail-order machine, Freud's letter arriving with a vengeance, over and over.[44]

If we are to believe Bergson, this sort of comic violence, far from producing a negative affect in viewers, appears to elicit (if not require) a kind of neurasthenia, a physically and emotionally numb response to the reality of that violence. The logic seems almost contradictory: in order to experience the pleasure of laughter we invoke the displeasure of violence *and* we withhold our sympathy for its victims. For Zupancic, even as she differs from Bergson, this is the necessary condition for approaching that metaphysical gap that comedy opens for us (or that we open for the comic). Our unbridled laughter, as Freud would have it, derives from a childish repetition compulsion, a need to witness the machine falter then recover itself, the object become a subject for a moment then be punished for that change—for a willful gesture it did not will: "The child demands repetition because its failure nevertheless realizes something, and this something is precisely what he wanted to see, appearing in the form in which he wanted, or was able, to see it. In other words: the failure of repetition itself fails at some point, or *something disturbs the pure failure of repetition*: something fleeting, elusive, something perceptible at one moment and

FIGS. C.20–C.21 A running gag in Warner Bros. Road Runner cartoons—here *The Fast and Furry-ous* (1949)—is Wile E. Coyote's misguided belief that ACME products such as these will allow him to overcome his own physical limitations.

gone the next. And this something is what the subject wants to see, again and again and again."[45] What the subject wants to see is the precariousness of its own subject status performed by something or someone else, again and again—not to confirm itself as subject but to safely witness a fetishistic act of alienation and disavowal, its misrecognition punished in the body of someone/something else, then forgotten until it happens again. For Rey Chow, writing on the importance of repetition to the coherent materiality of the commodity form—the meaning that inheres in an otherwise underdetermined object—that repetition compulsion is key not only to understanding the force of laughter behind the comic character but also for questioning whether simply ceasing the repetitive activity that produces an unwanted meaning (say, censoring a cartoon) is an effective means of producing change. If, Chow asks, "the signifier is recognized as what works by iteration, would iteration henceforth have to become the only viable way to imagine agency . . . ? As much as a potentiality for radical social transformation ('progress'; 'freedom'), such agency also embeds in it the potentiality for sustaining and reinforcing relations of subordination, subjugation, and social unevenness." If the animated minstrel stands in as the embodied revenge of the disembodied worker, one given form only to fail, will its suppression break that racist spell? "How, then," she asks, "should we rethink the hitherto presumed mutual—and arguably circular—linkages among materialism, agency, and change-as-improvement? What forms of disarticulation and rearticulation would be possible—indeed, would be necessary?"[46]

The hunter hunts the rabbit for the pleasure of the kill. There is only one rabbit. If the hunter succeeds, then he kills the pleasure in himself. So, he fails. Then, we laugh. What the comic repetition of cartoon violence performs is indeed the vengeance of the social. Yet it may be performed equally as an act of resistance and an act of repression because laughter—far from being a physical and emotional response trivial in comparison to the tears evoked by tragedy—is an orgiastic appreciation of the necessary violence of subjection and the gasping, grasping pleasure at its momentary failure. The Method beckons us to engage in the singular, distancing act of sympathy for the character; comedy offers the possibility of empathy with the character-actor-animator. After Wile E. Coyote turns to the "camera" and beseeches us, always, he falls. Or a rock falls on him. Or he falls and then a rock falls on him. And so on. The machine grinds on, but for a moment it stutters and stops, and then restarts. Our sadistic pleasure is not in it stopping but in knowing that it will start again. But perhaps that

FIG. C.22 Infantile sadism satisfied: in *To Beep or Not to Beep* (1963), Wile E. Coyote looks imploringly to his audience moments before the suffering begins—again.

pleasure is tempered by (mis)recognition, the sense of knowing that we, too, have been made to serve the machine. And even as we know that we have no control over that machine, its parts beseech us, offering in their repetition an illusion of control that will necessarily be taken from us— and that we will continue to try to reclaim, if only to feel the (un)pleasure of a shared futility.

CONCLUSION

To conclude, a rather offensive joke:

> The Lone Ranger and Tonto are riding across the desert, heading west, when suddenly their path is blocked by five hundred Arapaho warriors. The Lone Ranger turns to Tonto and says, "Well, Tonto, it looks like we'll have to turn north." They ride north for an hour or so until their path is blocked by one thousand Blackfeet warriors. The Lone Ranger says to Tonto, "Well, I guess we'd better head east." But after a half hour riding east, their path is blocked by five thousand Sioux warriors. The Lone Ranger says to Tonto, "Well, Tonto, I suppose we can only head south." But a couple of hours to the south finds them face to face with seven thousand Apache warriors. The Lone Ranger sighs and says, "Well, Tonto, I guess we'll just have to stand and fight." At which point Tonto turns to the Lone Ranger and says, "What do you mean 'we,' white man?"

An old joke, to be sure, but an apt one. It points out that the politics of affiliation cut both ways—if not particularly evenly. This book began to take shape before the election of Barack Obama (and well before that sorry re-make of *The Lone Ranger* [Verbinski, 2013]), but it has largely been framed by the course of the Obama presidency. Invoking notions of Hope and Change, the first Obama campaign stood, for many Americans, white and of color, as *the* watershed moment when the United States would finally overcome one of the most defining chapters in its (racial) history. Sadly, and predictably, those hopes have not been fully realized. Yet it is precisely because the election of Barack Obama did not change the underlying chain of signification between African Americans and the laboring body that there has been a resurgence of blackface minstrelsy—a set of practices that this book has been at pains to point out has never actually ceased, and certainly not as far as commercial animation has been concerned. An optimistic reading of this "new blackface" is that it is, like the deployment of the blackface minstrel in animation, an attempt to work through, via repetition, a shared investment in fantastic blackness as a liberatory force in democratic capitalist America, *and* the necessary backlash that requires its punishment for attempting exactly what has been asked of it. As Larry Wilmore pointed out on *The Daily Show* a year after Barack Obama took office, there was a shared delusion that Obama would somehow prove to be a Magical Negro—like Michael Clarke Duncan's John Coffey in *The Green Mile* (Darabont, 1999), Will Smith's eponymous *Bagger Vance* (Redford, 2000), or just about any character played by Morgan Freeman—a figure who could actually redeem the racist underpinnings of democratic capitalism through his own willing sacrifice at its hands.[47] Yet as long as the relationship between that fantasy and the commodity nature of anyone living in a democratic capitalist society goes unacknowledged, the magic can't work: we will continue to need black presidents and minstrels, vestigial and otherwise, to punish for our shortcomings. The "we" here, or in the joke above, or invoked by Kirk Lazarus/Lincoln Osiris and repudiated by Alpa Chino in *Tropic Thunder*, is not merely designated by circumstance or by performance but by repeated acts of affiliation and empathy, both failed and successful, by the *act*. It is acknowledged in this instance through the articulation of the animated minstrel as an avatar of alienation, a material manifestation in celluloid and ink of the labor taken to make it. The racist caricatures of the 1930s were a violent reaction to the potential disruption of that chain of signification—in which fantastic blackness stands in for alienated labor power—by the efflorescence of actual African American culture, especially in jazz. In spite of that rupture, and of the fading of stage traditions that supported

FIGS. C.23–C.24 At the end of *What's Opera Doc?* (1957), Elmer Fudd thinks that he has killed Bugs Bunny; Bugs, quite alive, reminds us that unlike cartoons, operas never end happily.

its live performance, blackface continues today, not as something new but as a continuation of that tradition of locating anxiety about the commodity in an imagined black body. The spate of "new blackface" performances in recent years does not speak to or for a postracial moment; far from it. Rather, it represents unfinished business that the 2008 election uncovered: the election of Barack Obama, as historically significant as it was, did not (could not) address systemic, institutional racism—the disproportionate rates of incarceration; unemployment; infant, youth, and senior mortality; and so on—nor the incredible semiotic weight of a fantastic blackness carried for an ostensibly white society by actual African Americans in a nearly post-neoliberal and almost neofeudal moment. The seeming resurgence of blackface now, to the degree that it is a return at all, is a return of the repressed. As Chow suggests, repetition may be a given, yet change without conscious disarticulation and rearticulation does not automatically equal improvement. To articulate the meanings of these moments of blackface, contemporary and historical, live and animated, is not to define them, hence lay them to rest, but to lay claim to their meaning in the service of that change, however imperfect and ephemeral it may be. At the end of *What's Opera Doc?* (Warner Bros., 1957), after a particularly violent romp through the pretenses and precincts of high culture, an ostensibly dead Bugs Bunny/Brunhilde rises up in Elmer Fudd/Siegfried's arms and says to us, "Well what did you expect in an opera? A happy ending?"[48] One can only hope.

NOTES

INTRODUCTION

To view all of the media discussed in this chapter, go to http://scalar.usc.edu/works /birthofanindustry.

1 In his discussion of *Mickey's Mellerdrammer*, Donald Crafton notes, citing the example of Bert Williams, that applying burnt cork did not necessarily confer whiteness to the skin beneath. While he does not go so far to suggest either that Mickey is black or a minstrel, he coyly suggests that Mickey's "blackened self is performative, different from his 'natural' ethnicity—whatever that may be." Crafton, *Shadow of a Mouse: Performance, Belief, and World Making in Animation* (Berkeley: University of California Press, 2013), 124.

2 For a detailed discussion of *Uncle Tom's Cabin* and its variations, see Linda Williams, *Playing the Race Card: Melodramas of Black and White from Uncle Tom to O.J. Simpson* (Princeton, NJ: Princeton University Press, 2001), 45–96.

3 See the discussion of *Lucky Ducky* (MGM, 1948) in chapter 4.

4 For one of many contested histories of "Dixie," see William J. Mahar, *Behind the Burnt Cork Mask: Early Blackface Minstrelsy and Antebellum American Popular Culture* (Chicago: University of Illinois Press, 1999), 37. Tap dance, of course, has as one of its antecedents the "eccentric dance" of blackface minstrelsy.

5 For a range of recent scholarship on blackface minstrelsy past and present, see Catherine M. Cole and Tracy C. Davis, eds., "Routes of Blackface," special issue, *Drama Review* 57:2 (summer 2013).

6 For a detailed and illuminating discussion of *Bamboozled*, see Kara Keeling, "Passing for Human: *Bamboozled* and Digital Humanism," *Women and Performance* 15:1 (2005), 237–50.

7 William Faulkner, *Requiem for a Nun* (New York: Vintage, 2011 [1950]). Barack Obama, in the speech "A More Perfect Union" (Philadelphia, 18 March 2008), said, "Understanding this reality requires a reminder of how we arrived at this point. As William Faulkner once wrote, 'The past isn't dead and buried.

In fact, it isn't even past.' We do not need to recite here the history of racial injustice in this country. But we do need to remind ourselves that so many of the disparities that exist in the African-American community today can be directly traced to inequalities passed on from an earlier generation that suffered under the brutal legacy of slavery and Jim Crow" (http://www.theatlantic.com /daily-dish/archive/2008/03/obamas-speech/218796/).

8 As a whiteface clown, it may not be immediately apparent why one should think of him as a minstrel. As will become evident, this study understands minstrelsy as comprising both gestural and visual elements, and it is in this light that one can perhaps understand Ko-Ko as a minstrel.

9 See later in this introduction for a detailed discussion of that scholarship.

10 For a comparison of the framing of the fight from the perspectives of the white and the black presses, see Dan Streible, *Fight Pictures: A History of Boxing and Early Cinema* (Berkeley: University of California Press, 2008), 195–239. Compare David A. Gerstner, *Manly Arts: Masculinity and Nation in Early Cinema* (Durham, NC: Duke University Press, 2006).

11 "Singing Minstrel Tops Keith's Bill," *Boston Herald*, 18 January 1929; "Eddie Leonard, Minstrel Man, Is Found Dead," *New York Herald Tribune*, 30 July 1941; "The Origin of 'Wha Wha,'" *Variety*, 10 December 1910; clippings in Billy Rose Theatre Division, New York Public Library.

12 "Thinks Jeffries Can Whip Johnson," *New York Telegraph*, 14 July 1910; "Eddie Leonard Likes the Pugilistic Game," n.d., unidentified newspaper clipping, Billy Rose Theatre Division, New York Public Library.

13 The NAACP was founded in 1909.

14 "Eddie Leonard, Minstrel Man, Is Found Dead." The article hints that Leonard came from a wealthy Virginian family whose fortunes were lost during Reconstruction. That narrative fits well with the plantation fantasy of the minstrel stage.

15 For a discussion of racial formation, see Michael Omi and Howard Winant, *Racial Formation in the United States from the 1960s to the 1990s* (New York: Routledge, 1994).

16 Jack Johnson died in a car crash in 1946, reportedly after angrily leaving a North Carolina diner that refused to serve him. "Two Champs Meet," *US News and World Report*, 9 January 2005.

17 "Eddie Leonard, Minstrel Man, Is Found Dead."

18 On the DVD commentary for the film, Downey claims he dubbed Swope's voice because Johnson had trouble with memorization and delivery. *Putney Swope*, DVD, eOne Films (2006 [1969]). In an interesting coincidence, Antonio Fargas, who plays The Arab in the film, was simultaneously appearing in a Broadway production of *The Great White Hope*, which is based on the Johnson–Jeffries fight.

19 Compare Fred Moten, *In the Break: The Aesthetics of the Black Radical Tradition* (Minneapolis: University of Minnesota Press, 2003), 119–20, 197. See also chapter 4.

20 See, for instance, Norman Mailer, "The White Negro," *Dissent* (spring 1957), 276–93. For a satirical look at the fantasy, see the film *Watermelon Man* (Van Peebles, 1970).

21 For a discussion of black anger, humor, and questions of authenticity, see Glenda Carpio, *Laughing Fit to Kill: Black Humor and the Fictions of Slavery* (New York: Oxford University Press, 2008), 3–28. See also Bambi Haggins, *Laughing Mad: The Black Comic Persona in Post-soul America* (New Brunswick, NJ: Rutgers University Press, 2007).

22 For instance, the need to locate black authenticity in relation to suffering drove Norman Lear, a contemporary of Downey, to situate genuine black experience in the ghetto. (On *The Jeffersons*, George Jefferson's success ["movin' on up"] was depicted as an act of betrayal and erasure; the theme song for *Good Times* offers a celebration of the ghetto as the crucible of the real.) Compare this to the depiction of black life in the 1980s on *The Cosby Show* and to critical arguments about wealth, blackness, and authenticity. See, for instance, Haggins, *Laughing Mad*, 14–69.

23 Act 3, scene 4. The entire line is "Thou art the thing itself: unaccommodated man is no more but such a poor bare, forked animal as thou art."

24 See, for instance, Daphne Brooks, *Bodies in Dissent: Spectacular Performances of Race and Freedom, 1850–1910* (Durham, NC: Duke University Press, 2006); Jayna Brown, *Babylon Girls: Black Women Performers and the Shaping of the Modern* (Durham, NC: Duke University Press, 2008); Saidiya Hartman, *Scenes of Subjection: Terror, Slavery, and Self-Making in Nineteenth-Century America* (New York: Oxford University Press, 1997); Fred Moten, *In the Break: The Aesthetics of the Black Radical Tradition* (Minneapolis: University of Minnesota Press, 2003).

25 See, for instance, Gregory S. Parks and Matthew Hughey, eds., *The Obamas and a (Post) Racial America?* (New York: Oxford University Press, 2012). For reactions in the popular press, simply type "post racial" into any search engine in the United States.

26 Tyler Perry's Madea series (2005–2012) is also parodied here. Compare this to the fart scene at the opening of *Tropic Thunder* (Stiller, 2008). For a detailed discussion of the latter, see the conclusion. A talking head on the online video entertainment news service SideReel declared that the episode had "seemed to make headlines, but not in a controversial way, since everyone knows that Jenna's character is a dimwit." "30 Rock TV News," *SideReel*, 20 December 2010, reeltv.com, http://www.youtube.com/watch?v=gp8NEpDKeOA2o.

27 Henry T. Sampson, *That's Enough, Folks: Black Images in Animated Cartoons, 1900–1960* (London: Scarecrow, 1998). This was updated slightly by Christopher Lehman, *The Colored Cartoon: Black Presentation in American Animated Short Films, 1907–1954* (Amherst: University of Massachusetts Press, 2007). For an intelligent take on the issue of racism in early cartoons, see Jeet Heer, "Racism as a Stylistic Choice and Other Notes," *Comics Journal*, 14 March 2011.

28 Richard Iton, *In Search of the Black Fantastic: Politics and Popular Culture in the*

Post–Civil Rights Era (New York: Oxford University Press, 2008), esp. 289–90. Sadly, Richard Iton succumbed to cancer during the writing of this book. He will be sorely missed.

29 In this case, for instance, small items such as the Trayvon Martin shooting target (see "Hate-Mongers Sell Paper Targets Depicting Trayvon Martin," *Daily Kos*, 11 May 2012, http://www.dailykos.com/story/2012/05/11/1090882/-Hate-mongers-sell-paper-targets-depicting-Trayvon-Martin) can go unnoticed yet can attach stereotype to affect in particularly effective ways.

30 Annemarie Bean, James Hatch, and Brooks McNamara, eds., *Inside the Minstrel Mask: Readings in Nineteenth-Century Blackface Minstrelsy* (Middletown, CT: Wesleyan University Press, 1996); Louis Chude-Sokei, *The Last "Darky": Bert Williams, Black-on-Black Minstrelsy, and the African Diaspora* (Durham, NC: Duke University Press, 2006); W. T. Lhamon, *Raising Cain: Blackface Performance from Jim Crow to Hip Hop* (Cambridge, MA: Harvard University Press, 1998), and *Jump Jim Crow: Lost Plays, Lyrics, and Street Prose of the First Atlantic Popular Culture* (Cambridge, MA: Harvard University Press, 2003); Eric Lott, *Love and Theft: Blackface Minstrelsy and the American Working Class* (New York: Oxford University Press, 1993); William J. Mahar, *Behind the Burnt Cork Mask: Early Blackface Minstrelsy and Antebellum American Popular Culture* (Chicago: University of Illinois Press, 1999); Dale Cockrell, *Demons of Disorder: Early Blackface Minstrels and Their World* (Cambridge: Cambridge University Press, 1997).

31 Lott, *Love and Theft*; David Roediger, *The Wages of Whiteness: Race and the Making of the American Working Class* (New York: Verso, 1991), and *Towards the Abolition of Whiteness: Essays on Race, Politics, and Working Class History* (New York: Verso, 1994); Michael Rogin, *Blackface, White Noise: Jewish Immigrants in the Hollywood Melting Pot* (Berkeley: University of California Press, 1996); Chude-Sokei, *Last "Darky"*; Tavia Nyong'o, *The Amalgamation Waltz: Race, Performance, and the Ruses of Memory* (Minneapolis: University of Minnesota Press, 2009), 103–35.

32 The exact authorship and provenance of "Old Zip Coon" and "Turkey in the Straw" are a matter of some dispute. As with many minstrel songs, versions of each intersected and overlapped during the nineteenth century, and attributing authorship to Foster, or to anyone else, requires ignoring the ongoing play of theme and variation that minstrel shows produced as performers made fast and loose with material. At the same time, treating these songs as "traditional" plays into minstrelsy's originary fantasies. See, for instance, Lott, *Love and Theft*, for a discussion of the tension between "folk" melodies and published songs.

33 Lhamon (*Jump Jim Crow*) gives the date of this invention as exactly 21 May 1830. As will become evident, the origin stories are more important than the origin itself. Compare, for instance, Alexander Saxton, "Blackface Minstrelsy," and Eric Lott, "Blackface and Blackness: The Minstrel Show in American Culture," in Bean et al., *Inside the Minstrel Mask*, 67–85 and 3–32, respectively.

34 See W. T. Lhamon, ed., *Jim Crow: American* (Cambridge, MA: Harvard University Press, 2009).

35 Following the Civil War there were increasing numbers of black minstrel troupes, but even these maintained the conventions of blackface and costume.

36 See Lott, *Love and Theft*, 140.

37 Roediger (*Wages* and *Towards the Abolition*) has argued that the minstrel should be understood in relation to a misdirected working-class impulse away from class struggle and toward racial tension. Mahar disagrees, seeing a more variable class composition in audiences, hence the impossibility of locating a singular reading of the minstrel show. See Mahar, *Behind the Burnt Cork Mask*, 27, 91, 192. Lott has argued for a more nuanced reading of minstrelsy that takes into account historical and local specifics in making sense of the intersection of class and race in the minstrel. Considering the twentieth century, Rogin (*Blackface*) has argued for seeing in minstrelsy a vehicle toward whiteness for members of the immigrant working class.

38 Roediger, *Wages of Whiteness*, 115–27.

39 See Sean Wilentz, *Chants Democratic: New York City and the Rise of the American Working Class, 1788–1850* (New York: Oxford University Press, 1984. See also Lawrence Levine, *Highbrow/Lowbrow: The Emergence of Cultural Hierarchy in America* (Cambridge, MA: Harvard University Press, 1990).

40 For a discussion of novelty, change, and mediation, see Lisa Gitelman, *Always Already New: Media, History, and the Data of Culture* (Cambridge, MA: MIT Press, 2006).

41 Barbara Lewis, "Daddy Blue: The Evolution of the Dark Daddy," in Bean et al., *Inside the Minstrel Mask*, 269–70.

42 Here, Stephen Jay Gould's essay on the neotyny of Mickey Mouse is instructive. See Gould, *The Panda's Thumb: More Reflections in Natural History* (New York: Norton, 1980).

43 Stuart Hall, "Racist Ideologies in the Media," in Paul Marris and Sue Thornham, eds., *Media Studies: A Reader* (New York: New York University Press, 2000); see also Stuart Hall, "The Spectacle of the 'Other'" in Hall, ed., *Representation: Cultural Representations and Signifying Practices* (London: Sage, 1997), 223–90.

1. PERFORMANCE

To view all of the media discussed in this chapter, go to http://scalar.usc.edu/works/birthofanindustry.

1 For a brief biography of McCay, see John Canemaker, *Winsor McCay: His Life and Art* (New York: Abrams, 2005). Canemaker's book remains the most complete history of McCay's work, and his collection of notes and interviews—the Canemaker Collection, Fales Library, New York University (hereafter Canemaker Collection)—has been invaluable to this project. See also Donald Craf-

ton, *Before Mickey: The Animated Film, 1898–1928* (Cambridge, MA: MIT Press, 1982).

2 The title card for *Little Nemo* reads *Winsor McCay, the Famous Cartoonist of the N.Y. Herald and His Moving Comics.* The title card for *Gertie* reads *Winsor McCay, America's Greatest Cartoonist, and Gertie.* Common usage has altered these to *Little Nemo* and *Gertie the Dinosaur.*

3 McCay kept a meticulous journal in code in which he recorded everything from the particulars and gate of each performance to whether he had sex with his wife on a given night. His stage show occupied a significant and prominent portion of this journal, indicating its importance to him. See Canemaker Collection.

4 Whether one finds in animation a practice significantly distinct from that of live cinema is a point of debate, of course. Compare, for instance, Lev Manovich, "Image Future," *Animation* 1:1 (2006), 25–44; Sean Cubitt, *The Cinema Effect* (Cambridge, MA: MIT Press, 2004), esp. 1–70; and Alan Cholodenko, "The Animation of Cinema," *Semiotic Review of Books* 18:2 (2008), 1–10. While these polemics by no means exhaust the topic, they offer a sampling of the reasoning that has emerged recently to confront the seeming ingestion of live cinematic practices by what has traditionally been called animation. For a rebuttal to Cubitt, see Dudley Andrew, *What Cinema Is!* (New York: Wiley-Blackwell, 2010), ch. 1.

5 In this vein, Scott Bukatman has challenged arguments that McCay's animation and his comic strips are of a piece with the chronophotography of the day. Even though McCay had a phenomenal ability to decompose the individual elements of locomotion, like Muybridge or Marey, his performative approach to the exercise disavowed the scientific or scientistic framing of those other efforts. See Bukatman, *The Poetics of Slumberland: Animated Spirits and the Animating Spirit* (Berkeley: University of California Press, 2012), ch. 1. See also Bukatman, "Comics and the Critique of Chronophotography, or 'He Never Knew When It Was Coming!,'" *Animation* 1:1 (2006), 83–103.

6 Donald Crafton, *Shadow of a Mouse: Performance, Belief, and World-Making in Animation* (Berkeley: University of California Press, 2013), 2, 6, 48–51.

7 For discussions of the social aspects of vaudeville, see, for instance, Henry Jenkins, *What Made Pistachio Nuts? Early Sound Comedy and the Vaudeville Aesthetic* (New York: Columbia University Press, 1993); Robert M. Lewis, *From Traveling Show to Vaudeville: Theatrical Spectacle in America, 1830–1910* (Baltimore: Johns Hopkins University Press, 2003); Anthony Slide, *New York City Vaudeville* (Chicago: Arcadia, 2006), and *The Encyclopedia of Vaudeville* (Oxford: University of Mississippi Press, 2012). Andrew Erdman has suggested that as consolidators such as Keith and Albee gained control of vaudeville they attempted to curtail that interaction, but he also suggests that this was a performance itself, designed to assuage reformers more than to stifle performers. Erdman, *Blue Vaudeville: Sex, Morals and the Mass Marketing of Entertainment, 1895–1915* (Jefferson, NC: McFarland, 2004), 2–4.

8 See, for instance, Canemaker, *Winsor McCay*, 24–34, 64. See also Bukatman, *Poetics of Slumberland*, 85–87.

9 Erwin Feyersinger has recently produced a very exacting analysis of this movement between levels in McCay's work, and in animation generally, through the narratological term "metalepsis." Feyersinger, "Diegetic Short Circuits: Metalepsis in Animation," *Animation* 5:3 (2010), 279–94.

10 See, for instance, Jane Lancaster, *Making Time: Lillian Moller Gilbreth—A Life beyond "Cheaper by the Dozen"* (Boston: Northeastern University Press, 2004); Laurel Graham, *Managing on Her Own: Dr. Lillian Gilbreth and Women's Work in the Interwar Era* (Norcross, GA: Engineering and Management Press, 1998), and "Domesticating Efficiency: Lillian Gilbreth's Scientific Management of Homemakers, 1924–1930," *Signs* 24:3 (1999), 633–75; see also Samuel Haber, *Efficiency and Uplift* (Chicago: University of Chicago Press, 1964); Daniel Nelson, *Frederick W. Taylor and the Rise of Scientific Management* (Madison: University of Wisconsin Press, 1980); Nicholas Sammond, "Picture This: Lillian Gilbreth's Industrial Cinema for the Home," *Camera Obscura* 21:3 (December 2006), 103–33.

11 Just as the production of cartoons in the industry's early days was almost exclusively a male affair, the characters, especially the popular continuing ones, tended to be male. In that many of the labor struggles of the late nineteenth and early twentieth centuries involved women workers, this creates an unfortunate ellipsis such that the animated embodiment of labor struggles was largely masculine, undermining a more gendered affective relationship to the issue.

12 For a discussion of Walt Disney and the performance of mastery through management, see Eric Smoodin, *Animating Culture: Hollywood Cartoons from the Sound Era* (New Brunswick, NJ: Rutgers University Press, 1993). See also Nicholas Sammond, *Babes in Tomorrowland: Walt Disney and the Making of the American Child, 1930–1960* (Durham, NC: Duke University Press, 2005).

13 The widely agreed-on account of American animation's early history, one carefully and masterfully constructed by John Canemaker, Donald Crafton, Paul Wells, Mark Langer, Maureen Furniss, and others, traces animation's development from craft to industry through the parallel venues of the vaudeville stage, comic strip, and trick film. Stephen Worth, the former head of the International Animated Film Society, Hollywood (ASIFA), suggested to me in 2011 that figure-painting on classical Greek pottery should properly be understood as animation. I am not trying to supplant this historical narrative as much as to understand it in relation to its larger historical moment and to make sense of trends and ideas that have been noted, if not explained or interpreted. For an essay on cave painting as animation, see Marc Azema and Florent Rivere, "Animation in Palaeolithic Art: A Pre-echo of Cinema," *Antiquity* 86:332 (2012), 316–24.

14 See Crafton, *Before Mickey*, 223–28. See also Tom Gunning, "'Primitive' Cinema—A Frame-Up? or The Trick's on Us," *Cinema Journal* 28:2 (winter 1989), 3–12, for a discussion of the splice of substitution.

15 See Erdman, *Blue Vaudeville*, 2–11.

16 Norman M. Klein, "Animation and Animorphs: A Brief Disappearing Act," in Vivian Sobchack, ed., *Meta-morphing: Visual Transformation and the Culture of Quick-Change* (Minneapolis: University of Minnesota Press, 2000), 24. For a discussion of the "shock of the modern," see Leo Charney and Vanessa Schwartz, eds., *Cinema and the Invention of Modern Life* (Berkeley: University of California Press, 1996).

17 Tom Gunning, "The Cinema of Attraction[s]," *Wide Angle* 8:3–4 (1986), 5–36. It is not insignificant that while trick photography was eventually subsumed under the rubric of special cinematic effects, animation became a form unto itself. While one could put this down to animation being drawn, it speaks also to the indexical link between the live substrate that trick cinematography shared with an emerging narrative, live-action cinema. Animation was photographed on the same film, but pointed toward a realm other than the photographic real.

18 See Crafton, *Shadow*, 6. We can see a similar sort of reflexivity at work in Méliès's trick films and in Emile Cohl's groundbreaking *Fantasmagorie* (1908) or *Hasher's Delirium* (1910).

19 Even Emile Cohl, whose *Fantasmagorie* puts the lie to McCay's claim of origination yet who did not perform live, played with this convention, inserting his hand into the film frame to manipulate his Pierrot character.

20 See Cholodenko, "Animation of Cinema."

21 As Crafton (*Before Mickey*, 178–84) has pointed out, McCay, McManus, and Powers were among a group of cartoonists working for Hearst or for Pulitzer, and both were happy to sponsor the conversion of the work of their artists to the screen by an emerging crop of young animators.

22 For a meditation on animation, the automaton, and the uncanny, see Alan Cholodenko, "Speculations on the Animatic Automaton," in Cholodenko, ed., *The Illusion of Life II: More Essays on Animation* (Sydney: Power, 2007), 486–528.

23 See Paul Wells, *Understanding Animation* (New York: Routledge, 1998), introduction and ch. 1.

24 See Canemaker, *Winsor McCay*, 157–61. See also Canemaker Collection for more detailed notes on McCay's relationship to Blackton.

25 Crafton, *Before Mickey*, 40–48.

26 Quoted in Alan Harding, "They Thought Him Crazy, but They Don't Think So Now," *American Magazine*, 194[?], Canemaker Collection.

27 McManus had actually left the *New York World* and *The Newlyweds* by the time Cohl animated it. So he had unwillingly turned the strip over to another artist, and that artist, Carmichael, turned it over to Cohl.

28 John Canemaker, interview with Otto Messmer, March 5, 1975, Canemaker Collection.

29 John Canemaker, interview with Otto Messmer, January 29, 1979, Canemaker Collection.

30 John Canemaker, "Otto Messmer Interview, March 5 1975, Fort Lee, NJ," Cane-

maker Collection. John Canemaker, "Otto Messmer and Felix the Cat," *Cartoonist Profiles*, no. 37 (March 1978).

31 Crafton, *Shadow*, 99–101.

32 Mark Langer, "Polyphony and Heterogeneity in Early Fleischer Films: Comic Strips, Vaudeville, and the New York Style," in Daniel Goldmark and Charlie Keil, eds., *Funny Pictures: Animation and Comedy in Studio-Era Hollywood* (Berkeley: University of California Press, 2011), 29–50.

33 Joe Adamson, "Dave Fleischer Interview" (1970), folder 18, Oral Histories Collection, Mayer Library, American Film Institute, Los Angeles. See also Joe Adamson, "'Where Can I Get a Good Corned Beef Sandwich?': An Oral History with Dave Fleischer" (1969), folder 18, Oral Histories Collection, Mayer Library.

34 Timberg and Rooney were also a multigenerational act, with fathers training sons. See Lewis, *From Traveling Show to Vaudeville*; Slide, *Encyclopedia of Vaudeville*.

35 Klein, "Animation and Animorphs," 27.

36 Joe Adamson, "'From This We Are Making a Living?': An Oral History with Richard Huemer" (1969), folder 18, Oral Histories Collection, Mayer Library. Even Jack Warner, long before he became a movie magnate, got his start performing in blackface on the vaudeville stage. "Personal History, Experience and Duties of J. L. Warner" (1 May 1940), Warner Bros. History: 15494B, Warner Bros. Archives, University of Southern California, Los Angeles.

37 If we view *Gertie* as a minstrel show, then Gertie reads as Tambo or Bones, and McCay as the interlocutor, trying and failing to contain her. While the cartoon is not literally a minstrel show, the power dynamic, a sickly sweet combination of domination and affection, matches that of the white(r) interlocutor and his "black" informants.

38 Jenkins, *What Made Pistachio Nuts?*, 63–72.

39 McCay had an assistant, John Fitzsimmons, for these early films and had Blackton's help in the actual filming. See Canemaker, *Winsor McCay*, 157–61. See also Canemaker Collection.

40 John Canemaker, commentary, *Winsor McCay: The Master Edition* (Milestone Film and Video, 2004).

41 The same is true of Flip and Impy's mugging in front of the camera/audience before Nemo takes them in hand in *Winsor McCay, the Famous Cartoonist of the N.Y. Herald and His Moving Comics* (1911).

42 Willis O'Brien would achieve a similar effect in *The Lost World* (Hoyt, 1925). Consider also Ladislas Starevich's *The Cameraman's Revenge* (1912), which mockingly takes up some of the common filmmaking tropes of its day (such as the keyhole reveal) and places them in the hands of stop-action bugs.

43 See Crafton, *Before Mickey*, 111–12.

44 Stephen Kern suggests that early cinema's manipulation of space was of a piece with cubism and with Einsteinian understandings of the space-time continuum. While this suggestion is broadly reasonable, it compresses the tech-

nical and aesthetic history of film rather severely. In commercial cinema, the movement was toward creating a stable sense of spatial relations, not disrupting them. Kern, *The Culture of Time and Space 1880–1918* (Cambridge, MA: Harvard University Press, 1983), 42.

45 What is significant in this regard is that during the first two decades of the twentieth century, established notions of the relationship of time and space were being called into question on a number of fronts. For a somewhat compressed and homologous account, for instance, see Kern, *Culture of Time and Space*, 131–80. Still, arguably the first feature-length animated film in the United States was *The Einstein Theory of Relativity* (Fleischer, 1923).

46 Bukatman, "Comics and the Critique of Chronophotography," 83–103.

47 Canemaker, *Winsor McCay*, 132.

48 See Robert C. Allen, *Horrible Prettiness: Burlesque and American Culture* (Chapel Hill: University of North Carolina Press, 1991); Lawrence Levine, *Highbrow/Lowbrow: The Emergence of Cultural Hierarchy in America* (Cambridge, MA: Harvard University Press, 1990); Lewis, *From Traveling Show to Vaudeville*.

49 If this vestigial performativity is less evident in the animation of comic strips such as *The Newlyweds*, or in Powers's Phables series, that may be because they were translations of newspaper strips, not pieces conceived first as animation.

50 Vivian Sobchack, "At the Still Point of the Turning World," in Sobchack, ed., *Meta-morphing: Visual Transformation and the Culture of Quick-Change* (Minneapolis: University of Minnesota Press, 2000), 144.

51 See Crafton, *Shadow*, 101–4.

52 Michael Rogin, *Blackface, White Noise: Jewish Immigrants in the Hollywood Melting Pot* (Berkeley: University of California Press, 1996), 45–120.

53 See, for instance, Lary May, "Review: *Blackface, White Noise: Jewish Immigrants in the Hollywood Melting Pot*," *American Jewish History* 85:1 (1997), 115–19; or Richard M. Merelman, "Hollywood's America: Social and Political Themes in Motion Pictures" (review), *American Political Science Review* 91:3 (September 1997), 753–54. My thanks to Andrea Most for pointing me to this literature.

54 For an idealistic discussion of the American Creed, see, for instance, Arthur M. Schlesinger, *The Disuniting of America: Reflections on a Multicultural Society* (New York: Norton, 1998).

55 This is not to underestimate other legal maneuvers to regulate difference, such as the Chinese Exclusion Act of 1882. But while laws such as the Exclusion Act barred persons of a given race, legal interpretations such as *Plessy* derived from and spoke back to the question of the relationship of objecthood to subjecthood in African Americans, a question deriving from the discursive and practical histories of chattel slavery.

56 Scott Bukatman, "Taking Shape: Morphing and the Performance of Self," in Sobchack, *Meta-morphing*, 240.

57 Sobchack, introduction to *Meta-morphing*, xi–xxiii. On plasmaticity, see Sergei M. Eisenstein, *Eisenstein on Disney*, ed. Jay Leyda, trans. Alan Upchurch (Calcutta: Seagull Books, 1986).

58 See Crafton, *Before Mickey*, 48–58.

59 Ed James, *The Amateur Negro Minstrels Guide* (New York: Ed James, 1880), 23; Fred Atkinson Collection, University of Chicago Library.

60 See Daphne Brooks, *Bodies in Dissent: Spectacular Performances of Race and Freedom, 1850–1910* (Durham, NC: Duke University Press, 2006); and Jayna Brown, *Babylon Girls: Black Women Performers and the Shaping of the Modern* (Durham, NC: Duke University Press, 2008).

61 "Music and the Drama," *Chicago Record-Herald*, [1906?], clipping in Robinson Locke Collection, Billy Rose Theatre Division, New York Public Library (hereafter Robinson Locke Collection).

62 George Walker, "The Real 'Coon' on the American Stage," *Theatre Magazine*, August 1906, n.p., Robinson Locke Collection.

63 "Colored Actor Tells the Story of His Life from Kansas to Abyssinia," *Toledo (Ohio) Blade* [?], [23 January 1907?], Robinson Locke Collection.

64 "Negro Actors at Majestic," *New York Times*, 9 May 1911, n.p., Robinson Locke Collection.

65 Bert A. Williams, "The Negro on Stage," *Green Book Album* 2:6 (December 1910), 1341–44, Robinson Locke Collection.

66 For a discussion of minstrelsy and amalgamation, see Tavia Nyong'o, *The Amalgamation Waltz: Race, Performance, and the Ruses of Memory* (Minneapolis: University of Minnesota Press, 2009), 103–35.

67 Louis Chude-Sokei, *The Last "Darky": Bert Williams, Black-on-Black Minstrelsy, and the African Diaspora* (Durham, NC: Duke University Press, 2006). See also Brooks, *Bodies in Dissent*, 220–21; and Karen Sotiropoulos, *Staging Race: Black Performers in Turn of the Century America* (Cambridge, MA: Harvard University Press, 2006), 42–123.

68 Jenkins, *What Made Pistachio Nuts?*, 63–81.

69 Chude-Sokei (*Last "Darky"*) has pointed out that the construction of the notion of the "immigrant" of the late nineteenth and early twentieth centuries is often shorthand for the *European* immigrant, a move that excludes those arriving from Africa, the Caribbean, and Latin America from the category.

70 Caroline Caffin, *Vaudeville: The Book* (New York: Kennerly, 1914). See also Lary May, *Screening Out the Past* (Chicago: University of Chicago Press, 1980).

71 This distinguished early minstrels from other blackface performers who demonstrated dance and vernacular from less exotic locales such as New Jersey; W. T. Lhamon, *Raising Cain: Blackface Performance from Jim Crow to Hip Hop* (Cambridge, MA: Harvard University Press, 1998).

72 See Eileen Southern, "The Early Georgia Minstrels," in Annemarie Bean, James Hatch, and Brooks McNamara, eds., *Inside the Minstrel Mask: Readings in Nineteenth-Century Blackface Minstrelsy* (Middletown, CT: Wesleyan University Press, 1996), 163–74, for a history of the troupe.

73 For detailed discussions of the history of blackface minstrelsy, see Dale Cockrell, *Demons of Disorder: Early Blackface Minstrels and Their World* (Cambridge: Cambridge University Press, 1997); Bean et al., *Inside the Minstrel Mask*; and

William J. Mahar, *Behind the Burnt Cork Mask: Early Blackface Minstrelsy and Antebellum American Popular Culture* (Chicago: University of Illinois Press, 1999).

74 See, for instance, Paul Levitt, *Vaudeville Humor: The Collected Jokes, Routines, and Skits of Ed Lowry* (Carbondale: Southern Illinois University Press, 2002), 2–3. See also Frank Cullen, Florence Hackman, and Donald McNeilly, *Vaudeville Old and New: An Encyclopedia of Variety Performers in America*, vol. 1 (New York: Routledge, 2006), xxix–xxx.

75 Jenkins, *What Made Pistachio Nuts?*, 59–95.

76 See Robert W. Rydell, *World of Fairs: The Century-of-Progress Expositions* (Chicago: University of Chicago Press, 1993). See also Bernth Lindfors, ed., *Africans on Stage: Studies in Ethnological Show Business* (Bloomington: Indiana University Press, 1999).

77 *Theatre Magazine Advertiser*, n.d., Robinson Locke Collection, folder 2461, Special Collections, Performing Arts Library, New York Public Library.

78 See Brooks, *Bodies in Dissent*, 207–9, for an illuminating discussion of the illegibility of *In Dahomey* for British audiences.

79 Daniel Goldmark, *Tunes for 'Toons: Music and the Hollywood Cartoon* (Berkeley: University of California Press, 2005), 84.

80 Klein, "Animation and Animorphs," 27.

81 Although space doesn't permit a discussion here, another obvious and significant source for stereotyping in animation was print media.

82 See Goldmark, *Tunes for 'Toons*, 84; see also 77–106, 183n12, and 184–85n21.

83 Canemaker, "Otto Messmer Interview, March 5 1975, Fort Lee, NJ," Canemaker Collection.

84 For a detailed discussion of the performance of Topsy, see Brown, *Babylon Girls*, 56–91.

85 *Moving Picture World*, 9 December 1916, quoted in Crafton, *Before Mickey*, 174.

86 See Marx, *Capital*, trans. Ben Fowlkes, vol. 1 (New York: Penguin Classics, 1976), 125–77, esp. 163–65.

87 *Los Angeles Times*, 2 April 1916, 15 (reprint from *Omaha World-Herald*).

88 John R. Bray, "How the Comics Caper," *Photoplay* 11:2 (January 1917), 68. Walt Disney Productions would repeat this trope of one man becoming many in its public relations for *Snow White* (1937), for instance. See "The Big Bad Wolf," *Fortune*, November 1934; and "Mouse and Man," *Time*, 27 December 1937.

89 Bud Fisher, "'Here's How'—Says Bud," *Photoplay* 18:2 (July 1920), 58. For a brief history of Fisher's legal problems and outsourcing, see Crafton, *Before Mickey*, 196–200.

90 Of course, this trope continued into the sound era in the petulance of Bugs Bunny, Daffy Duck, and Woody Woodpecker.

91 John Canemaker, "Interview With: Shamus Culhane," 13 February 1973, copyrighted 1974, Canemaker Collection.

92 *Moving Picture World*, 26 March 1927, 426. For an account of Termite Terrace, see Donald Crafton, "The View from Termite Terrace: Caricature and Parody

in Warner Bros. Animation," in Kevin S. Sandler, ed., *Reading the Rabbit: Explorations in Warner Bros. Animation* (New Brunswick, NJ: Rutgers University Press, 1998); Martha Sigall, *Living Life inside the Lines: Tales from the Golden Age of Animation* (Oxford: University of Mississippi Press, 2005); or Tom Sito, *Drawing the Line: The Untold Story of Animation Unions from Bosko to Bart Simpson* (Lexington: University Press of Kentucky, 2006).

93 Crafton, *Before Mickey*, 298–99. For his discussion of the relationship of animator, animated, and audience, see Crafton, *Shadow*, esp. 15–58.

94 It is not necessary to view this shift through the lens of the commonly accepted narrative of a popular rejection of vaudeville by moviegoing audiences. The formal and structural alterations Crafton notes in the early history of animation indicate a change in taste, a desire to accommodate the more continuous experiences of narrative cinema—though whether the impetus for that change properly resided in audiences, exhibitors, or distributors remains a matter of debate, one not exclusive to animation; disagreement remains as to whether the rise of a narrative cinema over one of attractions in the early decades of the twentieth century was primarily influenced by audience demand, exhibitors' desires to exert more control over their programs, or producers' competitive exploration of new technological and practical means of production. See, for instance, Charles Musser, "The Nickelodeon Era Begins: Establishing the Framework for Hollywood's Mode of Representation," in Thomas Elsaesser, ed., *Early Cinema: Space, Frame, Narrative* (London: BFI, 1990 [1984], 256–73; and Tom Gunning, "The Cinema of Attraction[s]," *Wide Angle* 8:3–4 (1986), 5–36. For a discussion of animation and its audiences, see Wells, *Understanding Animation*, 10–67 and 222–43.

95 See Sito, *Drawing the Line*, 39–40; and Harvey Deneroff, "'We Can't Get Much Spinach!': The Organization and Implementation of the Fleischer Strike," *Film History* 1:1 (1987), 1–14.

96 For a detailed history of labor struggle in animation, see Sito, *Drawing the Line*.

97 Van Beuren's short was also called *In a Cartoon Studio*.

98 Sito, *Drawing the Line*, 77–100.

2. LABOR

To view all of the media discussed in this chapter, go to http://scalar.usc.edu/works /birthofanindustry.

1 This was roughly ten years before the beginning of labor troubles that would lead to a strike at the Fleischer Studios; the Fleischers also had trouble maintaining copyright over their own work. Richard Fleischer, *Out of the Inkwell: Max Fleischer and the Animation Revolution* (Lexington: University Press of Kentucky, 2005); Mark Langer, "Institutional Power and the Fleischer Studios: The 'Standard Production Reference,'" *Cinema Journal* 30:2 (winter 1991), 3–22.

2 Donald Crafton, *Shadow of a Mouse: Performance, Belief, and World-Making in Animation* (Berkeley: University of California Press, 2013), 6.

3 See Scott Bukatman, *The Poetics of Slumberland: Animated Spirits and the Animating Spirit* (Berkeley: University of California Press, 2012), 131.

4 For a discussion of displacement and condensation in animation, and particularly in the rotoscoping of the Fleischers, see Lisa Cartwright, "The Hands of the Animator: Rotoscopic Projection, Condensation, and Repetition Automatism in the Fleischer Apparatus," *Body and Society* 18:1 (2012), 47–78.

5 Robert S. Lynd and Helen M. Lynd, *Middletown: A Study in American Culture* (New York: Harcourt Brace, 1929), 75–76, 39–40.

6 Donald Crafton, *Before Mickey: The Animated Film, 1898–1928* (Cambridge, MA: MIT Press, 1982, 163–67. Yuriko Furuhata, "Rethinking Plasticity: The Politics and Production of the Animated Image," *Animation* 6:1 (2011), 25–38. See also Nicholas Sammond, *Babes in Tomorrowland: Walt Disney and the Making of the American Child, 1930–1960* (Durham, NC: Duke University Press, 2005), chs. 1–3. Crafton also briefly invokes the work of Lillian and Frank Gilbreth, whose cinematic time and motion studies deanimated workers in order to understand the component movements of specific tasks or reduced those movements to gestural streaks of light not unlike those used a generation later in what Norman Klein has called the "zip-crash" school of animating. See Laurel Graham, "Beyond Manipulation: Lillian Gilbreth's Industrial Psychology and the Governmentality of Women Consumers," *Sociological Quarterly* 38:4 (fall 1997), 539–65, and *Managing on Her Own: Dr. Lillian Gilbreth and Women's Work in the Interwar Era* (Norcross, GA: Engineering and Management Press, 1998). See also Nicholas Sammond, "Picture This: Lillian Gilbreth's Industrial Cinema for the Home," *Camera Obscura* 21:3 (December 2006), 103–33. Bukatman (*Poetics of Slumberland*, 58) also notes the importance of the regimes of attention that Jonathan Crary has delineated to the complex of animating, deanimating, and reanimating that was important to time and motion studies. Crary, *Suspensions of Perception: Attention, Spectacle, and Modern Culture* (Cambridge, MA: MIT Press, 2000).

7 See Graham, "Beyond Manipulation," and *Managing*; and Sammond, "Picture This."

8 See, for instance, Christine Frederick, *The New Housekeeping: Efficiency Studies in Home Management* (New York: Doubleday, Page, 1913), and *Household Engineering: Scientific Management in the Home* (Chicago: American School of Home Economics, 1920); Lillian Gilbreth, *The Home-Maker and Her Job* (New York: D. Appleton, 1927). See also Dolores Hayden, *Grand Domestic Revolution* (Cambridge, MA: MIT Press, 1981).

9 For contemporary instructions to the animator for observing and drawing, see Edwin G. Lutz's *Animated Cartoons: How They Are Made, Their Origin and Development* (New York: Scribner's, 1926 [1920]). Links to the entire work are available at scalar.usc.edu/works/birthofanindustry.

10 In spite of this, of course, animators would always find characters or situations they were more suited to, as well as ones they avoided.

11 The epitome of this trend would be the work of Hanna-Barbera in the 1960s. Complex backgrounds were possible in "long take" scenes, but excessive movement favored repeating backgrounds, and economy favored simplicity.

12 Fleischer, *Out of the Inkwell*, 15–18.

13 Fleischer, *Out of the Inkwell*, 1–30; Michael Barrier, *Hollywood Cartoons: American Animation in Its Golden Age* (New York: Oxford University Press, 1999), 22–29.

14 See Langer, "Institutional Power and the Fleischer Studios."

15 Langer, "Institutional Power and the Fleischer Studios," 6; see also Joe Adamson, "Working for the Fleischers: An Interview with Dick Huemer," *Funnyworld* 16 (1974–1975), 23–28.

16 Langer ("Institutional Power and the Fleischer Studios") has placed the introduction of in-betweening in 1923. Dick Huemer claims that he was using it as early as 1915; Joe Adamson, "'From This We Are Making a Living?': An Oral History with Richard Huemer" (1969), folder 18, Oral Histories Collection, Mayer Library, American Film Institute, Los Angeles.

17 Rob King, *The Fun Factory: The Keystone Film Company and the Emergence of Mass Culture* (Berkeley: University of California Press, 2008), 64. See also King, "The Art of Diddling: Slapstick, Science, and Antimodernism in the Films of Charlie Bowers," in Daniel Goldmark and Charlie Keil, eds., *Funny Pictures: Animation and Comedy in Studio-Era Hollywood* (Berkeley: University of California Press, 2011).

18 David Weinstein, "Interview with Otto Messmer, Creator of Felix the Cat," n.d., 2, Canemaker Collection, Fales Library, New York University (hereafter Canemaker Collection). Dick Huemer, describing his early days at Barré's studio, claimed that the output was one cartoon a week. Huemer, "Pioneer Portraits," *Cartoonist Profiles* 1:3 (summer 1969), 14–18.

19 Weinstein, "Interview with Otto Messmer."

20 Richard Huemer, "Pioneer Portraits," *Cartoonist Profiles* 1:3 (summer 1969), 14–18.

21 Thomas, quoted in John Canemaker, "Sincerely Yours, Frank Thomas," *Millimeter* 3:1 (January 1975), 16–17.

22 See Norman M. Klein, *7 Minutes* (London: Verso, 1993), 42–43; Leonard Maltin, *Of Mice and Magic: A History of American Animated Cartoons* (New York: Plume, 1980), 27; and Charles Solomon, *Enchanted Drawings: The History of Animation* (New York: Random House, 1994), 37. It goes almost without saying that art schools would also play a role in the conventional training of animators, from McCay's schooling at Michigan State Normal to Walt Disney's restructuring of the Chouinard Art Institute as the California Institute of Art in the early 1960s. On McCay, see John Canemaker, *Winsor McCay: His Life and Art* (New York: Abrams, 2005), 30–31.

23 Lutz, *Animated Cartoons*, 100; Lutz's book may be viewed at http://www.archive.org/stream/cu31924075701304#page/no/mode/2up.

24 Lutz, *Animated Cartoons*, 178.

25 Langer, "Institutional Power and the Fleischer Studios," 12.

26 Maltin, *Of Mice and Magic*, 30–38; Frank Thomas and Ollie Johnston, *The Illusion of Life: Disney Animation* (New York: Disney Editions, 1981), 80–85.

27 Thomas and Johnston, *Illusion of Life*, 84.

28 There is also a tradition among historians of animation of celebrating the antic behaviors of animators on the job, dating back to the early work of Adamson and Canemaker. This is not to discount this behavior as apocryphal; far from it: the animators themselves reported it. Rather, it is to note that if a historian has attempted to describe those hijinks it has usually been to indicate the individualism and idiosyncracy of animators, not as a response to demanding industrial piecework.

29 Huemer, "Pioneer Portraits."

30 This is not to say that there weren't scores of animated shorts that did not take up the theme of rebellion and resistance. There were many, many cartoons that played out the narratives of the comic strips on which they were based or that followed the basic vaudeville structure of stringing successive gags together with little or no reference to the animator or the conditions of production. But those themes and tropes that persisted in the form—between studios, across character lines, and over time—did feature those themes repeatedly, especially in the continuing characters of a number of studios. My thanks to Donald Crafton for raising this issue.

31 Adamson, "Working for the Fleischers"; Huemer ("Pioneer Portraits") put it this way: "While the dual role of storyman and animator was fun for the artist, it scarcely made for a complete and well-rounded story line. Frequently the picture would end with some hastily contrived gimmick, or the all-too-often iris down on the character running towards the horizon. For when the very strict footage limitations had been reached or the time allowed for production had been used up, whichever came first, it was THE END."

32 Jones, quoted in Michael Barrier and Bill Spicer, "An Interview with Chuck Jones," *Funnyworld* 13 (1971), http://www.michaelbarrier.com. In revisiting this interview, Barrier has suggested that Jones's antipathy for Schlesinger was not shared by other Warner animators and directors.

33 John Canemaker, "Otto Messmer Interview, March 5 1975, Fort Lee, NJ," Canemaker Collection. For an example of peripatetic animators, see Adamson, "Working for the Fleischers."

34 Barrier and Spicer, "Interview with Chuck Jones."

35 Donald Crafton, "The View from Termite Terrace: Caricature and Parody in Warner Bros. Animation," in Kevin S. Sandler, ed., *Reading the Rabbit: Explorations in Warner Bros. Animation* (New Brunswick, NJ: Rutgers University Press, 1998), 112.

36 Tom Sito, *Drawing the Line: The Untold Story of Animation Unions from Bosko to Bart Simpson* (Lexington: University Press of Kentucky, 2006), 15.

37 Interview by John Canemaker, 13 February 1973, Canemaker Collection; pub-

lished as John Canemaker, "Animation History and Shamus Culhane," *Film-makers Newsletter* 7:8 (June 1974), 23–28.

38 Joe Adamson, "With Disney on Olympus: An Interview with Dick Huemer," *Funnyworld* 17 (1978), 39.

39 Grim Natwick, "Dick Huemer 1898–1979: Homage to a Star," *Cartoonist Profiles* 45 (March 1980), http://www.huemer.com/animate2.htm.

40 Joe Adamson, "Interview with Dick Huemer" (1968–1969), Mayer Library, American Film Institute. For a detailed discussion of how certain cartoon characters changed in the hands of different animators, see Adamson's 1971 interview with Chuck Jones, reprinted in Maureen Furniss, ed., *Chuck Jones: Conversations* (Jackson: University Press of Mississippi, 2005), esp. 59–63.

41 *Publix Opinion*, 26 September 1930, Mayer Library, American Film Institute.

42 The "slash" method of animation is usually attributed to Raoul Barré, and involves the time-saving device of tearing off and replacement of moving parts from an otherwise static figure in order to minimize the amount of redrawing. For a discussion of the Brays' aggressive use of patents (both their own and others') and licensing, see, for instance, Crafton, *Before Mickey*, 145–60; or Maltin, *Of Mice and Magic*, 7–22.

43 Karl Marx, *Capital*, vol. 1, trans. Ben Fowlkes (New York: Penguin Classics, 1976), 163–64.

44 For a more detailed discussion of free will and the slave's body, see chapter 4.

45 See Bukatman, *Poetics of Slumberland*, 108.

46 See Klein, *7 Minutes*, 3–18. See also Crafton, *Before Mickey*, 174–75.

47 Crafton, *Before Mickey*, 272.

48 Dick Huemer notes the Fleischer Studios' insistence on the use of a certain pen nib, the same used by Charles Dana Gibson and McCay, to produce a finer line in order to differentiate its products. But the fact that a difference in line weight would mark a brand is indication of an otherwise uniform set of practices. Adamson, "Interview with Dick Huemer" (1968–1969), Mayer Library, American Film Institute.

49 For a discussion of communities of practice, see Barbara Rogoff, *Everyday Cognition: Its Development in Social Context* (Cambridge, MA: Harvard University Press, 1984); and Jean Lave and Etienne Wenger, *Situated Learning: Legitimate Peripheral Participation* (Cambridge: Cambridge University Press, 1991).

50 This generational process offers a detailed example of the Bourdieuian notion of habitus. See Pierre Bourdieu, *Outline of a Theory of Practice* (Cambridge: Cambridge University Press, 1977).

51 See Mark Langer, "The Disney-Fleischer Dilemma: Product Differentiation and Technological Innovation," *Screen* 33:4 (winter 1992), 343–58.

52 See Donald Crafton, *Emile Cohl, Caricature, and Film* (Princeton, NJ: Princeton University Press, 1990); Scott McCloud, *Understanding Comics* (New York: Kitchen Sink Press, 1993); David Carrier, *The Aesthetics of Comics* (University Park: Penn State University Press, 2000); Scott Bukatman, "Comics and the

Critique of Chronophotography, or 'He Never Knew When It Was Coming!,'"
Animation 1:1 (2006), 83–103; Drew Morton, "Sketching under the Influence?
Winsor McCay and the Question of Aesthetic Convergence between Comic
Strips and Film," *Animation* 5:3 (2010), 295–312.

53 Henry Jenkins, *What Made Pistachio Nuts? Early Sound Comedy and the Vaudeville Aesthetic* (New York: Columbia University Press, 1993), 59–95.

54 For discussions of the disappearance of the animator in early animation, see
Crafton, *Before Mickey*, 298–99; Bukatman, *Poetics of Slumberland*, 113–31.

55 See, for instance, Donald Crafton, *The Talkies: American Cinema's Transition
to Sound, 1926–1931* (Berkeley: University of California Press, 1997); Douglas
Gomery, *The Coming of Sound* (New York: Routledge, 2003); Edwin M. Bradley,
The First Hollywood Sound Shorts, 1926–1931 (London: McFarland, 2005); Brian
Winston, "How Are Media Born?," in Michele Hilmes, ed., *Connections: A
Broadcast History Reader* (Belmont, CA: Wadsworth, 2003), 3–18; James Lastra,
*Sound Technology and the American Cinema: Perception, Representation, Moder-
nity* (New York: Columbia University Press, 2000), 107–35.

56 Space does not permit a discussion of Blanc's and Warner Bros.' interesting
choice to make most of its trademark characters suffer a speech defect, marking them as simultaneously defective yet powerful.

57 See Richard Schickel, *The Disney Version: The Life, Times, Art and Commerce of
Walt Disney* (New York: Simon and Schuster, 1968). It may also be what led
Paul Wells to title a book that is largely about Disney *Animation and America*
(2002).

58 See Maltin, *Of Mice and Magic*, 34–39; and Barrier, *Hollywood Cartoons*,
48–107.

59 "Mouse and Man," *Time*, 27 December 1937. See Bukatman, *Poetics of Slumberland*, 113–17.

60 Klein, *7 Minutes*, 110–46.

61 For an interpretation of cartoons' role in the transition to sound, see Hank
Sartin, "From Vaudeville to Hollywood, from Silence to Sound: Warner Bros.
Cartoons of the Early Sound Era," in Kevin Sandler, ed., *Reading the Rabbit*
(New Brunswick, NJ: Rutgers University Press, 1998). For a discussion of the
notion of Bazinian realism, see Philip Rosen, *Change Mummified: Cinema, History, Theory* (Minneapolis: University of Minnesota Press, 2001), 3–43. For a
recent defense of Bazin, see Dudley Andrew, *What Cinema Is!* (London: Blackwell, 2010); for a Bergsonian discussion of the organization of space, memory,
and time in cinema, see Gilles Deleuze, *Cinema 1: The Movement Image*, trans.
Hugh Tomlinson and Barbara Habberjam (Minneapolis: University of Minnesota Press, 1986), and *Cinema 2: The Time Image*, trans. Hugh Tomlinson
and Robert Goleta (Minneapolis: University of Minnesota Press, 1989). For
a discussion of animation as engaged in something other than the teleologi-
cal process of approaching a receding real, see Thomas LaMarre, *The Anime
Machine: A Media Theory of Animation* (Minneapolis: University of Minnesota
Press, 2009).

62 One need only look at the progression of the Marx Brothers' films and the brothers' unease with the drive toward narrative stability as they moved from Paramount to MGM, for example, to see the diminishing place vaudeville aesthetics had in the new regime once they had done the heavy lifting of ushering in the new technology. See Jenkins, *What Made Pistachio Nuts?*, 6–10. While early sound musicals and comedies would seem to offer exceptions to this trend, even they underwent at least a degree of diegetic containment, one lampooned, for instance, in *Singin' in the Rain* (Donen/Kelly, 1952).

63 In an otherwise exhaustive study of reflexivity in film and literature, Robert Stam, *Reflexivity in Film and Literature: From Don Quixote to Jean-Luc Goddard* (New York: Columbia University Press, 1992), devotes a scant two pages to animation, and then only to sound animation of the thirties through the fifties.

64 See, for instance, Dana Polan, "Brecht and the Politics of Self-Reflexive Cinema," *Jump Cut* 17 (1978), 29–32; or Cartwright, "Hands of the Animator."

65 Sullivan studios produced the Chaplin series between 1918 and 1919. Other Chaplin cartoons had been produced earlier in the decade by the Movca company, and as a result the provenance of early Chaplin cartoons is sometimes up for debate.

66 John Canemaker, "Otto Messmer and Felix the Cat," *Cartoonist Profiles*, no. 37 (March 1978), Canemaker Collection. See also the 1923 short *Felix in Hollywood*, in which the cat imitates Charlie Chaplin, much to Chaplin's annoyance.

67 Canemaker, "Otto Messmer Interview, March 5 1975, Fort Lee, NJ," Canemaker Collection.

68 For discussions of the rise of movie fan culture, see, for instance, Kathryn Fuller, *At the Picture Show: Small-Town Audiences and the Creation of Movie-Fan Culture* (Washington, DC: Smithsonian Institution Press, 1996); or Shelley Stamp, *Movie-Struck Girls: Women and Motion Picture Culture after the Nickelodeon* (Princeton, NJ: Princeton University Press, 2000). For a case study of the organization and mobilization of fan culture in the 1930s, see Eric Smoodin, *Regarding Frank Capra: Audience, Celebrity, and American Film Studies, 1930–1960* (Durham, NC: Duke University Press, 2004), 1–50.

69 See Bukatman, *Poetics of Slumberland*, 136.

70 See the introduction. Compare David Roediger, *The Wages of Whiteness: Race and the Making of the American Working Class* (New York: Verso, 1991); and Eric Lott, *Love and Theft: Blackface Minstrelsy and the American Working Class* (New York: Oxford University Press, 1993).

71 For a discussion of rationalization and its effect on convention, see Crafton, *Before Mickey*, 271–72. Bukatman (*Poetics of Slumberland*, 106–35) also treats the rebelliousness of the animated character in relation to the mode of production but seems to see that rebellion as a compulsion located in the very force of automatism and automation itself rather than as a sublimated protest over the automation of the labor process.

72 Bukatman, *Poetics of Slumberland*, 108.

73 Bukatman, *Poetics of Slumberland*, 21. Bukatman builds a significant portion

of his analysis around Sianne Ngai's influential discussion of labor and minstrelsy. See Sianne Ngai, *Ugly Feelings* (Cambridge, MA: Harvard University Press, 2005), 89–125.

74 Most recently, see, for instance, Furuhata, "Rethinking Plasticity."

75 "Mouse and Man."

76 Bosley Crowther, "Cartoons on the Screen: A Momentary Consideration of Who Makes Them, How Many, and Why," *New York Times*, 13 February 1938, 158. Crowther apparently did not know that the Fleischers, having lost a bitter unionization battle, had just announced to their staff that they were about to decamp to Miami in a bid to break the new union shop.

77 Eric Smoodin, *Animating Culture: Hollywood Cartoons from the Sound Era* (New Brunswick, NJ: Rutgers University Press, 1993), 96–135.

78 Anne O'Hare McCormick, "Hollywood: Weird Factory of Mob Art," *New York Times Magazine*, 6 December 1931, 5.

79 Klein, *7 Minutes*, 172–80.

80 The Popeye series (1933–1957), which eventually eclipsed Betty Boop, signaled that transition in the same way that Disney's *Egyptian Melodies* (1931) had indicated that studio's move away from the presentational and toward the representational. Although more contained and less self-referential, many Popeye shorts had their share of winks and asides to the audience. By the time of the Superman series (1941–1943), the Fleischer Studios were on their way to bankruptcy and takeover by Paramount. For this history, see Barrier, *Hollywood Cartoons*, 292–306.

81 For a discussion of labor struggles in the American animation industry, see Sito, *Drawing the Line*.

82 Walter Benjamin, "Mickey Mouse," in *The Work of Art in the Age of Its Technological Reproducibility and Other Writings on Media*, ed. Michael W. Jennings, Brigid Doherty, and Thomas Y. Levin, trans. Rodney Livingstone (Cambridge, MA: Harvard University Press, 2008 [1931]), 338.

83 Walter Benjamin, "The Work of Art in the Age of Its Technological Reproducibility," in *Work of Art in the Age of Its Technological Reproducibility*, 38.

84 Benjamin, "Work of Art in the Age of Its Technological Reproducibility."

85 Benjamin, "Work of Art in the Age of Its Technological Reproducibility," 51–52n29. Since Mickey Mouse's first outing in color was in *The Band Concert* (1935), it is likely that Benjamin refers to the Silly Symphonies.

86 This sort of interpretive overreaching has been repeated less lyrically and thoughtfully in recent scholarship outside of animation studies proper that imagines, for instance, that the output of a single studio such as Pixar can describe in and of itself—and without regard for any history of cinema generally or of animation more specifically—significant changes in social and material relations that a more grounded analysis would at the least trouble and at most actually contradict.

87 For a brilliant analysis of the spatial dynamics of *Egyptian Melodies* and its relationship to changing animation technologies, see Crafton, *Shadow*, 144–53.

88 Walt Disney, quoted in Irving Wallace, "Mickey Mouse, and How He Grew," *Colliers* 123:15 (9 April 1949), 20–21.

3. SPACE

To view all of the media discussed in this chapter, go to http://scalar.usc.edu/works /birthofanindustry.

1 "200 Publix Houses Get 'Talkies,'" *Publix Opinion*, 21 May 1928, 2; Mayer Library, American Film Institute, Los Angeles.

2 "Sales Slant Correct!," *Publix Opinion*, 2 May 1930, 9; Mayer Library, American Film Institute. While the film did feature scenes in the fields, the action was not confined to that locale.

3 One could argue that the plot of *Hallelujah!* features a cotton field and so, like other tie-ins, the lobby display simply extended the film's diegetic world into the house. Yet just as the need to set the dramatic action in and around a cotton field was driven by stereotype, so was the lobby art. In both cases, legibility also meant comfort for white audiences. Hence the nod toward "local tradition."

4 *Hallelujah!* featured scenes in cotton fields, but they were not the sole location for the film, nor its narrative center. Conversely, given the rapid ascendancy of the "mid-Atlantic" accent in Hollywood sound films (a trend parodied in *Singin' in the Rain* [1952]), anxiety about the undermining of regional accents was not unreasonable.

5 Stuart Hall, "Racist Ideologies and the Media," in Paul Marris and Sue Thornham, eds., *Media Studies: A Reader* (New York: New York University Press, 2000), 271–82. See also Stuart Hall, "The Spectacle of the 'Other,'" in Hall, ed., *Representation: Cultural Representations and Signifying Practices* (London: Sage, 1997), 223–90.

6 See Michael Rogin, *Blackface, White Noise: Jewish Immigrants in the Hollywood Melting Pot* (Berkeley: University of California Press, 1996), 3–44; and Thomas Cripps, "Review: *Blackface, White Noise: Jewish Immigrants in the Hollywood Melting Pot*," *Journal of American History* 83:4 (March 1997), 1462–63.

7 Hank Sartin, "From Vaudeville to Hollywood, from Silence to Sound: Warner Bros. Cartoons of the Early Sound Era," in Kevin Sandler, ed., *Reading the Rabbit: Explorations in Warner Bros. Animation* (New Brunswick, NJ: Rutgers University Press, 1998), 67–85. See also Charles Wolfe, "'Cross Talk': Language, Space, and the Burns and Allen Comedy Film Short," *Film History* 23:3 (2011), 300–312.

8 Donald Crafton, *Shadow of a Mouse: Performance, Belief, and World-Making in Animation* (Berkeley: University of California Press, 2013), 103.

9 See, for instance, Edward F. Albee, "Twenty Years of Vaudeville," *Variety* 72:3 (6 September 1923).

10 See Daniel Goldmark, *Tunes for 'Toons: Music and the Hollywood Cartoon* (Berkeley: University of California Press, 2005), 32.

11 See Norman M. Klein, *7 Minutes* (London: Verso, 1993), 186–99.

12 See Goldmark, *Tunes for 'Toons*; and Joel Dinerstein, *Swinging the Machine: Modernity, Technology, and African American Culture between the World Wars* (Boston: University of Massachusetts Press, 2003).

13 Donald Crafton, *Before Mickey: The Animated Film, 1898–1928* (Cambridge, MA: MIT Press, 1982), 272.

14 See Scott Bukatman, *The Poetics of Slumberland: Animated Spirits and the Animating Spirit* (Berkeley: University of California Press, 2012), 114–18.

15 For the foreclosure of diegetic space in the emerging conventions of classical Hollywood, see Miriam Bratu Hansen, *Babel and Babylon: Spectatorship in American Silent Film* (Cambridge, MA: Harvard University Press, 1991), esp. 81–83.

16 *San Francisco Call*, 9 February 1914, n.p., folder 30, Eddie Leonard Minstrels, Billy Rose Theatre Division, New York Public Library.

17 For an overview of this phenomenon, see, for instance, Richard Kozarski, *An Evening's Entertainment: The Age of the Silent Feature Picture, 1915–1928* (Berkeley: University of California Press, 1994); or Sheldon Hall and Steve Neale, eds., *Epics, Spectacles, and Blockbusters: A Hollywood History* (Detroit: Wayne State University Press, 2010), ch. 3. For a hagiographic account of Sam "Roxy" Rothafel's role in the rise of combination shows, see Ross Melnick, *American Showman: Samuel "Roxy" Rothafel and the Birth of the Entertainment Industry, 1908–1935* (New York: Columbia University Press, 2012).

18 This studio went under a number of different names, including Red Seal, Out of the Inkwell, and Fleischer Studios, at different times.

19 For a concise and complementary reading of this cartoon, see Crafton, *Shadow*, 104–15.

20 The intertitle is actually from a 2003 reissue by Inkwell Images. Still, in the original Max yells at Ko-Ko, and we can assume that the meaning of the original title card was roughly equivalent.

21 This moment seems a nice illustration of Rogin's (*Blackface, White Noise*) claim that Jews in the early twentieth century used performances of racial transformation as a way of demonstrating their whiteness.

22 See Henry Jenkins, *What Made Pistachio Nuts? Early Sound Comedy and the Vaudeville Aesthetic* (New York: Columbia University Press, 1993), 63–85. See also Robert M. Lewis, *From Traveling Show to Vaudeville: Theatrical Spectacle in America, 1830–1910* (Baltimore: Johns Hopkins University Press, 2003); and Andrew Erdman, *Blue Vaudeville: Sex, Morals and the Mass Marketing of Entertainment, 1895–1915* (Jefferson, NC: McFarland, 2004).

23 See Bukatman, *Poetics of Slumberland*, 113–18; and Erwin Feyersinger, "Diegetic Short Circuits: Metalepsis in Animation," *Animation* 5:3 (2010), 279–94.

24 Perhaps the best example of this in the Out of the Inkwell series is *Ko-Ko's Earth Control* (1928), in which Ko-Ko and his sidekick, Fitz, actually destroy the real world through their antics in the drawn one. For more clearly racialized and troubling versions of this trope, see, for instance, *The Ouija Board* (1920) or *Ko-Ko the Barber* (1925).

25 For an insightful discussion of the complexities of modeling the moviegoing experience, see Robert C. Allen, "Reimagining the History of the Experience of Cinema," in Richard Maltby, Daniel Biltereyst, and Philippe Meers, eds., *Explorations in New Cinema History: Approaches and Case Studies* (Malden, MA: Wiley-Blackwell, 2011).

26 Appropriately, the first of these was *My Old Kentucky Home* (1924), based on a classic minstrel tune penned by Stephen Foster originally titled "Poor Uncle Tom, Goodnight." See Steven Kanfer, *Serious Business: The Art and Commerce of Animation in America from Betty Boop to "Toy Story"* (New York: Da Capo, 1997), 69. Kanfer found the "Talkartoons" (a term he seems to use interchangeably with "Song Car-Tunes" and "Screen Songs") drab compared to Disney. See also Donald Crafton, *The Talkies: American Cinema's Transition to Sound, 1926–1931* (Berkeley: University of California Press, 1997), 395–400; or Richard Fleischer, *Out of the Inkwell: Max Fleischer and the Animation Revolution* (Lexington: University Press of Kentucky, 2005), 43.

27 The principal difference between the Song Car-Tunes and Screen Songs was that the latter often, though not always, featured popular musical and vaudeville acts of the day, such as the Mills Brothers or Boswell Sisters, in live interludes. Only approximate numbers are given because of disagreements over release dates and because some shorts were issued first as Song Car-Tunes and then rereleased as Screen Songs. See Leonard Maltin, *Of Mice and Magic: A History of American Animated Cartoons* (New York: Plume, 1980); or Leslie Carbarga, *The Fleischer Story* (New York: Da Capo, 1988).

28 Rogin, *Blackface, White Noise*, 121–56. For critiques of Rogin's argument, see Cripps, "Review: *Blackface, White Noise*"; David Nasaw, "Review: *Blackface, White Noise: Jewish Immigrants in the Hollywood Melting Pot*," *American Historical Review* 102:4 (October 1997), 1244–45; Richard M. Merelman, "Hollywood's America: Social and Political Themes in Motion Pictures" (review), *American Political Science Review* 91:3 (September 1997), 753–54; and Lary May, "Review: *Blackface, White Noise: Jewish Immigrants in the Hollywood Melting Pot*," *American Jewish History* 85:1 (1997), 115–19.

29 Saidiya Hartman, *Scenes of Subjection: Terror, Slavery, and Self-Making in Nineteenth-Century America* (New York: Oxford University Press, 1997), 17–23, 106. See also Hortense J. Spillers, "Mama's Baby, Papa's Maybe: An American Grammar Book," *Diacritics* 17:2 (summer 1987), 65–81; and Michelle M. Wright, *Becoming Black: Creating Identity in the African Diaspora* (Durham, NC: Duke University Press, 2004).

30 C. S. Sewell, "Dolly Gray," *Moving Picture World*, 6 February 1926, 565. See Maltin, *Of Mice and Magic*, 358. Maltin does not include *Dolly Gray* in his list of Song Car-Tunes, but he does mention *Darling Nellie Gray* (1926). The description offered by Sewell, however, better fits the former.

31 "'The Children's Hour' at the Plaza Theatre," *New York Times*, 26 December 1926, x7.

32 "My Bonnie," *Film Daily*, 20 September 1925, 32.

33 Melnick, *American Showman*, 57–65.

34 See Erdman, *Blue Vaudeville*, 2–3, 21–23, 48–53, on Keith's rules.

35 "Stages Epilogue with 40 People for Song Car-Tune 'My Bonnie,'" *Moving Picture World*, 17 October 1925, 574.

36 Fleischer, *Out of the Inkwell*, 39.

37 Douglas Gomery, *The Coming of Sound* (New York: Routledge, 2003), 11–12. For Rothafel, see Melnick, *American Showman*, 2012.

38 Gomery suggests that up until the 1925/1926 season, first-run theaters had offered vaudeville combinations but not full presentations. A survey of *Wid's* and *Film Daily* from 1920 on suggests that Broadway houses were offering presentations much earlier.

39 "At Broadway Theaters," *Wid's Daily*, 15 September 1920, 4.

40 "At Broadway Theaters," *Film Daily*, 16 April 1925, 6. This was only a few months before the Fleischers premiered their feature-length film *Evolution* at the nearby Rivoli, presenting it in both full-length and short form. "Evolution Film," *Film Daily*, 21 June 1925, 1.

41 "Pictures at Keith's Palace, Cleveland," *Film Daily*, 7 July 1925, 2.

42 Keith-Albee would, of course, become part of RKO Pictures in 1928.

43 Charles Hynes, "How B'way Does It," *Film Daily*, 9 October 1927, 8.

44 Fleischer, *Out of the Inkwell*, 30–45.

45 "'Ko-Ko' a Presentation Knockout," *Moving Picture World*, 8 May 1926, 183.

46 "'Ko-Ko' a Presentation Knockout."

47 "'Ko-Ko' a Presentation Knockout," 184.

48 Bergson has described mechanical behavior such as this as at the root of comedy. See the conclusion. Henri Bergson, *Laughter: An Essay on the Meaning of the Comic*, trans. Cloudesly Brereton and Fred Rothwell (St. Paul, MN: Green Integer, 2003 [1911]).

49 Bergson, *Laughter*. For a discussion of mechanical movement and comedy, see Bergson, *Laughter*, 12–18, 22–30. For the mechanical in relation to animation, see Bukatman, *Poetics of Slumberland*, 136–43. See also the conclusion.

50 "'Felix the Cat' Cartoon Prologues to Be a Feature of Short Subject Month," *Moving Picture World*, 24 October 1925, 637–38.

51 Mary Ann Doane, "The Voice in the Cinema: The Articulation of Body and Space," *Yale French Studies* 60 (1980), 33–50.

52 Gomery, *Coming of Sound*, xii–xxi. Gomery is responding to Crafton, *Talkies*.

53 For an excellent discussion of race more broadly conceived in relation to space and the cinema, see Alice Maurice, *The Cinema and Its Shadow: Race and Technology in Early Cinema* (Minneapolis: University of Minnesota Press, 2013).

54 Consider, for instance, the Fleischers' *The Chinaman* (1920), Disney's *Alice Chops the Suey* (1925), Iwerks's *Chinaman's Chance* (1933), Terrytoons' *Hungarian Goulash* (1930) or *Scotch Highball* (1930), or Van Beuren's *Hot Tamale* (1930) or *Gypped in Egypt* (1930), to name but a few.

55 Crafton, *Shadow*, 109.

56 Crafton suggests that after an initial fascination with accents, in both early

sound features and shorts the major studios moved away from ethnicity when the economic dictates of the Depression demanded a broader appeal (*Talkies*, 417). In this vein, Bradley notes that the second Warner Bros. short, *The Better Ole* (1926), featured Al Jolson in blackface making a joke about an Irish tenor, and the Jewish act of the Howard brothers. Edwin M. Bradley, *The First Hollywood Sound Shorts, 1926–1931* (London: McFarland, 2005), 5. While Bradley makes the unfortunate slip of imagining that blackface minstrelsy borrows directly from African American culture, he also notes the early fascination with race and ethnicity in early sound shorts.

57 See Donald Bogle, *Toms, Coons, Mulattoes, Mammies, and Bucks: An Interpretive History of Blacks in American Films* (New York: Continuum, 2006); Thomas Cripps, *Slow Fade to Black: The Negro in American Films, 1900–1942* (New York: Oxford University Press, 1995).

58 Crafton, *Talkies*, 412.

59 Phil Wagner points out that this was not universally true, with the Maurice and Fanchon players performing for Publix long after the company had closed down other presentations. Wagner, "'An America Not Quite Mechanized': Fanchon and Marco, Inc. Perform Modernity," *Film History* 23:3 (2011), 251–67.

60 Gomery, *Coming of Sound*, 11–13.

61 "Warner Brothers History," box 1549B, folder 1, p. 12, Warner Bros. Archive, University of Southern California, Los Angeles. See also *Variety*, August 1926, 3.

62 Crafton, *Talkies*, 76.

63 "'Metro Movietone Acts,'" *MGM Distributor*, 19 January 1929, n.p.; Margaret Herrick Library, Academy of Motion Picture Arts and Sciences, Beverly Hills.

64 The notion of "generic" depends, of course, on the assumption that acts that feature whites are not racial while those that feature nonwhites are.

65 *Exhibitor's Herald*, 2 March 1929, 22.

66 *Exhibitor's Herald*, 29 June 1929, 162.

67 *Exhibitor's Herald*, 29 June 1929, 162. Thanks to Rob King for bringing these articles to my attention.

68 "Eliminate Unit Shows in 6 Theatres," *Publix Opinion* 3:26 (7 March 1930), 1; Mayer Library, American Film Institute.

69 Jack White quoted in "Audien Shorts," *Exhibitor's Herald*, 27 April 1929, 36.

70 Of course, as a producer of short talking comedies (which were different from variety shorts), White had a vested interest in describing even filmed vaudeville acts as passé; they also were the competition.

71 "Short Comedies," *Exhibitor's Herald*, 24 March 1928, 31.

72 Note also in this promo the tie-in to Amos 'n' Andy's feature film *Check and Double Check* (1930).

73 Crafton, *Talkies*, 400.

74 Mark Langer, "The Disney-Fleischer Dilemma: Product Differentiation and Technological Innovation," *Screen* 33:4 (1992), 343–59.

75 See Henri Lefebvre, *The Production of Space*, trans. Donald Nicholson-Smith

(London: Blackwell, 1974), 31–33. See also Crafton, *Talkies*; Doane, "Voice in the Cinema"; Hansen, *Babel and Babylon*; James Lastra, *Sound Technology and the American Cinema: Perception, Representation, Modernity* (New York: Columbia University Press, 2000), 61–91.

76 See, for instance, Lastra, *Sound Technology*, 92–122.

77 In contrast, live shorts that showcased popular musical acts were often simply static visual records of performances, sometimes enlivened by quirky sets or costumes, with a perfunctory framing narrative. For instance, in the Vitaphone Variety *The Police Quartette* (1927) a desk sergeant receives a call and explains to three other officers that the chief wants them to perform at an orphanage but that they should practice first. Thus begins a barbershop quartet number. Another Variety, *Paul Tremaine and His Aristocrats* (1929), opens with stock footage of trains and then crossfades to a series of static shots of the orchestra doing a jazzed-up version of "I've Been Working on the Railroad." The novelty of such shorts was in their use of synchronized sound and simple juxtaposition of sounds and images, certainly not in their relatively rudimentary cinematography.

78 Norman M. Klein, "Animation and Animorphs: A Brief Disappearing Act," in Vivian Sobchack, ed., *Meta-morphing: Visual Transformation and the Culture of Quick-Change* (Minneapolis: University of Minnesota Press, 2000), 29.

79 Goldmark, *Tunes for 'Toons*, 1–6, 10–16.

80 A slightly earlier version of this shift in spatial ontology is the Fleischers' *Swing You Sinners!* (1930), an animated interpretation of "Sing You Sinners," a popular tune in the 1930 Paramount catalogue.

81 An interesting difference between this cartoon and the last is that while the Fleischer Studios had grown out of J. R. Bray's animation operation, the Van Beuren studio was purchased from the Keith-Albee vaudeville chain, which had bankrolled Paul Terry's output throughout most of the 1920s, only to sell the company to Amedee Van Beuren in 1928 at the dawn of the sound era. Maltin, *Of Mice and Magic*, 195. See also Michael Barrier, *Hollywood Cartoons: American Animation in Its Golden Age* (New York: Oxford University Press, 1999), 168–69.

82 This is a perfect example of what Crafton refers to as the clash between the "parthenogenesis" and "autophagy" of cartoons that create and consume their own narratives. See Crafton, *Shadow*, 70.

83 Amedee Van Beuren was neither an animator nor a particularly hands-on producer, and the Van Beuren studio barely survived the transition to sound, folding in 1936 amid squabbles between animators and managers, after marginally successful experiments with color in its Rainbow Parade series, a revival of Felix the Cat, and a sideline of live adventure films, including the Frank Buck series.

84 Doane, "Voice in the Cinema," 35.

85 Specifically, Doane is concerned with the voice, and not only the synchronous voice but also the voice off and the voice-over. Each offers the possibility of a

richer sense of cinematic realism, of the fluid movement through narrative time and space, yet at the same time through the potential for dislocation each poses a greater threat to the sense of harmonious unity at the center of the Lacanian model of spectatorial pleasure. The voice that does not match its body undermines the potential for identification. (The classic example is *Singin' in the Rain* [1952], in which the central gag and plot point involves a silent movie star whose voice is so grating that she is overdubbed without her knowledge.) For a discussion of voice and access to the Real in film, see Slavoj Žižek, "Grimaces of the Real, or When the Phallus Appears," *October* 58 (1991), 44–68.

86 See also Kaja Silverman, *The Acoustic Mirror: The Female Voice in Psychoanalysis and Cinema* (Bloomington: Indiana University Press, 1988); and Britta Sjogren, *Into the Vortex: Female Voice and Paradox in Film* (Chicago: University of Illinois Press, 2006), for a more detailed discussion of voice, gender, and cinema.

87 It was as if the Lacanian threat of castration that purportedly powers suture was made good, yet the audience survived to view again. Rather than obliterating the fantasmatic wholeness of the viewing subject, the cartoon derided that figure's solitary provenance, invoking a collective subjectivity in its place. See, for instance, Daniel Dayan, "The Tutor Code of Classical Cinema," *Film Quarterly* 28:1 (fall 1974), 22–31; Jean-Pierre Oudart, "Cinema and Suture," trans. Kari Hanet, *Screen* 18 (winter 1978), 35–47; and Kaja Silverman, *The Subject of Semiotics* (New York: Oxford University Press, 1983), ch. 5.

88 See Bukatman, *Poetics of Slumberland*, 129–36; and Gilles Deleuze, *Immanence: A Life*, trans. Ann Boyman (New York: Zone, 2001), 25–35.

89 In the 1930s, Warner Bros. in particular would play on the atrophy of this space through a gag involving a silhouetted audience member in front of the action of the cartoon. In this gag, an argument would break out between a character on-screen and a "real" audience member (who appeared as a shadow). For a discussion of the organization of spectatorship in these gags, see Sartin, "From Vaudeville to Hollywood."

90 Crafton, *Shadow*, 150.

91 Not every cartoon indulged in this sort of racist stereotyping, but a surprising number that participated in the swing craze from the late twenties onward did. This number is surprising now because most of these cartoons were withdrawn from general circulation and the nostalgic canon we normally associate with cartooning's "golden age." Much of this happened when Ted Turner bought the Warners prewar and Fleischer collections. Rereleases of older cartoons now often feature warnings about changing standards of racial decorum, as in Disney's use of Leonard Maltin's live, short, instructive lectures, in which he explains how something so offensive today could have been considered just good fun when it was made. These interludes, as well-meaning as they are, stop short of implicating early animators and producers in the structural processes of racism.

92 For a thorough discussion of this relationship, see Goldmark, *Tunes for 'Toons*, 77–106.

93 Dempsey J. Travis, "Chicago's Jazz Trail, 1893–1950," *Black Music Research Journal* 10:1 (spring 1990), 82–85.

94 For a detailed study of the relationship of vaudeville to early sound film comedy, see Jenkins, *What Made Pistachio Nuts?* It is worthwhile to note that even as it faded as a live performance form, vaudeville had a second life on radio and a third life on television.

95 An ongoing site for the nostalgic practice of blackface minstrelsy in the 1930s was in charity shows, and there was a proliferation of minstrel manuals specifically designed for amateurs during the decade. See Samuel Goldman Papers, University of Chicago Special Collections Research Center, University of Chicago Library; or Harris Collection, John Hay Library, Brown University.

96 Klein, *7 Minutes*, 172–80.

97 Klein, "Animation and Animorphs," 27.

98 Crafton, *Shadow*, 48–49.

99 Again, to concentrate on the black/white binary is not to deny the operations of other racial formations at the time. The focus on that binary here is due to its strong association with a history of slavery, labor, and the commodified body and because of its dominance in the racial imaginary of the time. A study of the place of stereotypical Chinese, Mexican, or Irish figures during this time would add much to a discussion of the depiction of the laboring body and would be extremely worthwhile. But given that none of these stereotypes informed the trademark characters of the era, they are beyond the scope of this work.

100 While figures such as Zip Coon or Jim Dandy complicated this scenario, it was often through their juxtaposition to these plantation figures.

101 James Naremore, "Uptown Folks: Blackness and Entertainment in *Cabin in the Sky*," in Krin Gabbard, ed., *Representing Jazz* (Durham, NC: Duke University Press, 1995).

102 In the same light, we can read Lead Belly's "Bourgeois Blues" (1938) as a repudiation of the aspirations of the American Folklore project as a profoundly bourgeois fantasy of racial harmony through education and understanding rather than through aggressive economic and social action.

103 Alvin Lucier, *I Am Sitting in a Room*, LP/CD 1013 (Lovely Music, Ltd., 1981/1990). Lucier first performed this piece in 1969. The exact phrases Lucier used were "I am sitting in a room different from the one you are in now. I am recording the sound of my speaking voice and I am going to play it back into the room again and again until the resonant frequencies of the room reinforce themselves so that any semblance of my speech, with perhaps the exception of rhythm, is destroyed. What you will hear, then, are the natural resonant frequencies of the room articulated by speech. I regard this activity not so much as a demonstration of a physical fact, but more as a way to smooth out any irregularities my speech might have."

104 Michel Foucault, "Of Other Spaces" [1967], *Architecture/Mouvement/Continuité* (October 1984), 46–49.

105 Lefebvre describes these as "spatial practice, which embraces production and reproduction, and the particular locations and spatial sets characteristic of each social formation. . . . Representations of space, which are tied to the relations of production and to the 'order' which those relations impose, and hence to knowledge, to signs, to codes, and to 'frontal' relations . . . [and] representational spaces, embodying complex symbolisms, sometimes coded, sometimes not, linked to the clandestine or underground side of social life, as also to art (which may come eventually to be defined less as a code of space than as a code of representational spaces)" (*Production of Space*, 33). For other approaches to the spatialization of practice, see, for instance, Foucault, "Of Other Spaces" (Lefebvre takes Foucault to task in his work); David Harvey, *Spaces of Capital: Towards a Critical Geography* (New York: Routledge, 2001); and Anthony Giddens, *The Constitution of Society* (Berkeley: University of California Press, 1984), 110–45. For a discussion of material practice and social geography, see Chandra Mukerji, *Territorial Ambitions and the Gardens of Versailles* (Cambridge: Cambridge University Press, 1997).

106 William Paul, for instance, has made reference to the multiplex as the physical instantiation of cable television. While this may be slightly reductive, it does point to a relationship between viewers and content that has correlates in the immaterial space of cable programming and the material space of the mall and cineplex. Paul, "The K-Mart Audience at the Mall Movies," *Film History* 6:4 (winter 1994), 487–501.

107 Homi K. Bhabha, *The Location of Culture* (New York: Routledge, 1994), 302–35. See Fredric Jameson, *Postmodernism, or The Cultural Logic of Late Capitalism* (Durham, NC: Duke University Press, 1991); Harvey, *Spaces of Capital*. See also Jacques Derrida, *Spectres of Marx* (New York: Routledge, 1994), 62–63. For a problematic but useful discussion of the applicability of Lefebvre, see Jason Edwards, "The Materialism of Historical Materialism," in Diana Coole and Samantha Frost, eds., *New Materialisms: Ontology, Agency, and Politics* (Durham, NC: Duke University Press, 2010), 288–92.

108 John L. Jackson, *Real Black: Adventures in Racial Sincerity* (Chicago: University of Chicago Press, 2005), 4; Fred Moten, *In the Break: The Aesthetics of the Black Radical Tradition* (Minneapolis: University of Minnesota Press, 2003), 251–52.

109 Sergei M. Eisenstein, *On Disney*, trans. Jay Leyda (London: Methuen, 1988).

110 For a discussion of the relationship of the real and the ideal in the commodity form and of the process of commodification as consciousness, see David Bakhurst, *Consciousness and Revolution in Soviet Philosophy: From the Bolsheviks to Evald Ilynenkov* (Cambridge: Cambridge University Press, 1991).

111 The operations of gender and sexuality, while very important to the history of American animation, are beyond the scope of this project.

4. RACE

To view all of the media discussed in this chapter, go to http://scalar.usc.edu/works /birthofanindustry.

1 The year 1937 marked the release of Disney's feature-length cartoon *Snow White*. At least two feature-length animated films are widely accepted as predating *Snow White*: the Fleischers' *The Einstein Theory of Relativity* (1923) and Lotte Reininger's *The Adventures of Prince Achmed* (1926).

2 For discussions of the relationship between immigration, assimilation, and fantasies of blackness, see, for instance, Michael Rogin, *Blackface, White Noise: Jewish Immigrants in the Hollywood Melting Pot* (Berkeley: University of California Press, 1996); David Roediger, *The Wages of Whiteness: Race and the Making of the American Working Class* (New York: Verso, 1991), and *Towards the Abolition of Whiteness: Essays on Race, Politics, and Working Class History* (New York: Verso, 1994); Eric Lott, *Love and Theft: Blackface Minstrelsy and the American Working Class* (New York: Oxford University Press, 1993); Daphne Brooks, *Bodies in Dissent: Spectacular Performances of Race and Freedom, 1850–1910* (Durham, NC: Duke University Press, 2006). For discussions of stereotype and fantasy, see, for instance, Stuart Hall, "Racist Ideologies and the Media," in Paul Marris and Sue Thornham, eds., *Media Studies: A Reader* (New York: New York University Press, 2000), and "Stereotyping as a Signifying Practice," in Hall, ed., *Representation: Cultural Representations and Signifying Practices* (London: Sage, 1997); Richard Iton, *In Search of the Black Fantastic: Politics and Popular Culture in the Post–Civil Rights Era* (London: Oxford University Press, 2010); or James C. Davis, *Commerce in Color: Race, Consumer Culture, and American Literature, 1893–1933* (Ann Arbor: University of Michigan Press, 2007).

3 For an overview of eugenics in the United States, see Wendy Kline, *Building a Better Race: Gender, Sexuality, and Eugenics from the Turn of the Century to the Baby Boom* (Berkeley: University of California Press, 2001); or Laura L. Lovett, *Conceiving the Future: Pronatalism, Reproduction, and the Family in the United States, 1890–1938* (Durham, NC: University of North Carolina Press, 2007). For a relatively recent example of a eugenic argument, see Richard J. Herrnstein and Charles Murray, *The Bell Curve: Intelligence and Class Structure in American Life* (New York: Free Press, 1994). For the ongoing potency of this discourse, see Sam Roberts, "A Nation of None and All of the Above," *New York Times*, 16 August 2008.

4 See Jacqueline Najuma Stewart, *Migrating to the Movies: Cinema and Black Urban Modernity* (Berkeley: University of California Press, 2005), 23–90; and Alice Maurice, *The Cinema and Its Shadow: Race and Technology in Early Cinema* (Minneapolis: University of Minnesota Press, 2013), ch. 1. For an intelligent discussion of racism in early cartoons, see Jeet Heer, "Racism as a Stylistic Choice and Other Notes," *Comics Journal* 301, online (posted 14 March 2011).

5 For a detailed musicological discussion of this segment, see Daniel Goldmark,

Tunes for 'Toons: Music and the Hollywood Cartoon (Berkeley: University of California Press, 2005), 77–106.

6 For discussions of African Americans and fantasies of the jungle and of African-ness, see, for instance, Thomas Cripps, *Slow Fade to Black: The Negro in American Films, 1900–1942* (New York: Oxford University Press, 1995); or James Naremore, "Uptown Folks: Blackness and Entertainment in *Cabin in the Sky*," in Krin Gabbard, ed., *Representing Jazz* (Durham, NC: Duke University Press, 1995). For a detailed analysis of real and imagined African Americans in American musicals, see Arthur Knight, *Disintegrating the Musical: Black Performance and American Musical Film* (Durham, NC: Duke University Press, 2002).

7 See Amelia Holberg, "Betty Boop: Jewish Film Star," *American Jewish History* 87:4 (December 1999), 291–312.

8 Henry T. Sampson, *That's Enough, Folks: Black Images in Animated Cartoons, 1900–1960* (London: Scarecrow, 1998), 81.

9 See Robert O'Meally, "Checking Our Balances: Ellison on Armstrong's Humor," *boundary 2* 30:2 (2003), 115–36.

10 Of course, this is a racial binary only if we consider Ko-Ko's literalized Jewishness as "white." Otherwise, we are actually dealing with racial triangulation. See Rogin, *Blackface, White Noise.*

11 Norman M. Klein, *7 Minutes* (London: Verso, 1993), 66.

12 Knight, *Disintegrating the Musical*, 32.

13 For a discussion of *Plessy v. Ferguson* and the racial formation "separate but equal," see James T. Patterson, *Brown v. Board of Education: A Civil Rights Milestone and Its Troubled Legacy* (New York: Oxford University Press, 2002); or Waldo E. Martin, *Brown v. Board of Education: A Brief History with Documents* (New York: Bedford St. Martin's, 1998).

14 For an excellent reading of "animatedness" and racialized resistance, see Sianne Ngai, *Ugly Feelings* (Cambridge, MA: Harvard University Press, 2005), 89–125.

15 Compare Sigmund Freud, "The Relation of Jokes to Dreams and to the Unconscious," in Freud, *Jokes and Their Relation to the Unconscious*, trans. and ed. James Strachey (New York: Penguin Books, 1991 [1905]), with Sigmund Freud, "Humor," in Freud, *Art and Literature*, ed. James Strachey, trans. Joan Riviere (New York: Penguin Books, 1990 [1928]), discussed here. For a discussion of this comparison, to which space does not permit a detailed reply, see Simon Critchley, *On Humour* (London: Routledge, 2002). For the sake of argument, Freud's 1928 essay collapses humor and joking somewhat, considering the similarities more important to the topic than the differences. It is important to note that in the earlier work, Freud does discuss empathy (see *Jokes and Their Relation to the Unconscious*, 239–59). However, that discussion centers more on naïve utterances, especially by children, and on jokes in which a lack of ill intent on the part of the teller is assumed.

16 For an excellent account of animation and swing, see Goldmark, *Tunes for*

'*Toons*. See also Joel Dinerstein, *Swinging the Machine: Modernity, Technology, and African American Culture Between the World Wars* (Boston: University of Massachusetts Press, 2003), for a discussion of swing, race, and modernism.

17 Comedians such as Costello and Allen (and the writers who crafted their material) also made heavy use of the sort of wordplay found in minstrelsy's stump speech. For a collection of vaudeville scripts, see the Library of Congress collection, http://memory.loc.gov/ammem/vshtml/vshome.html.

18 Charles Wolfe reports that Burns and Allen tried several different routines without success before falling into the smart/dumb dichotomy with which they became synonymous. Wolfe, "'Cross-Talk': Language, Space, and the Burns and Allen Comedy Film Short," *Film History* 23:3 (2011), 300–312.

19 The association between minstrels and trademark animated characters is long-standing. Even in the sound era, as Lehman points out, that relationship continued: "Iwerks also adapted Sambo and company to the animation trends of the mid-1930s. Sambo looks and acts just like Mickey Mouse—hardly a surprise, given that Iwerks helped to create the mouse. The boy is dressed in short pants and huge oval shoes just like Mickey's"; Christopher Lehmann, *The Colored Cartoon: Black Presentation in American Animated Short Films, 1907–1954* (Amherst: University of Massachusetts Press, 2007), 54. See also the discussion of Felix later in this chapter.

20 Lott, *Love and Theft*, 38–63; Hall, "Racist Ideologies."

21 Saidiya Hartman, *Scenes of Subjection: Terror, Slavery, and Self-Making in Nineteenth-Century America* (New York: Oxford University Press, 1997), 29.

22 Lehman, *Colored Cartoon*, 47.

23 For a discussion of torture and humor in relation to the American conquest of Iraq, see Schuyler Henderson, "Disregarding the Suffering of Others: Narrative, Comedy, and Torture, *Literature and Medicine* 24:2 (fall 2005), 181–208.

24 This offers a counter to Benjamin's fears of the desire of the masses appropriated by film producers and crystallized in the body of the star. Walter Benjamin, "The Work of Art in the Age of Its Technological Reproducibility," in *The Work of Art in the Age of Its Technological Reproducibility and Other Writings on Media*, ed. Michael W. Jennings, Brigid Doherty, and Thomas Y. Levin (Cambridge, MA: Harvard University Press, 2008), 34.

25 This phenomenon is found today in the "heel turn" in professional wrestling, in which a heroic wrestler turns bad and the quality of her or his performance is celebrated by booing. For an overview of the concept of "community of practice," see Barbara Rogoff, *Everyday Cognition: Its Development in Social Context* (Cambridge, MA: Harvard University Press, 1984); or Jean Lave and Etienne Wenger, *Situated Learning: Legitimate Peripheral Participation* (Cambridge: Cambridge University Press, 1991).

26 For a detailed meditation on the place of empathy in public life, see Martha Nussbaum, *Upheavals of Thought: The Intelligence of Emotions* (Cambridge: Cambridge University Press, 2001).

27 For an overview of suture and its literature, see Kaja Silverman, *The Subject*

of Semiotics (London: Oxford University Press, 1983), 194–236. Discussing comic performance, Alenka Zupancic describes this bifurcation from the perspective of the comic actor, pointing out that while epic performance is a narration of relations and tragic performance the representation of relations, comic performance offers the collapse of performer and character into one imperfect object that performs its lack for us. Zupancic, *The Odd One In: On Comedy* (Cambridge, MA: MIT Press, 2008), 23–39.

28 Freud's gallows joke ("Humor," 427) involves a criminal walking to the gallows on a Monday remarking, "Well the week's beginning nicely." For Freud, the joke converts the listener's unexpected, empathic expectation that the condemned man will be enraged or grieving his own end into laughter at his defensive humor. Compare this with *Jokes and Their Relation to the Unconscious* (291), in which Freud brackets empathy in quotation marks, limiting its ambit to the situation of the joke itself and linking it to a shared sense of infantile helplessness in the face of the reality principle and laughter in a shared sense of involuntary infantile transgression. Compare with *Jokes*, 245 and 255–57, and with "Humor," 429–30.

29 For a reading of this condition as that which allowed early twentieth-century Jewish performers to enter into whiteness, see Rogin, *Blackface, White Noise*.

30 For a discussion of problems of cross-racial identification, see Noel Ignatiev, *Race Traitor* (New York: Routledge, 1996).

31 One example of a Mickey Mouse short that makes direct reference to minstrelsy is *Mickey's Mellerdrammer* (1933). One can also read the early Warner Bros. Bosko shorts as intentional minstrel performances.

32 The radio program *Amos 'n' Andy* (1928–1960) seems a signal exception. Interestingly, of course, this radio program relied on auditory markers to signal its minstrelsy and, set in contemporary Chicago, eschewed the classic minstrel-show format. Creators Gosden and Correll attempted to bring their characters to the screen in both live and cartoon versions yet failed to extend their otherwise successful franchise to cinema. Also significant is the 1948 premier episode of the television program, in which Gosden and Correll introduced the black actors who would take their places as the living embodiment of the minstrel characters they had created. See Melvin P. Ely, *The Adventures of Amos 'n' Andy: A Social History of an American Phenomenon* (New York: Free Press, 1991); and William Barlow, *Voice Over: The Making of Black Radio* (Philadelphia: Temple University Press, 1999).

33 See Brooks, *Bodies in Dissent*; Wesley Brown, *Darktown Strutters* (Amherst: University of Massachusetts Press, 2000); Knight, *Disintegrating the Musical*; Karen Sotiropoulos, *Staging Race: Black Performers in Turn of the Century America* (Cambridge, MA: Harvard University Press, 2006); and Louis Chude-Sokei, *The Last "Darky": Bert Williams, Black-on-Black Minstrelsy, and the African Diaspora* (Durham, NC: Duke University Press, 2006).

34 A portion of that campaign involved reminding fans that the early Mickey had an edge, framing the new version as merely an act of reclamation. According

to Jerome Christensen, Disney later abandoned this campaign and resoftened the Mickey of *Epic Mickey*. Christensen, *America's Corporate Art: The Studio Authorship of Hollywood Motion Pictures* (Palo Alto: Stanford University Press, 2012), 314–40.

35 Richard deCordova, "The Mickey in Macy's Window: Childhood, Consumerism, and Disney Animation," in Eric Smoodin, ed., *Disney Discourse* (New York: Routledge, 1994), 203–13.

36 Robert Sklar, "The Making of Cultural Myths—Walt Disney," in Gerald Peary and Danny Peary, eds., *The American Animated Cartoon: A Critical Anthology* (New York: Dutton, 1980), 58–65. See also Frank Nugent, "That Million Dollar Mouse," *New York Times*, 21 September 1947, SM22.

37 For a discussion of the metaphysics of early animation, see Donald Crafton, *Before Mickey: The Animated Film, 1898–1928* (Cambridge, MA: MIT Press, 1982), 32–33. See also Sergei M. Eisenstein, *On Disney*, trans. Jay Leyda (London: Methuen, 1988). For a dense, interesting, and sometimes ambitious discussion of animation and animism, see Alan Cholodenko, "Speculations on the Animatic Automaton," in Cholodenko, ed., *The Illusion of Life II: More Essays on Animation* (Sydney: Power, 2007), 486–528.

38 See Karl Marx, *Capital*, vol. 1, trans. Ben Fowlkes (New York: Penguin Classics, 1976), 178–97, 270–80. See also Nicholas Sammond, *Babes in Tomorrowland: Walt Disney and the Making of the American Child, 1930–1960* (Durham, NC: Duke University Press, 2005), for a discussion of the trope of Walt Disney the self-made man. See Eric Smoodin, *Animating Culture: Hollywood Cartoons from the Sound Era* (New Brunswick, NJ: Rutgers University Press, 1993), for a discussion of Walt's production through public relations.

39 Coincidentally, the Frank Buck films were produced by animation studio head Amedee Van Beuren.

40 This broad-stroke history admits many variations and contradictions. T. D. Rice claimed to have learned to "jump Jim Crow" from an old, perhaps disabled, stable hand who may or may not have been a former slave; likewise, Zip Coon was a fantasy of the northern black dandy whose pretensions ostensibly revealed the overreaching and uncivilizable nature of some African Americans. See, for example, Dale Cockrell, *Demons of Disorder: Early Blackface Minstrels and Their World* (New York: Cambridge University Press, 1997), 62–138. For discussion of the anthropological conceit, see Lott, *Love and Theft*, 38–62. See also Hans Nathan, "The Performance of the Virginia Minstrels," in Annemarie Bean, James Hatch, and Brooks McNamara, eds., *Inside the Minstrel Mask: Readings in Nineteenth-Century Blackface Minstrelsy* (Middletown, CT: Wesleyan University Press, 1996); or W. T. Lhamon, *Jump Jim Crow: Lost Plays, Lyrics, and Street Prose of the First Atlantic Popular Culture* (Cambridge, MA: Harvard University Press, 2003), 31.

41 Fredric Jameson, *The Political Unconscious* (London: Routledge, 1983), 172–93. See also Peter Stallybrass and Elon Whyte, *The Politics and Poetics of Transgres-*

sion (London: Methuen, 1986), for a discussion of the carnivalesque and coded resistance.

42 From the journal of George Christy, Codex and Manuscript Collection, Special Collections Research Center, University of Chicago Library. The aphorism is not clearly attributed but is usually credited to the English poet John Clare, who may have meant to paraphrase Aristotle. Lewis Carroll inverted the phrase in his poem "Poeta Fit Non Nascitur."

43 *Christy's New Songster and Black Joker* (New York: Dick & Fitzgerald, 1868), 19, copy in Lincoln Collection, Special Collections Research Center, University of Chicago Library.

44 Mickey also makes use of the tune in *The Shindig* (1930). By 1935, it is Donald Duck who plays it as he disrupts Mickey's rendition of the *William Tell* Overture in *The Band Concert*.

45 As has often been noted, the film was not the first sound cartoon, merely the first cartoon to successfully demonstrate the potential of synchronized sound (and to link that performance to an effective public relations campaign). Of particular note were experiments by the Fleischer brothers in sound animation that predated Disney's work by several years. Yet in efforts such as their Song Car-Tunes and Screen Songs, the Fleischers also relied on standards from the vaudeville and minstrel stages, encouraging audiences to sing along by following the bouncing ball to songs such as "Dixie," "My Old Kentucky Home," "Sleepy Time Down South," and "Old Black Joe" (see chapter 3).

46 For a contemporary example that makes a visual analogy between mules and African Americans, see *I Am a Fugitive from a Chain Gang* (LeRoy, 1932). For Br'er Rabbit, see Joel Chandler Harris, *Uncle Remus and His Legends of the Old Plantation* (London: David Bogue, 1881).

47 Dennis Childs, "'You Ain't Seen Nothin' Yet': *Beloved*, the American Chain Gang, and the Middle Passage Remix," *American Quarterly* 61:2 (June 2009), 279.

48 Quoted in Alex Lichtenstein, *Twice the Work of Free Labor: The Political Economy of Convict Labor in the New South* (New York: Verso, 1996), 180. See also Debra Walker King, *African Americans and the Culture of Pain* (Charlottesville: University of Virginia Press, 2008), 8.

49 Hartman, *Scenes of Subjection*, 31.

50 Hartman, *Scenes of Subjection*, 31–32. For discussion of the intersection of this racial dynamic with the emerging class politics of the nineteenth and early twentieth centuries, see Lott, *Love and Theft*; or Roediger, *Wages of Whiteness*.

51 One could argue that because he is a clown, Ko-Ko isn't a minstrel. Yet as a character Ko-Ko operates within a tradition of animation that favors continuing characters as tricksters and draws on a variety of both visual and performative minstrel tropes (blacking up being only one of them). Ko-Ko has a white face but performatively acts the minstrel. He is created by Max (the animators working under Max and Dave) to rebel against the conditions of his making,

to disrupt the social order, and to be punished for his rebellion. In that, he performs the role of the minstrel.

52 See, for instance, Crafton, *Before Mickey*, 169–77.

53 Crafton, *Shadow*, 7.

54 The figure of the "laughing coon" was extremely popular with white audiences in the early days of the twentieth century. See Laura Wexler, "'Laughing Ben' on 'The Old Plantation,'" in Elizabeth Abel and Leigh Raiford, eds., "Photography and Race Forum," in *English Language Notes* 44.2 (fall/winter 2006). See also O'Meally, "Checking Our Balances," 282. For a fictional interpretation of laughter as violence and violence averted, see Brown, *Darktown Strutters*.

55 See, for example, Rogin, *Blackface, White Noise*, 140; Goldmark, *Tunes for 'Toons*, 80–81; and Corin Willis, "Blackface Minstrelsy and Jazz Signification in Hollywood's Early Sound Era," in Graham Lock and David Murray, eds., *Thriving on a Riff: Jazz and Blues Influences in African American Literature and Film* (Oxford: Oxford University Press, 2009), 41.

56 Goldmark, *Tunes for 'Toons*, 88–89.

57 Marx, *Capital*, vol. 1, 167.

58 Marx, *Capital*, vol. 1, 125–77. Sigmund Freud, "Fetishism," in Freud, *Sexuality and the Psychology of Love*, ed. Phillip Rieff, trans. Joan Riviere (New York: Touchstone Books, 1997 [1927]). See also Jameson, *Political Unconscious*, 271–90, for a discussion of the role of mass culture in representing, hence working through, repressed relations. See also Slavoj Žižek, *The Sublime Object of Ideology* (London: Verso, 1989), 11–53.

59 The same may be said for "free" or "northern" minstrel characters such as Zip Coon or Jim Dandy. They may pretend to civilization, but the joke is premised on their falling short of the mark.

60 In this light, Ko-Ko's efforts to draw himself independent of Max's hand or Felix's use of his tail to reinscribe his landscape speak of (failed) attempts to claim possession of their selves as useful and independent objects/agents.

61 This short was directed by Manny Gould for Charles Mintz.

62 See Marx, *Capital*, vol. 1, 270–306.

63 Fredric Jameson, *Signatures of the Visible* (New York: Routledge, 1992), 18–23.

64 For an elaboration on this point in the same essay, one that posits the repetitive use of cultural icons as a mass working through of repressed political impulses, see 32–34.

65 Fred Moten, *In the Break: The Aesthetics of the Black Radical Tradition* (Minneapolis: University of Minnesota Press, 2003), 1–24.

66 Moten, *In the Break*, 251.

67 In the rare cases of manumission or the ability to buy one's freedom, that sense of one's own value did revert to the body of the slave. See, for instance, Amy Dru Stanley, *From Bondage to Contract: Wage Labor, Marriage, and the Market in the Age of Slave Emancipation* (Cambridge: Cambridge University Press, 1998), 60–97.

68 Moten, *In the Break*, 251.

69 Moten, *In the Break*, 251.

70 Willis, "Blackface Minstrelsy and Jazz Signification," 48–50.

71 In the case of Warner Bros., those continuing characters almost always had a speech impediment. It is beyond the scope of this essay to discuss this peculiar feature of Warner's interpretation of the animate minstrel, except to note that it seems that the impediment was usually linked to the characters' cries of objection or proximity to crisis.

72 See Lisa Cartwright, "The Hands of the Animator: Rotoscopic Projection, Condensation, and Repetition Automatism in the Fleischer Apparatus," *Body and Society* 18:1 (2012), 47–78.

73 See Lott, *Love and Theft*; Roediger, *Wages of Whiteness*; and Rogin, *Blackface, White Noise*.

74 Consider Gilles Deleuze, *Masochism: Coldness and Cruelty* (New York: Zone Books, 1989), 91–101.

75 See Leopold Sacher-Masoch, *Venus in Furs* (New York: Zone Books, 1989 [1870]), esp. 222–26.

76 See Hall, "Stereotyping as a Signifying Practice," and "Racist Ideologies"; and Lott, *Love and Theft*.

77 Cholodenko, "Speculations," 486–528. See Scott Bukatman, *The Poetics of Slumberland: Animated Spirits and the Animating Spirit* (Berkeley: University of California Press, 2012), 108.

78 Marx, *Capital*, vol. 1, 125–77; Freud, "Fetishism." See Bukatman, *Poetics of Slumberland*, 143; and Cartwright, "Hands of the Animator," 50.

79 This is not to say that there is a *true* set of relations based in empathy. As Lacan makes clear, the formation of the ego and its defenses are built alike on a chain of miscognitions or misunderstandings (*meconnaisance*), which, if we trace them backward, lead not to an initial error that we can then easily correct but to a realization that the formation of the ego-in-relation depends on that mistake. Empathy at that moment must then be for the object of our (mis) understanding and for ourselves as the producer and production (alongside the object) of that misunderstanding. Jacques Lacan, "The Function and Field of Speech and Language in Psychoanalysis," in *Ecrits: A Selection*, trans. Alan Sheridan (New York: Norton, 1977 [1948]), 41–42. See Nussbaum, *Upheavals of Thought*, 297–351.

80 For a detailed history of the animation work of Blackton and of McCay, see Crafton, *Before Mickey*. McCay consulted with Blackton when he began animating and shot his early films at Blackton's studio. John Canemaker, "The Birth of Animation," *Millimeter* 3:4 (April 1975).

81 Canemaker, quoted in Charles Solomon, "The Oscars: The Penguins and People Look Great, but Are They Animation?," *New York Times*, 7 January 2007.

82 In the image of the cast member in the Mickey suit we have an apt metaphor for Adam Smith's invisible hand producing the fantasy of Marx's commodity fetish: that which we see as alive but whose outward expression of life is inter-

esting to itself only in terms of exchange. As Fred Moten puts it, referring to Frederick Douglass's description of witnessing his Aunt Hester being beaten by her master: "To think that the possibility of an (exchange-) value that is prior to exchange, and to think the reproductive and incantatory assertion of that possibility as the objection to exchange that is exchange's condition of possibility, is to put oneself in the way of an ongoing line of discovery, of coming upon, of invention. . . . It is an achievement we'll see given in the primal scene of Aunt Hester's objection to exchange, an achievement given in speech, literary phonography, and their disruption. What is sounded through Douglass is a theory of value—an objective and objectional, productive and reproductive ontology—whose primitive axiom is that commodities speak" (Moten, *In the Break*, 11). The difference between Mickey as drawn and the Mickey suit is that Mickey as drawn both acknowledges and denies his status as a product in his attempts to live for himself. This is truer of the early Mickey than of his later incarnations. See Sklar, "Making of Cultural Myths—Walt Disney."

83 This tag line was also used in *The Wacky Worm* (Warner Bros., 1941) and is muttered by a crow as he gives up trying to catch a worm. To hear a recording of this routine, visit the Internet Archive at http://ia301504.us.archive.org/2/items/MoranMackTwoBlackCrows/MoranMackTwoBlackCrows-Part-1.mp3 (accessed 6 November 2014).

84 For Freud's take on the meaning of caricature as an expression of desire turned toward sadistic aggression, see Freud, *Jokes and Their Relation to the Unconscious*, 262.

85 Lehman, *Colored Cartoon*, 39.

86 See Rob King, *The Fun Factory: The Keystone Film Company and the Emergence of Mass Culture* (Berkeley: University of California Press, 2008), ch. 2; Henry Jenkins, *What Made Pistachio Nuts? Early Sound Comedy and the Vaudeville Aesthetic* (New York: Columbia University Press, 1992), 59–95; and David Nasaw, *Going Out: The Rise and Fall of Public Amusements* (New York: Basic Books, 1993), 19–34.

87 The class dynamics of burlesque and vaudeville were complicated. Performers of varied class origins performed roles indebted to working-class performance aesthetics for audiences who were, as vaudeville established itself, imagined by producers as representative of middle-class ideals and sensibilities. Compare Andrew Erdman, *Blue Vaudeville: Sex, Morals and the Mass Marketing of Entertainment, 1895–1915* (Jefferson, NC: McFarland, 2004); Robert C. Allen, *Horrible Prettiness: Burlesque and American Culture* (Chapel Hill: University of North Carolina Press, 1991); Lawrence Levine, *Highbrow/Lowbrow: The Emergence of Cultural Hierarchy in America* (Cambridge, MA: Harvard University Press, 1990); and Robert M. Lewis, *From Traveling Show to Vaudeville: Theatrical Spectacle in America, 1830–1910* (Baltimore: Johns Hopkins University Press, 2003).

88 See Rogin, *Blackface, White Noise*.

89 See *The Ouija Board* (1920) or *Ko-Ko the Barber* (1925).

90 Joe Adamson, "'Where Can I Get a Good Corned Beef Sandwich?': An Oral History of Dave Fleischer," 1969, 78, American Film Institute Oral History Project (now housed in the University of California, Los Angeles, Oral History Project).

91 See Ely, *Adventures of Amos 'n' Andy*; or Knight, *Disintegrating the Musical*.

92 "Music and the Drama," *Chicago Record*, c. 1910, Robinson Locke Collection, New York Public Library. Needless to say, there are issues of freedom of speech and of permissible discourse that may have shaped Williams's public pronouncements. What seems notable here is that in order to protect and further his career, Williams entered into and furthered that discourse.

93 Jim Crow was voiced by Cliff Edwards, a vaudeville performer who sometimes did a blackface minstrel act. Huemer, quoted in Joe Adamson, "With Disney on Olympus: An Interview with Dick Huemer," *Funnyworld* 17 (1978), 37–43.

94 Chude-Sokei, *Last "Darky,"* 82–113.

95 In his graphic retelling of this story, *Breakdowns: Portrait of the Artist as a Young %@&*!* (New York: Pantheon, 2008), 13, Spiegelman is more specific, pegging it to insights gained in film classes he took with Ken Jacobs at the State University of New York in the early 1970s. More recently, Niall Ferguson, with his usual subtlety, compared President Obama to Felix the Cat, stating that both were "not only black . . . [but] also very, very lucky." Ferguson, "A Runaway Deficit May Soon Test Obama's Luck," *Financial Times*, 10 August 2009.

96 Conversation with Ray Pointer, July 2006; conversation with Jerry Beck, August 2007. See also Klein, *7 Minutes*, 192–99.

97 Hall, "Racist Ideologies."

98 *Time*, 13 February 1928.

99 For a discussion about elite anxiety around immigrants, popular culture, and social life, see Lawrence Levine, *Highbrow/Lowbrow: The Emergence of Cultural Hierarchy in America* (Cambridge, MA: Harvard University Press, 1990), 169–242; and Sammond, *Babes in Tomorrowland*, 81–134. For a discussion of vaudeville and tensions with "polite society," see Erdman, *Blue Vaudeville*, 21–42. For an overview of social reform and anxiety around class, race, and immigration, see, for instance, John Whiteclay Chambers II, *The Tyranny of Change: Americans in the Progressive Era, 1890–1920* (New York: St. Martins, 1992), esp. 274–98. For a discussion of the production of jazz in dominant discourse and cinema, respectively, see Krin Gabbard, *Jammin' at the Margins: Jazz and the American Cinema* (Chicago: University of Chicago Press, 1996), and *Representing Jazz*. For a discussion of jazz and modernity/technology, see Dinerstein, *Swinging the Machine*. Regarding jazz as reproduced through contemporary criticism, see John Gennari, *Blowin' Hot and Cool: Jazz and Its Critics* (Chicago: University of Chicago Press, 2006). See also Carol Clover, "Dancin' in the Rain," *Critical Inquiry* 21:4 (summer 1995), 722–47; and Naremore, "Uptown Folks." While Erdman and others have argued that by the teens vaudeville had

become a thoroughly middle-class enterprise, they also describe it as the first truly mass entertainment, hence a source of anxiety over the regulation of behavior.

100 See Freud, *Jokes and Their Relation to the Unconscious*, and "Humor." See notes 15 and 28, this chapter.

101 For critiques of Rogin, see Thomas Cripps, "Review: *Blackface, White Noise: Jewish Immigrants in the Hollywood Melting Pot*," *Journal of American History* 83:4 (March 1997), 115–19; or Knight, *Disintegrating the Musical*.

102 See W. E. B. Du Bois, *The Souls of Black Folk* (New York: Oxford University Press, 2007 [1903]); Paul Gilroy, *The Black Atlantic: Modernity and Double Consciousness* (Cambridge, MA: Harvard University Press, 1993); and Frantz Fanon, *Black Skin, White Masks* (New York: Grove, 1967). For a detailed historical analysis and critique of this idea, see Michelle M. Wright, *Becoming Black: Creating Identity in the African Diaspora* (Durham, NC: Duke University Press, 2004), 66–110.

103 Glenda Carpio, *Laughing Fit to Kill: Black Humor in the Fictions of Slavery* (New York: Oxford University Press, 2008), 74.

104 For a more critical take on the limits of empathy in the face of racism, see Bambi Haggins, *Laughing Mad: The Black Comic Persona in Post-soul America* (New Brunswick, NJ: Rutgers University Press, 2007), 192–93.

105 For a useful discussion of identity and subjectivity around injury, see Wendy Brown, "Wounded Attachments," *Political Theory* 21:3 (August 1993), 390–410. While Brown's discussion of wounded identity is by no means exhaustive, it does frame issues of race, gender, ability, and sexuality in terms of the regimes of legitimation and avenues to power that have grown around and within racial formations in the United States over the last two centuries.

106 Rogin (*Blackface, White Noise*, 182–89) makes a similar move to link the Freudian and Marxist fetish in the act of blacking up. But this link is made primarily in the context of the oedipal dynamics Rogin locates in the Jewish use of blackface, and is soon after dropped. Žižek (*Sublime Object of Ideology*, 49) suggests that the Marxian and Freudian fetishes are different because the Marxian fetish stands in for a positive network of social relations, while the Freudian replaces a lack. Space does not permit a detailed discussion of this supposed difference.

107 Compare Marx, *Capital*, vol. 1, 411–16 and 544–64; and Audre Lorde, "Age, Race, Class and Sex: Women Redefining Difference," in R. Ferguson et al., eds., *Out There: Marginalization and Contemporary Cultures* (Cambridge, MA: MIT Press, 1990), 287.

108 Klein, *7 Minutes*, 192, italics in original.

109 See Crafton, *Shadow*, 48–51.

CONCLUSION

To view all of the media discussed in this chapter, go to http://scalar.usc.edu/works /birthofanindustry.

The epigraph to the first section is from George W. Walker, "The Real 'Coon' on the American Stage," *Theatre Magazine*, August 1906, Robinson Locke Collection, Billy Rose Theatre Division, New York Public Library.

1 For a discussion of the episteme, see Michel Foucault, *The Order of Things: An Archaeology of Human Knowledge* (New York: Routledge, 2005). For a discussion of racial formation, see Michael Omi and Howard Winant, *Racial Formation in the United States from the 1960s to the 1990s* (New York: Routledge, 1994).

2 Productive in that contradiction produces instabilities that in their resolution produce new meanings and relations.

3 Stephanie Zacharek, "Tropic Thunder," *Salon*, 13 August 2008, http://www .salon.com/2008/08/13/tropic_thunder/.

4 On 2 September 2005, on an NBC telethon for Katrina survivors, West said, "George Bush doesn't care about black people." See also Bambi Haggins, *Laughing Mad: The Black Comic Persona in Post-soul America* (New Brunswick, NJ: Rutgers University Press, 2007), 237–43.

5 Roger Ebert, "Tropic Thunder: The Ultimate War-Movie Movie," *Chicago Sun-Times*, 12 August 2008.

6 Lisa Schwarzbaum, "Movie Review: Tropic Thunder," *Entertainment Weekly*, 12 August 2008, http://www.ew.com/ew/article/0,,20218776,00.html.

7 Manhola Dargis, "War May Be Hell, but Hollywood Is Even Worse," *New York Times*, 12 August 2008.

8 *The Daily Show* also deploys comedian Larry Wilmore as "senior black correspondent" to further its self-reflexive credentials by mocking both knee-jerk identity politics and Stewart's seeming racial naïveté.

9 See Constantin Stanislavsky, *My Life in Art*, trans. J. J. Robbins (London: Bles, 1924); Lee Strasberg and Toby Cole, *Acting: A Handbook of the Stanislavski Method* (New York: Lear, 1947).

10 Henri Bergson, *Laughter: An Essay on the Meaning of the Comic*, trans. Cloudesly Brereton and Fred Rothwell (St. Paul, MN: Green Integer, 2003 [1911], 71.

11 Bergson, *Laughter*, 26–27. For another detailed discussion of this passage in relation to minstrelsy, see Louis Chude-Sokei, "The Uncanny History of Minstrels and Machines, 1835–1923," in Stephen Johnson, ed., *Burnt Cork: Traditions and Legacies of Blackface Minstrelsy* (Boston: University of Massachusetts Press, 2012), 122.

12 According to Bergson, even though one's reason knows the difference between a black man and a man in blackface, one's imagination cannot entirely be persuaded. Amusingly, given the context here, Bergson later makes the same claim about disability. Bergson, *Laughter*, 18–19, 34.

13 Alenka Zupancic, *The Odd One In: On Comedy* (Cambridge, MA: MIT Press, 2008), 35–36.

14 The term is not Zupancic's own but borrowed from Hegel. Zupancic, *Odd One In*, 26–27.

15 "ABC" here stands for the Australian Broadcasting Company, not the American Broadcasting Company.

16 See Wendy Brown, "Wounded Attachments," *Political Theory* 21:3 (August 1993), 390–410.

17 Zupancic, *Odd One In*, 180–81.

18 Zupancic, *Odd One In*, 150–63.

19 Sergei M. Eisenstein, *Eisenstein on Disney*, ed. Jay Leyda, trans. Alan Upchurch (Calcutta: Seagull Books, 1986), 7.

20 See Scott Bukatman, *The Poetics of Slumberland: Animated Spirits and the Animating Spirit* (Berkeley: University of California Press, 2012), 58.

21 See *Falling Hare* (Warner Bros., 1943).

22 Sigmund Freud, *Beyond the Pleasure Principle*, ed. and trans. James Strachey (New York: Norton, 1961 [1920]), 41–42.

23 Sigmund Freud, "The Relation of Jokes to Dreams and to the Unconscious," in Freud, *Jokes and Their Relation to the Unconscious*, ed. and trans. James Strachey (New York: Penguin Books, 1991 [1905]), 291.

24 Walter Benjamin, "The Work of Art in the Age of Its Technological Reproducibility," in *The Work of Art in the Age of Its Technological Reproducibility and Other Writings on Media*, ed. Michael W. Jennings, Brigid Doherty, and Thomas Y. Levin (Cambridge, MA: Harvard University Press, 2008), 38.

25 See Bukatman, *Poetics of Slumberland*, 106–34.

26 Commenting on Klein's reading of the narrative convention of struggle in cartoons, Bukatman, *Poetics of Slumberland*, 136.

27 See Rob King, "The Art of Diddling: Slapstick, Science, and Antimodernism in the Films of Charlie Bowers," in Daniel Goldmark and Charlie Keil, eds., *Funny Pictures: Animation and Comedy in Studio-Era Hollywood* (Berkeley: University of California Press, 2011), 191–210.

28 See Donald Crafton, *Before Mickey: The Animated Film, 1898–1928* (Cambridge, MA: MIT Press, 1982), 298–99; Norman M. Klein, "Animation and Animorphs: A Brief Disappearing Act," in Vivian Sobchack, ed., *Meta-morphing: Visual Transformation and the Culture of Quick-Change* (Minneapolis: University of Minnesota Press, 2000), 24; Bukatman, *Poetics of Slumberland*, 136.

29 Norman M. Klein, *7 Minutes: The Life and Death of the American Animated Cartoon* (New York: Verso, 1993), 75.

30 Miriam Bratu Hansen, "The Mass Production of the Senses: Classical Cinema as Vernacular Modernism," in Christine Gledhill and Linda Williams, eds., *Reinventing Film Studies* (London: Arnold, 2000), 332–50. See Henry Jenkins, "'I Like to Sock Myself in the Face': Reconsidering 'Vulgar Modernism,'" in Daniel Goldmark and Charlie Keil, eds., *Funny Pictures: Animation and Comedy in Studio-Era Hollywood* (Berkeley: University of California Press, 2012), 153–74.

31 Bergson, *Laughter*, 97.

32 See Donald Crafton, *Shadow of a Mouse: Performance, Belief, and World-Making in Animation* (Berkeley: University of California Press, 2012), 50–51.

33 See Sigmund Freud, *Jokes and Their Relation to the Unconscious*, ed. and trans. James Strachey (New York: Penguin Books, 1991 [1905]), 239–41, 296.

34 Simon Critchley, *On Humour* (New York: Routledge, 2002), 56.

35 Critchley, *On Humour*.

36 For a discussion of the public celebration of Disney as the apotheosis of the commodity form, see Eric Smoodin, *Animating Culture: Hollywood Cartoons from the Sound Era* (New Brunswick, NJ: Rutgers University Press, 1993); and Nicholas Sammond, *Babes in Tomorrowland: Walt Disney and the Making of the American Child, 1930–1960* (Durham, NC: Duke University Press, 2005).

37 Zupancic, *Odd One In*, 28.

38 Keaton sent Felix creator Otto Messmer and Pat Sullivan photos of some of his signature gestures so that the popular cat could use them and circulate them. See John Canemaker, "Otto Messmer Interview, March 5 1975, Fort Lee, NJ," Messmer Interview Folder 18/203, Canemaker Collection, Fales Library, New York University; this interview later became "Otto Messmer and Felix the Cat," *Cartoonist Profiles*, no. 37 (March 1978).

39 Bergson, *Laughter*, 31.

40 For a discussion of the place of music in this operation, see Daniel Goldmark, "Sounds Funny/Funny Sounds: Theorizing Cartoon Music," in Daniel Goldmark and Charlie Keil, eds., *Funny Pictures: Animation and Comedy in Studio-Era Hollywood* (Berkeley: University of California Press, 2011), 257–71. See also Crafton, *Shadow of a Mouse*, 15–57.

41 Zupancic, *Odd One In*, 35–36.

42 Zupancic, *Odd One In*, 27.

43 That is the fundamental joke of the series; where traditionally cartoon characters have violently assaulted each other and remained relatively unscathed, Itchy regularly dismembers Scratchy before his very eyes . . . at least as long as they remain in the cat's head.

44 Crafton, *Shadow*, 294. See Slavoj Žižek, *Enjoy Your Symptom: Jacques Lacan in Hollywood* (New York: Routledge, 2001), 1–30.

45 Zupancic, *Odd One In*, 172.

46 Rey Chow, "The Elusive Material, What the Dog Doesn't Understand," in Diana Coole and Samantha Frost, eds., *New Materialisms: Ontology, Agency, and Politics* (Durham, NC: Duke University Press, 2010), 231.

47 *The Daily Show*, 19 January 2010. For an example of the distance between Barack Obama as symbol and as practicing politician, see Paul Tough, "What Does Obama Really Believe In?," *New York Times Magazine*, 15 August 2012.

48 See Sianne Ngai, *Our Aesthetic Categories: Zany, Cute, Interesting* (Cambridge, MA: Harvard University Press, 2012), 187–91.

BIBLIOGRAPHY

Adamson, Joe. "With Disney on Olympus: An interview with Dick Huemer." *Funnyworld* 17 (1978), 37–43.

Adamson, Joe. "Working for the Fleischers: An Interview with Dick Huemer." *Funnyworld* 16 (1974–1975), 23–28.

Allen, Robert C. *Horrible Prettiness: Burlesque and American Culture.* Chapel Hill: University of North Carolina Press, 1991.

Allen, Robert C. "Reimagining the History of the Experience of Cinema." In Richard Maltby, Daniel Bilteryst, and Philippe Meers, eds., *Explorations in New Cinema History: Approaches and Case Studies.* Malden, MA: Wiley-Blackwell, 2011, 41–57.

Andrew, Dudley. *What Cinema Is!* New York: Wiley-Blackwell, 2010.

Azema, Marc, and Florent Rivere. "Animation in Palaeolithic Art: A Pre-echo of Cinema." *Antiquity* 86:332 (2012), 316–24.

Bakhurst, David. *Consciousness and Revolution in Soviet Philosophy: From the Bolsheviks to Evald Ilynenkov.* Cambridge: Cambridge University Press, 1991.

Barlow, William. *Voice Over: The Making of Black Radio.* Philadelphia: Temple University Press, 1999.

Barrier, Michael. *Hollywood Cartoons: American Animation in Its Golden Age.* New York: Oxford University Press, 1999.

Barrier, Michael, and Bill Spicer. "An Interview with Chuck Jones." *Funnyworld* 13 (1971). http://www.michaelbarrier.com.

Bean, Annemarie, James Hatch, and Brooks McNamara, eds. *Inside the Minstrel Mask: Readings in Nineteenth-Century Blackface Minstrelsy.* Middletown, CT: Wesleyan University Press, 1996.

Benjamin, Walter. "Mickey Mouse." In *The Work of Art in the Age of Its Technological Reproducibility and Other Writings on Media*, ed. Michael W. Jennings, Brigid Doherty, and Thomas Y. Levin, trans. Rodney Livingstone. Cambridge, MA: Harvard University Press, 2008 [1931], 338.

Benjamin, Walter. "The Work of Art in the Age of Its Technological Reproducibility." In *The Work of Art in the Age of Its Mechanical Reproducibility and Other Writings on Media*, ed. Michael W. Jennings, Brigid Doherty, and Thomas Y. Levin, trans. Rodney Livingstone. Cambridge, MA: Harvard University Press, 2008 [1931], 19–55.

Bergson, Henri. *Laughter: An Essay on the Meaning of the Comic*. Trans. Cloudesly Brereton and Fred Rothwell. St. Paul, MN: Green Integer, 2003 [1911].

Bhabha, Homi K. *The Location of Culture*. New York: Routledge, 1994.

"The Big Bad Wolf." *Fortune*, November 1934.

Bogle, Donald. *Toms, Coons, Mulattoes, Mammies, and Bucks: An Interpretive History of Blacks in American Films*. New York: Continuum, 2006.

Bourdieu, Pierre. *Outline of a Theory of Practice*. Cambridge: Cambridge University Press, 1977.

Bradley, Edwin M. *The First Hollywood Sound Shorts, 1926–1931*. London: McFarland, 2005.

Bray, John R. "How the Comics Caper." *Photoplay* 11:2 (January 1917), 68.

Brooks, Daphne. *Bodies in Dissent: Spectacular Performances of Race and Freedom, 1850–1910*. Durham, NC: Duke University Press, 2006.

Brown, Jayna. *Babylon Girls: Black Women Performers and the Shaping of the Modern* Durham, NC: Duke University Press, 2008.

Brown, Wendy. "Wounded Attachments." *Political Theory* 21:3 (August 1993), 390–410.

Brown, Wesley. *Darktown Strutters*. Amherst: University of Massachusetts Press, 2000.

Bukatman, Scott. "Comics and the Critique of Chronophotography, or 'He Never Knew When It Was Coming!'" *Animation* 1:1 (2006), 83–103.

Bukatman, Scott. *The Poetics of Slumberland: Animated Spirits and the Animating Spirit*. Berkeley: University of California Press, 2012.

Bukatman, Scott. "Taking Shape: Morphing and the Performance of Self." In Vivian Sobchack, ed., *Meta-morphing: Visual Transformation and the Culture of Quick-Change*. Minneapolis: University of Minnesota Press, 2000, 225–49.

Caffin, Caroline. *Vaudeville: The Book*. New York: Kennerly, 1914.

Canemaker, John. "Animation History and Shamus Culhane." *Filmmakers Newsletter* 7:8 (June 1974), 23–28.

Canemaker, John. "The Birth of Animation." *Millimeter* 3:4 (April 1975), 14–16.

Canemaker, John. Commentary. *Winsor McCay: The Master Edition*. DVD. Milestone Film and Video, 2004.

Canemaker, John. "Otto Messmer and Felix the Cat." *Cartoonist Profiles*, no. 37 (March 1978).

Canemaker, John. "Sincerely Yours, Frank Thomas." *Millimeter* 3:1 (January 1975), 16–18.

Canemaker, John. *Winsor McCay: His Life and Art*. New York: Abrams, 2005.

Carbarga, Leslie. *The Fleischer Story*. New York: Da Capo, 1988.

Carpio, Glenda. *Laughing Fit to Kill: Black Humor and the Fictions of Slavery*. New York: Oxford University Press, 2008.

Carrier, David. *The Aesthetics of Comics*. University Park: Penn State University Press, 2000.

Cartwright, Lisa. "The Hands of the Animator: Rotoscopic Projection, Condensation, and Repetition Automatism in the Fleischer Apparatus." *Body and Society* 18:1 (2012), 47–78.

Chambers, John Whiteclay, II. *The Tyranny of Change: Americans in the Progressive Era, 1890–1920*. New York: St. Martins, 1992.

Charney, Leo, and Vanessa Schwartz, eds. *Cinema and the Invention of Modern Life*. Berkeley: University of California Press, 1996.

Childs, Dennis. "'You Ain't Seen Nothin' Yet': *Beloved*, the American Chain Gang, and the Middle Passage Remix." *American Quarterly* 61:2 (June 2009), 271–97.

Cholodenko, Alan. "The Animation of Cinema." *Semiotic Review of Books* 18:2 (2008), 1–10.

Cholodenko, Alan. "Speculations on the Animatic Automaton." In Cholodenko, ed., *The Illusion of Life II: More Essays on Animation*. Sydney: Power, 2007, 486–528.

Chow, Rey. "The Elusive Material, What the Dog Doesn't Understand." In Diana Coole and Samantha Frost, eds., *New Materialisms: Ontology, Agency, and Politics*. Durham, NC: Duke University Press, 2010, 221–33.

Christensen, Jerome. *America's Corporate Art: The Studio Authorship of Hollywood Motion Pictures*. Palo Alto: Stanford University Press, 2012.

Chude-Sokei, Louis. *The Last "Darky": Bert Williams, Black-on-Black Minstrelsy, and the African Diaspora*. Durham, NC: Duke University Press, 2006.

Chude-Sokei, Louis. "The Uncanny History of Minstrels and Machines, 1835–1923." In Stephen Johnson, ed., *Burnt Cork: Traditions and Legacies of Blackface Minstrelsy*. Boston: University of Massachusetts Press, 2012, 104–32.

Clover, Carol. "Dancin' in the Rain." *Critical Inquiry* 21:4 (summer 1995), 722–47.

Cockrell, Dale. *Demons of Disorder: Early Blackface Minstrels and Their World*. Cambridge: Cambridge University Press, 1997.

Cole, Catherine M., and Tracy C. Davis, eds. "Routes of Blackface." Special issue, *Drama Review* 57:2 (summer 2013).

Crafton, Donald. *Before Mickey: The Animated Film, 1898–1928*. Cambridge, MA: MIT Press, 1982.

Crafton, Donald. *Emile Cohl, Caricature, and Film*. Princeton, NJ: Princeton University Press, 1990.

Crafton, Donald. *Shadow of a Mouse: Performance, Belief, and World-Making in Animation*. Berkeley: University of California Press, 2013.

Crafton, Donald. *The Talkies: American Cinema's Transition to Sound, 1926–1931*. Berkeley: University of California Press, 1997.

Crafton, Donald. "The View from Termite Terrace: Caricature and Parody in Warner Bros. Animation." In Kevin S. Sandler, ed., *Reading the Rabbit: Explorations in Warner Bros. Animation*. New Brunswick, NJ: Rutgers University Press, 1998, 101–20.

Crary, Jonathan. *Suspensions of Perception: Attention, Spectacle, and Modern Culture*. Cambridge, MA: MIT Press, 2000.

Cripps, Thomas. "Review: *Blackface, White Noise: Jewish Immigrants in the Hollywood Melting Pot.*" *Journal of American History* 83:4 (March 1997), 1462–63.

Cripps, Thomas. *Slow Fade to Black: The Negro in American Films, 1900–1942.* New York: Oxford University Press, 1995.

Critchley, Simon. *On Humour.* London: Routledge, 2002.

Cubitt, Sean. *The Cinema Effect.* Cambridge, MA: MIT Press, 2004.

Cullen, Frank, Florence Hackman, and Donald McNeilly. *Vaudeville Old and New: An Encyclopedia of Variety Performers in America.* Vol. 1. New York: Routledge, 2006.

Davis, James C. *Commerce in Color: Race, Consumer Culture, and American Literature, 1893–1933.* Ann Arbor: University of Michigan Press, 2007.

Dayan, Daniel. "The Tutor Code of Classical Cinema." *Film Quarterly* 28:1 (autumn 1974), 22–31.

deCordova, Richard. "The Mickey in Macy's Window: Childhood, Consumerism, and Disney Animation." In Eric Smoodin, ed., *Disney Discourse.* New York: Routledge, 1994, 203–13.

Deleuze, Gilles. *Cinema 1: The Movement Image.* Trans. Hugh Tomlinson and Barbara Habberjam. Minneapolis: University of Minnesota Press, 1986.

Deleuze, Gilles. *Cinema 2: The Time Image.* Trans. Hugh Tomlinson and Robert Goleta. Minneapolis: University of Minnesota Press, 1989.

Deleuze, Gilles. *Immanence: A Life.* Trans. Ann Boyman. New York: Zone Books, 2001.

Deleuze, Gilles. *Masochism: Coldness and Cruelty.* New York: Zone Books, 1989.

Deneroff, Harvey. "'We Can't Get Much Spinach!': The Organization and Implementation of the Fleischer Strike." *Film History* 1:1 (1987), 1–14.

Derrida, Jacques. *Spectres of Marx.* New York: Routledge, 1994.

Dinerstein, Joel. *Swinging the Machine: Modernity, Technology, and African American Culture between the World Wars.* Boston: University of Massachusetts Press, 2003.

Doane, Mary Ann. "The Voice in the Cinema: The Articulation of Body and Space." *Yale French Studies* 60 (1980), 33–50.

Du Bois, W. E. B. *The Souls of Black Folk.* New York: Oxford University Press, 2007 [1903].

Edwards, Jason. "The Materialism of Historical Materialism." In Diana Coole and Samantha Frost, eds., *New Materialisms: Ontology, Agency, and Politics.* Durham, NC: Duke University Press, 2010.

Eisenstein, Sergei M. *Eisenstein on Disney.* Ed. Jay Leyda. Trans. Alan Upchurch. Calcutta: Seagull Books, 1986.

Eisenstein, Sergei M. *On Disney.* Trans. Jay Leyda. London: Methuen, 1988.

Ely, Melvin P. *The Adventures of Amos 'n' Andy: A Social History of an American Phenomenon.* New York: Free Press, 1991.

Erdman, Andrew. *Blue Vaudeville: Sex, Morals and the Mass Marketing of Entertainment, 1895–1915.* Jefferson, NC: McFarland, 2004.

Fanon, Frantz. *Black Skin, White Masks.* New York: Grove, 1967.

Faulkner, William. *Requiem for a Nun*. New York: Vintage, 2011 [1950].

"'Felix the Cat' Cartoon Prologues to Be a Feature of Short Subject Month." *Moving Picture World*, 24 October 1925, 637–38.

Ferguson, Niall. "A Runaway Deficit May Soon Test Obama's Luck." *Financial Times*, 10 August 2009.

Feyersinger, Erwin. "Diegetic Short Circuits: Metalepsis in Animation." *Animation* 5:3 (2010), 279–94.

Fisher, Bud. "'Here's How'—Says Bud." *Photoplay* 18:2 (July 1920), 58.

Fleischer, Richard. *Out of the Inkwell: Max Fleischer and the Animation Revolution*. Lexington: University Press of Kentucky, 2005.

Foucault, Michel. "Of Other Spaces" [1967]. *Architecture/Mouvement/Continuité* (October 1984), 46–49.

Foucault, Michel. *The Order of Things: An Archaeology of Human Knowledge*. New York: Routledge, 2005.

Frederick, Christine. *Household Engineering: Scientific Management in the Home*. Chicago: American School of Home Economics, 1920.

Frederick, Christine. *The New Housekeeping: Efficiency Studies in Home Management*. New York: Doubleday, Page, 1913.

Freud, Sigmund. *Beyond the Pleasure Principle*. Ed. and trans. James Strachey. New York: Norton, 1961 [1920].

Freud, Sigmund. *The Complete Introductory Lectures on Psychoanalysis*. Ed. and trans. James Strachey. New York: Norton, 1966 [1920].

Freud, Sigmund. "Fetishism." In Freud, *Sexuality and the Psychology of Love*, ed. Phillip Rieff, trans. Joan Riviere. New York: Touchstone Books, 1997 [1927], 204–9.

Freud, Sigmund. "Humor." In Freud, *Art and Literature*, ed. James Strachey, trans. Joan Riviere. New York: Penguin Books, 1990 [1928], 425–33.

Freud, Sigmund. "The Relation of Jokes to Dreams and to the Unconscious." In Freud, *Jokes and Their Relation to the Unconscious*, ed. and trans. James Strachey. New York: Penguin Books, 1991 [1905], 215–302.

Fuller, Kathryn. *At the Picture Show: Small-Town Audiences and the Creation of Movie-Fan Culture*. Washington, DC: Smithsonian Institution Press, 1996.

Furniss, Maureen, ed. *Chuck Jones: Conversations*. Jackson: University Press of Mississippi, 2005.

Furuhata, Yuriko. "Rethinking Plasticity: The Politics and Production of the Animated Image." *Animation* 6:1 (2011), 25–38.

Gabbard, Krin. *Jammin' at the Margins: Jazz and the American Cinema*. Chicago: University of Chicago Press, 1996.

Gabbard, Krin, ed. *Representing Jazz*. Durham, NC: Duke University Press, 1995.

Gennari, John. *Blowin' Hot and Cool: Jazz and Its Critics*. Chicago: University of Chicago Press, 2006.

Gerstner, David A. *Manly Arts: Masculinity and Nation in Early Cinema*. Durham, NC: Duke University Press, 2006.

Giddens, Anthony. *The Constitution of Society*. Berkeley: University of California Press, 1984.

Gilbreth, Lillian. *The Home-Maker and Her Job*. New York: D. Appleton, 1927.

Gilroy, Paul. *The Black Atlantic: Modernity and Double Consciousness*. Cambridge, MA: Harvard University Press, 1993.

Gitelman, Lisa. *Always Already New: Media, History, and the Data of Culture*. Cambridge, MA: MIT Press, 2006.

Goldmark, Daniel. "Sounds Funny/Funny Sounds: Theorizing Cartoon Music." In Daniel Goldmark and Charlie Keil, eds., *Funny Pictures: Animation and Comedy in Studio-Era Hollywood*. Berkeley: University of California Press, 2011, 257–71.

Goldmark, Daniel. *Tunes for 'Toons: Music and the Hollywood Cartoon*. Berkeley: University of California Press, 2005.

Gomery, Douglas. *The Coming of Sound*. New York: Routledge, 2003.

Gould, Stephen Jay. *The Panda's Thumb: More Reflections in Natural History*. New York: Norton, 1980.

Graham, Laurel. "Beyond Manipulation: Lillian Gilbreth's Industrial Psychology and the Governmentality of Women Consumers." *Sociological Quarterly* 38:4 (fall 1997), 539–65.

Graham, Laurel D. "Domesticating Efficiency: Lillian Gilbreth's Scientific Management of Homemakers, 1924–1930." *Signs* 24:3 (spring 1999), 633–75 .

Graham, Laurel. *Managing on Her Own: Dr. Lillian Gilbreth and Women's Work in the Interwar Era*. Norcross, GA: Engineering and Management Press, 1998.

Gunning, Tom. "The Cinema of Attraction[s]." *Wide Angle* 8:3–4 (1986), 63–70.

Gunning, Tom. "'Primitive' Cinema—A Frame-Up? or The Trick's on Us." *Cinema Journal* 28:2 (winter 1989), 3–12.

Haber, Samuel. *Efficiency and Uplift*. Chicago: University of Chicago Press, 1964.

Haggins, Bambi. *Laughing Mad: The Black Comic Persona in Post-soul America*. New Brunswick, NJ: Rutgers University Press, 2007.

Hall, Sheldon, and Steve Neale, eds. *Epics, Spectacles, and Blockbusters: A Hollywood History*. Detroit: Wayne State University Press, 2010.

Hall, Stuart. "Racist Ideologies and the Media." In Paul Marris and Sue Thornham, eds., *Media Studies: A Reader*. New York: New York University Press, 2000, 271–82.

Hall, Stuart. "The Spectacle of the 'Other.'" In Hall, ed., *Representation: Cultural Representations and Signifying Practices*. London: Sage, 1997, 223–90.

Hall, Stuart. "Stereotyping as a Signifying Practice." In Hall, ed., *Representation: Cultural Representations and Signifying Practices*. London: Sage, 1997.

Hansen, Miriam Bratu. *Babel and Babylon: Spectatorship in American Silent Film*. Cambridge, MA: Harvard University Press, 1991.

Hansen, Miriam Bratu. "Benjamin, Cinema and Experience: 'The Blue Flower in the Land of Technology.'" *New German Critique* 40 (winter 1987), 179–224.

Hansen, Miriam Bratu. "The Mass Production of the Senses: Classical Cinema as Vernacular Modernism." In Christine Gledhill and Linda Williams, eds., *Reinventing Film Studies*. London: Arnold, 2000, 332–50.

Harris, Joel Chandler. *Uncle Remus and His Legends of the Old Plantation*. London: David Bogue, 1881.

Hartman, Saidiya. *Scenes of Subjection: Terror, Slavery, and Self-Making in Nineteenth-Century America*. New York: Oxford University Press, 1997.

Harvey, David. *Spaces of Capital: Towards a Critical Geography*. New York: Routledge, 2001.

Hayden, Dolores. *Grand Domestic Revolution*. Cambridge, MA: MIT Press, 1981.

Heer, Jeet. "Racism as a Stylistic Choice and Other Notes." *Comics Journal* 301, online (posted 14 March 2011).

Henderson, Schuyler. "Disregarding the Suffering of Others: Narrative, Comedy, and Torture." *Literature and Medicine* 24:2 (fall 2005), 181–208.

Herrnstein, Richard J., and Charles Murray. *The Bell Curve: Intelligence and Class Structure in American Life*. New York: Free Press, 1994.

Holberg, Amelia. "Betty Boop: Jewish Film Star." *American Jewish History* 87:4 (December 1999), 291–312.

Horkheimer, Max, and Theodor Adorno. *The Dialectic of Enlightenment*. San Francisco: HarperCollins, 1975.

Huemer, Dick. "Pioneer Portraits." *Cartoonist Profiles* 1:3 (summer 1969), 14–18.

Ignatiev, Noel. *Race Traitor*. New York: Routledge, 1996.

Iton, Richard. *In Search of the Black Fantastic: Politics and Popular Culture in the Post–Civil Rights Era*. New York: Oxford University Press, 2008.

Jackson, John L. *Real Black: Adventures in Racial Sincerity*. Chicago: University of Chicago Press, 2005.

James, Ed. *The Amateur Negro Minstrels Guide*. New York: Ed James, 1880.

Jameson, Fredric. *The Political Unconscious*. London: Routledge, 1983.

Jameson, Fredric. *Postmodernism, or The Cultural Logic of Late Capitalism*. Durham, NC: Duke University Press, 1991.

Jameson, Fredric. *Signatures of the Visible*. New York: Routledge, 1992.

Jenkins, Henry. "'I Like to Sock Myself in the Face': Reconsidering 'Vulgar Modernism.'" In Daniel Goldmark and Charlie Keil, eds., *Funny Pictures: Animation and Comedy in Studio-Era Hollywood*. Berkeley: University of California Press, 2011, 153–74.

Jenkins, Henry. *What Made Pistachio Nuts? Early Sound Comedy and the Vaudeville Aesthetic*. New York: Columbia University Press, 1993.

Kanfer, Steven. *Serious Business: The Art and Commerce of Animation in America from Betty Boop to "Toy Story."* New York: Da Capo, 1997.

Keeling, Kara. "Passing for Human: *Bamboozled* and Digital Humanism." *Women and Performance* 15:1 (2005), 237–50.

Kern, Stephen. *The Culture of Time and Space 1880–1918*. Cambridge, MA: Harvard University Press, 1983.

King, Debra Walker. *African Americans and the Culture of Pain*. Charlottesville: University of Virginia Press, 2008.

King, Rob. "The Art of Diddling: Slapstick, Science, and Antimodernism in the Films of Charlie Bowers." In Daniel Goldmark and Charlie Keil, eds., *Funny*

Pictures: *Animation and Comedy in Studio-Era Hollywood*. Berkeley: University of California Press, 2011, 191–210.

King, Rob. *The Fun Factory: The Keystone Film Company and the Emergence of Mass Culture*. Berkeley: University of California Press, 2008.

Klein, Norman M. "Animation and Animorphs: A Brief Disappearing Act." In Vivian Sobchack, ed., *Meta-morphing: Visual Transformation and the Culture of Quick-Change*. Minneapolis: University of Minnesota Press, 2000, 21–40.

Klein, Norman M. *7 Minutes: The Life and Death of the American Animated Cartoon*. London: Verso, 1993.

Kline, Wendy. *Building a Better Race: Gender, Sexuality, and Eugenics from the Turn of the Century to the Baby Boom*. Berkeley: University of California Press, 2001.

Knight, Arthur. *Disintegrating the Musical: Black Performance and American Musical Film*. Durham, NC: Duke University Press, 2002.

"Ko-Ko a 'Presentation Knockout.'" *Moving Picture World*, 8 May 1926, 183.

Kozarski, Richard. *An Evening's Entertainment: The Age of the Silent Feature Picture, 1915–1928*. Berkeley: University of California Press, 1994.

Lacan, Jacques. "Aggressivity in Psychoanalysis." In Lacan, *Ecrits: A Selection*, trans. Alan Sheridan. New York: Norton, 1977 [1948], 8–28.

Lacan, Jacques. "The Function and Field of Speech and Language in Psychoanalysis." In Lacan, *Ecrits: A Selection*, trans. Alan Sheridan. New York: Norton, 1977 [1948], 30–113.

LaMarre, Thomas. *The Anime Machine: A Media Theory of Animation*. Minneapolis: University of Minnesota Press, 2009.

Lancaster, Jane. *Making Time: Lillian Moller Gilbreth—A Life beyond "Cheaper by the Dozen."* Boston: Northeastern University Press, 2004.

Langer, Mark. "The Disney-Fleischer Dilemma: Product Differentiation and Technological Innovation." *Screen* 33:4 (winter 1992), 343–59.

Langer, Mark. "Institutional Power and the Fleischer Studios: The 'Standard Production Reference.'" *Cinema Journal* 30:2 (winter 1991), 3–22.

Langer, Mark. "Polyphony and Heterogeneity in Early Fleischer Films: Comic Strips, Vaudeville, and the New York Style." In Daniel Goldmark and Charlie Keil, eds., *Funny Pictures: Animation and Comedy in Studio-Era Hollywood*. Berkeley: University of California Press, 2011, 29–50.

Lastra, James. *Sound Technology and the American Cinema: Perception, Representation, Modernity*. New York: Columbia University Press, 2000.

Lave, Jean, and Etienne Wenger. *Situated Learning: Legitimate Peripheral Participation*. Cambridge: Cambridge University Press, 1991.

Lefebvre, Henri. *The Production of Space*. Trans. Donald Nicholson-Smith. London: Blackwell, 1974.

Lehman, Christopher. *The Colored Cartoon: Black Presentation in American Animated Short Films, 1907–1954*. Amherst: University of Massachusetts Press, 2007.

Levine, Lawrence. *Highbrow/Lowbrow: The Emergence of Cultural Hierarchy in America*. Cambridge, MA: Harvard University Press, 1990.

Levitt, Paul. *Vaudeville Humor: The Collected Jokes, Routines, and Skits of Ed Lowry.* Carbondale: Southern Illinois University Press, 2002.

Lewis, Barbara. "Daddy Blue: The Evolution of the Dark Daddy." In Annemarie Bean, James Hatch, and Brooks McNamara, eds., *Inside the Minstrel Mask: Readings in Nineteenth-Century Blackface Minstrelsy.* Middletown, CT: Wesleyan University Press, 1996, 257–74.

Lewis, Robert M. *From Traveling Show to Vaudeville: Theatrical Spectacle in America, 1830–1910.* Baltimore: Johns Hopkins University Press, 2003.

Lhamon, W. T., ed. *Jim Crow: American.* Cambridge, MA: Harvard University Press, 2009.

Lhamon, W. T. *Jump Jim Crow: Lost Plays, Lyrics, and Street Prose of the First Atlantic Popular Culture.* Cambridge, MA: Harvard University Press, 2003.

Lhamon, W. T. *Raising Cain: Blackface Performance from Jim Crow to Hip Hop.* Cambridge, MA: Harvard University Press, 1998.

Lichtenstein, Alex. *Twice the Work of Free Labor: The Political Economy of Convict Labor in the New South.* New York: Verso, 1996.

Lindfors, Bernth, ed. *Africans on Stage: Studies in Ethnological Show Business.* Bloomington: Indiana University Press, 1999.

Lorde, Audre. "Age, Race, Class and Sex: Women Redefining Difference." In Russell Ferguson, Martha Gever, Trinh T. Minh-ha, and Cornel West, eds., *Out There: Marginalization and Contemporary Cultures.* Cambridge, MA: MIT Press, 1990, 281–88.

Lott, Eric. "Blackface and Blackness: The Minstrel Show in American Culture." In Annemarie Bean, James Hatch, and Brooks McNamara, eds., *Inside the Minstrel Mask: Readings in Nineteenth-Century Blackface Minstrelsy.* Middletown, CT: Wesleyan University Press, 1996, 3–34.

Lott, Eric. *Love and Theft: Blackface Minstrelsy and the American Working Class.* New York: Oxford University Press, 1993.

Lovett, Laura L. *Conceiving the Future: Pronatalism, Reproduction, and the Family in the United States, 1890–1938.* Durham, NC: University of North Carolina Press, 2007.

Lutz, Edwin G. *Animated Cartoons: How They Are Made, Their Origin and Development.* New York: Scribner's, 1926 [1920].

Lynd, Robert S., and Helen M. Lynd. *Middletown: A Study in American Culture.* New York: Harcourt Brace, 1929.

Mahar, William J. *Behind the Burnt Cork Mask: Early Blackface Minstrelsy and Antebellum American Popular Culture.* Chicago: University of Illinois Press, 1999.

Mailer, Norman. "The White Negro." *Dissent* (spring 1957), 276–93.

Maltin, Leonard. *Of Mice and Magic: A History of American Animated Cartoons.* New York: Plume, 1980.

Manovich, Lev. "Image Future." *Animation* 1:1 (2006), 25–44.

Martin, Waldo E. *Brown v. Board of Education: A Brief History with Documents.* New York: Bedford St. Martin's, 1998.

Marx, Karl. *Capital.* Trans. Ben Fowlkes. Vol. 1. New York: Penguin Classics, 1976.

Maurice, Alice. *The Cinema and Its Shadow: Race and Technology in Early Cinema.* Minneapolis: University of Minnesota Press, 2013.

May, Lary. "Review: *Blackface, White Noise: Jewish Immigrants in the Hollywood Melting Pot.*" *American Jewish History* 85:1 (1997), 115–19.

May, Lary. *Screening Out the Past.* Chicago: University of Chicago Press, 1980.

McCloud, Scott. *Understanding Comics.* New York: Kitchen Sink Press, 1993.

McCormick, Anne O'Hare. "Hollywood: Weird Factory of Mob Art." *New York Times Magazine,* 6 December 1931, 5.

Melnick, Ross. *American Showman: Samuel "Roxy" Rothafel and the Birth of the Entertainment Industry, 1908–1935.* New York: Columbia University Press, 2012.

Merelman, Richard M. "Hollywood's America: Social and Political Themes in Motion Pictures." (Review.) *American Political Science Review* 91:3 (September 1997), 753–54.

Morton, Drew. "Sketching under the Influence? Winsor McCay and the Question of Aesthetic Convergence between Comic Strips and Film." *Animation* 5:3 (2010), 295–312.

Moten, Fred. *In the Break: The Aesthetics of the Black Radical Tradition.* Minneapolis: University of Minnesota Press, 2003.

"Mouse and Man." *Time,* 27 December 1937.

Mukerji, Chandra. *Territorial Ambitions and the Gardens of Versailles.* Cambridge: Cambridge University Press, 1997.

Musser, Charles. "The Nickelodeon Era Begins: Establishing the Framework for Hollywood's Mode of Representation." In Thomas Elsaesser, ed., *Early Cinema: Space, Frame, Narrative.* London: BFI, 1990 [1984], 256–73.

"My Bonnie." *Film Daily,* 20 September 1925, 32.

Naremore, James. "Uptown Folks: Blackness and Entertainment in *Cabin in the Sky.*" In Krin Gabbard, ed., *Representing Jazz.* Durham, NC: Duke University Press, 1995, 169–92.

Nasaw, David. *Going Out: The Rise and Fall of Public Amusements.* New York: Basic Books, 1993.

Nasaw, David. "Review: *Blackface, White Noise: Jewish Immigrants in the Hollywood Melting Pot.*" *American Historical Review* 102:4 (October 1997), 1244–45.

Nathan, Hans. "The Performance of the Virginia Minstrels." In Annemarie Bean, James Hatch, and Brooks McNamara, eds., *Inside the Minstrel Mask: Readings in Nineteenth-Century Blackface Minstrelsy.* Middletown, CT: Wesleyan University Press, 1996, 35–42.

Natwick, Grim. "Dick Huemer 1898–1979: Homage to a Star." *Cartoonist Profiles* 45 (March 1980). http://www.huemer.com/animate2.htm.

Nelson, Daniel. *Frederick W. Taylor and the Rise of Scientific Management.* Madison: University of Wisconsin Press, 1980.

Ngai, Sianne. *Our Aesthetic Categories: Zany, Cute, Interesting.* Cambridge, MA: Harvard University Press, 2012.

Ngai, Sianne. *Ugly Feelings.* Cambridge, MA: Harvard University Press, 2005.

Nussbaum, Martha. *Upheavals of Thought: The Intelligence of Emotions.* Cambridge: Cambridge University Press, 2001.

Nyong'o, Tavia. *The Amalgamation Waltz: Race, Performance, and the Ruses of Memory.* Minneapolis: University of Minnesota Press, 2009.

O'Meally, Robert. "Checking Our Balances: Ellison on Armstrong's Humor." *boundary 2* 30:2 (2003), 115–36.

Omi, Michael, and Howard Winant. *Racial Formation in the United States from the 1960s to the 1990s.* New York: Routledge, 1994.

Oudart, Jean-Pierre. "Cinema and Suture." Trans. Kari Hanet. *Screen* 18 (winter 1978), 35–47.

Parks, Gregory S., and Matthew Hughey, eds. *The Obamas and a (Post) Racial America?* New York: Oxford University Press, 2012.

Patterson, James T. *Brown v. Board of Education: A Civil Rights Milestone and Its Troubled Legacy.* New York: Oxford University Press, 2002.

Paul, William. "The K-Mart Audience at the Mall Movies." *Film History* 6:4 (winter 1994), 487–501.

"Pictures at Keith's Palace, Cleveland." *Film Daily,* 7 July 1925, 2.

Polan, Dana. "Brecht and the Politics of Self-Reflexive Cinema." *Jump Cut* 17 (1978), 29–32.

Roediger, David. *Towards the Abolition of Whiteness: Essays on Race, Politics, and Working Class History.* New York: Verso, 1994.

Roediger, David. *The Wages of Whiteness: Race and the Making of the American Working Class.* New York: Verso, 1991.

Rogin, Michael. *Blackface, White Noise: Jewish Immigrants in the Hollywood Melting Pot.* Berkeley: University of California Press, 1996.

Rogoff, Barbara. *Everyday Cognition: Its Development in Social Context.* Cambridge, MA: Harvard University Press, 1984.

Rosen, Philip. *Change Mummified: Cinema, History, Theory.* Minneapolis: University of Minnesota Press, 2001.

Rydell, Robert W. *World of Fairs: The Century-of-Progress Expositions.* Chicago: University of Chicago Press, 1993.

Sacher-Masoch, Leopold. *Venus in Furs.* New York: Zone Books, 1989 [1870].

Sammond, Nicholas. *Babes in Tomorrowland: Walt Disney and the Making of the American Child, 1930–1960.* Durham, NC: Duke University Press, 2005.

Sammond, Nicholas. "Picture This: Lillian Gilbreth's Industrial Cinema for the Home." *Camera Obscura* 21:3 (December 2006), 103–33.

Sampson, Henry T. *That's Enough, Folks: Black Images in Animated Cartoons, 1900–1960.* London: Scarecrow, 1998.

Sartin, Hank. "From Vaudeville to Hollywood, from Silence to Sound: Warner Bros. Cartoons of the Early Sound Era." In Kevin Sandler, ed., *Reading the Rabbit: Explorations in Warner Bros. Animation.* New Brunswick, NJ: Rutgers University Press, 1998, 67–85.

Saxton, Alexander. "Blackface Minstrelsy." In Annemarie Bean, James Hatch, and

Brooks McNamara, eds., *Inside the Minstrel Mask: Readings in Nineteenth-Century Blackface Minstrelsy*. Middletown, CT: Wesleyan University Press, 1996, 67–85.

Schickel, Richard. *The Disney Version: The Life, Times, Art and Commerce of Walt Disney*. New York: Simon and Schuster, 1968.

Schlesinger, Arthur M. *The Disuniting of America: Reflections on a Multicultural Society*. New York: Norton, 1998.

Schwarzbaum, Lisa. "Movie Review: *Tropic Thunder*." *Entertainment Weekly*, 12 August 2008. http://www.ew.com.

Sewell, C. S. "Dolly Gray." *Moving Picture World*, 6 February 1926, 565.

Shapiro, Fred, ed. *The Yale Book of Quotations*. New Haven: Yale University Press, 2006.

Sigall, Martha. *Living Life inside the Lines: Tales from the Golden Age of Animation*. Oxford: University of Mississippi Press, 2005.

Silverman, Kaja. *The Acoustic Mirror: The Female Voice in Psychoanalysis and Cinema*. Bloomington: Indiana University Press, 1988.

Silverman, Kaja. *The Subject of Semiotics*. New York: Oxford University Press, 1983.

Sito, Tom. *Drawing the Line: The Untold Story of Animation Unions from Bosko to Bart Simpson*. Lexington: University Press of Kentucky, 2006.

Sjogren, Britta. *Into the Vortex: Female Voice and Paradox in Film*. Chicago: University of Illinois Press, 2006.

Sklar, Robert. "The Making of Cultural Myths—Walt Disney." In Gerald Peary and Danny Peary, eds., *The American Animated Cartoon: A Critical Anthology*. New York: Dutton, 1980, 58–65.

Slide, Anthony. *The Encyclopedia of Vaudeville*. Oxford: University of Mississippi Press, 2012.

Slide, Anthony. *New York City Vaudeville*. Chicago: Arcadia, 2006.

Smoodin, Eric. *Animating Culture: Hollywood Cartoons from the Sound Era*. New Brunswick, NJ: Rutgers University Press, 1993.

Smoodin, Eric. *Regarding Frank Capra: Audience, Celebrity, and American Film Studies, 1930–1960*. Durham, NC: Duke University Press, 2004.

Sobchack, Vivian. "At the Still Point of the Turning World." In Sobchack, ed., *Meta-morphing: Visual Transformation and the Culture of Quick-Change*. Minneapolis: University of Minnesota Press, 2000, 144.

Sobchack, Vivian. Introduction to Sobchack, ed., *Meta-morphing: Visual Transformation and the Culture of Quick-Change*. Minneapolis: University of Minnesota Press, 2000, xi–xxiii.

Solomon, Charles. *Enchanted Drawings: The History of Animation*. New York: Random House, 1994.

Sotiropoulos, Karen. *Staging Race: Black Performers in Turn of the Century America*. Cambridge, MA: Harvard University Press, 2006.

Southern, Eileen. "The Early Georgia Minstrels." In Annemarie Bean, James Hatch, and Brooks McNamara, eds., *Inside the Minstrel Mask: Readings in Nineteenth-Century Blackface Minstrelsy*. Middletown, CT: Wesleyan University Press, 1996, 163–74.

Spiegelman, Art. *Breakdowns: Portrait of the Artist as a Young %@&*!* New York: Pantheon, 2008.

Spillers, Hortense J. "Mama's Baby, Papa's Maybe: An American Grammar Book." *Diacritics* 17:2 (summer 1987), 65–81.

"Stages Epilogue with 40 People for Song Car-Tune 'My Bonnie.'" *Moving Picture World*, 17 October 1925, 574.

Stallybrass, Peter, and Elon Whyte. *The Politics and Poetics of Transgression.* London: Methuen, 1986.

Stam, Robert. *Reflexivity in Film and Literature: From Don Quixote to Jean-Luc Goddard.* New York: Columbia University Press, 1992.

Stamp, Shelley. *Movie-Struck Girls: Women and Motion Picture Culture after the Nickelodeon.* Princeton, NJ: Princeton University Press, 2000.

Stanislavsky, Constantin. *My Life in Art.* Trans. J. J. Robbins. London: Bles, 1924.

Stanley, Amy Dru. *From Bondage to Contract: Wage Labor, Marriage, and the Market in the Age of Slave Emancipation.* Cambridge: Cambridge University Press, 1998.

Stewart, Jacqueline Najuma. *Migrating to the Movies: Cinema and Black Urban Modernity.* Berkeley: University of California Press, 2005.

Strasberg, Lee, and Toby Cole. *Acting: A Handbook of the Stanislavski Method.* New York: Lear, 1947.

Streible, Dan. *Fight Pictures: A History of Boxing and Early Cinema.* Berkeley: University of California Press, 2008.

Thomas, Frank, and Ollie Johnston. *The Illusion of Life: Disney Animation.* New York: Disney Editions, 1981.

Tough, Paul. "What Does Obama Really Believe In?" *New York Times Magazine*, 15 August 2012. http://www.nytimes.com/2012/08/19/magazine/obama-poverty.html?pagewanted=all.

Travis, Dempsey J. "Chicago's Jazz Trail, 1893–1950." *Black Music Research Journal* 10:1 (spring 1990), 82–85.

Wagner, Phil. "'An America Not Quite Mechanized': Fanchon and Marco, Inc. Perform Modernity." *Film History* 23:3 (2011), 251–67.

Wallace, Irving. "Mickey Mouse, and How He Grew." *Colliers* 123:15 (9 April 1949), 20–21.

Wells, Paul. *Animation and America.* New Brunswick, NJ: Rutgers University Press, 2002.

Wells, Paul. *Understanding Animation.* New York: Routledge, 1998.

Wexler, Laura. "'Laughing Ben' on 'The Old Plantation.'" In Elizabeth Abel and Leigh Raiford, eds., "Photography and Race Forum," *English Language Notes* 44.2 (fall/winter 2006), n.p.

Wilentz, Sean. *Chants Democratic: New York City and the Rise of the American Working Class, 1788–1850.* New York: Oxford University Press, 1984.

Williams, Linda. *Playing the Race Card: Melodramas of Black and White from Uncle Tom to O.J. Simpson.* Princeton, NJ: Princeton University Press, 2001.

Willis, Corin. "Blackface Minstrelsy and Jazz Signification in Hollywood's Early

Sound Era." In Graham Lock and David Murray, eds., *Thriving on a Riff: Jazz and Blues Influences in African American Literature and Film*. Oxford: Oxford University Press, 2009, 40–61.

Winston, Brian. "How Are Media Born?" In Michele Hilmes, ed., *Connections: A Broadcast History Reader*. Belmont, CA: Wadsworth, 2003, 3–18.

Wolfe, Charles. "'Cross-Talk': Language, Space, and the Burns and Allen Comedy Film Short." *Film History* 23:3 (2011), 300–312.

Wright, Michelle M. *Becoming Black: Creating Identity in the African Diaspora*. Durham, NC: Duke University Press, 2004.

Zacharek, Stephanie. "Tropic Thunder." *Salon*, 13 August 2008. www.salon.com.

Žižek, Slavoj. *Enjoy Your Symptom: Jacques Lacan in Hollywood*. New York: Routledge, 2001.

Žižek, Slavoj. "Grimaces of the Real, or When the Phallus Appears." *October* 58 (1991), 44–68.

Žižek, Slavoj. *The Sublime Object of Ideology*. London: Verso, 1989.

Zupancic, Alenka. *The Odd One In: On Comedy*. Cambridge, MA: MIT Press, 2008.

INDEX

Bimbo (animated character), 5, 28,
106–7, 125, 161, 175–82, 205–8, 232,
240, 264, 267–68, 293. *See also*
Fleisher Studios
Bimbo's Initiation, 175–78. *See also*
Bimbo; Fleischer Studios
Black Power movement, 11
blackface minstrelsy: as appropriation,
21; as art form, 18; and the body,
24–27, 68, 139–42, 151, 171, 221,
226, 245–60, 273; and class tension, 24; contemporary examples,
4, 15–16, 30, 270–305; critiques of,
6; decline of, 3, 7, 11, 18, 25, 29–30,
61–64, 205–65; and discourses of
power, 19; early instances of, 18–19,
89; and the emergence of moving
images, 25; fantasy of black persona,
5–6, 13, 27, 63–66, 250–51, 267–
305; nostalgia for, 5, 10–12, 181–82;
and racial formation, 64; and radio,
5, 19, 169–70, 183, 213, 250–52; and
rag-time's influence, 65; resistance
to regulation, 4, 80–90, 215–65;
and role of interlocutor, 24–27, 34,
46–48, 61–62, 68, 88–90, 120, 140,
182, 185, 213, 222, 246, 298; scholarship on, 6, 19, 29; and sound, 160;
trickster figure in, 66, 216–65; and
vaudeville, 5, 33–39; Walker and
Williams, performance of, 62–66;
white performers, 65
Black Swan, 15–16
Blackton, James Stuart (J. S.), 41–45,
61, 73, 79, 92, 124, 146, 180, 199,
244; *The Enchanted Drawing*, 45, 115;
The Haunted Hotel, 41; *Lightning-
Sketches*, 41–42
Blake, Eubie, 163–64
Blanc, Mel, 116
Bobby Bumps (animated series), 111,
116, 256. *See also* Bray Productions;
Hurd, Earl
Booth, Walter R., 44

Bosko the Talk-Ink Kid, 119, 140–41,
289. *See also* Harman, Hugh; Ising,
Rudolf (Rudy)
Bosko the Talk-Ink Kid (animated char-
acter), 21, 28, 119, 140–41, 161, 182–
84, 209, 236, 255, 264, 267–68,
289, 294, 339n31. *See also* Harman,
Hugh; Ising, Rudolf (Rudy)
Boswell Sisters, 329n27
"Bourgeois Blues," 334n102
Bowers, Charles (Charlie), 76, 290
Bradley, Scott, 183
Brando, Marlon, 281–83
Bray, John Randolph, 44–45, 54, 75,
78, 91, 94–97, 103, 118, 124, 161,
236, 332n81. *See also* Bray Produc-
tions
Bray, Margaret, 44, 54, 124. *See also*
Bray, John Randolph; Bray Produc-
tions
Bray Productions, 44, 54, 73–80, 91,
94–97, 103–8, 111, 118, 124, 150, 161,
236–37, 332n81; *The Artist's Dream*,
44; Colonel Heeza Liar (animated
series), 54, 117, 255–56, 290
Br'er Rabbit (symbolic figure), 224,
341n46
Bring 'Em Back Alive, 221
Brooker and Clayton's Georgia Min-
strels, 66–67
Brooks, Daphne, 14
Buck, Frank, 221
Bugs Bunny (animated character), 3,
32, 34, 46, 107, 183, 214–18, 223,
236–41, 248–52, 261–64, 267, 295,
298, 304–5, 318n90. *See also* Avery,
Tex; Jones, Charles (Chuck); Schle-
singer, Leon
Bug Vaudeville, 33–39, 51, 79. *See also*
McCay, Winsor
Bukatman, Scott, 54–55, 61, 114, 125,
312n5, 325n71
Bunny, John, 49
Burns, George. *See* Burns and Allen

Mighty Mouse (animated character), 107. *See also* Terry, Paul

Miller, Flournoy E. *See* Miller and Lyles

Miller and Lyles, 163, 167–69, 213

Mills Brothers, 235, 329n27

Minnelli, Vincent, 182

Minnie Mouse (animated character), 1, 127. *See also* Walt Disney Productions

Minnie the Moocher, 232–36, 253. *See also* Betty Boop; Fleischer Studios

"Minnie the Moocher," 235, 255. *See also* Calloway, Cab

Minstrel Show, The, 181. *See also* Krazy Kat; Mintz, Charles B.

Mintz, Charles B., 104, 128–30

Mississippi Swing, 188–89, 196–97

Moran, George. *See* Moran and Mack

Moran and Mack, 169–70, 183, 250–51, 268

Minstrel Man, The, 183

minstrelsy. *See* blackface minstrelsy

Morgan, Tracy, 15–17

Morton, Drew, 114

Moten, Fred, 14, 200, 237–41, 344n82

Mother Goose Goes Hollywood, 122. *See also* Walt Disney Productions

Movietone (series), 165. *See also* MGM

Moving Picture World, 153–59

Murphy, Eddie, 15

Mussolini, Benito, 200

Mutt and Jeff (animated series), 76, 82, 113, 154–55, 242, 297. *See also* Fisher, Bud

Muybridge, Eadweard, 102, 312n5

My Bonnie Lies Over the Ocean, 150, 153. *See also* Fleischer Studios; Song Car-Tunes

My Old Kentucky Home, 152. *See also* Fleischer Studios; Song Car-Tunes

"My Old Kentucky Home," 152. *See also* Foster, Stephen

Mysto the Magician (animated character), 296. *See also* Avery, Tex

"Nagasaki," 195

Naremore, James, 189–91

National Association for the Advancement of Colored People (NAACP), 308n13

Natwick, Grim, 106. *See also* Betty Boop

Newlyweds, The, 43, 113, 316n49. *See also* Cohl, Emile; McManus, George

Newman Laugh-O-Grams, 74. *See also* Disney, Walt

Newton, Huey, 13

New York Morning Telegraph, 7

New York Times, 64, 80, 127, 153, 276

New York Times Magazine, 127

New York World, 314n27

Nicholas, Fayard. *See* Nicholas Brothers

Nicholas, Harold. *See* Nicholas Brothers

Nicholas Brothers, 163–64, 169

Nolan, Bill, 54, 104

Nutty Professor, The, 15

Obama, Barack: election and presidency of, 4, 14–17, 32, 273, 283, 303–5, 345n95; and the "postracial" era, 14–15, 283–85, 305

O'Brien, Willis, 315n42

"Of Other Spaces," 196–98

Old Black Joe, 150. *See also* Fleischer Studios; Song Car-Tunes

"Old Folks at Home," 21

Old Man of the Mountain, The, 253. *See also* Betty Boop; Calloway, Cab; Fleischer Studios

"Old Zip Coon," 21–26, 46, 66, 70, 132, 142, 175, 223–24, 287, 310n32. See also *Steamboat Willie*

On Strike, 76, 242. *See also* Mutt and Jeff

Opry House, The, 175. *See also* Mickey Mouse; Walt Disney Productions

Oswald the Lucky Rabbit (animated